Donkey Work

Donkey Work

CONGRESSIONAL DEMOCRATS
IN CONSERVATIVE AMERICA,
1974–1994

Patrick Andelic

University Press of Kansas

Published by the University Press of Kansas (Lawrence, Kansas 66045), which was
organized by the Kansas Board of Regents and is operated and funded by Emporia State
University, Fort Hays State University, Kansas State University, Pittsburg State University,
the University of Kansas, and Wichita State University.

Library of Congress Cataloging-in-Publication Data
Names: Andelic, Patrick, 1987– author.
Title: Donkey work : congressional Democrats in conservative America, 1974–1994 /
    Patrick Andelic.
Description: Lawrence, Kansas : University Press of Kansas, [2019] | Includes
    bibliographical references and index.
Identifiers: LCCN 2018058810
    ISBN 9780700628032 (cloth)
    ISBN 9780700638093 (paper)
    ISBN 9780700628049 (ebook)
Subjects: LCSH: Democratic Party (US)—History—20th century. | Conservatism—
    United States—History. | United States—Politics and government—20th century. |
    Political parties—United States—History—20th century.
Classification: LCC JK2316 .A62 2019 | DDC 324.2736/09048—dc23
LC record available at https://lccn.loc.gov/2018058810.

British Library Cataloguing-in-Publication Data is available.

The paper used in this publication is acid free and meets the minimum requirements of
the American National Standard for Permanence of Paper for Printed Library Materials
Z39.48-1992.

For my parents, Rosemary and Steven

CONTENTS

ACKNOWLEDGMENTS

Though a cliché, it is nonetheless true that the writing of any book is a collective endeavor. I have incurred a great many debts in researching and writing this book, and I am glad to recognize some of them here.

The first person to thank is my graduate supervisor, Dr. Gareth Davies, of St. Anne's College, Oxford. Gareth was a tolerant, wise, and encouraging mentor throughout my studies, and it would be impossible to fully account for all that I owe to his efforts. I am only sorry that I could not even fake an interest in either cricket or rugby by way of recompense. Gareth was one of several academics at a range of institutions who offered insight and guidance. I would therefore like to thank Jonathan Bell, Nigel Bowles, Pekka Hämäläinen, Fabian Hilfrich, Mara Keire, Robert Mason, Iwan Morgan, Mark Newman, Paul Quigley, Timothy Stanley, and Stephen Tuck.

As a graduate student, I was fortunate to be part of the Rothermere American Institute (RAI) at Oxford, which sustains as fine a community of scholars as any to which I could have hoped to belong. Research can be a lonely pursuit, and I am grateful for the valued friendships that I made there. I am also deeply grateful for the friends and colleagues I made in the wider Americanist community, both their criticism and their camaraderie. My sincere thanks go to Dominic Barker, Christopher Brown, Todd Carter, Malcolm Craig, Tom Cutterham, Huw David, Jane Dinwoodie Ushiyama, Rivers Gambrell, Ursula Hackett, Karen Heath, Nadia Hilliard, Louisa Hotson, Mandy Izadi, Oenone Kubie, Robbie Maxwell, Mark McLay, Alison Skye Montgomery, Kathryn Olivarius, Tom Packer, Sebastian Page, Jane Rawson, Mitchell Robertson, Daniel Rowe, and Joe Ryan-Hume.

I also wish to acknowledge the vital support of the administrative and technical staff who make the work of researchers possible. I would like to single out for special mention the staff of the RAI and Vere Harmsworth Library, Oxford, particularly Johanna O'Connor, Richard Purkiss, Joanne Steventon, Martin Sutcliffe, and Judy Warden.

I am deeply grateful to the archivists at various archives, libraries, and institutions across the United States for their forbearance and generosity. I would like to offer particular thanks to the staff at the John W. Kluge Center at the Library of Congress in Washington, DC, where I spent six months as an Arts and Humanities Research Council (AHRC) fellow. I am also grateful to the staff at the Center for Lowell History at the University of Massachusetts Lowell, the John F. Kennedy Presidential Library (Boston, MA), the John J. Burns Library at Boston College, the Jimmy Carter Presidential Library (Atlanta, GA), the University of Arizona (Tucson, AZ), the Minnesota Historical Society, the University of Colorado Boulder, the University of California, Berkeley, and the University of California, Los Angeles.

Many organizations provided the funding that made the research for this book possible. First and foremost, I wish to thank the AHRC, whose doctoral award enabled me to embark on this project in the first place. I am grateful also to the RAI, St. Anne's College, the Oxford History Faculty, and Northumbria University, without whose generous grants I would not have been able to make research trips to the United States, attend conferences, and complete my research.

A great many colleagues have listened patiently to my papers, however poorly conceived, at various conferences—including those of the American Politics Group (APG), British Association for American Studies (BAAS), Historians of the Twentieth Century United States (HOTCUS), and Policy History—and offered invaluable feedback. I am grateful to them all.

Special thanks must also go to the staff of the University Press of Kansas, and particularly to David Congdon, Kelly Chrisman Jacques, and Penelope Cray, who shepherded this manuscript to publication with patience, dexterity, and sound judgment. I would also like to thank UPK's reviewers, Jennifer Delton and Kevin Mattson, who read drafts of the manuscript with great care and offered incisive and thoughtful comments.

Finally, I would like to thank my family—Finola, Rory, and especially my parents, Rosemary and Steven—without whose love and support I would not have made it this far.

This book would not have been possible without those mentioned above. Only the mistakes are solely my own work.

When I first conceived of the project that would eventually lead to this book—as an aspiring graduate student struggling to write applications for various postgraduate programs back in 2009—my understanding of US politics was naively cyclical. As a starting point, I speculated that just as Franklin D. Roosevelt had ushered in a Democratic ascendancy in the 1930s and Ronald Reagan had established a Republican hegemony in the 1980s, so too might the newly elected Barack Obama consolidate a new Democratic majority that would dominate US politics for years, if not decades. Therefore, it was, I claimed, important to explore what Democrats had done during their wilderness years in order to better understand their coming hegemony. A year later, the rise of the Tea Party and the Democrats' midterm "shellacking" would brutally undermine that assumption.[1] I wince a little when I remember the confidence with which I used to explain this planned framework to others.

In my defense, I was far from alone in thinking like this. Indeed, it was not a particularly original conclusion. Many commentators had drawn the same comparisons to FDR and Reagan and suggested that Obama might be presiding over a realignment.[2] There was still considerable enthusiasm for the "emerging Democratic majority" thesis that had been advanced by journalist John B. Judis and political scientist Ruy Teixeira in 2002.[3] Their work had cited the growth of Asian, Latino, and African American populations, the rise in levels of college and postgraduate education, and the growing number of Americans working white-collar, "knowledge economy" jobs—all Democratic-leaning voter blocs—to suggest that the Democrats had the opportunity to create a durable electoral majority. Many pundits condensed this to the slogan "demography is destiny," though Teixeira would later disavow that as a "dangerous misinterpretation" of their thesis.[4]

We are still waiting for the emerging Democratic majority to emerge. It is just about plausible to argue that a Democratic majority of sorts exists, though it is one that is misaligned with US institutions, particularly the Electoral College and the Senate. After all, the Democratic candidate has won the popular vote (majority or plurality) in seven of the last eight presidential elections.[5] However, other developments, such as the gains Donald Trump made among African American and Latino voters between 2016 and 2020, have undermined the conventional wisdom that a more diverse electorate would always favor the Democrats.[6] Few people repeat the mantra "demography is destiny" with much confidence anymore.

I had to perform a *volte-face* to write this book. The volatile politics of the 2010s and 2020s would suggest that there are serious flaws in a straightforwardly cyclical understanding of US politics. In researching the congressional Democratic Party in the 1970s and 1980s, I concluded that this framework was equally unsatisfactory in explaining how the politics of these decades unfolded. Put simply, it became clear to me that liberalism had not been swept aside by an all-conquering conservative movement. That the Democratic Party had maintained a secure foothold in Congress even while losing the White House in comically lopsided landslides suggests that the political dynamics of this era are more complicated.

As a young scholar, I benefitted from both the rich and burgeoning literature on modern American conservatism and the relative lack of attention to liberalism since the 1960s. By the time I was writing this book, an army of historians had taken up the infamous Alan Brinkley's challenge. Once an "orphan in historical scholarship," as Brinkley had memorably described it in 1994, by the 2010s, American conservatism had a detailed and expanding genealogy.[7] As an undergraduate at the University of Edinburgh, I had studied the crisis of liberalism in the 1960s in a module taught by Dr. Robert Mason, an outstanding scholar of conservatism. I realized that while there was a growing amount of material on conservatism, there was far less on what had happened to liberals after 1968. It was as though historians, embarrassed by their neglect of mid-twentieth-century conservatism, had decided to give late-twentieth-century liberalism a taste of the wilderness.

This book was therefore an effort to take liberalism seriously in a period when it was often portrayed as cowed and marginalized. I also wanted to argue that there were stronger connections between the modern Democratic Party and the party as it existed in the 1970s and 1980s. Other scholars had been inclined to present this period as something of a dead end for the Democrats. Jeffrey Bloodworth, for example, had argued in *Losing the Center* that the Democrats had collapsed into self-indulgence in the years between 1968 and 1992 and had allowed conservatives to dominate US politics.[8] This is likewise an animating theme of Kenneth Baer's meticulous history of the Democratic Leadership Council, which credits the DLC with having wrested control of the party away from extremists and made the Democrats electable again.[9] Instead, I intended for this book to show the underappreciated continuities between the Democratic Party of the 1970s and 1980s and that of the present day. Indeed, Bradford Martin argued that this could have gone further, asking in his review of the book if "[Edward] Kennedy's effort to keep health-care reform alive as a national priority represented the continuation of a fundamental part of a liberal agenda that began with Truman's Fair Deal, sputtered during the Clinton administration, and culminated with Obamacare?"[10]

I approached the University Press of Kansas for the simple reason that when I looked at my bibliography, I realized that UPK had published many works that I admired and had engaged with during my research. This included Timothy Stanley's bracingly revisionist account of Senator Edward M. Kennedy's 1980 primary challenge to incumbent President Jimmy Carter.[11] In Stanley's account, Kennedy's campaign was not a quixotic howl of rage in the face of liberalism's imminent failure, but a credible effort to unseat an unpopular president that failed because of contingent factors like the flaws in Kennedy's character and campaign strategy and the foreign policy crises that defined that campaign. Among its other strengths, UPK has published a number of revisionist works on American liberalism in the late twentieth century and will publish more in the future. I am proud that this book is alongside those fine works.

The first reviews of this book, when they began to emerge, ranged from the warm to the politely muted, but they were all thoughtful, generous, and much kinder than I feared they would be. I am grateful to every reviewer who took the time to engage with my arguments, and I must concede— begrudgingly and with ill grace—that they all made fair criticisms of this book.[12] Bradford Martin, for example, noted that this narrative did not do enough to acknowledge the work of female legislators. Though the book discusses the "quantum leap of Democratic women in Congress" in the 1992 elections, he noted that the "grassroots organizational efforts to elect more women began earlier, with modest gains."[13] Men dominated Congress in these years, but I agree that I could have done more to prevent them from dominating the narrative. Marjorie Randon Hershey suggested that the book did not fully account for the role played by "the strength of Democratic loyalties among southerners" in "the exceedingly slow pace of the secular party realignment in the South."[14] While southern Democrats make appearances at key points in the book, it perhaps does not fully do justice to their place in the wider coalition. These are lacunae that other historians will be able to fill. Joe Ryan-Hume, for example, has (in my estimation at least) more effectively explored the links between the Democratic Party's institutions and its progressive, activist base.[15]

Inevitably when looking back on a first book, I have some other regrets, but these are generally minor and concerned with the roads not taken. I still wonder, for instance, if this book would have worked better if I had structured it as a collective biography of the Watergate Babies: the cohort of legislators first elected in 1974. These figures dominate the early pages but start to recede somewhat in the later chapters, though their influence continues to be felt in the narrative. For that book, you'd need to read John A. Lawrence's *The Class of '74*.[16] I also feel I could have engaged more directly with the emerging scholarship on neoliberalism. Though neoliberalism does make an appearance in the final chapter of this book, it is in reference to the reformist ideas of Democrats like Paul Tsongas, which should be understood as distinct from neoliberalism as most other scholars would use it. My handling of neoliberalism received a sceptical mention in an otherwise terrific review article by Ariane Leendertz, which described my ideas as "rather odd."[17] I think there was some confusion in that article's characterization of those ideas for which I take full responsibility. It is nevertheless flattering to have made the cut for a "State of the Field" review article, even if it was only to gently chastise me for the state I was making of this field.

It is now clear that this book was part of a wave of new works that focus on liberalism after the 1960s and seek to understand the ways that liberalism and the Democratic Party have transformed in the post–New Deal era. Lily Geismer has produced two stellar books on, respectively, the role of affluent suburban Democratic activists in the party's transformation and the party's failure to tackle poverty and inequality since the Clinton era.[18] Paul Sabin has explored the way that progressive "public interest" activists on the left were effective in undermining confidence in government, an assault that "helped to break apart the New Deal coalition that supported—and relied on—a strong and active federal government, and made it harder for the government to do big things."[19] These are just two standout examples in an expanding and vibrant subfield.[20] I attended the American Political History Conference at Vanderbilt University, Nashville, Tennessee, in June 2024 and found myself surrounded by scholars working on liberalism and the Democratic Party, many of them graduate students.[21] The future of this subfield looks very bright to me.

One of the major themes of this book is a paradox that continues to warp American politics: widespread distrust of "big government" among US citizens in the abstract, alongside high expectations of government on a wide array of specific issues. (Given that my doctoral advisor was Dr. Gareth Davies, whose works you will also find in UPK's collections, it is perhaps not a surprise that I became preoccupied with this conundrum.)[22] Ordinary Americans continue to expect a great deal from a government that they regard with disdain, and this paradox creates challenges for both parties. While Republicans have at times successfully resisted further expansions of the federal government, they have repeatedly struggled to roll back existing programs. The challenge has, however, been more acute for a Democratic Party that has, since the New Deal, been organized around the principle that government can be a force for positive social and economic change. Recent events have perhaps provided some hope for supporters of "big government" liberalism, with the administration of President Joe Biden, at least in domestic policy, pursuing arguably one of the most progressive and interventionist agendas of any White House since the 1960s.[23]

The other major theme of this book was the inadequacy of Congress as a platform for any party to reshape its public philosophy and take control of the political agenda. Although this book sought to push back on the "presidential synthesis" as the dominant organizing principle of US political history, it was ultimately quite pessimistic about the prospect of coordinating political action from the legislative branch as opposed to the executive branch. Yet, as I finish writing this preface, a loosely organized rebellion among congressional Democrats and the wider party has succeeded in persuading President Joe Biden to step down from the national ticket. According to some reports, former Democratic Speaker of the House of Representatives, Nancy Pelosi, was a critical figure in this effort, as were the party's current congressional leadership, House Majority Leader Hakeem Jeffries and Senate Majority Leader Chuck Schumer.[24] Other Democratic members of Congress were vocal in their demands for Biden to leave the race.[25] It would be too early to conclude that this prefigures a fundamental rebalancing of the relationship between the president and Congress—or the transformation of the Democrats into a conventional parliamentary-style party where a "backbench" rebellion can force out a leader—but these events are to some extent uncharted territory for the Democratic Party and we will only understand the ramifications in the years ahead. It may be that I was too cynical about the effectiveness of Congress.

Notes

1. Liz Halloran, "Obama Humbled by Election 'Shellacking,'" *NPR*, November 3, 2010, https://www.npr.org/2010/11/03/131046118/obama-humbled-by-election-shellacking.

2. Steven F. Hayward, "Obama: The New Reagan," *Forbes*, August 14, 2009, https://www.forbes.com/2009/08/13/barack-obama-ronald-reagan-leadership-opinions-contributors-steven-hayward.html.

3. John B. Judis and Ruy Teixeira, *The Emerging Democratic Majority* (Scribner, 2002).

4. Kevin Drum, "Demography is Destiny," *Mother Jones*, July 9, 2010, https://www.motherjones.com/kevin-drum/2010/07/demography-destiny/; Ruy Teixeira, "Demography Is Not Destiny," *Persuasion*, July 16, 2020, https://www.persuasion.community/p/demography-is-not-destiny.

5. Nicolas Riccardi, "Democrats Keep Winning the Popular Vote. That Worries Them," *AP News*, November 14, 2020, https://apnews.com/article/democrats-popular-vote-win-d6331f7e8b51d52582bb2d60e2a007ec.

6. Christian Paz, "Can the Party of Trump Really Become a Multiracial Coalition?" *Vox*, December 1, 2023, https://www.vox.com/2024-elections/23982907/trump-democrats-republicans-working-class-voters-latino-black-voters.

7. Alan Brinkley, "The Problem of American Conservatism," *American Historical Review* 99 no. 2 (April 1994): 409, https://doi.org/10.2307/2167281.

8. Jeffrey Bloodworth, *Losing the Center: The Decline of American Liberalism, 1968–1992* (University Press of Kentucky, 2013).

9. Kenneth S. Baer, *Reinventing Democrats: The Politics of Liberalism from Reagan to Clinton* (University Press of Kansas, 2000).

10. Bradford Martin, "Review of *Donkey Work*," *American Historical Review* 126, no. 1 (March 2021): 359, https://doi.org/10.1093/ahr/rhab021.

11. Timothy Stanley, *Kennedy vs. Carter: The 1980 Battle for the Democratic Party's Soul* (University Press of Kansas, 2010).

12. Marcus M. Witcher, "Witcher on Andelic, 'Donkey Work: Congressional Democrats in Conservative America, 1974–1994,'" *H-1960s, H-Net Reviews*, July 2020, https://

networks.h-net.org/node/19474/reviews/6246279/witcher-andelic-donkey-work
-congressional-democrats-conservative.

13. Bradford Martin, "Review of *Donkey Work*," *American Historical Review* 126, no. 1 (March 2021): 359, https://doi.org/10.1093/ahr/rhab021.

14. Marjorie Randon Hershey, "*Donkey Work: Congressional Democrats in Conservative America, 1974–1994* by Patrick Andelic (review)," *Journal of Southern History* 87, no. 1 (February 2021): 158, https://doi.org/10.1353/soh.2021.0036.

15. Joe J. Ryan-Hume, "The National Organization for Women and the Democratic Party in Reagan's America," *The Historical Journal* 64 no. 2 (2021): 454–476, https://doi.org/ 10.1017/S0018246X20000175.

16. John A. Lawrence, *The Class of '74: Congress after Watergate and the Roots of Partisanship* (Johns Hopkins University Press, 2018).

17. Ariane Leendertz, "State of the Field: A View from Abroad: Post-1968 US History, the End of the New Deal Order, and Neoliberalism," *Reviews in American History* 49 no. 4 (December 2021): 640, https://doi.org/10.1353/rah.2021.0061.

18. Lily Geismer, *Don't Blame Us: Suburban Liberals and the Transformation of the Democratic Party* (Princeton University Press, 2015); Lily Geismer, *Left Behind: The Democrats' Failed Attempt to Solve Inequality* (PublicAffairs, 2022).

19. Paul Sabin, *Public Citizens: The Attack on Big Government and the Remaking of American Liberalism* (W. W. Norton, 2021), xvi.

20. See, for instance, Adam Hilton, *True Blues: The Contentious Transformation of the Democratic Party* (University of Pennsylvania Press, 2021); Cory Haala, "The Progressive Center: Midwestern Liberalism in the Age of Reagan, 1978–1992," (PhD diss., Marquette University, 2020); Joe J. Ryan-Hume, "Standing in Reagan's Shadow: Liberal Strategies in the 1980s," (PhD diss., University of Glasgow, 2017).

21. American Political History Conference, "Reconstructing Democracy: Power, Politics, and Participation (June 6–8, 2024 at Vanderbilt University)," accessed July 22, 2024, https://as.vanderbilt.edu/history/american-political-history-conference/.

22. Gareth Davies, *From Opportunity to Entitlement: The Transformation and Decline of Great Society Liberalism* (University Press of Kansas, 1999); Gareth Davies, *See Government Grow: Education Policy from Johnson to Reagan* (University Press of Kansas, 2012).

23. Perry Bacon Jr., "Biden Is Learning That Being Progressive Is Good Policy – and Good Politics," Opinion, *Washington Post*, March 15, 2024,https://www.washington post.com/opinions/2024/03/15/four-biden-presidencies-progressive-centrist-inter nationalist/.

24. Jill Filipovic, "How Nancy Pelosi Got This Done," *Slate*, July 22, 2024, https://slate.com/news-and-politics/2024/07/nancy-pelosi-kamala-harris-endorse ment-biden-jeffries-schumer.html; Seema Mehta, "Public Deference, Private Power: How Nancy Pelosi Navigated the Biden Withdrawal," *Los Angeles Times*, July 23, 2024, https://www.latimes.com/politics/story/2024-07-23/public-deference-private-power -how-pelosi-navigated-the-biden-withdrawal; Tyler Page and Michael Scherer, "Jeffries, Schumer Privately Warned Biden He Could Imperil Democrats," *Washing-*

ton Post, July 17, 2024, https://www.washingtonpost.com/politics/2024/07/17/jeffries
-schumer-biden-hurting-democrats/.

25. June Kim, Blacki Migliozzi, K. K. Rebecca Lai, Neil Vigdor, and Lily Boyce,
"How the Pressure Grew for Biden to Drop Out," *New York Times*, July 21, 2024,
https://www.nytimes.com/interactive/2024/us/elections/biden-drop-out-democrats.
html.

It was 2:45 A.M. by the time the party's nominee took to the stage
to give his acceptance speech. Peak time for Guam.[1] That day, the
fourth and final of the 1972 Democratic National Convention, had
been taken up with a frantic search for a running mate for George
McGovern, the party's presidential candidate. The McGovern campaign had been rebuffed again and again by their preferred choices,
eventually enlisting Missouri senator Thomas Eagleton only minutes before the 3 P.M. convention filing deadline. Usually the nomination of a vice president is a pro forma affair, a rubber-stamp of
the nominee's choice, but not that evening. When the convention
opened the session for nominations and supporting speeches, the
raucous delegates placed name after name in contention, including
antiwar activist Jerry Rubin, CBS anchor Roger Mudd, Hispanic labor organizer Cesar Chavez, sitcom character Archie Bunker, and
China's Communist leader, Mao Tse-tung. When McGovern finally
made it to the podium, he opened with a joke: "I assume that everyone here is impressed with my control of this Convention in that my
choice for Vice President was challenged by only 39 other nominees."
The TV audience for his remarks, which had peaked earlier in the
evening at 70 million, had shrunk to around 15 million.[2]

The three previous days had been no less chaotic. McGovern's
campaign had arrived at the convention still battling a "stop Mc-
Govern" movement, coordinated principally by labor leaders, determined to deny him the nomination. The McGovern campaign
spent the first days fighting a series of obscure parliamentary challenges intended to deny him victory on the first ballot.[3] Though
McGovern's nomination was assured by the end of the first night,
the various challenges meant that the convention's first day ended
at 5:20 A.M. Day two, given over the party's platform, underscored
the openness of the convention, for good and ill, "with participatory democracy in all of its glorious messiness on public display."
The convention considered a series of minority planks from various wings of the party: for abortion rights, for gay marriage, for a
constitutional amendment permitting school prayer, and for a ban

on busing. Almost all were defeated, sometimes thanks to the machinations of the McGovern forces.[4] The second day finished at 6:24 A.M. Some delegates joked that the Democratic convention might not be over in time for the Republicans to hold theirs, also scheduled for Miami Beach, on August 21.[5] "More and more, you get the feeling that the secret purpose of this Democratic national convention is to ensure the re-election of Richard M. Nixon," wrote columnist Joseph Alsop.[6]

The tumult at Miami Beach was in some respects the logical end point of the desire of many reformist Democrats to introduce more participatory democracy into the presidential selection process. That reform spirit, dubbed the "New Politics," had been born in opposition to the Vietnam War in the 1960s and soon evolved into a broader critique of establishment liberalism. It had been given expression in the insurgent presidential campaigns of Senators Eugene McCarthy and Robert F. Kennedy in 1968 that forced President Lyndon B. Johnson into an early retirement. However, the New Politics faction was unable to prevent party brokers from bestowing the nomination on Johnson's vice president, Hubert Humphrey, without his having entered a single primary.[7] What it did succeed in doing at the 1968 Chicago convention, however, was passing a resolution to establish the Commission on Party Structure and Delegate Selection, to reform the rules by which the Democratic Party selected its presidential nominees and convention delegates.

Also known as the McGovern-Fraser Commission, after its two chairmen, this body was charged with devising recommendations to democratize the primary process and open the party's structures to previously marginalized groups—primarily women, African Americans, and the young. The commission report made a series of recommendations, most of which were enacted, for state delegations to be more demographically representative, for delegation selection procedures to be codified, and to strip state party leaders of the power to nominate delegates.[8] McGovern-Fraser was the first of a series of reforming commissions that transformed the rules governing the national Democratic Party in the 1970s and 1980s (some of them, such as the 1981 Hunt Commission, were established to correct perceived excesses in the results of earlier commissions). The 1972 Democratic primary race was the first to be conducted under the new rules. The convention in Miami Beach was the most open in the party's history. The ill-discipline on display was in part the result of the cork coming off the bottle of pent-up radical energies that had been building within the party for years.

By the time he arrived at Miami Beach, George McGovern, the unassuming senator from South Dakota, had become more of an avatar of the New Politics contingent than McCarthy or even Robert Kennedy had been. An outspoken critic of the Vietnam War and ally of the antiwar movement, McGovern had briefly stepped into the presidential race in 1968, at the request of the Kennedy family, following Robert F. Kennedy's assassination. As first chair of the reform commission, he had witnessed the restructuring of the primary process and was well prepared for the new institutional context when he announced his own bid for the presidency in 1971. McGovern ran a strategically dazzling campaign, relying on an army of enthusiastic grassroots volunteers and exploiting the new rules that had created a mass-participation primary system. The motivation and discipline of the McGovern campaign enabled a candidate whose national name recognition had been mired in the low single digits in 1971 to leapfrog many more established candidates and amass a commanding delegate lead by the time of the convention.[9]

As far as many regular Democrats were concerned, McGovern was the leader of a dangerous radical insurgency that threatened not only established Democratic traditions but also their political careers. Members of Congress were particularly disturbed by the chaos on display in Miami Beach. Most concluded, rightly as it transpired, that it was a harbinger of McGovern's likely defeat in that November's presidential election. A sufficiently heavy McGovern defeat might also lead to heavy Democratic losses in Congress. At the beginning of August, at McGovern's request, the candidate met with a caucus of House Democrats in a closed-door session. The ostensible purpose of the meeting, according to one report, was to show his former colleagues that "he has no horns and will not take them down to defeat on Nov. 7." This was the first time a presidential nominee had been moved to take such a step.[10]

There was similar concern among key Democratic constituencies, particularly organized labor. No other bloc was more implacably opposed to McGovern's nomination and, if they had no desire to see McGovern win the presidency, labor leaders also fretted that a disastrous McGovern showing would ripple outward to damage the rest of the party. "We have been able to live—not very well—through the Nixon years because the Democrats control Congress," said one official of the American Federation of Labor and Congress of Industrial Organizations (AFL-CIO), the largest and most powerful trade union collective in the United States. "So what we have probably got to do is try to save Congress."[11]

On Election Day, as expected, McGovern went down to defeat in one of the biggest landslides in US history, the sort of which Democrats had, since the New Deal, become accustomed to being on the other side. Nixon won all but one state (Massachusetts) and the District of Columbia and bested McGovern by almost twenty million popular votes. Postelection postmortems seemed to confirm that the Democratic Party had disintegrated. Though the party's black support remained solid, as Timothy Thurber has put it, "other members of the New Deal coalition deserted their party like passengers on a sinking ship." For the first time in the party's history, a Republican presidential candidate swept the South, winning some states with over 70 percent of the vote. More ominously, in the North, 55 percent of blue-collar workers opted for Nixon over McGovern, an alarming increase on the 41 percent who had voted for the Republican in 1968. A majority of Catholics opted for the Republican over the Democrat, and among union families, Nixon achieved a 17 percent increase on his 1968 tally, which testified to the failure of union leadership to rally to McGovern.[12]

The only bright spot was that Nixon's coattails, despite his tremendous victory, had failed to deliver control of either house of Congress to the Republican Party. In the Senate, the Democrats made a net gain of two seats, pushing their total Senate conference to fifty-seven. In the House, they lost only thirteen seats, which still left them with 242 seats to the Republicans' 192.[13] McGovern's candidacy may have been an electoral catastrophe, but at least it had been effectively contained. The *New York Times* speculated that perhaps the Democrats had benefited from what it characterized as the "penance" vote: "Democrats who defected to vote for the President were nevertheless firm enough in their commitment to the party to make up for that major unorthodoxy by being ultraloyal everywhere else on the ticket."[14]

The people had spoken, but it was not immediately clear what they had said. The voters had rejected McGovern, but the fact that they had returned solid Democratic majorities to both houses of Congress suggested that they were hardly making a decisive break with liberalism. The Democrats increased their Senate majority by two, from fifty-five to fifty-seven. The GOP fared better in the House, but the thirteen additional seats they won was well short of the thirty-nine needed to take control, and so the Democratic advantage remained substantial at 244 to 191. Indeed, given the relative moderation of Nixon's first term—the passage of unprecedented environmental legislation, the steady desegregation of the southern school system, the imposition of wage/price controls and general adherence to Keynesian economics, a guaranteed income plan, and a proposed national health insurance reform—observers could be forgiven for thinking that liberalism remained the nation's dominant ideology.

The year 1972 was convulsive for the Democratic Party. On the face of it, the Miami Beach convention was little more than self-indulgent and self-destructive. However, it also represented the profound transformation that the Democratic Party was undergoing. "McGovern's landslide defeat in 1972 became a negative touchstone for Democrats," writes Bruce Miroff, "a grim warning sign of what would happen to the party if it let its liberal wing prevail again."[15] However, the McGovern-Fraser Commission and the McGovern campaign would reshape the party in profound and lasting ways. Alongside the televised bedlam was another story of a party's voter base and legislative priorities evolving.

Though the party had not yet met the representation goals mandated by the reform commissions, it seemed to have made considerable strides toward them. Around 33 percent of the delegates to the convention were women—a significant increase on the 13 percent at the 1968 convention but still below the 50 percent target that all delegations were expected to achieve by 1976.[16] The convention nominated Jean Westwood as chair of the Democratic National Committee, the first woman to head a national party organization.[17] It was also the first national party convention to offer childcare facilities to its delegates.[18] Fifteen percent of the delegates to the convention were African American, more than double the number who had attended in 1968.[19] Representative Shirley Chisholm, congresswoman from New York's twelfth district, became the first woman to run for the Democratic Party's presidential nomination and the first African American to seek the presidential nomination of either party.[20]

If Congress had insulated itself from the immediate electoral consequences of McGovern, it was not untouched by the reform spirit that had animated his campaign. Indeed, within two years, Congress would witness the climax of a decades-long reform movement to democratize the institution, transferring power from conservative committee "barons" to the individual members. The success of that reform movement would coincide not with a political catastrophe for the Democratic Party but with a historic success, in the midterm congressional elections of 1974. The aftermath of those elections, and their legacy for the Democratic Party in Congress, is the subject of this book.

For many historians, the McGovern defeat of 1972 is one of the first set pieces in the decline and marginalization of the Democratic Party after the 1960s. In most political histories, the narrative is one of declension: Democratic politicians were swept from office as they found that their ideals no longer aligned with those of the average American. Columnist E. J. Dionne's largely supportive Bill Clinton–era assessment of liberal politics was titled *They Only Look Dead.*[21] Bruce Miroff has described a Democratic Party that has been trapped in an identity crisis since the early 1970s, "torn between their hearts and their heads, between idealistic convictions about equality and peace originally forged in the struggles over civil rights and the war in Vietnam, and practical calculations of how to win elections in a country whose majority evidently does not share such convictions."[22] Jeffrey Bloodworth has condemned "decades of ideological incoherence and political ineptitude" as Democrats discarded Vital Center liberalism (defined as "an antiutopian fighting faith committed to national greatness at home and human freedom abroad") and embraced a creed that was beloved by activists and despised by voters.[23] In more strident terms, Ronald Radosh has declared that since 1968 "the Democrats [have] stood in the public's eye for a new kind of liberalism, one that spelled permissiveness and moral nihilism."[24] Michael Tomasky has accused the American left of having "completely lost touch with the regular needs of regular Americans" and having come to be viewed "as pursuing narrow agendas that don't speak either to their basic needs in day-to-day life or to any larger vision for that society as a whole."[25]

By contrast, histories of the Republican Party concentrate on explaining its late twentieth-century ascendancy, asking how it was able to sweep aside the last vestiges of the "liberal consensus" that had sustained the Democratic Party's midcentury hegemony. Jefferson Cowie and Nick Salvatore have gone so far as to argue that the New Deal order should be understood as "a long exception" in the twentieth century, "a byproduct of the massive crisis of the Great Depression rather than the linear triumph of the liberal state." In fact, they argue, the continuities between the pre-1930s and the post-1970s United States are so striking as to negate the idea of an enduring liberal transformation of the nation's political economy.[26] Political historians who are loath to go as far as Cowie and Salvatore accept that American politics have moved decisively rightward since the 1970s and that conservative Republican ideas have shaped the choices available to policy-makers in the latter third of the twentieth century. Steven Hayward and Sean Wilentz have both published works under the title *The Age of Reagan*. Between them, that era spans 1964 to 2008.[27]

These analyses are based on a cyclical interpretation of American politics, in which political outcomes are shaped by alternating right and left majority coalitions. This interpretation owes a great deal to the father-and-son historians Arthur Schlesinger Sr. and Arthur Schlesinger Jr., who elaborated a similar theory of the "cycles of American history."[28] They also draw on V. O. Key and Walter Dean Burnham's "critical election" theories, in which "critical" realigning elections disrupt established voting patterns and reshape the balance of political power within the American system at regular intervals.[29] In the twentieth century, the "critical" elections are 1932, which heralded the coming of the New Deal coalition, and either 1968 or 1980, which brought the conservative coalition to power. Thus, in these models, Franklin Roosevelt inaugurates the great era of reform and either Nixon or Reagan the great era of reaction. Liberal reformers and conservative reactionaries dominate policy-making in roughly forty-year chunks.

This book proceeds from the assumption that this idea of "realignment" cannot fully encapsulate the political situation in the United States between 1974 and 2008. There is certainly evidence to support a narrative of conservative, and Republican, political triumph after the 1960s. For instance, excluding Jimmy Carter's narrow 50.1 percent victory in 1976, no Democratic candidate would win more than 50 percent of the vote in a presidential election between 1968 and 2008. By contrast, the Republican candidate carried all states but one in the presidential elections of 1972 and 1984, a feat not equalled by any Democrat since.

The political story of the last third of the twentieth century is more complicated than a straightforward one of liberal collapse and conservative resurgence. Since Alan Brinkley's declaration in 1994 that "twentieth century American conservatism" was "something of an orphan in historical scholarship," there has been an explosion of outstanding scholarship on the history of conservatives.[30] Historians have explored a range of conservative activists, organizations, leaders, ideas, and institutions. To take a representative sample: Mary C. Brennan has posited an alternative history of the 1960s focusing on the conservative activists who spent the decade infiltrating the Republican Party and isolating its liberal northeastern wing.[31] Thomas Sugrue and Dan Carter have argued for the centrality of race to the conservative ascendancy.[32] Lisa McGirr has explored the world of the highly motivated suburban conservatives in California's Orange County.[33] Kevin M. Kruse has traced an alliance of Christian conservatives and business leaders back to the New Deal.[34] Nicole Hemmer has anatomized the vast and diverse conservative media network that has emerged since the 1940s.[35] Steven M. Teles has dissected the multifaceted, largely elite-level assault on the "liberal legal regime" by conservative judges, academics, public interest law firms, and think tanks.[36] Michael Flamm has identified the rise of "law and order" politics and the widespread fear of social breakdown at the end of the 1960s as a key motor of the conservative ascendancy.[37]

The literature on late twentieth-century American liberalism is as underdeveloped as the scholarship on post-1960s conservatism is rich. The continued endurance of liberalism after the 1960s has been ignored in favor of a clean teleological story of Republican triumph as the American people embraced conservative remedies and rejected liberal reform.[38] This is not to suggest that conservatives have not enjoyed considerable political and policy successes: tax reform was vigorously and successfully implemented; private sector unions were diminished; deregulation advanced steadily; government-sponsored affirmative action was essentially halted; and defense outlays were dramatically increased. Whereas considerable energy has been spent on explaining the "rise of conservatism," historians have too often neglected the vital task of seeking out its limits and reversals. The result has been to reduce liberals, inadvertently, to bit players in a drama in which they were in fact leading characters.

This book focuses on the US Congress, where Democratic strength proved most durable over this period. The Democrats retained control of the House of Representatives for the entirety of the Nixon and Reagan eras (indeed until the "Republican Revolution" of 1994) and maintained a similar hold on the Senate for all but six years of the same period. Congress became a redoubt for the Democratic Party. Though they seemed incapable of winning the presidency except under abnormal circumstances, they seemed equally incapable of losing Congress. By 1990, political scientist Norman Ornstein was describing "the persistence of firm Democratic Party majorities in Congress" as one of "the most enduring, puzzling, and contentious phenomena of modern American political life."[39] This stands in stark contrast to the substantial Republican congressional losses in the 1930s and 1960s, the two supposed apotheoses of twentieth-century liberal reform foment. In the "Age of Reagan," conservatives were forced to reckon with a Democratic Party that stubbornly refused to collapse and proved surprisingly adept at frustrating their legislative ambitions.

Congress has been chronically understudied by historians, save in reference to a presidential agenda. Indeed, presidencies remain at the forefront of twentieth-century political history, despite the "presidential synthesis" having been dismissed as "a failure" by the historian Thomas Cochran as early as 1948.[40] Dividing US political history into discrete four- or eight-year chunks often has the effect of obscuring longer trends. For example, between 1955 and 1995, while the White House passed from Republican to Democrat and back again, the House of Representatives remained firmly in Democratic hands.[41] This book does not entirely shatter the "presidential synthesis," as evidenced by several of the chapter titles. Nor does it argue that a presidency is always a misleading way to organize political time. Nonetheless, it does aspire to give Congress a more prominent place in US political history and to argue that turning the lens away from the White House reveals forces and developments that might otherwise be overlooked.

In focusing on Congress, this book explores how Democrats perceived and reacted to the rising conservative movement. It begins by treating the 1974 elections as a moment of genuine historical contingency, rather than a post-Watergate aberration. From the perspective of the mid-1970s, the triumph of conservatism was by no means a foregone conclusion. At the time, many Democrats remained complacently confident that they were members of the nation's majority party, a status that seemed fundamentally unchallenged. This book follows various Democratic factions within Congress as they competed to take advantage of political opportunities, pushed their own legislative priorities, and reacted to a rising conservative movement that continued to grow after 1974.

One of the key themes of this book is the unsuitability of Congress as an arena for the discussion and refinement of a party's public philosophy. It seeks to show how grander liberal ambitions were often subordinated to the logic of legislative politics and policy-making, especially after a series of institutional reforms in the 1970s had the unintended effect of intensifying the centrifugal forces that fragmented both Congress and the Democratic Party. Again and again, the legislature displayed a remarkable facility for undermining iconoclasm and stalling policy experimentation. However, the enduring Democratic strength in Congress meant that Capitol Hill remained at the center of the party's efforts to reclaim its preeminent position in American politics. This was further complicated by the ideological heterogeneity of the Democratic Party, which similarly militated against Democratic efforts to recast liberalism to meet the problems of the age.

By "liberalism," this book principally means an ideology of social and economic interventionism that came to define the Democratic Party after the New Deal. In a broad sense, Democrats were united by a shared belief in the capacity of the federal government to solve social and economic problems. By the 1970s, the Democratic Party was confronting a political climate that was increasingly hostile to government, at least in the abstract. In 1964, for instance, the University of Michigan's National Election Study found that 76 percent of respondents believed government could be trusted "to do what is right . . . just about always [or] most of the time." By 1980, that figure had slumped to an anemic 25 percent.[42] One of the most pressing problems that confronted the Democratic Party in this era—and the one that they found most difficult to solve—was how to build public support for a fundamentally pro-government ideology among an electorate that was so much more disdainful of government as a tool of amelioration and advancement.

Paradoxically, it was in defending the existing government that Democrats enjoyed some of their greatest policy successes in this era. Nowhere are the limitations of American conservatism more apparent than in the failure of Republicans to significantly roll back the responsibilities of the welfare state. As R. Shep Melnick has noted, the welfare and regulatory state has become embedded in American society because the American public's expectations of the government's responsibilities remain remarkably high. Melnick notes that while Americans might cheer denunciations of tyrannical big government, the only federal programs they seem to oppose "are foreign aid (whose cost they substantially overestimate) and something called 'welfare.'"[43] As can be seen in later chapters, while the Democrats struggled to make a positive case for new government interventions, they had comparatively little difficulty defending the existing ones from conservative antistatists.

Despite the casual use of the term so far (and indeed throughout this book) there is, in fact, no single "Democratic Party." The party has national institutions (the Democratic National Committee, most notably), but those institutions have limited control over the actions of other cogs within the party machine. There is a Democratic Party in the House of Representatives and another in the Senate; there are fifty state parties; there are the networks surrounding presidential, gubernatorial, congressional, and sundry other state-level candidates; there are activist groups and labor unions; there are innumerable caucuses, coalitions, committees, and conferences that are, to a greater or lesser extent, Democrat-associated. When the party does not the control the White House, it has no formally, or even informally, recognized leader. Even a Democratic President, nominally the party's leader, struggles to impose his will on its membership. Though this book focuses primarily on the congressional wing of the Democratic Party, even this can be subdivided by region, state, and ideological predilection. As the entertainer Will Rogers once famously joked, "I am not a member of an organized political party—I'm a Democrat."[44]

Less than two years after the McGovern debacle, the Democratic ship was looking distinctly more buoyant. In the 1974 midterm elections, with the GOP bogged down by the Watergate scandal and economic downturn, the party garnered some of its best results since Johnson's glory days. The share of the electorate registered as Republicans slumped to 18 percent.[45] If the Democrats had to undergo an identity crisis and civil war, it must have seemed fortuitous that the Republican Party was reeling at the same time, having spectacularly failed to capitalize on the opportunity they had been handed by the Nixon administration. That same year, Lanny Davis, a New Politics activist (and a future member of the Clinton administration), published *The Emerging Democratic Majority*, an explicit rejoinder to Kevin Phillips's book of five years earlier that sported a nearly identical title, *The Emerging Republican Majority*.[46]

Within Congress, where Democratic majorities had swelled to remarkable proportions, the 1974 elections led directly to the climax of a long reform movement that both defenestrated conservative committee "barons" and empowered individual representatives with new resources and outlets to pursue a variety of programmatic commitments. The first chapter of this book explores those elections and their aftermath. The class of 1974, soon dubbed the "Watergate Babies," constituted a generational shift within the institution, introducing a distinct breed of legislator—young, media-savvy, ambitious, impatient, and entrepreneurial—that Burdett Loomis would identify as "the new American politician" in 1988.[47] Their influence would be felt in the Democratic Party for decades, and they loom large in this book. The Watergate Babies joined a Congress that was becoming increasingly determined to assert its own prerogatives against an overmighty executive. The circumstances were therefore promising not only for a Democratic recovery but also for a congressionally driven Democratic recovery.

The second chapter will show how those hopes began to falter almost immediately. Focusing on the efforts of the Democratic Congress to pass legislation over a veto-happy President Gerald Ford, it will demonstrate how fragile the unity of the Democratic majorities proved to be. With new resources at their disposal, many new members proved more concerned with winning reelection than with party-building activities. I pay particular attention in this chapter to the California congressman, Phillip Burton, who sought unsuccessfully to transform the House Democratic Caucus into an instrument of liberal reform. This chapter will explore why the Democratic Congress, despite a series of advantages, was unable to seize the legislative agenda from Ford.

The third chapter turns its attentions to the early years of Jimmy Carter's presidency and to his relationship with the Democratic Congress. Initially, the situation seemed brighter. On the surface, with the Democrats in control of the White House and Capitol Hill, the political context bore comparison with the heyday of FDR or LBJ. However, this chapter will show how Carter failed to provide the forceful liberal leadership for which many congressional Democrats had hoped. Much of this chapter is given over to a case study of the revival of national planning ideas in the face of the prolonged economic crisis of the 1970s and the legislative battle to pass the Humphrey-Hawkins Full Employment Act, one of the most ambitious pieces of legislation to come before Congress in this period.

The fourth chapter continues to follow the breakdown of relations between Carter and the Democratic Congress. It considers the emergence of several popular and viable alternatives to Carter within the congressional party—most notably New York senator Pat Moynihan, Massachusetts senator Ted Kennedy, and Arizona representative Mo Udall—and explores how they reacted to the challenges of the 1970s and, both implicitly and explicitly, rejected the governing philosophy that Carter was pursuing. Congressional disillusionment with Carter would curdle into Kennedy's unsuccessful primary challenge to the former's presidency, which both Moynihan and Udall endorsed.

Chapter five opens with the Democratic Party at perhaps its lowest ebb since the 1920s. With Reagan in the White House and the party having lost control of the Senate, Democrats were forced to confront the loss of their majority status. Yet even here, the party staged a remarkable, and remarkably swift, recovery. Though polling showed considerable ideological support for

Reagan's antigovernment agenda, this would translate into meagre political support in programmatic terms. When the Reagan administration sought to retrench one of the largest entitlement programs, Social Security (an episode that forms a key case study in this chapter), it became embroiled in a damaging and ultimately futile political controversy. The administration's mishandling of the Social Security issue stands as one of the most spectacular political blunders in recent political history. Throughout the Reagan years, the Democratic-controlled Congress played a vital role in obstructing and delaying the ambitions of the ascendant conservatives.

The sixth chapter follows a parallel story that unfolded across the 1980s and into the 1992 election but that had its roots in the 1974 elections. It begins with the Democratic Party struggling to come to terms with the Reagan Revolution and the fact that the Republicans had become, in Moynihan's words, the "party of ideas." There was no shortage of Democrats seeking to claim the party's intellectual mantle, however. The chapter follows the rise of the "neoliberal" movement, a cohort of young legislators, journalists, academics, and policy thinkers who sought to reconceptualize liberalism around the virtues of pragmatism and realism. In the words of one of the doctrine's founders, neoliberalism was devised by liberals who "decided to retain our goals but to abandon some of our prejudices."[48] The doctrine of neoliberalism was one of the most ideologically substantive contributions that the Watergate Babies made to debates within the Democratic Party. The neoliberal critique inspired a fierce backlash, and debate over the value and desirability of its "new ideas" filled op-ed pages. Neoliberal candidates sought the presidency in the 1984, 1988, and 1992 elections, but neoliberalism proved as incapable as traditional liberalism of defeating Reaganism. From 1984, attention would increasingly turn to extra-congressional bodies as a means of getting the party back into the White House, particularly the Democratic Leadership Council (DLC), a group of moderate and conservative Democrats who drew some inspiration from the neoliberals. This chapter concludes with the Democratic primary contest that pitted the neoliberal former senator Paul Tsongas against the DLC-affiliated New Democrat Bill Clinton to demonstrate the extent to which this ideology had come to dominate the party's mainstream.

In the years after 1974, Congress was the Democrats' most effective weapon and perhaps also its most significant weakness. The continued existence of solid Democratic congressional majorities throughout the 1970s and 1980s meant that it was able to resist the ambitions of resurgent conservatives quite effectively. Ultimately, the Democratic Party's surprising strength may have been a key part of its undoing in these years. Ironically, the very absence of a decisive realignment may have been a key factor working against the party. Democrats were not moved, as Republicans had been, to construct an alternative infrastructure to advance their cause. The very absence of a stable beachhead in the political establishment forced conservatives to pursue innovative strategies. The Republican Party greeted the 1980s supported by an extensive network of politically minded think tanks and policy institutes, while the Democrats had to scramble to catch up. The mentality of a minority party accompanied the Republicans into office and was supplemented in important ways by the Democrats' failure to collapse in the face of the conservative onslaught. Opposition is often the best place for a political party to redefine itself, to develop and hone new ideas. For more than a decade after 1984, the Democrats never truly experienced it.

Donkey Work

"We Came Here to Take the Bastille"

The Midterm Elections of 1974
and the Watergate Babies

John Hazuda Sr. had voted Democratic in every presidential election in which he had been eligible. A boilermaker from Pittsburgh,
Hazuda had spent half his life in the trade. He had worked hard to
provide for his family, and by the early 1970s he was settling into
comfortable middle age. Dark haired and well-built, Hazuda lived in
a one-family brick house halfway up a hill in the suburb of Beech-
view. His home had multiple televisions and wrought-metal pea-
cocks on the wall. In 1972, he was working on a project installing
antipollution devices on a power plant in Ohio. He rose at 5:30 A.M.
each day to drive the sixty miles to the site in his white-and-green
1972 Oldsmobile. On weekends, he golfed, hunted, or (during base-
ball season) watched Pittsburgh Pirates games at the Three Rivers
Stadium. He owned a plot of land and a trailer at a nearby mountain
lake to which he could retreat in summer, and each winter he spent
two to three weeks vacationing in Florida. And in that year's presidential election, he planned throw his support to Richard Nixon.
In fact, he intended to vote for the straight Republican ticket and
was even contemplating a permanent switch in his party affiliation. Though unenthused by the election, the issues that had driven
Hazuda into Nixon's coalition were busing ("If they can force me to
send my kids to a different school, well, then they could force me to
go to a different church"), welfare ("They wouldn't be in poverty if
they went out and got a job"), and amnesty for draft evaders ("These
guys that went off to Canada better not come back. I'd hang them
if they did").

As the *New York Times* correspondent sent to interview Hazuda noted, the Pennsylvania native was "one of millions of blue-collar workers . . . who [were] abandoning their habitual allegiance to the Presidential nominee of the Democratic Party."[1] Dissolving those ties of allegiance between the Democratic Party and the white working class had been central to Nixon's efforts to construct his New Majority. The blue-collar Republican voter would be bound to the GOP by cultural rather than economic ties. Nixon was particularly concerned with winning "white ethnic" voters—generally defined as the descendants of southern and eastern European immigrants—to the Republican side.[2] These voters were to be persuaded that the Democratic Party, in the words of conservative Democrat Ronald Radosh, had come to represent "a new kind of liberalism, one that spelled permissiveness and moral nihilism, and that ignored and ridiculed the conservative desires" of working-class America.[3] The Nixon campaign, according to its own "Assault Book," sought to "portray McGovern as the pet radical of Eastern Liberalism, the darling of the New York Times, the hero of the Berkeley Hill Jet Set" in contrast to Nixon, who was to be represented as "the Candidate of the Common Man, the working man."[4] The Slovakian-descended Hazuda was an ideal target for the Nixon strategy, and, as his interview suggests, it was apparently vindicated in that year's presidential election results.

Hazuda was part of what many historians have termed the "backlash," the rejection of the Democratic Party, and of liberal politics more broadly, by substantial portions of the white working class.[5] Voters like Hazuda were vital to Nixon's efforts to construct a new Republican governing coalition, and the remarkable tallies that Nixon ran up among blue-collar voters, Catholics, and union families was a testament to the apparent success of the strategy.

But if Hazuda was a symbol of the fracturing of the New Deal coalition, there were other voters who seemed to offer hope of a reinvigorated majority for the Democrats. Almost a year after the 1972 election, the *Washington Post* featured a profile of another suburban family, the Perlsteins, as part of its Washington Today series. Harvey Perlstein was a thirty-seven-year-old systems analyst for the Westinghouse Electric Corporation who, when transferred to Annapolis, Maryland, had moved with his wife, Muriel, and their two young children to a new development in Montgomery County, on the outskirts of Washington, DC. Perlstein became a "reverse commuter," traveling from his suburban home on Randolph Road to Annapolis, and, living in the "inner suburbs," the Perlsteins sought to combine the urban with the rural. They were regular attendees at Washington's museums, theaters, and historic sites, and they tended tomatoes, corn, peanuts, and watermelons in their garden. Harvey and Muriel were both graduates, holding degrees from the Massachusetts Institute of Technology and Boston University, respectively. Both were politically engaged; Harvey had been a Democratic precinct chairman in Baltimore while Muriel had been a fund-raiser for the local unit of the Parent Teacher Association. They were contemptuous of "rednecks" from whom they had experienced anti-Semitism and professed their ease in "integrated" communities. They were "fascinated" by Watergate and expressed concern about inflation, which they felt was doing the most harm to the middle class.[6]

It was voters like the Perlsteins who flipped Maryland's fifth congressional district from Republican to Democratic control in 1974.[7] The victorious Democrat there, Gladys Noon Spellman, was in some ways an unusual "Watergate Baby." She was older than many other members of the incoming class, a grandmother in her midfifties. She also had significantly more political experience than some of her colleagues, having served for more than a decade on the Prince George's County Board of Commissioners, of which she ultimately became chairwoman, and then on its successor body, the County Council, after the latter was established in 1970.[8] In other respects, she was a typical member of the class of '74, both in her demographic background and ideology. A New York native, Spellman had studied at George Washington University (though left without taking a degree) before becoming an elementary school teacher in Maryland. She came to electoral politics as an activist on her school's Parent Teacher Association and through civic associations, and when she ran for county commissioner the first time, it was as a reform-minded "Independent Democrat," running against the local Democratic machine. She worked for Robert F. Kennedy's presidential campaign in 1968, and Massachusetts senator Edward M. Kennedy repaid the favor by appearing at one of her fund-raisers in 1974.[9] As a politician, Spellman cultivated what one colleague called a "mother hen" quality to conceal her political skills in an environment that was not always favorable to forceful female politicians. She often boasted that she had never raised her voice in the pursuit of any objective. She became known familiarly as "Gladys" to colleagues and constituents (an affectation that would continue in Congress). She recalled that, as a member of the County Council, to avoid being "trampled," she would casually suggest her ideas to one of the male councilors. "He'd bring it up and I'd say, 'Gee, that's a good idea. I think it's marvelous.' Pretty soon, they began to think I had pretty good judgement."[10]

As the Democratic candidate for the Maryland fifth in 1974, Spellman courted the district's predominantly suburban electorate. She announced her candidacy from the front lawn of her suburban home in Laurel, calling the incumbent Republican, Lawrence Hogan, "a White House echo" and accusing him of trying to undermine House Judiciary Committee investigations into President Nixon.[11] She made corruption and inflation the keystones of her campaign, both issues that appealed to Maryland's affluent suburbanites. As a candidate, she spent a day working as a cashier at a Pantry Food Market, scanning and bagging purchases in front of the TV cameras and commiserating with the shoppers about the rising food prices.[12] These strategies seemed to pay dividends on Election Day. In 1972, the Republican incumbent had carried the seat with 61 percent of the vote; in 1974, Spellman won the seat with 52.6 percent.[13]

The suburban voters who swept Spellman and others into office were an attractive prize for the Democrats. Since 1966, the number of House districts that were more than half suburban had risen from 92 to 131 (by contrast, the number of seats that were predominantly rural had fallen from 181 to 130).[14] For some Democrats, these seats were a key part of the party's post-1968 evolution. Jack Newfield of the *Village Voice* had suggested that the Democratic Party's future lay in an alliance of "campus, ghetto, suburb."[15] He believed that the foundations of a new Democratic majority were to be found in bringing college students, impoverished nonwhite urbanites, and affluent suburbanites to the cause of liberalism. With such a coalition, it was reasoned, the party could afford to make losses among white, working-class voters who stifled racial progress and looked askance at emerging liberal priorities like environmentalism. The new Democratic coalition was impossible, however, if the party did not make inroads into suburbs that had once been Republican strongholds.

The 1974 congressional elections went some way toward vindicating those predictions. Democrats made gains in suburbs across the nation, picking up seats in the environs of New York City, Chicago, Philadelphia, Atlanta, Indianapolis, Detroit, Denver, Los Angeles, and San Francisco.[16] The "class of '74" represented one of the most significant generational shifts in the history of Congress and the Democratic Party. The new legislators—young, media-savvy, ambitious, impatient, and with their own distinct sensibility—

would enter an institution that was becoming increasingly jealous of its own prerogatives and determined to assert itself as the first branch of government once more. That sensibility was informed by the years that had shaped their political consciousness and often also by their suburban constituents (almost half of the new Democratic intake in the House came from seats with predominantly suburban electorates). They would immediately join forces with a movement that had been agitating to reform Congress for decades, effectively guaranteeing it final victory by 1975. After its humiliation in 1972, the Democratic Party appeared to be staging a remarkable comeback. Yet by 1975, even with this sudden arrival of Democratic talent into Congress, the party would find itself struggling with how to reformulate liberalism to grapple with the challenges of the 1970s and adapt to the post–New Deal order. Before the glow of victory had faded, the Democrats were struggling with the inherent limitations of Congress as an arena for refashioning a party's public philosophy and with the new barriers that their reforms had put in the way of that task.

Congressional Government

Even before the 1974 elections, there were signs that Congress was becoming more restive and confrontational. Nixon had been elected in 1968 as the first president since Zachary Taylor 120 years earlier not to carry at least one house of Congress for his party. At the beginning of his second term, with a thumping personal victory that had done little for his party's congressional wing, Nixon began signaling his intention to pursue more aggressively conservative policies. His new cabinet, according to the *New York Times*, suggested "a White House retreat from progressive social action," as did the president's description of many welfare programs as "all fat, too bloated" and his attacks on "permissiveness" in civil liberties and criminal justice.[17] The conciliatory and pragmatic Nixon of 1968–1972, it seemed, was being jettisoned in favor of a more hard-line approach.

Democratic fears of a more aggressively conservative Nixon meshed with growing disquiet over the president's aggrandizement of executive power, and in particular his encroachments on Congress's role in determining budgetary priorities and on its war powers. Domestically, Democrats were especially incensed by Nixon's habit of "impounding" congressionally appropriated funds for federal programs.[18] Senator Sam Ervin Jr., the "simple country lawyer" who would find fame as the chairman of the select committee that investigated Watergate, denounced impoundment as "contemptuous of the role of Congress in our tripartite system."[19] By March, even the normally temperate Senate majority leader Mike Mansfield was warning that the issue of executive privilege "may be approaching a crisis stage."[20]

The same year Nixon's second term began, Arthur Schlesinger Jr., historian and former advisor to President John F. Kennedy, published *The Imperial Presidency*, which gave a conceptual skeleton to these complaints. The trend of the twentieth century, said Schlesinger, had been toward "presidential primacy." However, in recent years, this had lurched toward "presidential supremacy" and produced "a conception of presidential power so spacious and peremptory as to imply a radical transformation of the traditional polity." Under Nixon, Schlesinger contended, the presidency had so outstripped its constitutional limits as to be a practically revolutionary entity. A Kennedy partisan, Schlesinger acknowledged his own role in nurturing "the presidential mystique" but largely shielded JFK from culpability. Instead, he placed most of the blame for unwelcome recent developments at the feet of Kennedy's successors: Johnson and Nixon.[21]

As James Sundquist has written, the enhanced powers of the modern presidency were not "wrested by self-seeking chief executives from a struggling but ultimately yielding Congress" but rather were wrested by "mutual consent, for the shifts were made pursuant to law, and Congress wrote and passed the laws."[22] Now Congress was being confronted with the consequences of its dereliction. Even before evidence of law-breaking by the Nixon administration came to light, Democrats in Congress found themselves facing a president who impounded funds that they had appropriated and who claimed the right to unilaterally conduct a war in Indochina. The stirrings of the Watergate investigation only emboldened an already bullish Congress looking to reclaim some of the prerogatives that had been ceded to the president. Against that backdrop, Congress and the White House spent much of 1973–1974 snarling at each other across the capital.

In late 1973, Congress passed the War Powers Act, over a presidential veto, to reclaim some of its foreign policy prerogatives. The act required the president to notify Congress within forty-eight hours of the deployment of American forces to any action and then to seek further congressional authorization within sixty days for that military action to continue. In July 1974, Congress followed up with the Congressional Budget Control and Impoundment Act, which clarified the process by which Congress formulated a budget and established the Congressional Budget Office to assist in doing so.[23] Against a weakening Nixon, Congress was mounting a challenge to the president's role as the prime mover in the legislative process. For the pre-1977 Democratic Party, this outcome was fairly agreeable. Let the Republicans control the White House; the Democrats would control the political agenda. And they seemed well placed, institutionally at least, to attempt this. In August 1974, the month Nixon resigned, Gallup recorded its highest approval ratings for Congress in months. Forty-seven percent of respondents approved of the way Congress was "handling its job."[24] This was hardly an overwhelming endorsement, but, considered within a broader crisis of authority afflicting the United States, it was certainly encouraging.

Landslide!

There were tremors before November's earthquake. In January 1974, six senior House Republicans, who would likely have occupied leadership positions or committee chairs in the event of a GOP takeover, announced their plans to retire.[25] That pessimism was borne out as the year unfolded. There were seven special elections in 1974. All were in traditionally Republican seats, and in all but one the Democratic candidate triumphed.[26] In February, Richard F. Vander Veen, a corporate lawyer and former chair of the Michigan fifth district Democratic Party, won the special election to fill the House seat vacated by Vice President Gerald Ford, beating the latter's handpicked successor. Vander Veen had sought to make the special election a referendum on Richard Nixon's continuation in office and upon his victory declared that the president had "lost the moral right to govern." Vander Veen was the first Democrat elected to Congress from Michigan's fifth congressional district since 1912. Senator Robert Griffin, a Republican from Michigan and minority whip, admitted that it was "something of a disaster" for the state party. Senator Mark Hatfield, a liberal Republican of Oregon, echoed Griffin: "The signal is pretty clear that Watergate has infected the entire scene. No Republican can be considered safe this year."[27] In another special election, John Burton, the younger brother of the House panjandrum Phillip Burton, was elected in California's sixth district. The RNC had invested next to nothing in the seat, and Burton's opponent gloomily told the *New York Times* that he would be "lucky" to get 25 percent of the vote. He managed just over 21 percent.[28]

For a brief moment, the arrival of President Gerald Ford seemed to offer the Republicans a way out of the morass. To the dismay of many Democrats, Ford enjoyed considerable public goodwill when he entered the White House. He was affable, forthright, and popular on Capitol Hill. Indeed, it was for these very qualities, combined with the expectation of an uncontroversial congressional confirmation, that he was tapped by Nixon to succeed the disgraced Vice President Agnew. Unlike Nixon and Agnew, Ford was, at least initially, a much less effective fund-raising tool for Democrats. Satirists might have portrayed the new president as slow-witted and clumsy, but at least that meant he was unlikely to be fomenting criminal conspiracies in the Oval Office. However, Ford squandered much of the goodwill he had banked when, almost one month to the day after Nixon's resignation, he issued a "full, free and absolute pardon" to his predecessor for "all offenses . . . which he . . . has committed or may have committed or taken part in" during his presidency.[29] However necessary Ford believed the pardon was to bring a definitive end to the "long national nightmare," it proved wildly unpopular. Senator Abraham Ribicoff, a Democrat of Connecticut, accused Ford of casting "great doubt on the principle that all persons are equal before the law."[30] Suspicions were voiced about the pardon's breadth, and accusations of a quid pro quo soon began to circulate. The *St. Louis Post-Dispatch* spoke for many when it asked, "Is Ford Protecting Nixon?" The *New York Times* chastised Ford for an "act of monumental folly" that had "wiped out the era of good feelings that he himself had inaugurated."[31]

In October, Ford appeared before a House Judiciary subcommittee to answer questions on the pardon, the first chief executive to do so since Lincoln. A fortnight earlier, Congress had reduced the $850,000 allocated to manage Nixon's transition expenses to $200,000.[32] "No President could ever agree to allow the counsel to the President to go down and testify before a committee," Nixon had declared bullishly at a press conference in March 1973.[33] Now a president had gone *personally* to Congress, effectively as a supplicant. Ford appeared for two hours, and he was received with warmth and civility. The only truly sharp line of questioning came from first-term New York Democrat Elizabeth Holtzman, who made reference to the nation's "dark suspicions" that President Ford had cut some sort of "deal" with Nixon.[34]

Demographically and temperamentally, Holtzman was in many respects a forerunner of the class of '74, embodying the traits that would define their actions in Congress. A Brooklyn native from a prosperous family, Holtzman had gotten her start in electoral politics in high school, running for student body vice president on the same ticket as her twin brother, Robert.[35] Although it was some years before Holtzman ran in another election, she remained politically engaged. She studied at Radcliffe College and then Harvard Law School, where she became involved with the Student Nonviolent Coordinating Committee (SNCC) and spent some time clerking on civil rights cases in Georgia. After a few years in private law practice, and following a recommendation from her law school colleagues, in 1967 Holtzman became a bureaucratic liaison in the office of New York mayor John Lindsay, an aristocratic liberal Republican who would switch allegiance to the Democratic Party in time to mount a presidential bid in 1972. In 1970, Holtzman moved into Democratic Party politics and was elected a district leader (Democratic state committeeperson) for Flatbush (the Brooklyn neighborhood that contained her parents' home) on a Reform ticket.[36]

In 1972, Holtzman launched an insurgent primary challenge to incumbent representative Emanuel Celler for the Democratic nomination in New York's sixteenth district. At eighty-three years old, Celler was venerable even by congressional standards. Having first been elected to Congress in 1922, almost twenty years before Holtzman was born, he was the chair of the Judiciary Committee and the "Dean of the House"—a title bestowed on the member with the longest continuous service. Though on most issues a liberal (he had opposed discriminatory immigration restrictions, denounced McCarthyism, and supported gun control), Celler had been a supporter of the Vietnam War and a sceptic of environmentalism. He was also unsympathetic to the women's liberation movement and had opposed the Equal Rights Amendment. These put him out of step with his district, and Holtzman, a cofounder of the Brooklyn Women's Political Caucus, made his "high-handed opposition" to those liberal causes a key part of her campaign.[37] Holtzman defeated Celler narrowly in the primary, by a margin of 609 votes out of almost 35,000 cast. That contest would drag on bitterly for several months, as Celler sought to have the primary vote nullified on the grounds of voter fraud. However, he eventually abandoned his dwindling hopes of reelection, and in November, the thirty-one-year-old Holtzman became the youngest woman ever elected to Congress (a title she would keep until 2014).[38]

Holtzman's confrontational questioning of President Ford in October 1974 was of a piece with her style as a legislator. In this she prefigured the assertive approach of the Watergate Babies and seemed to be the embodiment of a Congress determined to constrain the "imperial presidency." Though Holtzman joked, shortly before she was elected, that she had yet to resolve her "Don Quixote problem" (i.e., whether she should embark on a potentially fruitless quest to accomplish her political goals), she took political risks more readily than the average new House member.[39] In early 1974, Holtzman gave a speech, later excerpted in the *New York Times*, that reflected on her first term and discussed the exercise of "'freshperson' power," a neologism with "a delightful dual connotation" implying "newness and new approaches" as well as "a wholesome impertinence and impatience."[40] She was appointed to replace Celler on the Judiciary Committee, which made her a key player in the unfolding Watergate scandal.[41] She endeavored to block Ford's nomination as vice president, suggesting that he had misled the House Judiciary Committee in testimony and even that his nomination might itself be unconstitutional.[42] On the campaign trail in 1974, constituents excitedly declared that they had seen her on the television and thanked her for having "the guts" to make a stand. One admiring voter she encountered while campaigning in a supermarket told her, "Boy, you really chopped up what's his name—Chrysler? Pinto?"[43] If any first-time candidates had taken note of her career, they would have received an object lesson in the benefits of political independence and audacity and of the importance of comparatively new forms of media, like television, in cultivating a profile.

The significance of Ford's pardon would recede—by 1976 it was apparently no barrier to Ford nearly repelling the ostentatiously righteous Jimmy Carter in a presidential election—but in late 1974, public outrage at being cheated of catharsis was still fresh. At the beginning of October, the pollster Louis Harris told the Democratic Steering and Policy Committee that "anyone who tries to get out politically this fall and defend that pardon in any part of this country, North or South, is almost literally going to have his head handed to him."[44] With Ford's apparent political self-destruction and the nation's continued economic woes, one journalist noted that the "free wheeling euphoria of the Democrats" was rising once more.[45] For the first time in years, it was good to be a Democrat again.

"The Republicans are mounting major threats to continued Democratic control of Alaska and Maine," wrote David Broder in early October. "But in between those two states, there is a very big country that looks Democratic in election '74."[46] On the campaign trail, President Ford warned of a possible "legislative dictatorship" by the Democratic Party.[47] His warnings went unheeded. In November, the Democratic Party recorded its biggest wins since 1964. The party made a net gain of forty-nine seats in the House of Representatives and four in the Senate. With 291 seats to the GOP's 144, the Democrats now commanded a technically veto-proof majority in the House. The last time Democrats had done this well in the House, LBJ had been in the White House and Gerald Ford had been the frustrated minority leader. Reforms to the cloture rules at the beginning of 1975 would make their sixty-seat Senate majority at least theoretically capable of overruling a presidential veto. Democratic success was also reflected at the subcongressional level. For instance, the Democrats gained four governorships, taking their total to thirty-six against the Republicans' thirteen.[48]

More than the swelling majorities, the sheer size of the incoming Democratic class drew the attention of the press. In January 1975, seventy-five new Democratic representatives and eight new Democratic senators took their seats. It was the largest class since 1948. Fifteen of the seventy-five were from districts that had not elected a Democratic representative since 1945. Three of those were the first Democrats to represent their district in the twentieth century and a further three were the first Democrats elected in their district since its creation. The press was fascinated with the class of '74. Countless articles and profiles exploring their cultural and demographic similarities appeared. "The stories solidified the perception of a cohesive generation," writes Julian Zelizer, "as opposed to a disparate group who were brought in because of local concerns."[49] They swiftly acquired a nickname: the "Watergate Babies." In a 1984 retrospective, *Congressional Quarterly* acknowledged that while the Watergate Babies had received more attention than they deserved, there were "certain features," beyond their size, that explain why they proved so irresistible to the media.[50]

Most noteworthy was their youth. The Ninety-Fourth Congress was the youngest since World War II. Eighty-seven members (or one-fifth) of the House were under forty when Congress convened. Six new House members were under the age of thirty, including Thomas Downey of New York who, at twenty-five years old, only just cleared the age requirement for incoming representatives. Downey, a former Suffolk County legislator, had graduated from law school and won a seat in Congress in the same year. For the first time since World War II, the average age of the House dropped below fifty. A similar, though less dramatic, shift occurred in the notoriously venerable Senate. Though the average age remained unchanged, the upper chamber welcomed eleven new members, eight of whom were in their thirties or forties. The youngest member, thirty-four-year-old Patrick Leahy, the first Democrat elected to the Senate from Vermont, was young enough to be the grandson of his predecessor, eighty-two-year-old George D. Aiken. Leahy, the youngest senator in Vermont's history, had been less than a year old when Aiken first arrived on Capitol Hill.[51]

As arresting as the new members' youth was their relative political inexperience. Of the seventy-five new House members, almost half—thirty-one in total—had never held elective office before. Many had not followed the conventional career path for new congresspersons: serving in state legislatures or similar institutions, guided by state party machines. There were some extreme manifestations of this. Bob Edgar, for instance, a United Methodist minister from suburban Philadelphia and United Protestant Chaplain at Drexel University, had been politicized by Nixon's dismissal of special prosecutor Archibald Cox in October 1973. Until that point, he had never even attended a political meeting. "I literally looked up the word Democrat in the phone book," Edgar recalled. Having located the state party, he ran successfully as its candidate in Pennsylvania's seventh congressional district, becoming the first Democrat to represent the seat in thirty-six years and only the second that century.[52] In Indiana's second congressional district, Republican incumbent Earl F. Landgrebe—a three-term congressman who had declared that he would stand by Nixon "if he and I have to be taken out of this building and shot"—fell to Democrat Floyd J. Fithian, a history professor at Purdue University.[53]

The class reflected the nation's evolving demographics in other ways. All fifteen black incumbents in the House were reelected, and they increased their caucus by one.[54] Though the Senate would remain all-male until 1979, the Ninety-Fourth Congress would see a record eighteen female members, fourteen of whom were Democrats (though this still gave half the population control of some 4.1 percent of the seats available in the House). All female House incumbents who sought reelection, twelve in total, retained their seats. In the aftermath, Frances Farenthold, chairwoman of the National Women's Political Caucus, dubbed 1974 "the year of the breakthrough for women." Minority ethnic groups also made advancements. California, for instance, elected its first Japanese American representative, Norman Y. Mineta, the former mayor of San Jose who had spent several years in a US internment camp during World War II.[55]

Though the class took its name from the Watergate scandal, the issues upon which many of its members had campaigned centered on the flagging economy as much as the corrupt political system. Here Democrats were on safe territory. In 1974, the intellectual foundations of postwar liberalism had yet to feel the full devastating impact of stagflation. Since the New Deal, Democrats had won elections as the guarantors of the average American's economic stability. This shared commitment had held together a diverse and fractious political coalition through similarly turbulent times. It had apparently been eclipsed by cultural issues toward the end of the 1960s, but now oil shocks and recession brought it decisively back to the top of voter consciousness. The resurgence of economic issues, notes David Broder, had "brought signs of increased Democratic cohesion."[56] This gave the Democrats particular appeal in the rising suburbs where newly prosperous workers felt economic insecurity most sharply. Twenty-one of the forty-nine Democratic gains in the House had been in districts with majority suburban populations.[57] "The new blue-collar suburbs," observed *Congressional Quarterly*, "are made up largely of middle-income families with newly acquired houses and jobs vulnerable to an economic slowdown. These voters are often unionized, working in such places as automobile plants around Detroit or aerospace plants near Los Angeles. They are often registered Democrats or from a Democratic background."[58] It seemed that these voters, who had been driven into Nixon's arms in 1972, were coming home.

Of the seventy-five new Democrats elected to the House of Representatives, forty-four were from the Northeast or the Midwest. Democrats had a particularly good run in the Northeast. In that region, they won seven of the nine governorships contested.[59] After sixteen years of Republicans, New York State elected a Democratic governor in Hugh Carey. Ella T. Grasso became not only the first woman to be elected governor of Connecticut but also the first woman to be elected governor of any state without having been the spouse of a previous incumbent.[60] In Massachusetts's fifth congressional district, a thirty-three-year-old lawyer and city councilor, Paul E. Tsongas, defeated first-term Republican Paul W. Cronin. Largely by his own design, Tsongas would emerge as one of leading intellectual lights of the class of '74.[61] Raised in the textile town of Lowell, Massachusetts, Tsongas was the son of an immigrant Greek dry cleaner. He grew up in a largely apolitical household—his parents, he remembered, had little in the way of political commitments beyond a vague liking for their senator, Republican Henry Cabot Lodge, and Richard Nixon. Tsongas likewise had little in the way of a political consciousness until shortly before he finished his undergraduate degree at Dartmouth. Student life had consisted of mostly swimming (he swam varsity for the college), working part-time in his father's dry cleaners, and occasionally studying economics.[62]

Tsongas was inspired to a life of public service by the example of JFK, which persuaded him to enroll in the Peace Corps after graduating, much like his fellow Watergate Baby, Christopher Dodd of Connecticut. Tsongas served two stints with the Peace Corps, in Ethiopia and the West Indies, breaking up his time overseas with postgraduate study at Yale Law School and Harvard's newly renamed Kennedy School of Government. Returning to the United States and his hometown, Tsongas was elected to the Lowell City Council in 1969, moving on to become a county commissioner before jumping into the congressional race in 1974. Tsongas campaigned as a representative of the wisdom to be found in "the homes of the American people" and sought to portray his opponent, Cronin, as a tool of corporate elites who was "insensitive and unmoved by the abuses of the [Nixon] Administration."[63] The fifth district was solidly Democratic in November 1974 (44 percent of registered voters were Democrats according to the *Boston Globe*, compared to 18 percent Republicans and 38 percent independent) but had not elected a Democratic representative since 1895.[64] Nonetheless, Tsongas won handily, defeating Cronin by a staggering twenty-one points.

One of the biggest celebrity members of the class of '74 was former astronaut John H. Glenn, elected to fill one of Ohio's Senate seats having never previously held elective office. Once a combat pilot in the Marine Corps, Glenn had joined NASA in 1959 and became the first American to orbit the Earth and the fifth human being in space.[65] Glenn's career, writes Evans and Novak, was "unique in the post-Watergate politics of mass voter disillusionment: A national hero, unencumbered with the ideological baggage that has fragmented the Democratic Party, who seems eminently acceptable to blue-collar hard-hats and left-of-center intellectuals." A GOP leader in the state complained that Glenn was drawing in Republican voters "without half trying."[66] Glenn had made morality a key issue of his primary campaign against real estate millionaire Howard Metzenbaum, attacking his opponent for his use of tax shelters. A bumper sticker, disavowed by the Glenn campaign, was circulated purporting to advertise "Nixon/Metzenbaum—Tax Consultants." The genius of Glenn's campaign, exulted one of his aides after that primary victory, was "to put together a good political operation and have him come off as a nonpolitician."[67] Before he had even won his Senate seat, reported a *Washington Post* correspondent, "fanciful crystal ball gazers [were] predicting a 1976 ticket of John Glenn for president, [and New York gubernatorial candidate] Hugh Carey for vice president." If that ticket sounded "like science fiction," well "anything is possible in the age of television."[68]

Though the Democratic Party enjoyed its strongest gains in the Northeast and the Midwest, it could boast of advances in all the nation's sections. While only sixteen of the new Democrats in the House were from the South, the region was much better represented in the upper chamber, with four of the eight new senators hailing from below the Mason-Dixon Line. "Democrats Put Halt to Republican Momentum in South," declared the *Washington Post*.[69] Democrats had captured two southern Senate seats from Republican incumbents and made a net gain of five House seats in the region. If the monolithic southern Democracy was dead, this did not necessarily mean that the region would march en bloc into the Republican column. After a protracted and difficult labor, perhaps a new Democratic South was being born. Moreover, many of the Democrats winning races across the South looked remarkably like their colleagues in other regions.

In Arkansas, Dale Bumpers, one of Jimmy Carter's gubernatorial contemporaries, won the Democratic Senate primary contest against J. William Fulbright, a hero to many liberals for his principled stance against the Vietnam War. Fulbright, however, had served in the Senate since 1945 and had a less than spotless record on civil rights, both of which had been factors in Bumpers' decision to mount a challenge. Fulbright had been a signatory to the Southern Manifesto in 1956, which pledged staunch resistance to desegregation efforts. Anxious to demonstrate his integrity, Bumpers promised that he would accept out-of-state contributions only from family members and former classmates. When falsely accused by a Fulbright supporter of mishandling his official expense accounts, Bumpers had the records spread out on the dining room table of the governor's mansion and invited any interested constituents to inspect them for as long as they pleased.[70] Bumpers was not an isolated case. Florida's new senator was Richard Stone, a folksy Miami resident who mixed impromptu performances of the harmonica and the spoons on the campaign trail with denunciations of the "oil ransom" and the "high interest ransom" as the primary causes of inflation. Stone also boasted of having removed the door to his office while serving as Florida's secretary of state, a post to which he was elected in 1970, in a flamboyant demonstration of his commitment to open government.[71]

Populist reforming Democrats enjoyed similar triumphs out West. For those who hailed the emergence of a new species of liberal, few states returned more encouraging results than Colorado. In a remarkable sweep, the Democratic Party took every top statewide office, with the exception of secretary of state. The party won that year's contested Senate seat and shifted the balance of the state's delegation to the US House of Representatives in their favor, three Democrats to two Republicans. The pugnacious environmentalist Richard Lamm, who had walked the state during the campaign to protest the prohibitively high cost of running for office, was elected as governor. Majorities in the state House of Representatives and on the Board of Regents were flipped, and the Republican margin in the state senate was reduced. The *New Republic*'s Paul Wieck reported that an influx of retired couples and activists into the state had given these candidates ample raw material, but what mattered more was the tone and issue agendas of the campaigns they ran. In common with Watergate Babies nationwide, all had run aggressively populist campaigns, and many placed environmentalism at the core of their pitches. Many also came from nontraditional political backgrounds. The new state treasurer, Sam Brown, for example, had been a youth organizer for McCarthy in 1968 and a coordinator in the Moratorium to End the War in Vietnam movement. "There's a new breed of Democrats here, issue-minded, young, aggressive, [and] adept at organization. They're going to be heard from," wrote Wieck in a pair of sentences that could have stood as a commentary on the election as a whole.[72]

The newest senator from Colorado, Gary Hart, was in many respects an archetypal Watergate Baby. The serious-minded son of devout Nazarene parents, young Hart had intended to make a career in the clergy before the presidential campaign of John F. Kennedy turned him toward earthly concerns. He transferred from Yale Divinity School to Yale Law School and set himself up in law practice in Denver after graduation. In 1971, he was plucked by George McGovern to manage the senator's long shot candidacy for the White House. Subsequently Hart was often (in particular during his first bid for office) at pains to point out that his role in the McGovern campaign was concerned more with strategy than with issue formulation.[73] Hart was a key figure in assembling the diverse grassroots coalition—which he dubbed "the McGovern army"—that would win the presidential nomination for the senator.[74] A firm belief in the virtue of mass civic participation defined Hart's politics. After McGovern's defeat, Hart wrote, in ten weeks, a memoir of the campaign, *Right from the Start*, in which he conducted his own autopsy. The problem, he reflected, was that "the fount of specific proposals and programs was running dry. . . . By 1972, American liberalism was near bankruptcy." The Democratic Party was in need of new thinking and new leadership.[75]

Alongside this nebulous call for new leaders, Hart made trust in government and public officials central to his 1974 campaign. "We must make the restoration of public confidence in government the highest order of public business." He pledged an "open and honest" campaign, promising to fully disclose all donations from and financial dealings with contributors and not to accept money from "special interests." He charged his opponent, Peter Dominick, with supporting "an untouchable and undemocratic political aristocracy."[76] Castigating political elites was just one component of a broader populism that undergirded Hart's campaign. He took aim at private conglomerates that he accused of taking advantage of the hard-pressed American consumer. "Why Do the Big Oil Companies Want to Stop Gary Hart?" asked one campaign flier.[77] In this, Hart was echoing the class-based politics of the New Deal. However, Hart's populism was directed at calcified federal bureaucracies as frequently as it was at commercial monopolies. One stump speech, titled "Now It's Our Turn," ended with a rousing call to arms: "The time is here for *all* of us to rise up and take our country back from the power-hungry corrupters, the fat cats and special interest boys, the inter-locked institutional interests, the comfortable, complacent, backward-looking, out-dated old men, many of whom inhabit the United States Senate like a private club. Now it's *our* turn!"[78] Hart used his campaign to critique orthodox Democratic liberalism and to offer his own revisions. He was articulating more systematically a sentiment shared in some form by many of the Watergate Babies. This puzzled those who had not expected such apostasy from McGovern's onetime campaign manager. Several commentators noted Hart's efforts to distance himself from his former boss, much to the consternation of his opponent. "Expecting to run against a junior George McGovern whom he could label a big spender," noted a *Wall Street Journal* correspondent, "the conservative Senator [Dominick] is nonplused as Mr. Hart joins him in denouncing big government."[79] Hart's stump speech bore the title "The End of the New Deal." The approach to national problems since the end of World War II, the candidate told audiences across the state, had been defined by the intellectual parameters of the New Deal. There had been "little creative thinking," merely a continual recourse to bureaucratic solutions to a diverse array of social and economic problems. "The pragmatism of the New Deal has become doctrine—if there is a problem, create an agency and throw money at the problem." The Democratic Party had to rediscover, argued Hart, the experimental pragmatism that had defined Franklin Roosevelt's presidency.[80]

Colorado was not the only state that seemed to be witnessing a generational passing of the torch. That was perhaps most vividly, and literally, represented in California, where Jerry Brown, son of the former governor Pat Brown, won the gubernatorial election by a surprisingly close margin. The contrasts between father and son as politicians underscore the changes underway in the national Democratic Party's coalition and ideology. The elder Brown, "Pat" (both father and son were christened Edmund Gerald Brown), was an avuncular glad-hander, never happier than when demonstrating the positive impact that state government could have on the lives of ordinary Californians. His governorship, from 1959 to 1967, saw an unprecedented expansion of California's system of public colleges and networks, the passage of fair employment legislation, the establishment of a consumers' council, and the financing of a statewide network of dams and waterways, then the largest public works project that any single state had embarked upon.[81] Pat Brown's California was the embodiment of the ebullient liberal confidence then in the ascendant in the Washington of the New Frontier and Great Society. In a microcosm of the 1960s crisis of liberalism, Pat Brown was defeated for reelection in 1966, as the state was roiled by campus discontent and urban rebellions, by the former Hollywood actor Ronald Reagan running on a law-and-order platform.[82]

The younger Brown came to his political career via a very different route to that of his father—through a brief stint at a Jesuit seminary and then a more conventional education at UC Berkeley and Yale Law School. Where Pat was a product of California party politics (moving from the San Francisco district attorney's office to that of the state district attorney and finally ending up in the governor's mansion), Jerry, like many Watergate Babies, got his start in extra-party activism, aiding the civil rights effort in Mississippi in 1962 and joining the anti–Vietnam War movement in 1967. In 1968, he served as Southern California vice chairman and treasurer for Senator Eugene Mc-

Carthy's dark horse presidential candidacy. In 1970, Brown struck out on his own, entering the race for California secretary of state. Easily winning election alongside Reagan, Brown would use his office to fashion an image as a tireless crusader for the strict enforcement of campaign finance laws. He instigated, and won, prosecutions against private corporations and individual candidates for the making and receiving of illicit campaign contributions.

In 1974, buoyed by the reputation he had gained as secretary, Brown leapt into the Democratic gubernatorial primary to replace Ronald Reagan. In a split field, Brown was able to secure the nomination with relative ease. He did so by relying on the favorable memories evoked by his surname and by burnishing his liberal credentials. California, Brown said, needed "an activist Democratic governor," not the "passivity" that had defined Reagan's tenure. His literature stressed his role in the McCarthy campaign and in the antiwar movement.[83] Brown's campaign was "old-fashioned politics—dressed up to sell in the 1970s," declared an *LA Times* reporter.[84] Like Hart in Colorado, Brown made the restoration of trust in public officials a mainstay of his campaign. "He Could Make You Believe in Government Again," declared one leaflet.[85] Brown's victory over his Republican opponent in the general election, Houston I. Flournoy, was less convincing, and the Democrat only just managed to break 50 percent. The new governor would soon establish that he was certainly not the second coming of Pat Brown. Though recognizably a Democrat, Brown Jr. would exhibit considerably less confidence in the ameliorative capacities of government. They were even physically dissimilar. Tall, thin, angular-featured, and handsome, Brown cut a more dashing figure as governor than his stocky, bespectacled father.

With this infusion of Democratic talent, *Congressional Quarterly* confidently predicted that the Ninety-Fourth Congress would be noticeably more liberal than its predecessor.[86] In some senses this was certainly true. The Watergate Babies were profoundly influenced by counterculture-inflected sixties liberalism. They were, in the main, sensitive to minority rights, champions of the suburban consumer, environmentally conscious, and dovish on foreign policy. In other instances, they explicitly rejected the liberal doctrines of their forebears. Days before the election, David Broder reported a remark of Gary Hart's that Broder felt neatly summarized the incoming class but that would land Hart in hot water before he had even arrived in Washington: "We're not a bunch of little Hubert Humphreys."[87] In December, Hart wrote to Humphrey to apologize for the clumsiness of the language he used, explaining that he had merely been trying to affirm that the incoming legislators would be a diverse and independent-minded cohort.[88] This was disingenuous, though, as was revealed by another letter to a supporter who had been troubled by his apparent disrespect. "I believe the New Deal philosophy of a dominant federal government did much good for tens of millions of people. But that does not mean we . . . must worship it forever."[89] In this, Hart exemplified a shared belief among many younger Democrats that New Deal liberalism was defunct and that a replacement was needed. In this, at least, they were entirely in agreement with the mobilizing ranks of New Right activist groups.

Many felt the disappointments of the Johnson years keenly. The Great Society, as Eric Alterman and Kevin Mattson have put it, "articulated a fundamental faith of 1960s liberalism: America had entered a new, potentially perpetual cycle of economic abundance, and that abundance could be deployed to ensure the creation of a fairer and more equal society without any segment of society being asked to endure significant sacrifice."[90] Lighting the White House Christmas tree in 1964, President Johnson had declared, with characteristic modesty, "These are the most hopeful times since Christ was born in Bethlehem."[91] By November 1974—with the nation having endured war, urban rioting, once unthinkable economic turbulence, political scandal, and the resignation of a president—this assessment must have seemed like a perverse joke. The Watergate Babies, recalled Congressman James Florio, had been "burned by Great Society programs. . . . We were naive in believing that the creation of these programs was going to enable us to address these problems. We had to be smarter and less naive about what government can do."[92] Colorado representative Tim Wirth echoed those sentiments in one of his first constituent newsletters: "People are increasingly alienated by the distance and bigness of the giant institutions in our society."[93] If the besetting sin of liberalism since the Great Society was what Daniel Patrick Moynihan dubbed "the malaise of overpromising," the next generation of liberals would consciously move in the opposite direction, restoring trust in government by the managing of expectations.[94] The advocates of hardheaded, pragmatic liberalism—a liberalism of limits better suited to a chastened nation—had arrived in Washington.

This wariness of federal remedies to the nation's ills drew the ire of many old guard Democrats. One such Democrat was Senator Henry Jackson, who within two years would be running a presidential campaign rooted in New Deal statism. "I don't buy the idea that because something is big it's bad," he told audiences at campaign events. Jackson enjoyed claiming that he was the only candidate in the 1976 race willing to call himself a "liberal."[95] By contrast, many of the Watergate Babies eschewed conventional political labels. Those that they did, reluctantly, adopt stressed pragmatism above ideological commitments. Paul Tsongas preferred to characterize his politics as "compassionate realism," while Gary Hart opted for the rather more convoluted "Prairie Populist Jeffersonian democracy."[96] Most sought to define themselves in relation to the supposed doctrinaire liberals whose naive schemes had damaged the credo. As Tsongas would later recall, "A lot of us were instinctively more reformers than liberals. Watergate was tailor-made for that instinct."[97]

The Watergate Babies brought with them a distinctive sensibility. To a large extent, this was grounded in culture. Unlike older Democrats, the defining experiences of their childhoods had not been depression and a world war but rather prosperity and the Cold War. It was Tim Wirth, the newly elected representative from Colorado, who perhaps better than any other Watergate Baby encapsulated the generational and cultural shift that the class of '74 represented: "JFK was our first vote, and we went through Vietnam. The others came of age during World War II and revered Ike. We are accustomed to television. . . . We're part of the supermarket age, the quick fix, and the fast shot."[98] Most had come to maturity during the political and social upheavals of the 1960s. Steven Gillon is hardly alone among historians in understanding the upheavals of the 1960s as something akin to a civil war that "produced a generation that was scarred by the memory of the struggle, deeply divided over its meaning, and determined to win a long-term fight for the hearts and minds of the American people."[99] The rise of assorted civil rights movements, the disappointments of the Great Society, and the traumas of Vietnam defined their political identities. Their anti-authority, reformist instincts made the Watergate Babies natural allies of the congressional reform movement. However, they would struggle to create a unifying political agenda to take advantage of those reforms in the aftermath. Many would not see any pressing need to even try.

Taking the Bastille

In the aftermath of the 1974 elections, new Maryland representative Gladys Noon Spellman was among those who called for the incoming class to act in concert. "We can just be swallowed up and be one of hundreds," she said, "or we can work together and have some clout."[100] And from the first, the Watergate Babies exhibited a remarkable cohesion. Before the end of November, the class had rented their own office near the Capitol and begun hiring staff.[101] They were also much more aggressive than previous generations. Sam Rayburn, the convivial Texas pol who had served as Speaker from 1947 to 1949 and 1953 to 1955, would famously advise new members "to get along, go along."[102] However, quietly working their way up congressional hierarchies held little appeal for the new legislators. Such an uncontroversial career path cut across the class's revolutionary spirit. As California representative George Miller put it, "We came here to take the Bastille."[103] Many new members shared the outlook of Michigan's Bob Carr, who professed no real passion for a life in professional politics. "If I was a one-term member of Congress, that was fine with me" he recalled. "I was young and brash and was not looking for a long-term political career. I wanted to get something done."[104]

The first thing to get done was the reform of Congress itself. This was by no means a new issue. Since the New Deal, liberals had been frustrated by the ability of Republicans and conservative southerners to exploit the legislature's ossified institutional architecture to derail their legislative agendas. In 1965, Richard Bolling, a liberal congressman from Missouri, was moved to publish *House Out of Order*, a diatribe against the legislative inertia that resulted from the essentially unrepresentative nature of Congress. As far as Bolling was concerned, reform was too great a burden to be borne by "a few enlightened and energetic Members." Decades of venality and parochialism had corrupted the legislative apparatus beyond the point of internal rejuvenation, and only a tide of public outrage could cleanse Congress.[105] By 1974, it seemed that tide was about to hit DC. According to New York congressman Richard Ottinger, "the Watergate fallout [meant that] everyone—whether liberal or conservative—felt they were here to do congressional reform."[106] Bruce Wolpe, a staffer for Congressman Henry Waxman, recalled that some new members were so keen to demonstrate their commitment to open government that, like Richard Stone, they had their office doors removed.[107] Reforming Congress to make it more responsive to its membership, and therefore to the will of the American people, was the first step toward the reemergence of Congress as the prime mover in the constitutional system.

Liberal reformers nursed a particular grievance against the seniority system, the convention that dictated that committee chairmanships would be apportioned based solely on length of service. Because the South was essentially a one-party state for much of the twentieth century, conservative Dixiecrats exercised an effective veto power on the national party's ambitions. "When Will the Old Men of Congress Be Forced to Quit?" the acerbic columnist and investigative journalist Jack Anderson asked in 1970. Cataloging some of the more egregious examples of Congressional infirmity, Anderson wrote that the seniority system guaranteed that Congress was "dominated by old men who march in slow cadence behind the nation."[108] In forcing these old men out, Democratic reformers could count on burgeoning single-issue pressure groups for welcome support and unwelcome scrutiny. For instance, Common Cause, the liberal watchdog organization founded in 1970, conducted an "Open Up the System" campaign in advance of November's elections, sending questionnaires to incumbent and prospective representatives to gauge their position on a variety of reform issues and then publicizing the results. When the dust cleared, it had secured pledges of support from a majority of congresspersons on nearly all of its major issues. "Pat yourselves on the back CC members," began its last Washington Report of the year.[109]

The reformers' first target was the House Committee on Ways and Means, which exercised control over committee assignments and was presided over by the fearsome Arkansan Wilbur D. Mills. Described as the "steering wheel of the House" and the "second most powerful man in America," Mills had helmed the Committee on Ways and Means since 1958. In 1968, he had all but single-handedly forced LBJ to accept deep cuts to key Great Society programs in exchange for a tax surcharge to finance the Vietnam War.[110] Understandably, Democratic reformers and their extra-congressional allies approached the confrontation with some disquiet. They were fortunate that Mills obliged them with a spectacular personal implosion that became a bizarre symbol of the end of the committee era. On October 9, 1974, US Park Police pulled over a limousine driving without lights. Inside they discovered an intoxicated Mills bleeding from his nose and cheek. Also in the car was Annabelle Battistella, a stripper who went by the stage name "Fanne Foxe, the Argentine Firecracker." Startled by the official presence, Battistella, who was sporting facial bruises, leapt from the car and had to be fished out of the Tidal Basin. A television cameraman who had chanced to hear the police reports arrived on the scene in time to record the congressman's arrest. Mills was humiliated and political Washington was stunned.[111] Yet Mills clung on. A few weeks later, he was narrowly reelected. Had the scandal ended there, he could well have survived.

However, on the evening of November 30, days before the organizational caucus was scheduled to meet, at a Boston club where Foxe was performing, journalists were astonished when Mills staggered onto the stage. He followed this up with an impromptu press conference in Foxe's dressing room, where he called her "my little ole Argentine hillbilly" and pledged to help her to a career in the movies.[112] When the House Democratic Caucus met on December 2, Ways and Means was stripped of its power to make committee appointments. The caucus voted to relocate its Committee on Committees to the Steering and Policy Committee, which consisted of the Speaker, the House majority leader, the caucus chair, twelve regional representatives, and nine additional members chosen by the Speaker. This committee would make recommendations that the caucus would then ratify or modify. Ways and Means was also enlarged from twenty-five to thirty-seven members.[113] Soon afterward, Carl Albert announced that Mills would lose his chairmanship in the Ninety-Fourth Congress.[114] A Herblock cartoon produced in response showed a figure marked "Reform Democrats" tugging a royal robe from Mills's shoulders while the chairman protested, "Wait! Let Go—Not That Kind of Strip Routine."[115]

Other scalps would soon follow. Having denuded Mills, the class of '74 invited committee chairmen expecting reappointment to be quizzed in closed sessions. Some did not react prudently to the supposed disrespect of being summoned before their juniors. Edward Hébert of Louisiana, chairman of the House Armed Services Committee, began one answer with, "Okay, boys and girls. Let me tell you what it's like around here."[116] When the caucus reconvened in January, he was removed, along with William Poage and Wright Patman of Texas, chairmen of the House Agriculture Committee and the House Banking and Currency Committee, respectively.[117] A furious Hébert appeared on NBC's *Today Show* to fume, "Common Cause is running Congress. Who elected them?"[118] However, not every chairman that Common Cause had marked out for retirement was removed. One who survived the cull was Ohio's Wayne Hays, the sixty-three-year-old chair of the House Administration Committee and a particular target of good government organizations' anger. Hays had reportedly impressed the younger members during his interview, but he also enjoyed the support of Phillip Burton, the newly elected caucus chairman. During the election, Hays had been chair of the Democratic Congressional Campaign Committee while Burton had been head of the Democratic Study Group, and both had directed significant funds to Democratic challengers. Those challengers now discovered that the chits were being called in. Many incumbent Democrats were grateful to Hays for, as one unnamed representative put it, "talk[ing] back to Common Cause and Ralph Nader, who screech every time we get a new allowance and call our recesses 'vacations.' He takes a lot of heat for us, and we appreciate it."[119]

More reforms followed the deposition of the committee barons. In one particularly potent symbolic gesture, for example, the Democratic Caucus dissolved the House Un-American Activities Committee, which was largely defunct by this point in any case.[120] Alongside the dethroning of the chairmen, the caucus's most significant reform was to vote to increase the resources and staff members available to individual congresspersons. This was coupled with a rapid proliferation of subcommittees as reformers sought to decentralize power and democratize the institution. By 1984, for example, thirty of the thirty-seven remaining Watergate Babies in the House of Representatives were subcommittee chairs.[121] Mo Udall, liberal Democrat from Arizona, once joked that if he ever failed to recognize a fellow congressman, he would greet him as "Mr. Chairman."[122] Political scientist Burdett Loomis argued that this expansion of resources and legislative positions had "produced a new style of policy-based activism that emphasizes both a serious consideration of issues and a fresh approach to the traditional rules of the game."[123] These reforms, Loomis continued, had facilitated the emergence of "policy entrepreneurs," legislators who were able to develop substantial issue portfolios using Congress's decentralized structures and its surfeit of additional resources, as well as a media context that favored such publicity-hungry types. Not everyone was so complimentary, however. By 1977, Illinois representative John Anderson would complain, "The House less and less addresses itself to the great issues of policy. Everybody's got a little subcommittee, and everything is terribly fragmented. We've become a body of tinkerers."[124]

However, decentralization had never been the reformers' sole, or even overriding, intent. In some instances, they took steps to strengthen the leadership at the expense of the members. For instance, by the lopsided margin of 132–38, the caucus defeated a resolution that would have made the position of majority whip an elected rather than appointed post. The reformers argued that this change would unduly weaken the Speaker, who selected the whip

(Majority Leader Tip O'Neill had complained that such a move would "cut off my right arm").[125]

Similar changes were underway in the Senate. The day after the House's chairman cull, the upper chamber voted to select committee heads by secret ballot, after nomination by the Steering Committee. If a minimum of 20 percent of Democrats opposed a particular nominee, another secret ballot would be taken. Moreover, individual senators were given the right to hire three staffers to report to them on the work of their committees. Previously, such clerical assistance had been within the gift of the chairman. As in the House, the net effect was to augment the average senator as a legislative entrepreneur. The tendency of senators to adopt "an activist style based on a full exploitation of senatorial prerogatives" had been increasingly commonplace since the 1960s and these reforms only accelerated that process.[126] However, the principal target of liberal resentment in the Senate was the filibuster. In 1950, Senator Humphrey had even gone so far as to condemn the filibuster as "an evil."[127] Democrats had warmed to it since discovering its utility as a tool to frustrate Nixon's legislative ambitions, but it remained a liberal bugaboo. In 1975, it was the subject of one of the fiercest confrontations of the legislative session. Humphrey's protégé and fellow Minnesotan, Walter Mondale, along with Kansas Republican James B. Pearson, proposed a reform that would allow a simple majority to invoke cloture. After a vicious tussle between reformers and institutionalists, the Senate embraced a resolution reducing the number of senators required to break a filibuster from two-thirds to three-fifths.[128] By happy coincidence, this meant that the Democrats were now in possession of a filibuster-proof majority in the Senate, a fact that caused no little trepidation to the Ford administration.

What's Next?

Some older legislators understood the brash reformism of their new colleagues to be motivated largely by political calculation. They saw uneasy Democrats in marginal districts that they were never supposed to win hoping that some aggression would help their career prospects. Neal Smith, first elected to the House of Representatives from Iowa's fourth congressional district in 1958, complained that the new members "decided the most important thing in the world was to get re-elected, no matter what. The day they hit here they started campaigning for the next election instead of helping legislate."[129] This was unfairly cynical, but there was some truth to it. New members did have to worry about reelection, particularly those in formerly Republican constituencies. This problem was particularly pressing in the House, where the number of potential rivals for media attention and the brevity of the electoral terms would effectively concentrate the mind. In February 1975, George Miller and Toby Moffett organized a weekend retreat for the class. Moffett estimated that some 80 percent of the freshmen were in attendance. After smashing the committee system and augmenting the caucus, the purpose of the retreat was to devise future legislative strategies. Moffett was surprised when "conversation turned immediately to incumbency protection. That's what the weekend was spent on. . . . There were workshops on issues, but those were not nearly as popular. Everybody wanted to know how to get re-elected."[130] Hardly surprising, given how many members of the class had won in historically Republican-leaning districts. The high water could not last indefinitely.

Herein lies the essential problem that confronted the Watergate Babies as they surveyed the post-reform Congress. For all their cultural similarities, their populist attacks on a collection of corrupt elites, and their shared insistence on the need to find new solutions for the 1970s, there was precious little agreement over how to proceed and few attempts to approach systematically the question of just what a "liberalism of limits" might look like. In this, the class of '74 presented a stark contrast to the group of Democrats who had made up the last generational shift within Congress, the class of 1948. Superficially, there were striking similarities between the two classes. In 1946, it had seemed a foregone conclusion that 1948 would be a Republican year. In the 1946 midterm congressional elections, the Republican Party regained control of both the House and the Senate for the first time since 1932 and was blithely confident that in new president Harry S. Truman it had found an opponent who could be swatted aside with comparative ease. However, in a historic electoral upset, Truman held the White House, and the Democrats recaptured the House and the Senate. As in 1974, these elections saw the injection into Congress of a group of young, ambitious, and emphatically liberal politicians. Their fervor and disdain for congressional institutions earned them the nickname "bomb-throwers."[131] In his memoirs, Harry McPherson, then assistant to Majority Leader Lyndon Johnson, had disdainfully summarized "bomb-throwing" Illinois senator Paul Douglas, and indeed the whole class, as "a liberal Saint George [fighting] against the vested-interest dragon."[132]

The bomb-throwers were united in the belief that the most dramatically liberal legislative moves were being strangled by the conservative coalition within Congress, composed of southern Democrats and Republicans. They raged that these reactionaries, though numerically superior, did not command the loyalty of the American electorate, who had voted overwhelmingly for liberal reform. The fact that the people had put Truman back into office was surely evidence enough that they expected the "Fair Deal" to be enacted. Liberal conviction was only strengthened as they watched a recalcitrant Congress kill or castrate major components of the "Fair Deal." The legislative agenda, the liberals realized, was in the hands of those who understood the arcane procedures of Capitol Hill. In response, these bomb-throwers began the guerrilla war against the institutional weaponry wielded by the conservative coalition that would see final victory at the beginning of 1975.[133]

Like the Watergate Babies more than two decades later, the bomb-throwers entered Congress at a moment of existential crisis for liberalism. The stalling of New Deal reformism after its mid-1930s heyday, and then its eclipse by the imperatives of war in the Pacific and Western Europe, had induced a profound feeling of drift in congressional Democrats by VJ day. The death of Franklin Roosevelt some months earlier had only exacerbated that. The Democratic Party found itself confronted with a disturbing question: What happens now? Roosevelt was dead, the major architecture of the New Deal was in place, and the loss of an imminent national emergency, alongside a recalcitrant southern bloc, made further ambitious extensions of the federal prerogative unlikely. What was there to do now other than wait for an increasingly confident Republican Party to supplant them? The answer was to be found, according to many allied intellectuals, in a recalibration of liberalism's priorities. This would be best expressed some years later by Arthur Schlesinger, who, in a 1956 article for the *Reporter*, summarized a credo he called "qualitative liberalism," which was to be understood as distinct from the "quantitative liberalism" of the New Deal. The evils that the latter had been thought up to combat, most notably widespread and pervasive economic distress, had been largely vanquished. The new liberalism must turn its attention to "quality of life" issues, such as clean air and water, a better transport infrastructure, urban regeneration, health care, and various other "social justice" concerns. Liberals of the 1950s must fight "for individual dignity, identity, and fulfillment in a mass society."[134]

In some senses, Schlesinger's prescriptions were rather evanescent. Guaranteeing a secure home or a living wage are comparatively easy undertakings when set against the problem of formulating public policy that can ensure "identity" or "fulfillment." Nonetheless, this doctrinal update proved a vital lodestar for congressional Democrats during the Eisenhower years, when they could conceive of themselves as custodians of a legacy of unfinished business awaiting the return of a Democratic president to offer legislative leadership. This shared agenda—rooted in the New Deal and the Fair Deal and encompassing health-care reform, civil rights legislation, federal aid to education, and the restraining of the nuclear arms race—would become the foundation stone of the New Frontier and the Great Society around a decade and a half later. Likewise, the extra-congressional interest groups that sustained them—the ACLU, Americans for Democratic Acton, and the National Association for the Advancement of Colored People—had agendas that went beyond institutional reform. By contrast, the Watergate Babies were supported largely by public advocacy groups that pursued reform for its own sake, most notably Common Cause. These aims were no doubt laudable, but they masked a failure to grapple with the problem of what these bumper Democratic majorities would do once freed from the shackles imposed on them by the conservative coalition.

"Democrats beware!" remarked Hubert Humphrey as the returns were coming in on election night. "Now you have to deliver."[135] However, and in spite of their self-confident iconoclasm and their shared social and cultural characteristics, the Watergate Babies arrived in Congress without a broadly agreed-upon legislative agenda and would exhibit little inclination to establish one. Had the Republican challenge been more pressing at that moment, perhaps Democratic minds would have been concentrated on the problem. It may seem remarkable given the events that were to come, but many Democrats felt that they could safely ignore the GOP. "The Republicans were pathetic," recalled Bruce Wolpe. "After Watergate, they were nothing, they were beaten, they were cowed. They didn't have any ideas, the country wasn't listening to them. So we didn't have to pay any attention to them."[136] The reforms that the class of '74 helped enact erected additional barriers to those who sought to think seriously about the party's future. Moreover, a substantial number of congressional Democrats never quite embraced the idea of their branch's supremacy over the executive. Fighting Nixon was one matter, but with him removed from office, much of the energy drained away. Many were content to wait for their party's victory in the 1976 presidential election and then, with a Democrat in the White House, to react to his initiatives. With reform accomplished, the congressional party was simply unable to agree on a future agenda.[137] For a host of reasons, institutional and political, Congress would not be the engine of a post-Watergate Democratic revival.

"The Last Election Means the Buck Stops Here"

The Democratic Congress Struggles with Ford, 1975–1976

"The most puzzling aspect of the Democratic Party today," wrote columnist David Broder in early 1974, "is its tendency to alternating fits of neurotic gloom and unjustified euphoria."[1] When the party met for its first midterm convention in Kansas City, Missouri, in early December 1974, it was in the grips of one of those periodic euphoric fits. The midterm convention was a consequence of the McGovern-Fraser commission's proposal for a biennial "national policy conference"—"a national convention every two years" according to the *Washington Post*.[2] The nominal purpose of this first convention was to approve the party's new charter and to formally resolve those issues of representation and access that had not been settled by McGovern-Fraser or by the 1972 national convention. More importantly, at least for DNC chairman Robert S. Strauss, was the need for an ostentatious public display of unity that would erase painful memories of Miami Beach. It was in the interests of diminishing the political costs of any disharmony that the convention had been deliberately scheduled for one month *after* the congressional elections.[3]

The host city had been chosen with the same deliberate care. Kansas City was where Harry S. Truman, whose reputation was then undergoing an extraordinary posthumous rehabilitation, had started his political career. When Truman left office in 1953, his personal ratings had been even lower than Nixon's, a consequence of the Korean War and of accusations of corruption and Communist infiltration of his administration. Twenty years later, these failings had been all but eclipsed. What mattered were not so much Truman's policy accomplishments, although they certainly came in for reappraisal. Rather, as one commentator put it, the nostalgists admired Truman's "buoyancy of spirit, his gamecock combativeness, and his invincible faith in the United States and its people." Stories about Truman's blunt, even coarse, manner enhanced his standing. "Nobody who knew anything about him ever said there were two Trumans, the private man and the official man." For a scandal-beleaguered nation, the memory of the plain-speaking, earthy Missourian, who kept a sign on his Oval Office desk declaring, "The Buck Stops Here!" was deeply appealing. Merle Miller's *Plain Speaking*, a new oral biography based on a collection of interviews the author had conducted with Truman, was warmly received by critics and spent over a year on the *New York Times*'s bestseller list. Samuel Gallu's one-person play *Give 'Em Hell, Harry!*, set during the 1948 presidential campaign, won a Grammy and an Oscar nomination for its leading man, James Whitmore. This burst of "Trumanmania" spoke to a nation searching for trustworthy political leaders. "America needs you / Harry Truman," sang the progressive rock band Chicago in one of their most successful songs.[4]

Politicians rushed to claim Truman's mantle. Two days before Nixon resigned, the Senate sent to the House a bill to create the Harry S. Truman Scholarships, a federal memorial to the recently deceased president. Shortly afterward, newly inaugurated President Gerald Ford had a portrait of Truman hung in the Cabinet Room and a bust installed in the Oval Office, declaring that he had always admired the latter's "guts" and "straightforward" manner.[5] By the summer of 1975, the *New York Times* was reporting that Ford's closest advisors (his "kitchen cabinet") were preparing to market the president, in advance of his reelection bid, as "another Harry Truman, another honest, decent, friendly Middle Westerner who talks simply and acts on readily understandable human instincts."[6] Truman was likewise a prominent feature of the 1974 DNC campaign. One DNC fund-raising letter, signed by Robert Strauss, began, "President Truman used to be proud to say that the buck stopped at his desk, as indeed it did when he was in the White House."[7] By staging their midterm convention in a city so closely associated with Truman, the Democrats hoped to benefit from the nostalgia.

Midterm conventions had been mooted before. In 1937, for instance, former president Herbert Hoover had publicly endorsed the idea as a means of energizing the Republican Party against FDR's surging Democrats.[8] As a mechanism of policy formulation, the midterm convention enjoyed the support of many political scientists, and the question was intermittently taken up by the parties' national committees.[9] Robert Strauss hated the idea. An exuberant and colorful Texas pol, Strauss reveled in the political bear pit in a way that few of his contemporaries could match. Strauss reflected that being DNC chairman—a position to which he had ascended in December 1972—was "a little like makin' love to a gorilla. You don't quit when you're tired—you quit when the gorilla's tired."[10] With a keen understanding of just how little control he had over the party, he was less concerned with using his chairmanship to resolve bitter ideological disputes than with presenting a unified front to the public.

This was Strauss's strategy and the 1974 midterm convention was his first big public test. The previous year, his first as chairman, Strauss had embarked on a national unity tour with the intention, according to his biographer, of shaking hands "with every Democrat from Hawaii to Connecticut." Speaking to various groups around the country, Strauss would echo the same refrain: "I remain committed to the proposition that our conservatives are not bigots, our business community is not evil, that our young are not irresponsible, that our minorities are not selfish, our liberals are not foolish, and that our Democratic Party is not leaderless or without purpose."[11] He brought these conciliatory instincts to Kansas City. "Strauss moved like a rug merchant in the Casbah," one journalist reported, "cutting his deals with divided factions; placating, cajoling, begging, promising." Strauss delighted in engineering public rapprochements between seemingly natural adversaries. In Kansas City, he arranged for the liberal black congresswoman and civil rights champion Barbara Jordan of Texas to deliver a fulsome introduction for former Ku Klux Klan member Robert Byrd. He even persuaded Jesse Jackson and Richard Daley to publicly shake hands.[12] But for the journalists Rowland Evans and Robert Novak, the unity on display in Kansas City was "a gossamer façade." Nowhere was this more apparent than in the hostility and mutual suspicion exhibited by the proto-presidential campaigns. The convention, wrote the *New Republic*'s correspondent, was "a dry run for 1976, with candidates rushing from caucus to caucus, plying delegates with liquor and fighting for floor passes for staff."[13] Left-wing delegates remained implacably opposed to the candidacy of Washington senator Henry Jackson, and his fellow standard-bearer for the party's anti-McGovernite wing, Senator Lloyd Bentsen of Texas, and threatened to leave the party if he were to close in on the nomination. This unease was all the more pronounced because the party's liberals had yet to coalesce behind a candidate.[14]

There were issues of consequence that had to be settled at the convention, however, as the party processed its new rules. The most fraught issue among the delegates was that of representation, particularly the makeup of the delegations to the 1976 national convention. In the adoption of a new party charter, the language of the antidiscrimination provisions proved most contentious. That language, lifted verbatim from the rules adopted for the 1976 convention, prohibited "mandatory quotas" for previously marginalized groups but enjoined the state parties to pursue "affirmative action" policies to ensure "full participation by all Democrats, with particular concern for minority groups, native Americans, women and youth, in the delegate-selection process and in all party affairs . . . as indicated by their presence in the Democratic electorate." However, a further provision stated that convention delegations could not be challenged on the basis of "composition alone." While labor delegates objected to the "implied quotas" in the former provision, supporters of affirmative action opposed the latter, which they claimed deprived them of a vital enforcement mechanism. A day of tortured negotiations eventually produced a compromise, orchestrated by a group of governors, and the "composition alone" section was discarded.[15] Such confrontations led to intensified hostility between the forces of labor and the New Politics reformers.

Nonetheless, the general mood in Kansas City was one of exuberance. That was a marked contrast with the despondency of the conservatives who gathered at the Mayflower Hotel in downtown Washington, DC, a few months later for the second annual Conservative Political Action Conference (CPAC). There, the delegates were consumed by chatter about the possibility of a third party, an authentically conservative challenge to the supposedly impure Republicans. The chairman of the American Conservative Union, M. Stanton Evans, made an explicit call from the podium for work to begin on a new national conservative party. "The people at this conference," declared Ronald Docksai, the head of Young Americans for Freedom, "no longer reflexively see the Republican Party as home."[16] In early 1975, the publisher of *National Review*, William Rusher, began agitating for the creation of a new party, to be called the Independence Party, which should aim "to do to the Republican Party what the latter did to the Whigs: namely, replace it *in toto*."[17] For a time, this did not seem so outlandish. The share of the electorate registered as Republicans had slumped to 18 percent and the RNC had begun selling merchandise with the plaintive slogan "Republicans Are People Too."[18]

The momentum, it appeared to many observers, was with the Democratic Party and with Congress. Following November's elections, Strauss was quick to call on Ford to recognize "the congressional mandate" that the American people had conferred on the Democrats. The White House was unsettled by the speed and determination with which the newly expanded Democratic majorities had moved to enact sweeping institutional reforms. "It was a little startling to see how the Democrats marched in lock step," remarked one presidential aide.[19] Ford—a former House minority leader whose highest ambition had once been to become Speaker—had made efforts to mollify the legislature. Three days into his presidency, he gave his first address to a joint session of Congress and declared, "Part of my heart will always be here on Capitol Hill. I know well the co-equal role of the Congress in our constitutional process." Ford assured the assembled members, "I do not want a honeymoon with you. I want a good marriage."[20] The change from the bellicosity of Nixon to the conciliation of Ford reflected the different political styles of the two presidents but also revealed just how dramatically the political climate had shifted between 1972 and 1974. "I think the last election means the buck stops here," Rep. Carl Albert told the new members upon being reelected as Speaker of the House of Representatives in the organizational caucus of the Ninety-Fourth Congress.[21] A few weeks after the 1974 elections, *Time* magazine put a selection of the new Democratic congresspersons on its cover with the question, "What Next?"[22] For one moment, it seemed plausible that what was coming next was a Democratic and congressional renaissance.

King Caucus?

The House Caucus had once been the most potent entity in Congress. At the turn of the twentieth century, still an era of congressional government, the notorious Republican Speaker Joseph Cannon exercised such control over the House that his opponents spoke bitterly of "King Caucus."[23] In the final weeks of the 1974 campaign, Ford had stumped the country conjuring images of a return to those bad old days and warning of a coming "legislative dictatorship." This time, however, the Democrats would be running the show. A "runaway Congress" with the "wrong kind" of members, said the president, would jeopardize the administration's foreign policy and even peace itself.

Instead of an "imperial presidency," Ford now lamented an "imperilled presidency."[24] House Republicans sounded similar warnings. Congressman John
Anderson of Illinois spoke of "the trend toward what . . . has [been] termed
'congressional government' and . . . the re-emergence of 'King Caucus.'"[25]
The GOP had good reason to worry, and Ford's partisan attacks on Congress reflected not only rising Democratic confidence but also the growing
sense within the congressional Democratic Party, and in particular within
the House, that Congress should assert its constitutional right to set the legislative agenda for the nation.

An inherently majoritarian body, the House was theoretically better suited
than the Senate to give some direction to the congressional Democratic
Party. The reforms of early 1975 had strengthened the caucus—the conference of all Democratic members—against the conservative-leaning committees, which had throttled progressive legislation for decades. The beefed-up
caucus would be able to assume the legislative powers that had previously
been reserved to the committees and give the House a more unified voice on
matters of policy. Notwithstanding the comparable reform movement in the
Senate, there was no consistent drive to strengthen either the party leadership or the Conference. Senators remained essentially loyal to the individual-
istic, antimajoritarian ethos of the upper chamber, and power continued to
reside in the committees.

The efforts to turn the House Democratic Caucus into the catalyst for
Congress's resurgence were bound up in the 1970s with the career of the
brash California congressman Phillip Burton. An unabashed liberal and keen
student of power politics, Burton had been an enthusiastic supporter of the
congressional reform movement since arriving in Congress in 1964.[26] Tall,
burly, and permanently disheveled, Burton cut an unmistakable figure in the
corridors of the House. He chain-smoked unfiltered cigarettes, womanized
occasionally, and drank to excess. A staffer for Rep. Henry Waxman, Bruce
Wolpe, recalled that the congressman would keep a bottle of Stolichnaya
vodka in an office freezer for Burton. "Phil would come in at the end of the
day at 6 just to talk to him. And he would have half a bottle of vodka before going on his next rounds. And they would just talk and plot, and plot
and talk." Burton's biographer paints a vivid picture of his eccentric personal
behavior:

He towered over his fellow politicians in hallway encounters, thumping his finger on their chests, spitting saliva as he shouted, consuming, as one witness put it, "their very oxygen." He ate enormous portions of prime rib, pasta, and Dover sole with such unrepentant gusto that dinner companions said they needed an umbrella to protect their clothes. He did not think twice about spearing the chicken off the plate of a stranger seated next to him at an elegant dinner party, of taking columnist Jack Anderson, a religiously observant Mormon, on a late-night tour of San Francisco's strip joints, of calling Lady Bird Johnson, whom he barely knew, "Babe," or of trailing pillows from meeting to meeting to ease the pain of his haemorrhoids.[27]

Not since LBJ stalked the Senate corridors had a congressional politician wielded his vulgarity as such an effective political instrument. "He's got the personality of a Brillo pad," joked Arizona's Mo Udall. "But he gets a lot done."[28]

Throughout the 1970s, Burton schemed and maneuvered to strengthen the caucus and to ensure a leadership role for himself within it. He passed through the chairmanship of the Democratic Study Group (a legislative service organisation created as an informal whip for liberals) to the chairmanship of the caucus itself before finally mounting a campaign for House majority leader, so as to embed himself in the body's leadership and place himself in pole position to one day become Speaker. If there was to be a congressional dictatorship, as Ford had warned, there was no one better placed or more able to play its Il Duce than Burton.

Yet these efforts failed. Between Nixon's resignation and Jimmy Carter's inauguration, the House did not enact anything approximating a coherent liberal agenda—even with a huge and nominally veto-proof majority, a fairly cohesive class of reform-minded legislators, a Congress more favorable to liberalism than it had been in decades, and an ambitious and talented leader in the figure of Phillip Burton and facing a president for whom no one had yet cast a single vote. That failure reveals much about the congressional Democratic Party at mid-decade and about the institutional and political barriers faced by the legislative branch when it sought to supplant the executive as the prime mover in US politics. As the *New York Times*'s David Rosenbaum noted in December 1974, "You can't make an omelet without eggs and a pan. But Grade A eggs and the world's fanciest skillet do not guarantee that your omelet will be worth eating."[29]

One "Identity Crisis" among Many:
The Democratic Study Group

Founded in 1959, the Democratic Study Group (DSG) had been born out of liberal exasperation with Truman's thwarted Fair Deal, the cozy stagnation of the Eisenhower years, and the Democratic gains in the congressional elections of 1958.[30] It was intended as a coordinating body for liberals frustrated with being outmaneuvered by reactionary forces. Within a few years, the DSG would become one of the most formidable weapons that congressional liberals had at their disposal, honing the legislative agenda that would underpin the New Frontier and the Great Society. In late 1968, with president-elect Nixon preparing for his inauguration, outgoing chair James O'Hara convened a series of meetings to discuss strategies for dealing with "a tough, effective, hard-nosed [Republican] administration" that would be "hostile or at best apathetic to preserving many of the programs that had been enacted during the Kennedy-Johnson years." A number of proposals were entertained, including an open DSG challenge to the leadership and DSG-backed candidates for committee positions. It became apparent that congressional reform was the issue dominating most of the discussions. LBJ's huge mandate had left him free to disregard the conservative coalition within Congress, at least for a few crucial years, but by the late 1960s, with Democratic majorities diminished and a Republican in the White House, liberals found themselves at an institutional disadvantage once again.[31] They also confronted the task of ideological regrouping after the Great Society. Staff director Richard Conlon would recall the difficult adjustment that faced the DSG: "The glue that held [the DSG] together—Medicare, civil rights and the cluster of other Democratic issues—is gone now."[32]

O'Hara began informally polling representatives (he reportedly contacted 100 by telephone) and discovered shocking ignorance of the House rules. Most members canvassed believed that seniority had been officially codified or had some constitutional basis. O'Hara concluded that the DSG's highest priority ought to be meeting this education deficit with the intention of building a pro-reform coalition in the House.[33] Having settled on its post–Great Society mission—congressional reform—the DSG began pushing to democratize the House's antiquated structures and procedures, laying the foundations for the institutional revolution that would climax with the arrival of the Watergate Babies. But, for the most part, DSG liberals avoided the question of what the *purpose* of such reforms was. The greatest hope of Richard Conlon—described by John Jacobs as "one of the most important House staffers of the postwar era"—was that the DSG should become "a vehicle for discussion ventilation in terms of the issues." He prized the group's reputation as an impartial research tool above all else: "170-plus members of the Democratic Study Group [who] pay that $100 a year dues don't do it because they're committed liberals. They do it because they're getting damn good services that they can't get any place else and . . . that's what keeps them there."[34]

Over the next half decade, the DSG fought to revise the seniority system and strengthen the caucus. Allied with emerging public interest groups—most notably Common Cause, a watchdog organization founded in 1970 by John W. Gardner, a Republican who had served as secretary of Health, Education, and Welfare (HEW) under LBJ—the DSG mounted a succession of offensives to chip away at the autocratic power of the committee chairs. They enjoyed some success: in 1970, a committee was established to recommend ways that the chairmen could be made "more responsive to the Caucus and the House leadership"; in early 1971, the caucus approved a resolution giving it the formal power to approve committee chairmen (a power that it would struggle to wield until 1975); a Steering and Policy Committee was created in 1972 to set legislative priorities for the caucus. Yet there were also some significant reversals: a proposal to impose a seventy-year age limit on committee chairs was defeated; a liberal-backed effort to strip the seventy-two-year-old South Carolinian John C. McMillan of the chairmanship of the Committee on the District of Columbia, which the DSG had advanced as a test case, was decisively defeated; and an effort to place DSG chairman Donald Fraser on the Committee on Ways and Means failed.[35]

By 1969, Burton was establishing himself as a force within the DSG. Much of its membership overlapped with the anti–Vietnam War contingent in the House, and Burton soon muscled his way onto the Executive Committee. Almost immediately, he began "fatten[ing it] with his handpicked recruits."[36] It was a pattern that would recur throughout his career. In February 1971, Burton announced his intention of pursuing the chairmanship when incumbent Don Fraser retired. This represented a significant break in tradition for the still relatively young organization. Protocol had it that a nominating committee would select a slate of officers who would then be ratified unanimously. Now a contest was almost inevitable.[37] Burton's intervention was unprecedented and entirely predictable. He had chafed against the wait-your-turn traditions of the House since his arrival. As a member of the Interior Committee, he had made himself a persistent nuisance to Chairman Wayne Aspinall, disrespecting him during sessions and machinating to bring liberal allies onto the committee.[38] The DSG's nominating committee split, 7–7, between Burton and his opponent, fellow Californian and DSG secretary, James Corman. Both names went forward to a DSG-wide election on March 9.[39]

Bespectacled and dapper, Corman was a former Marine and Los Angeles city councilor and had served in Congress since 1961. From a seat on the Judiciary Committee, he had helped steer the 1964 Civil Rights Act to passage.[40] He had been effectively recruited by the anti-Burton faction within the DSG, who were motivated by a mixture of personal hostility and genuine concern over Burton's abrasiveness and uncompromising liberalism. Burton's campaign consisted mostly of convincing new members, and conservative southerners for whom he had done favors, to take up membership, and in the DSG-wide vote, Burton defeated Corman handily, seventy-three votes to forty-eight. Immediately following his election, Burton told the meeting that it had the "opportunity and obligation to lay the basis for the defeat of the Republican administration."[41] The House of Representatives, wrote reporter Lou Cannon, had rarely been perceived as a motor of liberal reform, and the DSG, "the voice of liberal policy in the House," had acquired its own establishment that was suspicious of boat-rockers. "Institutions, like people, tend to radicalism in youth and conservatism in old age." The election of the hard-charging Burton as DSG chair, a marked contrast to his predecessor Fraser, could change all that. Cannon concluded, "A new day may be dawning for liberals in the House."[42]

Initially, it seemed it was. "Almost overnight the DSG became an important center of House activities," wrote Burton's biographer, "the engine of reform and the instrument of Burton's power." Burton instituted daily strategy sessions, lubricated with large quantities of vodka, to which he invited representatives of various reform and good government groups, including Common Cause and the National Committee for an Effective Congress. In these sessions, Burton and his allies schemed to advance the reform agenda, a prerequisite for the passage of the legislation that was so dear to him. His major success was in drafting and passing a bundle of reforms that allowed for a secret-ballot caucus vote on every chairman, guaranteed every freshman

Democrat would receive at least one major committee assignment, and prohibited members of the Ways and Means, Rules, or Appropriations committees from holding other assignments. By early 1973, two Nixon aides wrote to the president that the "ultra-liberal" DSG was at the forefront of a Democratic effort to "McGoverniz[e] the House."[43] Yet the DSG was ultimately only a waystation for Burton, who had far grander ambitions.

This was obvious from his most significant innovation: the extent to which he involved the DSG in election financing. Having first "Burtonized" the DSG, he now sought to use the DSG to "Burtonize" the House. In 1972, the DSG raised some $200,000 for its candidates and reached out to others who struggled to receive funds from the organs of the party establishment.[44] Burton later concluded that, effective as this had been, too little had been done to target nonincumbents. Bob Carr, who would receive Burton's largesse during his successful 1974 bid to represent a Michigan district after being overlooked during a failed 1972 effort, later recalled that Burton "publicly stated at a meeting where I was present that he wished that he had listened to [Carr's appeals for financial assistance] because he felt that had we been targeted in '72, we would have won."[45] An ad placed by the DSG Campaign Fund ("the political arm of the Democratic Study Group") in the New York Times in September 1974 boasted, "in 1972, according to a Common Cause survey, DSG gave a greater share of its funds to non-incumbent candidates than any other Democratic, labor or liberal group. This year virtually all DSG funds will go to progressive **non-incumbent** candidates in close races."[46]

Even after moving on to pastures new, Burton continued to use the DSG for his own ends. Spotting earlier than most how the Watergate scandal could be exploited for Democratic gain in 1974, Burton resolved to use the DSG to swell and shape the House Caucus. Coordinating with labor unions and old ally Rep. Wayne Hays, then head of the Democratic Congressional Campaign Committee (DCCC), Burton directed DSG money to challengers. Through Hays, Burton also exercised considerable influence over the DCCC's $200,000 campaign budget, almost half of which was sent to nonincumbents. "Many thanks for your splendid DSG contribution," wrote Colorado's Tim Wirth to Burton in July. "Most welcome at a time of some real cash bind!"[47] Burton personally campaigned in more than forty districts.[48]

Other candidates reached out to Burton in search of support. Terry Moshenko, cochairman of Mark Hannaford's campaign for California's thirty-eighth district, wrote to Burton in July on behalf of his candidate. With

Burton's reelection "assured," Moshenko wrote, it was hoped that he would "assist other Democratic candidates in more difficult, yet promising, races," with fund-raising initiatives, "early money," and other forms of nonfinancial support. A day earlier, Jim Lloyd, the candidate for California's Republican-leaning thirty-fifth district, had sent Burton a form reply to a supportive telegram, annotated with the message, "I'll really need your help. I've placed your name on the mailing list. Also, I'll be in Wash D.C. within the next 3 weeks. I'll let you know!"[49] Both Hannaford and Lloyd were nonincumbents and both would go on to win their elections.

By 1973, the year Burton stepped down, the DSG was influential in a way that it had not been since the early 1960s. It was, claimed one headline, "Now [the] Dominant House Power."[50] The previous November, to general shock and excitement and at Burton's invitation, William "Fishbait" Miller, the House doorkeeper and "long a symbol of Dixiecrat power in the House," had made an unprecedented appearance at the DSG's freshman orientation session and spent several hours helping to pass out briefing papers, loudly praising the group's research activities, and glad-handing with new members.[51] Miller's attendance was a powerful reminder of the successes the DSG had enjoyed in bringing committee chairs (who Miller had formerly counted among his patrons) under the control of the caucus. However, the DSG would soon be eclipsed by the arrival of the Watergate Babies.

Though he had set his sights on bigger game, Burton continued to exercise considerable influence within the DSG. He had cultivated a loyal faction in the executive committee and the membership at large. Even by 1979, the Burton faction was regarded with some suspicion by the House Democratic leadership. "There's still a little bit of paranoia," remarked then chair Abner Mikva, a Burton ally, "that we're being masterminded by Phil."[52] Nonetheless, few successor chairs shared Burton's single-minded obsession with instrumentalizing the DSG, and without his attention the group sank into malaise. By the end of the decade, *Congressional Quarterly* was reporting on "The DSG's Identity Crisis." Once "on the cutting edge of social and congressional reform," the DSG now spent "most of its time these days cranking out impartial research papers."[53] A postmortem of the DSG, published by the *Nation* in 1981, quoted liberal New York representative Richard Ottinger (admittedly not an impartial observer, having been defeated in the 1978 chairmanship election) dismissing the DSG as "moribund" in terms of being "a vehicle for producing change."[54]

In some ways, this was how influential members of the group preferred the situation. In June 1977, Conlon had managed a review into the DSG's role within the House. It concluded that the DSG's primary mission had become to provide members "with accurate, comprehensive, objective and reliable research on legislation." It sought to "brief" not "lobby" members. The DSG membership had embraced this shift. A recent poll found that more than 90 percent of members "overwhelmingly rejected the suggestion that DSG place less emphasis on research and become more involved in pursuit of specific legislative objectives as in the past."[55] With Burton's focus elsewhere, the DSG slid toward nonpartisanship, depriving House liberals of a vital tool for formulating policy, buttressing their own ranks, and maintaining discipline. In mid-1977, Conlon wrote to Bill Hansel in the DNC's Campaign Services Office, "Please do not list the Democratic Study Group in the DNC Campaign Source Book. . . . The DSG is not a campaign organization."[56]

To Play the King: The Burton-Era Caucus

The dramatic institutional reforms that had been enacted within Congress after the 1974 elections were felt most profoundly in the House. The *Washington Post* was emphatic on that point: "There is no question that a revolution has occurred. The seniority system as the rigid, inviolable operating framework of the House has been destroyed. . . . The essence of the change is that the caucus has become both formally and actually the source of power and the ultimate instrument of discipline for all House Democrats."[57] If the caucus was to truly become "the source of power and the ultimate instrument of discipline" for the Democratic Party in the House, then it needed direction. Burton was determined to provide it. The polls had barely closed in November before he announced his candidacy for the caucus chairmanship. Key House allies, including freshmen like Henry Waxman and George Miller (both fellow Californians), were recruited as part of a "buddy system" to take soundings of caucus members.[58]

Many new members were already familiar with, and grateful to, Burton for directing funds to their campaigns or making personal appearances in their districts. He could also count on his liberal record to win him friends among the Watergate Babies. As a freshman congressman, Burton had antagonized LBJ by supporting the Mississippi Freedom Democratic Party's credential challenge at the 1964 convention and then, a year later, by becoming one of only three representatives to vote against funding for the Vietnam War.[59] That early opposition stood him in good stead with new members who had been elected on antiwar platforms. Burton could likewise rely on the support of vital activist groups. After Burton's retirement as DSG chair, Common Cause had publicly commended him for his leadership in the reform efforts and chair John Gardner had written to Burton to offer his personal thanks and congratulations.[60]

Burton's opponent for the chairmanship was a fellow Californian, Bernice F. "Bernie" Sisk. A Texan by birth, Sisk had represented California's twelfth and then sixteenth districts since 1955. Some fifteen years older, he had twice Burton's seniority and had won a position on the Rules Committee after its expansion in 1961. He and the ultraliberal Burton had clashed on numerous issues, at both the state and the national levels. Sisk had been a leading defender of the Vietnam War long after most Democrats had turned against it and an opponent of the United Farm Workers (UFW)–organized grape boycott. Burton, by contrast, had been a key supporter of the predominantly Hispanic and Filipino union and a friend of its leader, Cesar Chavez.[61] Sisk attracted support from those discomfited by Burton's ambitions and disrespect for House traditions. Deputy whip and Sisk backer Jim Wright found Burton's aggressive campaigning, and in particular his pursuit of support from new members, distasteful. "That had never been done before," he said. "People saw this as unbecoming. This should be an office that was bestowed rather than sought."[62] For the Watergate Babies, however, such niceties were features of the old, cozy politics. Even Sisk sensed the way the wind was blowing and promised that there would "be a place for a more active and aggressive Caucus" in the next Congress.[63]

Burton's becoming caucus chairman, wrote the *Wall Street Journal*'s John Pierson ominously, would represent "the first time in the memory of man that a real liberal with a taste for power and ability to exercise it will have gained a position of leadership in the House." If that were to happen, Pierson added, there was every chance that Burton would move to fill the "power vacuum" created by Speaker Carl Albert's "reluctance to lead and from the gradual decline of the authority of committee chairmen." Asked directly, Burton demurred, claiming that he would never compel any member to vote contrary to their conscience.[64] Pierson's divinations would soon be put to the test.

When the caucus convened on December 2 to select its officers, Burton defeated Sisk by 162 to 111 votes. The overwhelming majority of the new members sided with him. The assertive spirit of the body was clear from this organizing meeting. Reelected Speaker Albert told the caucus that the nation faced "a crisis in the economy, an energy crisis. We have had a moral crisis. We have had a crisis of confidence such as this country has never known before. It is up to you and to me to respond to the crises."[65] "It's self-evident the winds of change have arrived at the House," Burton told the press after the vote. "My election is a product of the electorate's decision in November." The caucus, he continued, would "provide the leadership with enough additional tools to encourage cooperation from the some-times recalcitrant committee chairmen." Others were anxious about the new chairman. Burton's defeated opponent, Representative Sisk, warned that "we may be in for a real rough session which could cause damage to the country and the Democrats in 1976. . . . [The American people] don't want to see us flying off into the wild blue yonder in too many innovations and spending schemes."[66]

Observers, friendly and unfriendly, were struck by the increased potency of the Democratic Congress, and particularly of the House, and uncertain as to how it would utilize its new power. Columnist William Safire had been so shocked by the transformation within Congress that he was moved to invoke Maoist Communism, declaring that the reforms constituted a "Great Congressional Cultural Revolution." Within months he was complaining that it was as if Nixon's opponent had won the presidential election of 1972: "'McGovernment' is upon us."[67] Others were more optimistic. A 1975 car-toon by Roll Call cartoonist Jim Orton depicted the Democratic Caucus as a gargantuan baby gnawing on a bar it had wrenched from its undersized cot and eyeing two nervous figures identified as "Dem. Leadership." One was remarking to the other, "Uh—growing right up, isn't he?" Orton sent the cartoon to Burton with the cheery inscription, "Best wishes and keep eating your spinach."[68]

The first significant flexing of caucus muscle on an issue of policy came in March with a resolution to oppose any additional military aid for Cam-bodia and South Vietnam. As so many new representatives had campaigned as opponents of further Asian adventurism, and as the war powers had been an issue of such contention with Nixon, this resolution was an obvious place to start. New York's Rep. Bella Abzug had been the leader of the antiwar movement in the House. On her first day as a congresswoman, in 1971, she introduced a resolution calling for the immediate withdrawal of all American troops.[69] By the mid-1970s, she was clearly identified as part of the militant antiwar left. Consequently, newly elected Rep. Bob Carr of Michigan was tapped by the antiwar congressional faction to put the measure to the caucus. Carr recalled that "Bella knew that she was just so controversial, that she had just burned so many bridges with others, that she couldn't . . . be the author of the resolution." Coming from a freshman member, the resolution would carry much greater symbolic authority. For his part, Carr claimed to have been comfortable with the risk.[70]

"Somewhere along the line," according to Carr, the resolution was "sanctioned" by Burton. "It could not have happened without the approval of Phil Burton."[71] The resolution offered, at a special caucus meeting convened on March 12, declared that it was "the sense of the Democratic Caucus that we firmly oppose the approval of any further military assistance to South Vietnam or to Cambodia in Fiscal Year 1975." Speaking in support, Carr told the caucus that the resolution "is imperative, it is timely, the time is now." The Congress had a duty to show that the responsibility for foreign policy rested not only with the White House and the executive branch. Democrats had been warned that the world would be watching to test America's commitment. "Well, the whole world is watching, not to test our commitment, but to test our sanity."[72] After a heated debate, the resolution was approved decisively, 189–49 votes.

Both Albert and Burton announced that this "sense of the caucus" resolution indicated that the House would almost certainly not approve any further requests for aid.[73] Some House members responded with fury. The caucus had directed the House on how to vote on an issue of policy before the relevant committee—in this case the House International Relations Committee—had been able to consider testimony from administration officials.[74] Discontent with this use of the caucus had been on display in the debate over Carr's defunding resolution. Wisconsin representative David Obey—a liberal reformer, and future DSG chair, who had opposed defense funding for Vietnam and Cambodia—distilled the hostility: "Jerry Ford is going to be able to run to the newspapers and be able to say, 'Look at that. Those Democrats are playing partisan politics on Cambodia. They voted in a secret caucus to bind their members on Cambodia.'"

Thomas Morgan, Pennsylvania congressman and chair of the Committee on International Relations, echoed Obey's concerns: "It does not make sense to me for the Caucus to try to take over the functions of the Legislative Committee. If the committee system does not work, that is another matter, but when the committees do their jobs and when you have a cooperative chairman like the guy you are looking at, then why should the Caucus try to upstage us?"[75] Even ardent reformer Richard Bolling declared publicly that he hated to see "the caucus function pitted against the committee function" and that he hoped "the present management . . . does not make the mistake of destroying the caucus before it's a year old."[76] Younger members were inclined to be dismissive of such concerns. Carr was among those who felt that the caucus should be used as an outlet for ambitious but frustrated freshmen. "The committee system is fine, but it doesn't always help us," he remarked. "The House needs a mechanism to proceed on an issue with much greater swiftness."[77]

Burton understood the concerns, telling the freshmen, "Some people were steamed. We have to lay off using the caucus for a while."[78] However, mere weeks after the passage of Carr's resolution, Burton was menacing the administration again. In late March, Burton was part of a group of congressmen, Democrats and Republicans, invited to a "three-course candlelit dinner" at Vice President Nelson Rockefeller's Washington, DC, mansion. Burton reportedly made "an impassioned plea" to Rockefeller for White House cooperation with Congress, before warning that he "had the votes" to override presidential vetoes of antirecession spending bills then under consideration.[79] The sense was growing in the Ford administration that Burton was the real power in the House.[80]

"The first few months of this Congress," boasted Burton's constituency newsletter in May 1975, "have been the most productive opening period of any Congress since World War II."[81] However, by the middle of 1975, it seemed the caucus was stalling. The most potent symbol of the Democratic House's impotence was the defeat, on June 4, of the motion to override Ford's veto of the Emergency Employment Appropriation Act, a $5.3 billion stimulus bill that the president had rejected as wasteful and inflationary.[82] Appealing for support in the special caucus meeting before the vote, Majority Leader Tip O'Neill told the assembled members that he hoped all Democrats would hold together on principle: "This is a bill that deals with the ideals that we believe in, jobs, wages and the incentive to get this economy moving. . . . I hope today we will all vote in the Democratic manner."[83] Albert took the unusual step of vacating the Speaker's chair so that he could argue for the bill from the floor, "plead[ing]" with the House "with all the urgency that I have in my body . . . to show that we are the legislative body of this Nation." Speaking for the bill, Burton denounced Ford's veto as "ill-advised" and made an appeal for Republican support that was half plea and half threat: "I would hope that when the totals on this bill are tallied that no one will be able to say that the Republican Party is the party of the cruel, the heartless, and the indifferent."[84] To no avail, however. The Democrats won the vote, 277 to 145, but fell five short of the majority needed to overturn the veto.

Later that month, a motion to override Ford's veto of a housing subsidy bill fell sixteen short of the two-thirds needed. Albert again took to the floor to denounce the president for designating "Pennsylvania Avenue as a one-way street with veto barricades against the overwhelming majority in every instance." Nonetheless, the inflated Democratic Caucus was supposed to have been able to batter through those barricades. In this instance, thirty-five Democrats joined with the Republicans to uphold the veto. This was Ford's fourth victory in veto-override confrontations with Congress.[85] The veto was Ford's most effective legislative weapon, and he wielded it often. Indeed, relative to time in office, Ford ranks fourth for the frequency with which he deployed his veto.[86] The press response to such stalemate was excoriating. "Ah, how June's reality has melted the optimisms of January!" wrote playwright and columnist Larry L. King. "Democrats, given opportunities to gladden the ghost of Franklin Roosevelt, have been unable to get together on their major schemes." In the same month, a *New York Times* editorial denounced both President Ford and the Democratic Congress for "Governing by Posture."[87]

The failure to override these vetoes was infuriating for those members who had expected the caucus to seize the legislative initiative in the Ninety-Fourth Congress. Some, younger members in particular, blamed the leadership, and complaints about generational disaffection were voiced more frequently. "Albert and O'Neill," said California's Norm Mineta, "can go in and tell a few jokes and buy a few rounds of drinks and people love them and they get re-elected. But we're the products of a different era and a different system."[88] Budget Committee chair Brock Adams recommended that the caucus take punitive action against defectors, such as stripping them of seniority. Burton publicly cautioned against "unleashing frustrations inward" and told members that that they had to "search for more carrots than sticks." Mo Udall, though he still hoped for more "vigorous" leadership, was equally circumspect: "You can't tell 289 [*sic*] independent Democrats to jump through a hoop. The whole thrust of reform was for independence and more individual intent. If they campaigned against an increase in the gas tax, no amount of brilliant leadership can make them vote for it."[89] Ultimately, it was unrealistic to expect members to vote against their districts, and thus against their own political careers.

David Broder came to a similar conclusion, writing that the House was "floundering" because it was "dominated by junior members so insecure about their political futures that they cannot see any issue in terms that reach beyond the next election. . . . No one can lead men and women who refuse to be led."[90] Given the unprecedented size of the freshman class, and the fact that so many members had won in marginal districts in a year when the Republican brand was peculiarly toxic, such anxieties were understandable. House Democrats could hardly expect the GOP to obligingly offer up a new Watergate every few years. Moreover, all things considered, the Democratic Caucus was remarkably cohesive. Veto-override resolutions almost always failed to pass by a handful of votes. With the total caucus only just clearing the magic two-thirds threshold, even a small rebellion could scupper the House Democrats' grand schemes. In this context, the much-feted "veto-proof majority" was as much a liability as an advantage, raising expectations of a congressional party facing a president who used his veto power as a bargaining tool.

Nonetheless, the caucus did struggle to clear the legitimacy hurdle, dogged constantly by accusations that it should not be used as an instrument of policy. This was characteristic of Burton's career. His successes were qualified by the manner in which he exploited House institutions to achieve them. He had forced the first contested election for caucus chairman in decades and made the chairmanship more prominent than it had ever been. Yet Burton understood that every bold use of the caucus antagonized both committee chairs and the existing leadership and invited backlash. His power base would be much more secure if he could penetrate the leadership hierarchy and guide House Caucus activities from a post where he would be expected to direct policy. In 1976, when the retirement of Speaker Albert prompted a leadership reshuffle that left the post of majority leader vacant, he got his chance.

The 1976 Majority Leader's Race

Of the Watergate Babies who sought reelection in 1976, all but two were returned to Congress, defying predictions that their election had been an aberration caused by the febrile political atmosphere of 1974. Reviewing the
returns from the 1976 elections, *Congressional Quarterly* psephologist Rhodes
Cook concluded that while the Republican Party remained formidable in
presidential races, at the state and local level it was "badly eroded." Steven
Stockmeyer, executive director of the Republican Congressional Campaign
Committee (RCCC), noted morosely, "Another showing like 1974 or 1976
would be close to fatal." By contrast, Paul Pendergast, executive director of
the DCCC was upbeat: "The Democratic Party around the country is health-
ier and bigger [than the GOP] and we have more talent to draw upon."[91]
Bumper Democratic congressional majorities had rarely proved so durable.
The majorities elected alongside LBJ in 1964, for instance, had all but been
wiped out by 1966 when the Great Society ran headlong into urban riots and
the Vietnam War. Moreover, few Democrats felt that they owed their election
to president-elect Jimmy Carter. Indeed, given that Carter ran behind many
congressional Democrats in their districts and the fact that he had apparently
squandered a large lead over Ford, congressional Democrats could be forgiven for thinking that Carter owed his election to the reverse coattails effect
that they had provided.[92] To that extent, the 1976 election only strengthened
the reformers' case for legislative leadership.

   Roll Call journalist Myron Struck reported that, having broken the congressional reform logjam, the class of '74—then making overtures to the
freshmen of the Ninety-Fifth Congress—now had the opportunity to reshape the House leadership in their image, if they could remain unified:
"Their relative ability to engender a spirit of cohesiveness is in their individual abilities to project a low-keyed concern for issues-oriented 'progressive' ideas and 'possibilities.' But their first serious test may be in the race
for House Majority Leader."[93] As early as June 1975, it was being reported
that freshmen Democrats were threatening open rebellion against the House
leadership in light of Congress's tepid legislative record. The possibility of a
resolution of no confidence in Albert was under discussion. Bob Carr had
gone so far as to publicly demand that the Speaker resign. Albert was, said
Carr, "not dynamic, [not] a strong personality, and [not] energetic in form-
ing a leadership figure around which the party can rally."[94] The attempts to

force Albert into premature retirement failed (Carr would later publicly regret his impetuousness), but relations between the Watergate Babies and the leadership remained cool. By contrast, Burton was as close as the class came to having its own leader.

In June 1976, with the Democratic Party poised to reclaim the two elected branches for the first time that decade, Albert announced his retirement. The Speakership would almost certainly pass to Albert's deputy, Majority Leader O'Neill, who was unlikely to face any serious opposition. The real race, then, was to replace O'Neill. Shortly after the announcement, Albert effectively endorsed O'Neill ("I'm recommending that he will make a great Speaker") but delicately declined to endorse any candidate in the majority leader's race. He did not believe, he added, that a "really great liberal" would emerge to lead the Ninety-Fifth Congress.[95] From the start, however, Burton was the presumed front-runner. Of the declared candidates, only he had won a caucus-wide election. In a letter to his House colleagues announcing his candidacy, Burton cast himself as a broker who was just as concerned with individual members' interests ("balancing the demands of Washington service with district time") as he was with the imperatives of party leadership ("forging a Democratic program through democratic means").[96]

The other candidates, at least initially, were John J. McFall, representative from California and majority whip, and Richard Bolling, Missouri congressman and elder statesman of the congressional reform movement. As majority whip, tradition had it that McFall would succeed O'Neill. He was a former lawyer who had represented a district that neighbored Burton's in northern California since the 1950s. McFall and Burton had gone head-to-head for the whip's position in early 1973, with the former winning out, a feat he hoped to replicate. He was damaged, however, by the "Koreagate" scandal, revelations that he had accepted thousands of dollars in gifts from a South Korean businessman, Tongsun Park, who was apparently a front for influence-buying by Korean officials. McFall was decent and well-liked but thought by some, as one member put it, as "just too nice to get things done." This was not a vice that the prickly and aloof Bolling shared. Bolling was a senior member of the Rules Committee, a former academic, and, according to the *New York Times*, "the Democrats' best parliamentarian and legislative theoretician." A onetime protégé of Sam Rayburn, Bolling had emerged as a formidable intellectual and legislator within the congressional reform movement, publishing, among other works, *House Out of Order* in 1965 in an effort to transform congressional reform into a public cause. He had been central to all manner of institutional reforms, and reform efforts, within the House and had challenged Albert for the majority leadership in 1962. However, though Bolling was generally respected, he was also regarded as arrogant.[97]

Over McFall and Bolling, Burton was confident that he had the edge, telling a San Francisco Chamber of Commerce delegation before Albert had even resigned that he would be the next majority leader. His allies boasted of the number of solid commitments he had received. "That's an old tactic of Burton's," countered McFall. "It's a pattern of his to say, 'I've got all the votes. Everyone else can go home.'"[98] In the Senate, a similar reshuffle was underway at the top. With the incumbent Mike Mansfield retiring, Hubert Humphrey had announced his intention to pursue the majority leadership.[99] "Most Democratic insiders agree," wrote Albert Hunt in the *Wall Street Journal*, "that if Rep. Burton wins in the House and Sen. Humphrey wins in the Senate, the outlook is for a more assertive Legislative branch." These two elections, thus, would "determine the disposition of the new Congress and its relationship with the Carter administration."[100]

No one was more dismayed by Burton's front-runner status than the man who was to succeed Albert: Thomas P. "Tip" O'Neill. Burton and O'Neill's mutual antipathy is in some respects surprising. Both were on the liberal wing of the caucus. Both drew accusations of excessive partisanship from House Republicans. Both had credibility with younger members, in large part because they had been early opponents of the Vietnam War and supporters of Eugene McCarthy's presidential campaign. O'Neill's infamous dictum "all politics is local" found near perfect expression in Burton's careful husbanding of his San Francisco constituency. Burton had publicly supported O'Neill's bid for the majority leadership in 1972, after the death of Hale Boggs, and O'Neill would later praise Burton as the "most abiding Democrat" he had ever known.[101]

Yet beneath the superficial comity, a deep rivalry had been intensifying between the two men throughout the 1970s. It dated to 1972 when DSG chairman Burton had made his first bid for a place in the Democratic leadership, in the elections precipitated by Majority Leader Hale Boggs's disappearance in a light aircraft over Alaska. Burton almost immediately announced his interest in succeeding O'Neill as majority whip.[102] As the whip's post was still within the gift of the leader, Burton understood that this was easier said than done. O'Neill and Burton had been involved in an altercation at a California fund-raiser only a few months earlier, which had climaxed in Burton challenging O'Neill to a fight.[103] O'Neill was hardly warm to the idea of having the volatile Californian as his deputy and had in fact told presumptive Speaker Albert that Burton was "crazy." O'Neill successfully obstructed a Burton-led caucus resolution to make the whip's post elective and promoted McFall instead.[104] From here, the animosity between the two men continued to fester.

The feud was more than a matter of clashing egos. There was a more substantive dispute between the two men, though it seemed more often strategic. Despite overlapping policy concerns, O'Neill was far more institutionally minded than Burton. He had greater respect for the House's traditions. California congressman Tony Coelho, who had worked for Bernie Sisk from 1965 until he succeeded to his seat in 1978, summarized the differences between O'Neill and Burton: "I don't think Tip ever got out ahead of the team too much. Burton wanted to educate. Burton wanted to convince. . . . [O'Neill] wanted to lead the troops, and help you accomplish things as opposed to having his own ideas of what needed to be done."[105] As the likelihood of a clash increased, O'Neill and Burton sniped at each other through the press. Questioned about possible intraleadership tensions, Burton remarked, "I can work with O'Neill. Ask him whether he can work with me." O'Neill replied soon afterward with a terse, "I can work with anyone."[106] An O'Neill-Burton double act seemed to promise near open warfare within the ranks of the Democratic leadership.

To derail the Burton locomotive, O'Neill and his allies cast around for a suitable log. They settled on Jim Wright of Texas. A ten-term veteran of the House, Wright was a liberal by his state's standards. He had declined to sign the "Southern Manifesto," circulated during his freshman term, and had voted for the 1957 Civil Rights Act. He never won his Texas seat with less than 60 percent of the vote. He had served on the Public Works Committee since his first term, distinguishing himself as a diligent and competent legislator, and was in line to become its chairman in the Ninety-Fifth Congress. In contrast to the often obnoxious and divisive Burton, Wright was, one reporter said, "Mr. Nice Guy, spelled in capital letters. It's virtually impossible to find a representative who has ever had a run-in with him." In 1972, Wright had published *You and Your Congressman*, which, in contrast to Bolling's excoriating polemics, was a gently laudatory defense of both his institution and his colleagues.[107] He was solicitous of his House colleagues in other ways, using his position on Public Works to steer infrastructure projects toward potential allies. Acknowledged as a fine orator, he was often sought out by other members as a campaigner.[108] Despite his late entry into the race, Wright brought formidable advantages with him, not the least of which was his membership in the large Texas delegation.[109] Wright announced his candidacy in late July. The role of the majority leader, he said in his announcement, was to be "advocate, conciliator, occasional innovator. Part evangelist, part parish priest, and every now and then, part prophet."[110]

Burton's objectionable legislative style and poor working relationship with O'Neill were significant obstacles to his leadership ambitions. An additional weakness was his association with Rep. Wayne Hays, the committee chair whom Burton had helped shield from the Watergate Babies' cull in early 1975 and who was, by mid-1976, embroiled in one of the worst congressional scandals of the decade. In May 1976, the *Washington Post* reported that Hays was keeping a young female clerk on his payroll, Elizabeth Ray, solely to offer him sexual favors. Ray—a one-time Miss Virginia, former waitress and stewardess, and aspiring actress—told the *Post* that she had never been asked to do any Congress-related work and appeared in the Capitol Hill office for only a few hours a week: "I can't type. I can't file. I can't even answer the phone."[111]

Initially, Hays denied the allegations, dismissing Ray as an "extremely sick young woman" and accusing the *Post* of pursuing "a political vendetta." Within days, however, Hays had reversed course, conceding the affair and referring himself to the House Committee on Standards of Official Conduct. The Justice Department and the FBI both embarked on their own investigations and a federal grand jury was impaneled to begin hearing testimony.[112] The scandal had been compounded by the considerable power that Hays wielded as chair of the House Administration Committee. This position gave Hays enormous power over the things congressional offices depended on day-to-day: stationery allowances, office space, telephones, mail franking, travel expenses, and even air-conditioning. Control of much of these privileges had come about as a direct result of Hays's efforts to expand the Administration Committee "from an obscure housekeeping agency into one of the most heavily staffed committees in the House."[113]

Cantankerous and penny-pinching, Hays was not shy about wielding his power. Hays's influence was augmented by his simultaneous chairmanship of the DCCC, a fact that drew the ire of several reform groups. In effect, Hays controlled a significant proportion of the resources that members would receive first as they sought office and then as they occupied it. "Allowing

Hays to chair both the Campaign Committee and the House Administration Committee," charged Fred Wertheimer, chair of Common Cause, "remains a scandal the Democrats have to deal with." It was, said Wertheimer, "the worst possible conflict of interest." Hays, in turn, sneeringly dismissed the organization as "Common Curse."[114] By contrast, Burton's congressional reform efforts meant that he was embraced as an ally by public advocacy groups like Common Cause.[115] The Hays affair placed those relationships under strain.

Almost immediately, House Democrats began agitating for Hays's removal, with some pressing for a special caucus meeting. By early June, O'Neill was demanding that Hays temporarily relinquish his committee chairmanships until the federal investigations had concluded. A week later, the Democratic National Congressional Committee voted unanimously to remove Hays as chair.[116] The next day, Hays was hospitalized following an overdose of sleeping medication, which he later claimed was accidental.[117] By the end of the month, he had resigned his chairmanship and the caucus had approved a recommendation from the Steering and Policy Committee to return some of the powers that had accrued to the Administration Committee to the full House.[118] In August, Hays announced his retirement, citing both health concerns and ongoing press "harassment," before resigning his seat entirely in September.[119]

As the scandal intensified, Hays had found himself with few defenders. Tensions had been running high between Hays and the leadership for some time. Despite pressure from Albert and O'Neill, Hays had refused to step aside as chair of the DCCC in January 1975. Hays blamed O'Neill for the Steering and Policy Committee recommendation to oust him from his chairmanship (repudiated, thanks to Burton, by the caucus).[120] Hays could count on little support from the rank and file. Well before the scandal had broken, the Watergate Babies had come in for significant criticism for their failure to remove Hays in the broader chairman cull. The *Washington Post* had been more forgiving than some, but even it had criticized the "self-styled congressional reformers" for seeking "to reallocate power within a system, rather than to remake the system itself." Removing Hays would have been "the first step to dismantling the internal spoils system of the House."[121]

Pressure came from both the Right and the Left. The House GOP seized on the issue enthusiastically, and Republican members took to referring to the scandal as a "Democratic Watergate." Minority Leader John Rhodes condemned it as "a black-eye on the whole Congress." President Ford, during a television interview, said both he and the nation were "disturb[ed]" by the allegations.[122] "If I were a Democratic congressman, I'd sleep nervously," said Minnesota Republican Bill Frenzel. "The majority has written the rules and runs the Congress. They've got to clean up the nest."[123]

Throughout Hays's prolonged public disgrace, Burton could do little to protect his old ally. He did take steps, however, to try to insulate himself from the scandal. For instance, in keeping with the mood of transparency, he produced a memorandum detailing his current assets and tax rates dating back to 1971. "As Majority Leader," he added, "it would be my intention to file such statements annually."[124] However, the scandal wounded him. Cartoonist Herblock depicted Burton as the proprietor of "Wheeler-Dealer Phil Burton's Congressional Used Cars" who, having already been responsible for a write-off marked "The Wayne Hays: A Burton Special," offers his ragged and bruised customer—"House Democrats"—the reassurance, "You lucky fellow—I just happen to have another great buy for you." The second car, leaking fluid and with a wonky front bumper, was marked "The Burton Leadership Deal."[125]

The calculation shifted in early November when Jimmy Carter won the presidency. Had Ford been narrowly returned to office—an eminently plausible outcome by November 1976—a noisy and aggressive partisan, to whip the ranks and override vetoes, might have made for a more appealing candidate. As it was, with a Democratic president-elect, the familiar paradigm of executive leadership in setting legislative priorities began to reassert itself. In that context, Burton struck an inclusive note, declaring in a newspaper interview that he hoped Carter would work with Congress as he pursued his reform agenda, paying attention to the membership as a whole and not just the leaders: "This is a rich national resource. We hope it will be called upon."[126]

Winning over the younger cohort was of vital importance. Burton was the youngest candidate in the race, and the most recently elected, and he had been cultivating relationships with many since his time at the DSG. Many felt they owed their congressional careers, at least in part, to Burton. He sought to nurture similar relationships with the new members. As usual, he flew to unfamiliar districts to campaign for new members and made sure he was the first congressman to welcome several to Washington.[127] The anti-Burton forces made similar overtures. O'Neill—along with Whip McFall and Deputy Whip John Brademas—organized the orientation for the forty-seven freshmen members, incurring the wrath of the DSG, which had traditionally been responsible for this. After tense negotiations, it was agreed that there would be two orientations. Doubtless, the House leadership was anxious to start molding the new intake, but there remained an abiding suspicion that the DSG was in some senses still a proxy for Burton.[128] However late, the leadership was moving to isolate Burton. Nonetheless, his support from the Watergate Babies, nearly all of whom had been reelected in 1976, remained solid. In the days before the caucus met, fourteen Democrats circulated a letter in support of Burton's candidacy. Fully half of those who signed had been elected in 1974. No other "class" had more than one member as a signatory.[129]

On December 6, the 296 members of the Democratic Caucus gathered on the floor of the House to elect their leaders for the upcoming Congress. In defiance of precedent, the caucus voted to open its session to the public. To no one's astonishment, O'Neill was elected unopposed as Speaker at the beginning of the session. During the two-hour, three-ballot election for House Majority Leader, the "packed galleries oohed and ahed as the returns were announced one by one."[130] One hundred and forty-nine votes were required for victory. Some observers had predicted that Burton would secure 130, perhaps even 140, in the first ballot.[131] It was therefore something of a surprise when Burton received only 106 votes in the first round, in which McFall was eliminated. When Bolling was knocked out in the second ballot (in which Burton's support crept up to 107), it would have been reasonable to assume that the reformist Missourian's supporters would flood over to the remaining liberal in the race, Burton. This would be to underestimate the extent to which Burton could antagonize his ideological bedfellows.

In the third and final ballot, Bob Carr was one of Burton's tellers. He recalled the tense atmosphere in the caucus toward the end of the count, when the four previous boxes had produced a tie, and he and Rep. Charlie Wilson of Texas, one of Wright's tellers, were alternately counting ballots: "It was Charlie and I counting the ballots. And he'd turn over one and I'd turn over one, and the clerks and everyone was watching this. It was like a very close sports match. And it came down, it literally came down, to the last ballot turned over. And Charlie turned it over, and it was for Jim Wright."[132]

Burton lost, with 147 votes to Wright's 148.[133] The implications of the result were obvious to observers. O'Neill's deputy would now not be the "tough, activist, ambitious Burton pushing O'Neill, pushing the House, pushing Jimmy Carter" but "a comfortable man with a soothing voice who sees his role as a builder of bridges between North and South, conservatives and liberals."[134]

"Given a choice of four office-seekers," wrote Jerry terHorst, former press secretary to President Ford, "[House Democrats] chose not to rush in where angels fear to tread."[135] In the Senate, Humphrey had suffered a similar fate, losing the majority leadership to Robert C. Byrd. In each case, the more activist liberal had lost to an institutionally conservative southerner.

Publicly, Burton was upbeat. "If you'd have predicted two years ago that I'd become majority leader, someone would have taken you off to an institution," he said afterward. "But I came within one vote of making it and I did it without waiting around to become the consensus candidate who spent years in one appointed House post after another, waiting for my turn to lead."[136] Nonetheless, this was the first election Burton had lost since 1954 and it proved a significant setback. His defeat was due to a combination of factors: O'Neill's opposition, the Hays scandal, Wright's southern support, and his own abrasive personality. Indeed, the very qualities that made him such an effective legislator may well have doomed him in the leadership election. "One word frequently heard in reference to Burton," reported one postmortem, "was 'instability.'"[137]

One anonymous Democratic congressman told the *San Francisco Examiner* that Carter might have played an indirect role in Burton's defeat: "There was a feeling that he would be in disharmony with the new administration as well as with the new Speaker. The Carter people thought he might not work well with them."[138] There was no indication that Carter took an active role in blocking Burton, but in such a tight race the undisguised suspicions of the president-elect's staff can hardly be discounted as a factor. If such considerations played a role in members' calculations, then it is clear that deference to the executive remained a tenacious force in Congress even after Watergate. One of the more illustrative remarks came from Senator John Glenn, who observed in June, "The outcome may depend on who is elected President. Will we need an articulate spokesman for the loyal Democratic opposition to a Republican President, or will we need a legislative mechanic to work with a Democratic president."[139] A similar orthodoxy prevailed in the House. Had Ford been elected, there would have been a far stronger case for taking a punt on Burton.

Burton did not entirely abandon his leadership ambitions after his maddeningly close defeat in 1976. By early 1978, Burton was intimating that he would challenge Wright for the majority leader's post again after that year's midterms. "I certainly don't expect to wait until next century," he told inquisitive journalists.[140] That challenge never materialized, however. By 1980, the Reagan landslide had put the House Democratic majority on the back foot, and by 1983, at the moment that a congressional pushback to the Reagan Revolution had begun in earnest, Burton was dead.

The Watergate Babies, under Burton's leadership, had failed to transform the caucus into an instrument of policy. Clearly, the Babies faced serious opposition from the institutionally minded in the House, especially those who felt that the caucus should not usurp functions properly exercised by the committees. However, the class had their own internal weaknesses. For all their cultural similarities, their populist attacks on a collection of corrupt elites, and their shared insistence on the need to find new solutions for the 1970s, there was precious little agreement over how to proceed and few attempts to systematically define these solutions. Clannish and fiercely protective of their independence, the Watergate Babies were not inclined to, for instance, colonize the DSG and renovate it as a tool for advancing their own legislative objectives.

Class cohesion, at least in ideological terms, broke down relatively quickly. Regular meetings ended for the Watergate Babies in 1979. By 1984, reported *Congressional Quarterly*, "the only time the members get together formally is for their annual Christmas party—and that event is organized by their wives." It had persisted as long as it had, recalled Toby Moffett, "partly out of nostalgia and partly out of fear of being swallowed up by the institution."[141] This disintegration was accelerated by the imperatives of reelection. Indeed, some older members understood the noisy reformism of their younger colleagues as the aggressive pursuit of high profiles by uneasy Democrats in marginal districts. The class's distinctive ideological leanings would not vanish, however. In fact, it would prove decisive in the early years of the Carter administration, as an older generation of congressional Democrats sought to seize control of the legislative initiative.

3

Peanuts
The Early Frustrations of the
Carter Years, 1976–1978

The defining feature of the Democratic Party's first midterm convention in Kansas City, according to the Catholic conservative-turned-liberal commentator Garry Wills, was the fear of a walkout by southern delegates and "the Northern liberal's hope that a Southerner will come along who talks just like the *New York Times*, a man to lead his benighted neighbors into civilization."[1] That hope was in some sense personified in Kansas City by the outgoing governor of Georgia, Jimmy Carter, fresh from a stint as the DNC's campaign chair for that year's congressional and gubernatorial campaigns.[2] Four years earlier, Carter had been one of a number of candidates for southern governorships who had apparently broken the race-baiting Dixiecrat mold, showing that Democrats who ran as trustworthy populists, eschewed racial demagoguery, and finessed the issue of desegregation could assemble winning coalitions of moderate whites and newly enfranchised African Americans.[3] In his inaugural address, Carter had declared, "The time for racial discrimination is over." *Time* magazine put Georgia's new governor on its cover—"soft voiced, assured, looking eerily like John Kennedy from certain angles"—and hailed him as the leader of a new generation of southern moderates "determined to resolve" some of the region's "paradoxes."[4] For Democrats, Carter represented the hope that even if the days of the deep blue "Solid South" were over, there was a Democratic-leaning, racially inclusive "New South" to be cultivated.

Carter's ambitions were national as well as regional. He began planning his own ascent to the White House from his earliest days in the governor's mansion. Carter had been a key figure in the Stop

McGovern forces at Miami Beach, giving the nomination speech for one of his opponents, Washington senator Henry "Scoop" Jackson.[5] Just over a week after the Kansas City convention concluded, Carter launched his presidential campaign, one of the first candidates out of the gates.[6] An early start was essential for Carter. Though he had been assiduously building a reputation within the Democratic Party, he was still considered a long shot for the presidency. With 1976 looking like a Democratic year, there were several more established candidates he would have to move aside and no shortage of similar long shot pretenders hoping that the unsettled political environment would open a path to the White House for them.

The 1976 Democratic presidential primaries were the most crowded in decades. In all, seventeen candidates sought the nomination. Few seemed to understand the political moment as well as Carter, though. He offered Americans not so much a political program as himself—trustworthy, self-effacing, and morally upstanding. His message, noted the *Atlantic*'s correspondent, was a "simple, comforting one. . . . Jimmy wasn't claiming to be better than everybody else, just one of us folks."[7] On the campaign trail, he emphasized his time managing his family's peanut farm rather than his background as a nuclear engineer in the US Navy. Carter's folksiness and personal integrity concealed his political skills and willingness to grab opportunities. His candidacy was deliberately packaged to appeal to a beleaguered, post-Watergate nation. "I will never lie to you," he told audiences across the country.[8] His rectitude was believable because of his unabashed religiosity. An evangelical himself, Carter was the first presidential candidate to bring born-again southern Christianity into mainstream American politics. This could make him seem exotic, even bizarre to many Americans, as when he suggested in an interview with *Playboy* magazine that he had "committed adultery in [his] heart many times" (Carter's chief of staff Hamilton Jordan called this the "weirdo factor").[9] Nonetheless, it gave him a substantial advantage with other white evangelicals, who turned out in droves for him in 1976.

Carter's victory in the Democratic primaries was the product of several factors. One was his distinctive political identity and the promise that he could be the Democratic candidate that could hold the party's traditional southern base without retreating on its commitment to civil rights. After Carter won the nomination, one of Ford's strategists, Tennessee-born Frances Kaye Pullen, noted in a confidential memo that Carter was "playing upon two essentially conflicting myths—the 'good ole boy' rural South and the 'black and white together' new South."[10] No other candidate occupied that space. When Carter defeated George Wallace in the Florida primary, it was treated by many commentators as an exorcism. He had repudiated the party's segregationist past and defended his claim to represent the new Democratic South.[11]

Carter also understood, in the way that few other candidates seemed to, how the McGovern-Fraser Commission had transformed the process by which the Democratic Party selected its standard bearer. His campaign recognized that it was not merely that the party had been further democratized but that the emerging *sequence* of the primaries (starting in states with small electorates like New Hampshire before moving to the larger, more delegate-rich states) created opportunities for candidates with few resources and even less name recognition.[12] The Carter campaign made a virtue of his unlikeliness as a candidate. "My name is Jimmy Carter and I'm running for president," the candidate told audiences across the country. This greeting— which underscored both his relative obscurity and his appealing modesty— became a catchphrase of sorts. As public faith in America's national political institutions declined, Carter enjoyed the cache of a Washington outsider who could run against the business-as-usual politics of Washington. This was not a posture that the presidential candidates who emerged from Congress could execute convincingly, although many tried to emphasize their distance from the cozy Beltway.

Neither Jimmy Carter nor the congressional Democratic Party felt any gratitude to the other after the elections of 1976. Although the presidential election was ultimately closer than many observers had expected it would be, Carter's victory was undoubtedly his own. For their part, most congressional Democrats did not feel they owed anything to Carter's coattails. Indeed, a substantial number had run *ahead* of Carter in their districts or states and felt that the new president owed his win to their coattails.[13] To a considerable extent, the election of Jimmy Carter and the reelection of the Democratic Congress were parallel rather than intertwined outcomes in 1976. This fact would define the relations between the Carter White House and Congress in the early years of Carter's first term. It was compounded by Carter's mishandling of the congressional Democratic Party. If congressional liberals had hoped that the election of a Democratic president would trigger a new burst of ambitious legislative reforms, they would be sorely disappointed. This was encapsulated in the effort to pass the Humphrey-Hawkins Full Employment

Act, which, though apparently uncontroversial in the Democratic primaries, would provoke one of the most tortured intraparty disputes between 1977 and 1978.

"Second-Place Mo": Mo Udall, Congress, and the 1976 Election

Carter was not the first candidate to announce his bid for the 1976 Democratic presidential nomination. That distinction belonged to Arizona congressman Morris K. "Mo" Udall. Despite a sprawling field of candidates, members of Congress were not particularly well represented in the 1976 Democratic presidential primaries. The three candidates who garnered the highest vote totals were all governors or former governors: Carter, Jerry Brown of California, and George Wallace of Alabama. Udall, an eight-term congressman from Arizona, was one of the best-performing congressional representatives and as close as the 1976 election came to having a full-fledged congressional Watergate Baby in the race. Although by most metrics he was one of the more conventional liberals running that year, Udall's campaign underlined the Democratic Party's growing reliance on affluent suburban voters and the concomitant transformation of its policy priorities.

Udall hailed from a sprawling family of Mormon pioneers who had settled in Arizona in the late nineteenth century. The Udalls were omnipresent in politics across the Southwest, occupying a plethora of offices at the state and the national levels. The Arizona town where Mo Udall was born in 1922, St. Johns, had been founded by his grandfather, David King Udall, on the orders of Brigham Young. Sited at a crossing on the Colorado River in the harsh northeastern uplands of Arizona, the arid desert climate of St. Johns would define Udall's childhood.[14] A naturally adventurous child, Udall would spend hours exploring the town's desert environs with his brothers. At the age of six, he lost his right eye in an accident involving a friend's pocket knife; he wore a glass prosthesis for the rest of his life.

After graduation from high school in 1940, Udall followed his older brother Stewart to the University of Arizona. He also joined his brother on the college basketball team, quickly emerging as a star player. At the outbreak of World War II, Udall was prevented by his disability from enlisting. When standards were later relaxed, he was admitted as a noncombat officer, serving in the army and air corps until mid-1946. He recalled later that the army was the first place he received a false eye that was both the right shape and the right color. Stationed in Louisiana, Udall was deeply affected by the segregated South, particularly in an unsuccessful stint as defense counsel for a black airman accused of murder. A demobbed Udall transferred to the University of Denver's law school after being offered a contract to play for a Colorado-based basketball team. In 1949, newly married and having passed the Arizona bar exam, Udall set up a law office in Tucson with his brother, Stewart. Udall swiftly established himself as a skillful trial lawyer, exploiting his natural quick wit to great effect in the courtroom.[15] Throughout his career, Udall's humor was one of his best political assets.[16] A member of the House Post Office Committee, he once joked, "Let's turn inflation over to the Post Office. That'll slow it down."[17]

In 1952, having successfully prosecuted a series of corrupt officials for bribery, Udall was elected the Pima County attorney. Two years later, he was defeated in the primary for a Superior Court judgeship, while his brother Stewart easily won election to the House from Arizona's second district. A crestfallen Udall returned to his practice, throwing himself into the law with renewed vigor. In 1961, Stewart was nominated as secretary of the interior in the incoming Kennedy administration, vacating his district. In the special election that followed, Mo Udall was pitted against Mac C. Matheson, a Tucson radio host with a fierce antipathy to the federal government and a penchant for racist jokes. Despite low turnout, Udall bested his Republican opponent, albeit by a narrow two thousand votes. In thirteen subsequent re-election campaigns, this would prove to be his closest result. What is perhaps most remarkable about Udall's political career is that a politically orthodox liberal ("a one-eyed Mormon Democrat," as he often described himself) was able to flourish in relatively conservative Arizona.[18]

In Congress, Udall became active in the Democratic Study Group and took up the cause of congressional reform, waging a decade-long offensive against the seniority system.[19] In 1964, he was chosen as the floor whip for northern and western members on the Civil Rights Act of 1964, his first congressional leadership role. In the late 1960s, he became one of the first Democrats to publicly condemn the administration's policy in Vietnam and was instrumental in triggering the congressional investigation into the My Lai massacre.[20] In 1969 and 1971, in an effort to accelerate House reform, Udall launched two unsuccessful bids for House leadership posts—Speaker and majority leader, respectively—earning him the enmity of the Democratic congressional establishment.[21] Nonetheless, in spite of those defeats, Udall's quixotic campaigns did at least succeed in further catalyzing the painfully slow reform of House procedures. "I used to say that you could exhume a congressman from 1920 and he'd never know he'd been gone," said Udall shortly after his second defeat. "You can't say that anymore."[22] By the mid-1970s, Udall had established a profile that guaranteed his standing in the eyes of the incoming freshmen reformers who had little time for other politicians of his generation. He was thus well placed to contribute to a debate within the Democratic Party about the best way to reinvigorate liberalism.

As the 1976 election approached, Udall set off in pursuit of the Democratic presidential nomination. With Ted Kennedy declining to run, Udall emerged as the preferred candidate of Democratic liberals. A relatively unknown House member, Udall understood just how formidable was the task that lay ahead.[23] He disputed the presumption that the Senate was the more suitable training ground for the presidency. "It's Senate snobbery," he said. "Hell, if you're under 65, a Senator, and not presently indicted, you're automatically assumed to be a presidential candidate."[24] Nonetheless, he was happy to joke about his struggles to be taken seriously as a candidate. He was fond of the self-deprecating anecdote in which he walked into a New Hampshire barber-shop and introduced himself to the proprietor. "Hi. I'm Mo Udall and I'm running for president." The barber responded, "Yes, we were just laughing about it."[25]

Udall's issue agenda—his support for congressional and campaign finance reform, civil rights, women's reproductive rights, and gay rights and his record as an early opponent of the Vietnam War—placed him squarely in the party's liberal wing. Only his support for right-to-work laws (a prerequisite for any ambitious politician in Arizona) gave liberals pause.[26] However, by 1976, Udall preferred to describe himself as a "progressive."[27] This represented more a concern with political branding than an ideological shift on Udall's part. "I haven't changed a speech or program or policy statement," he said, but the "liberal" moniker had become "a worry word" that caused otherwise sympathetic voters to "[tune] you out before you start."[28] He claimed that voters tended to associate "liberals" with "social issues such as abortion and drugs" or "big spenders and wasters in the Federal Government."[29]

In advance of the primaries, Udall had been carving out a niche for himself as one of his party's preeminent voices on environmental affairs. Adopting a public philosophy that belied his irreverent persona, Udall issued warnings about unrestrained economic growth, the energy crisis, and the population explosion, all of which signaled a coming "Age of Scarcity." With such portents, Udall endeared himself to the nascent environmentalist movement.[30] It was also an issue calculated to endear him to the party's growing bloc of suburban voters, who privileged environmentalism as a quality of life issue. The supporters of Udall's rival, Senator Henry M. "Scoop" Jackson, sneeringly called them "wine and cheese liberals" as opposed to Jackson's own stalwart base, the "lunch-pail Democrats."[31]

The antipathy between the Udall and Jackson campaigns turned on more than discordant lifestyles, however, and their division over issues played out most vividly in the Massachusetts primary in March 1976. One of the biggest points of contention, and one that was sharpened by the Bay State context, was that of school busing, the policy of transporting students across school districts to counteract racially segregated public school systems. Outraged white parents resisted this practice nationwide. In Boston, site of some of the most notorious antibusing demonstrations, the opposition was coordinated by a populist Democratic city councilor, Louise Day Hicks, who formed the organization Restore Our Alienated Rights (ROAR) in 1974 to protest (sometimes with violence) court-ordered busing plans.[32] With antibusing sentiment at a fever pitch, the issue played a decisive role in the primary.

Jackson took out ads that explicitly and directly announced his opposition to "forced busing," which he claimed would "resegregate" the public school system, as aggrieved white parents would simply remove their children. He also endorsed legislation that would require a three-judge panel to review any busing mandates issued by a federal court. Udall shot back that political leaders should "give the courts some help and not try to undercut them."[33] Udall was undoubtedly the most pro-busing candidate in the race, but even he held back from endorsing it as a positive good. He touted a bill he had cosponsored with South Carolina representative L. Richardson Preyer that directed municipalities to devise their own desegregation plans, "tailored to each community's needs," within a two-year period. Within those plans, busing could not be prohibited as a tool of integration, but nor did it have to be used if the community had more effective means.[34] The controversy over busing prefigured later intraparty fights over issues like affirmative action

and persuaded many Democrats to focus on policy approaches, like that embodied in the Humphrey-Hawkins Full Employment Act, that they hoped
could attack racial inequality without provoking a white backlash.

Whereas Jackson used the issue of busing to appeal to his "lunch-pail
Democrats," Udall made an aggressive pitch to a suburban constituency, cal-
culating that they made up around 25 percent of the Democratic primary
electorate, which would be enough to guarantee his victory in a split field.
His campaign concentrated on the well-heeled suburbs like Newtown, and
his message concentrated on environmentalism and government ethics, issues thought to be important to suburbanites. He touted an endorsement
from Archibald Cox, the Watergate special prosecutor whose firing by an embattled Nixon had fashioned him into a liberal hero. On Election Day, Udall
scored well in those suburbs—49 percent in one Lexington precinct, 53 percent in one Lincoln precinct—and took around one-third of the vote among
those with college degrees and families earning more than $25,000 per an-
num. These were no mean accomplishments in an eight-candidate field.[35] It
was enough to ensure that he ran a respectable second to Jackson, though
only narrowly ahead of the even more stridently antibusing George Wallace.
Carter trailed in fourth place. This left Udall, according to one roundup,
"king of the liberal, upper-income suburbs, but little else."[36]

Though Udall put in consistently solid performances throughout the primaries, he struggled to establish a convincing lead. Barreling from primary
to primary in a prop plane nicknamed the "Basler Bomber," Udall never
achieved his much-needed breakthrough.[37] He failed to win a single primary,
though he often came close, a predicament that earned him the nickname
"Second-Place Mo." His best chance came in April, in the Wisconsin primary.
Six of the original ten candidates had dropped out, leaving a four-way race
between Udall, Carter, Henry Jackson, and George Wallace. The Arizona congressman seemed poised to win and was buoyed when ABC news and many
early editions called the race for him. As the late returns trickled in, however,
Carter closed the gap with Udall and then overtook him. In the end, Udall
lost by one percentage point. "With exquisitely awful timing," said conservative columnist George Will, Udall had "established himself as the liberal
candidate at a moment when liberalism seems stale, less a public philosophy
than an incantation, a barren orthodoxy."[38] Richard Scammon put it more
bluntly: "The real problem for Udall is that the war is over."[39]

Jimmy Carter versus the Democratic Congress

As a candidate, Jimmy Carter sought to identify himself with the legacy of Franklin Roosevelt. He launched his campaign as the Democratic Party's presidential nominee in the fall of 1976 on the front porch of FDR's "Little White House" in Warm Springs, Georgia, the former president's favorite retreat.[40] Carter further encouraged those comparisons as he endeavored to portray Ford as a Herbert Hoover redux, incapable of addressing the nation's economic tribulations.[41] The geography of Carter's presidential coalition, relying so heavily on New Deal blocs, seemed to confirm this. However, there the similarities ended. Carter's approach to government, and his attitude to legislative politicking, was markedly different to those of FDR.

Carter brought into the White House a remarkable facility for understanding policy. Few other presidents in the twentieth century could match his grasp of policy detail. But he seemed to approach legislative problems with the mind-set of the engineer that he had been. For Carter, policy problems were questions to be answered with technocratic expertise, rather than finesse and the management of interests. This is not to say that he lacked political instincts or was incapable of compromise, but it did make him more inflexible, and moralistic, when confronting the demands of the Democratic Congress than was prudent.

From the outset, Carter's relationship with Congress was strained. "Congress will not be bludgeoned into submission, as Nixon learned to his cost," as Nigel Bowles wrote. "It must be courted into partnership, as Carter learned to his."[42] Carter disliked the courtship rituals, seeing them as emblematic of the business-as-usual politics he had campaigned against. The president's congressional liaison, Frank Moore, came in for particular criticism. A member of Carter's "Georgia mafia," Moore's selection seemed to confirm the administration's intention of standing aloof from political Washington. Moore had been Carter's legislative liaison when the latter was governor, but he had no connections on Capitol Hill. Carter's decision not to choose a more experienced Washington hand suggested a disdain for the traditional niceties of executive-legislative relations, which won him few friends in Congress.[43] Moore apparently compounded this by handling the Democratic caucuses clumsily. Within weeks, members were complaining that their calls went unreturned. Moore was likewise blamed by representatives when Carter made objectionable appointments without consultation. Tip O'Neill, for instance, held Moore responsible after Carter made Elliot L. Richardson, then a rising star in the Massachusetts Republican Party, an ambassador to the United Nations Convention on the Law of the Sea.[44] In a 1978 profile, Mary McGrory noted that the mention of Moore's name made O'Neill visibly "flinch."[45]

The first major confrontation between Carter and Congress, and in some ways the most damaging, came over the president's attempt in early 1977 to cancel a series of federal water resource projects. This clash was significant not only on substantive, policy grounds but also for what it seemed to reveal about Carter's attitude toward the legislative branch. In the confrontation over the water projects, Carter's belief in his technocratic grasp of policy detail and his superior democratic communion with the American people would run headlong into a resurgent Congress, fiercely protective of its constitutional prerogatives and the procedures that distributed valuable public works projects.

As a candidate, Carter had stressed his strong environmental credentials. His campaign reached out to several national environmental groups, recruiting volunteers to form Conservationists for Carter. Skepticism of federal water resource projects was a central theme. In July 1975, the Carter campaign had issued a press release declaring that "the Army Corps of Engineers ought to get out of the dam-building business."[46] Carter arrived in the White House determined to deny funding to wasteful or unnecessary water resource projects and to reform the procedures by which they were commissioned. Yet the Carter administration had grievously underestimated the importance of water to the desert states.[47]

In late February, Carter announced in a message to Congress that nineteen water projects had been identified for cancellation on "economic, environmental and/or safety grounds." While acknowledging the "critical role" that such projects had played in the development of the national economy, Carter asserted that many of the proposed schemes were "of doubtful necessity now, in light of new economic conditions and environmental policies." Their elimination would reduce the fiscal year 1978 budget by $289 million, with total potential savings projected to amount to $5.1 billion.[48] Carter directed the secretaries of the interior and the army, in concert with the Council on Environmental Quality (CEQ) and the Office of Management and Budget (OMB), to embark on a comprehensive review of each of the named projects and to deliver their report by April 15. On the day that the administration began notifying members of the cuts, Carter confided to his diary that he expected "a political furor" and "a pretty touchy legislative fight."[49] This proved to be prescient. If anything, it was an understatement.

As damaging to the Carter administration as the fact of the cancelations was the manner in which they were unveiled. Legislators in the affected states were not notified of the administration's decision until the Friday before Congress was officially informed. Some discovered that cuts were planned only through newspapers or television. Still more fumed that the administration had offered assurances that certain schemes were safe only to subsequently announce their elimination.[50] However justified on policy grounds, the administration's announcement had been badly bungled. Senators and representatives balked at the apparent high-handedness of the White House. Members were also infuriated by Carter's habit, as the controversy got underway, of announcing that he planned to bypass Congress and take his case to the people. As early as March, aide Bill Smith was advising Vice President Walter Mondale that the president's congressional relations would be improved if he "stopped *threatening* to go to the public." Smith noted that a public appeal could often be an effective and necessary tool for a president but that Carter "should occasionally just take his case to the people without threatening to do so or saying that is what he is doing."[51]

Carter's plans had their defenders. Wisconsin senator Gaylord Nelson, for instance, said that he believed Carter's instinct on the need to curb wasteful and unnecessary dam building was "absolutely correct" and called on the Senate not to obstruct the president's attempts to offer "some long-needed national leadership to force us to address ourselves very carefully to these projects and start rapidly cutting back on them, because we are wasting money."[52] Nelson's enthusiasm was exceptional, however. With his conference seething, Senate Majority Leader Robert Byrd was moved to write a letter of complaint to the president and followed up with another shot across the White House's bows through the Washington press corps. "The road can be smooth or the road can be rough," was his ominous remark to reporters.[53] Senator Gary Hart, ostensibly sympathetic to Carter's budgetary restraint, came out in defense of the projects that had been targeted for deletion in Colorado. "I could have helped pick some of those in my own state," he sighed to *Congressional Quarterly*. "I just think they picked the wrong ones."[54] He did go on to discuss which projects he would have eliminated. When he ran for reelection in 1980, Hart boasted of having opposed

Carter's "hit list" and claimed credit for having persuaded the administration to agree to hearings on each of the canceled projects and to have restored funding to two.[55]

The issue dragged on for much of 1977 without a satisfactory compromise being reached. On March 10, Carter recorded in his diary "a rough meeting" with around thirty-five members of Congress who were "raising Cain" because of the proposed cuts.[56] Less than a week later, in an effort to soothe bruised egos, Carter circulated a letter to members of Congress that set out his rationale for the water project cuts in greater detail and announced a meeting with congressional leaders from all affected committees "to establish a dialogue and close cooperation on this issue."[57] He did not, however, promise any concessions. In April, Frank Moore reported on a dispiriting meeting with leading Senate Democrats on the controversy. Moore had been told by "Dr. Byrd," that "the patient is in intensive care, has no discernible pulse, and prospects of survival are nil unless it receives an immediate Presidential transfusion."[58] Carter had yet to clear his first hundred days and already a signature policy was floundering.

In August 1977, Congress submitted to the president an appropriations bill that reinstated funding for all previously canceled projects. As the bill contained funds for vital elements of Carter's stimulus package, and in the knowledge that Congress had the votes to override a veto in any case, Carter reluctantly signed. Even as he did so, however, he announced that he remained "very concerned" about ten projects for which the bill guaranteed funding.[59] Carter would later say that he "still regret[ted] . . . weakening and compromising that first year on some of these worthless dam projects." In October 1978, apparently disgusted by his own earlier concessions, Carter vetoed the Energy and Water Development Authorization bill, which restored funding to many of the canceled projects.[60]

Bert Lance, director of the OMB, called the confrontation over the water resource projects "the worst political mistake [Carter] made, and its effects lasted the rest of his term and doomed any hopes we had of developing a good, effective working relationship with Congress."[61] The water projects debacle, Carter later reflected, "caused the deepest breach between me and the Democratic leadership."[62] Affronted members of Congress proved to have long memories. Robert Beckel, a White House special assistant, recalled that, on an occasion when he was trying to persuade a recalcitrant senator to support a foreign aid bill, he was reminded that it included appropriations for a dam in Pakistan. "Once I get my dam, you can have your dam," he was told.[63]

The Humphrey-Hawkins Full Employment Act

The water projects controversy set the pattern for relations between the Carter White House and the Democratic Congress: a cycle of conflicting incentives, misunderstanding, and recrimination. That pattern also defined the major legislative struggle of these years, the effort to pass the Humphrey-Hawkins Full Employment Act, which would, at least in its original form, have extended a legal right to a job to every American. That effort constituted the final legislative battle of one of the icons of liberalism's midcentury high-water mark: Hubert Humphrey.

Whereas water projects reform was a White House initiative, the Humphrey-Hawkins bill (named for its two principal sponsors, Senator Humphrey and Representative Augustus F. Hawkins) was congressionally driven and predated the Carter administration. It was a project embraced by Democrats whose response to the economic dislocations of the mid-1970s was to embrace ideas of national planning that had briefly been in vogue during the 1940s. However, to regard it solely, as many historians do, as no more than a retreat to familiar New Deal nostrums—an indicator of liberalism floundering in the face of unprecedented economic turbulence—is to underestimate both the radicalism of the act itself and the breadth of the political coalition that supported it.[64]

By embracing the national planning ideas embodied by the act, those Democrats who pushed for the passage of Humphrey-Hawkins were committing themselves to a fundamental reconfiguration of the relationship between state and society. They were moving beyond the assumptions of the postwar economic consensus—that judicious and intermittent government interventions could keep the economy stable and prosperous—and toward a more systematic role for the government in economic management.

Its sponsors also hoped the return to economic populism and to the emphasis on "security" that had defined the New Deal would reinvigorate and expand their party's coalition and drain the racial toxins that were enervating it. It sidestepped the solidifying impression among many white working-class Democrats that liberal reform had, as economic conditions deteriorated, become a zero-sum game, pitting white people against black people in a competition for diminishing resources. It similarly sought to meet the demands of rights conscious activist groups—civil rights, feminist, and gay rights organizations—whose pursuit of equality and dignity was always inextricably bound up with questions of economic citizenship.[65] The most radical provision of the original bill, the legally enforceable "right to a job," was an attempt to yoke the litigious rights consciousness of 1960s liberalism to the New Deal's preoccupation with material security.[66]

In the mid-1970s, the Humphrey-Hawkins bill was one of the most significant and ambitious pieces of legislation discussed in Washington. It was backed by a cross-racial coalition of extra-congressional pressure groups, and discussion of the bill's merits and failings filled op-ed pages. As well as becoming a liberal shibboleth, full employment commanded consistent support in most polls. Leadership on this reform came from two members of Congress—Humphrey and Hawkins—who had been further empowered by the congressional reforms of 1975 and a changing media context. With access to additional resources and staff, the chairmanships of newly created subcommittees, and TV and print media looking to fill pages and broadcast time, congresspersons found themselves with new powers to shape the policy agenda. Yet despite these advantages, the bill would founder without forceful and committed presidential leadership. Despite having endorsed it in the primaries, albeit reluctantly, the Carter administration would only throw its support behind gradualist legislation that kept costs to a minimum. Carter resisted pressure from key Democratic blocs—most notably labor and African American groups—for bolder action. As inflation began to edge out unemployment as the issue of greatest concern to American voters, the president became even more convinced of the need to rein in inflationary spending.

The Humphrey-Hawkins act represented, to poach Jefferson Cowie's phrase, "a New Deal that never happened."[67] It also underlines that many historians have been mistaken in drawing so sharp a dichotomy between sixties-era "rights liberalism" and New Deal–style "economic liberalism." If anything, it demonstrates two decidedly old-fashioned Democrats, in Humphrey and Hawkins, seeking a new political synthesis.

National planning ideas, which had enthused idealistic liberal reformers in the 1930s and 1940s, enjoyed a sudden revival in the 1970s, in the midst of the worst economic downturn since the Great Depression.[68] In response to the emergence of "stagflation," an increasing number of intellectuals and policy-makers concluded that a shift toward a planned economy was the way out of the crisis. At the 1973 meeting of the American Economic Association, Herbert Stein, chair of Nixon's Council of Economic Advisers (CEA), mused, "Maybe we need an economic planning agency."[69] The foremost academic champion of national planning was the Harvard economist and Nobel laureate Wassily Leontief, who began calling for "a well-staffed, well-informed and intelligently guided" national planning board.[70] In February 1975, Leontief joined with United Automobile Workers (UAW) president Leonard Woodcock to launch the Initiative Committee for National Economic Planning. At its first press conference, Woodcock declared that the United States could "no longer drift from one disaster to another." He called planning "compatible with democracy" and instructed, "If we don't take substantial steps toward planning, the days of democracy are very limited indeed." The committee also unveiled a proposal for legislation to create an Office of Economic Planning in the White House and a congressional Joint Planning Committee, sponsored by seventy businessmen, academics, and labor leaders.[71]

That legislation—the Balanced Growth and Economic Planning Act—was introduced in May 1975 by Senators Jacob Javits of New York, a liberal Republican, and Hubert Humphrey of Minnesota.[72] Humphrey, a former vice president and presidential candidate, had a longtime interest in planning that had crystallized during the early 1970s. Humphrey's political consciousness had been forged by the New Deal, which he saw as a lifeline for families like his. "Why am I what I am on economics?" he told a reporter in 1977. "I saw the Depression take ten years out of my father's life. . . . I have seen people who have just worked their hearts out and couldn't make it."[73] As a graduate student at Louisiana State University in 1939–1940, he wrote a master's thesis on the political philosophy that underpinned the New Deal. Humphrey understood the New Deal as a nonrevolutionary program, "thoroughly saturated with American ideals," that sought to save capitalism from itself and "to provide economic security without sacrificing political liberty." Its most significant innovation was "the acceptance by the state of the responsibility for keeping the economic machinery in operation."[74]

As a senator in the 1950s and 1960s, Humphrey built a record as a reliable liberal and an ardent supporter of activist government. Many of the causes he championed would later form the basis of the New Frontier and Great Society, among them civil rights, the Peace Corps, and Medicare. His cheerfully determined advocacy of liberal causes saw him nicknamed the "Happy Warrior." The crowning achievement of his legislative career may have been his service as floor manager of the 1964 Civil Rights Act.[75] In 1964, Lyndon B. Johnson made him the vice presidential nominee on the Democratic ticket. However, Humphrey's exclusion from serious policy-making as vice president, combined with his willingness to support LBJ's most controversial policies, particularly the Vietnam War, badly damaged his reputation.[76] When he ran for president in his own right in 1968, after Johnson declined to pursue renomination, he did so as the standard-bearer of the Democratic establishment against the insurgent New Politics candidacies of Eugene McCarthy and Robert Kennedy.[77] One journalistic account of the election compared Humphrey on the campaign trail—"bounc[ing] around the country with one hand always outstretched and his mouth usually open"—to Archie Rice, the protagonist of John Osborne's *The Entertainer*, a "plucky but pathetic" music hall performer unable to accept that his heyday has long since passed.[78]

The agonies of post-1960s liberalism did little to dent Humphrey's faith in big government, which was confirmed in his bid to return to the Senate in 1970. In announcing his candidacy, he castigated "the tragedy of government default on economic leadership" that had revived "something [he] had hoped never to see again—the fear of loss of jobs."[79] He had been deeply disturbed by his discovery of the anxiety and social conservatism, particularly among northern blue-collar whites, that George Wallace had been able to channel in 1968, however, and sought to answer that.[80] His announcement statement also called for "leadership that will stand calmly, but firmly, for reason against chaos." Humphrey also brought Ben Wattenberg on as a campaign speechwriter. Wattenberg, along with Richard Scammon, was the co-author of *The Real Majority*, a book released the same year that argued that Democrats were in danger of losing the nation's culturally conservative majority because of their perceived weakness on the "Social Issue" (an umbrella term covering crime, urban unrest, student protests, and general moral decline). Democrats, the authors argued, had to orient their politics around an electorate that was predominantly "unyoung, unpoor, and unblack."[81]

Wattenberg's influence on Humphrey's campaign soon became apparent. Humphrey's public statements on "law and order" were considerably more robust than they had been two years earlier. He set out to confront the issue head-on in a speech to the American Bar Association, "'Liberalism' and 'Law and Order': Must There Be a Conflict?"[82] No, Humphrey concluded. Both liberals and "hard hats" favored law and order. Nonetheless, he conceded that liberals had failed to get the political "atmospherics" right: "They must let the hard-hats, *Mr. and Mrs. Middle America*, know that they understand what is bugging them."[83] He wrote to Lawrence O'Brien soon afterward that the speech had attracted "a little heat from some of my liberal friends, but most of the reaction is good."[84]

However, Humphrey's newfound toughness on social issues was dwarfed by his continued enthusiasm for government interventions in the economy. In a memo to his staff, circulated in June 1970, Humphrey outlined policy suggestions for an "upbeat" campaign. These included, among others, a health insurance program for children ("Kiddicare"), a permanent youth opportunity program, a national service program, developing offshore shale oil deposits to finance an educational trust fund, and "develop[ing] the sea bed as means of international cooperation to provide a fund for the United Nations for economic development or for pollution control."[85] However much he trimmed under the influence of Wattenberg, Humphrey's lodestar remained the New Deal.

Humphrey won the election easily, but as congressional seniority was dependent on continuous service, he was subjected to the indignity of freshman status, denied a coveted appointment to the Foreign Affairs Committee, and given only minimal office space and staff.[86] He won a place on the Joint Economic Committee "because no one else wanted it," according to his biographer.[87] Humphrey was able to turn the Joint Economic Committee (JEC)—in part through his remarkable work ethic and enthusiasm for congressional politicking—into an effective platform. Serving on the committee, he said later, was "like going to a super-graduate school."[88] By 1973, the *Washington Post* was applauding his "re-emergence as a spirited leader on Capitol Hill."[89] It was from his perch as JEC chair that Humphrey would become one of the foremost congressional advocates of national economic planning. "All industrial nations plan and have planning systems," he wrote in 1975. "But the Federal Government continues to pursue an ad-hoc, piecemeal approach that is not only wasteful in its inefficiency but outright harmful in its short-sightedness."[90]

As well as his long-established policy commitments, Humphrey nursed a desire to reclaim some of the credibility he had lost with the liberal wing of the party, once his natural constituency. As LBJ's vice president, presidential nominee in 1968, and then principal rival to George McGovern in 1972, Humphrey had become, in the minds of many younger liberals, a symbol of the Democratic Party's corrupt, war-mongering establishment.[91] The Gonzo journalist and McGovern supporter Hunter S. Thompson spoke for many when he described Humphrey as "a treacherous, gutless old ward-heeler" and "a shallow, contemptible, and hopelessly dishonest old hack."[92] That alienation was a running sore for Humphrey and one he hoped to salve. At one point during the 1968 campaign—when he was being followed by angry protestors urging America to "Dump the Hump"—Humphrey reflected ruefully that he had "never left the liberals, even though some of them are disappointed in me."[93]

The Humphrey-Javits bill never came to a floor vote. Advocates of national planning found that they struggled to build public support for such legislation. The most pressing economic issue when the bill was introduced was recession—unemployment had peaked at 9 percent by the second quarter of 1975—but Humphrey-Javits offered little in the way of immediate relief. Leontief noted that a national planning board "could not possibly lead to the solution of the present crisis" but might "keep the country from stumbling into the next crisis."[94] This was cold comfort to those on the welfare lines in 1975. The supporters of planning found much more political traction when their aims were repackaged as a response to the unemployment crisis. This would bring Humphrey into an alliance with a California representative, Augustus F. Hawkins, in the first serious effort to enact full employment legislation since the 1940s.

Louisiana-born and California-raised, Gus Hawkins came from a family that embodied two migrations undertaken by African Americans in the first half of the twentieth century: first, from the states of the Jim Crow South to the North and West; and second, from the Republican Party to the Democratic Party. Hawkins's father had been a staunch "Hoover Republican," while his son supported FDR in 1932, predicting the movement of African American voters into the Democratic coalition.[95] Like Humphrey, the Depression made Hawkins a Democrat. His hopes of pursuing a postgraduate course in civil engineering had been shattered by the downturn of the 1930s. In 1934, he won a seat in the California State Assembly as a committed New Dealer, unseating an eight-term Republican incumbent.[96] In 1962, he sought and won election from a newly created, majority-black district, the twenty-first, becoming the first black member of Congress from any western state. At the heart of this district was the Watts neighborhood, which would erupt into riots in August 1965.[97]

In Congress, Hawkins made employment policy his area of expertise. He was the principal author of Title VII of the 1964 Civil Rights Act, which outlawed employment discrimination on the basis of race, religion, sex, or national origin, and established the Equal Employment Opportunity Commission. He became chairman of the Education and Labor Subcommittee on Employment Opportunities in 1972, using the position to strengthen the Equal Employment Opportunity Commission and to press for various jobs programs. He understood the issue of African American advancement as essentially an economic rather than a racial problem. For Hawkins, casting policy issues in racial terms was an impediment to building broad coalitions of support. "Racializing an issue defeats my purpose—which is to get people on my side," he once said.[98]

Hawkins's aversion to "racializing" issues created tensions with other members of the Congressional Black Caucus and black activists outside Congress. Although Hawkins had been a founder member of the Congressional Black Caucus, he often seemed slightly detached from the group. He had, for instance, only served briefly in a leadership role, as vice chairman, from 1971 to 1973. He was more comfortable than many black legislators with appealing to labor leaders for support. He was also critical of some black activists' turn in the mid-1960s toward militancy, calling for "clearer thinking and fewer exhibitionists in the civil rights movement." In 1972, he was involved in a confrontation with the Congress of Racial Equality (CORE), when fifty members of the organization briefly occupied his Washington office to demand a voice for anti-integration activists in an education conference he was organizing.[99]

Nonetheless, Hawkins, who identified strongly with the activism of A. Philip Randolph, represented a well-established tradition within the civil rights movement, which saw civil and economic rights as being intertwined.[100] Randolph had kept the March on Washington movement alive after 1941, and it had become the inspiration for the 1963 March on Washington (a march for "Jobs and Freedom"), at which Martin Luther King Jr. had told the American people about his dream. In 1966, Randolph and fellow activist Bayard Rustin had developed a "Freedom Budget" that contained a government-sponsored job guarantee. Martin Luther King Jr. had incorporated a federally backed right to a job into his "economic bill of rights" and his 1968 "Poor People's Campaign," and full employment had been one of the ten points of the Black

Panther Party's platform.[101] "Jobs for All" was an issue that had united African American activists across the political spectrum for decades.

The recession of 1973–1975 gave fresh impetus to the cause of full employment among black activists. The unemployment rate for African Americans was consistently double that of white Americans, often rising to almost 50 percent for young black men. Moreover, as Hawkins wrote, those statistics underestimated the extent of the problem for both black and white Americans by not including the "under-employed" (those in part-time work seeking full-time jobs) or the long-term unemployed.[102] Vernon Jordan, president of the National Urban League, said that by any available measurements African Americans were enduring "a major depression."[103] When the members of the Congressional Black Caucus met with President Gerald Ford a few weeks after his inauguration in late 1974, they requested a public employment program.[104]

The issue of full employment had brought together the civil rights movement and the advocates of national economic planning in the 1940s. By 1945, fearing that the end of World War II would bring a return of joblessness, some policy-makers had begun to argue that the federal government should retain the planning tools it had used to fight the war as the nation reconverted to a peacetime economy.[105] These ambitions dovetailed with the aims of a civil rights movement that had been growing in strength throughout the war years. More than one million African Americans served in the armed services, and major civil rights organizations sought to leverage that service in the ongoing freedom struggle. As the war drew to a close, activists pushed the cause of full employment, and a planned economy, alongside antidiscrimination.[106] Despite intensive lobbying from a liberal-labor coalition, and Truman's full-throated support, hopes for a robust bill ended in bitter disappointment with the passage of the anemic Employment Act in 1946.[107]

In August 1974, Humphrey and Hawkins joined together as cosponsors of the most ambitious full employment legislation since 1946. The Humphrey-Hawkins Full Employment Act directed the federal government to guarantee a job for all citizens over the age of sixteen. Though the preferred provider would be the private sector, those who remained without employment would be given public sector jobs in local government, financed from federal coffers. Perhaps the most radical component empowered those who found themselves neglected to sue the government for injunctive relief and damages. This provision yoked the litigious rights consciousness of 1960s liberalism to the New Deal's preoccupation with material security. Moreover, the original bill set no nominal unemployment rate for a "full employment" economy. The government would strive to provide jobs for all who sought them.[108]

The means by which full employment was to be achieved were rooted in national planning ideas. The president would be required to submit an annual full employment plan to Congress, setting targets for employment, national production, and purchasing power. Congress would have the power to review and revise that plan, and the federal budget and Federal Reserve's policies would have to be consistent with the finally agreed goals. The government would also be required to respond to economic distress with countercyclical measures such as increasing funding to state and local agencies, subsidizing private firms to take on more employees, financing public jobs, and establishing special youth programs. A permanent "full employment office" would be created within the Department of Labor to offer training programs, direct the unemployed toward jobs in the public and private sectors, and maintain a "jobs reservoir" for those who could not find work elsewhere.[109]

Alongside a significant overhaul of the nation's political economy, the Humphrey-Hawkins bill represented an effort to reunify the Democratic Party's coalition and ease the racial tensions that had been rupturing it. As the economy tanked, Democrats had found themselves struggling to balance their commitment to eradicating racial inequality against their historical relationship with, and organizational dependency on, organized labor. By the mid-1970s, relations between trade unions and the Democratic Party were at a low ebb. Stagflation produced uncomfortable trade-offs, intensifying racial conflict within the working class.[110] Younger Democrats, particularly New Politics types who had been politically awakened by the civil rights movement, were often disdainful of unions, viewing them as parochial and innately racist. Humphrey, a pro-labor and pro–civil rights Democrat, believed that the contradictions were reconcilable and that a return to the politics of economic uplift offered a way out of the quagmire. According to Judith Stein, Humphrey-Hawkins "simultaneously reinserted African American interests into mainstream economic policy making and advanced black and white working-class interests."[111]

The bill's drafters had been driven, Hawkins said, "out of sheer frustration with the disorderly management of our economic affairs to recognize the need for a coherent economic policy along the lines originally suggested in the Employment Act of 1946." The pretense "that such mismanaged policies are essential to maintain our freedom is sheer nonsense. This is as illogical as the assertion we must accept a recurring Watergate-type leadership failure as the price of democracy."[112] Its supporters were encouraged by the fact that the political pendulum seemed to be swinging back toward the Democrats in 1974. In March 1974, Hawkins had told a conference at Columbia University that "the winds of change are blowing towards liberalism" and confidently predicted the swift passage of full employment.[113]

Unsurprisingly, the Ford administration was entirely unsympathetic to the bill, dismissing it as ineffective and inflationary.[114] However, the bill's sponsors were not waiting for the White House to take the lead on the issue. Congress, Humphrey told the Senate Committee on Banking, Housing and Urban Affairs, "must assume more of the responsibility for managing the nation's economy."[115] In late 1975, Humphrey was invited by Oxford University Press to review Otis Graham's book *Towards a Planned Society*, a history of the national planning idea from FDR to Nixon.[116] Humphrey was so impressed that he had the review inserted into the *Congressional Record*, commending Graham for so "vividly" showing "that national planning should not be a partisan issue." He faulted Graham only for his portrayal of Congress as "a demonic force that has interfered with the creation of a planning capacity in the Federal Government." In fact, he said, many members "exhibit an increasing awareness of the need to set goals, to have a view that stretches beyond the reelection cycle, to foresee problems that will be upon us before we sometimes care to think, and to establish ways to design and coordinate Federal policies and activities in a more rational coherent way."[117]

In 1975–1976, utilizing his JEC chairmanship, Humphrey set out to turn these congressional efforts into a public campaign. The committee toured some of the worst-hit cities in the nation, gathering testimony on their economic woes. The first of these regional meetings was held in Chicago in October 1975. A month earlier, the Bureau of Labor Statistics had recorded an unemployment rate of 10.2 percent, around two points above the national rate (8.3 percent). Among black Chicagoans, the unemployment rate stood at 19.8 percent (rising to 36.4 percent when one factored in "discouraged workers" and the underemployed).[118] "It is obvious to me," declared Humphrey in his opening remarks, "that the old economic rules no longer apply." Endorsements of the Humphrey-Hawkins bill, or at least broad statements of support, came from academics, public officials, private citizens, and representatives from labor unions and activist organizations, including the National Organization for Women (NOW), the Chicago Urban League, and local chapters of the United Steelworkers, the UAW, and the United Electrical Workers (UE).[119] From Chicago, the Humphrey-Hawkins road show made appearances in New York, Atlanta, Los Angeles, and Boston.

This publicity blitz was supposed to make the bill an election issue for 1976. Humphrey and Hawkins planned for some version of the full employment bill to pass before November, to be greeted by a presidential veto, with which the Democratic candidate could beat Ford all the way to Election Day. The *New Republic* noted that Humphrey-Hawkins was "a Big Bertha of economic theory . . . a siege gun that will be used to lob criticisms at President Ford during the election campaign."[120] Even without a congressional vote, however, regular reports from the JEC condemned the Ford administration, demanded action on unemployment, and ensured that attention would be paid to the Democratic alternatives. A March report in response to the president's January Economic Report identified unemployment as the principal issue facing the nation, castigated the administration and the Federal Reserve for "misunderstanding and mismanagement," and declared America "the victim of misguided policies." It called for greater stimulative measures in response to the crisis and condemned Ford's fiscal conservatism: "The President's 1977 budget is so restrictive that it does not serve as a useful starting point for budget policy deliberations."[121] Later that month, the JEC led the commemoration of the thirtieth anniversary of the passage of the Employment Act of 1946, staging a two-day conference on full employment in Washington, DC.[122]

Humphrey was widely considered a front-runner for the Democratic presidential nomination in 1976. *U.S. News & World Report* surveyed 162 members of the Democratic National Committee in November 1975 and discovered that 49 percent expected Humphrey to be the next presidential nominee (a clear plurality, 41 percent, believed Jimmy Carter would be Humphrey's running mate).[123] Ford himself expected to face Humphrey in the election.[124] Humphrey refused to formally declare himself a candidate, but he did make clear his receptivity to a convention draft. Though this eventuality never arose, Humphrey had an outsize impact on the presidential primaries.[125] By 1976, according to one journalist, Humphrey-Hawkins had become the "current shibboleth of Democratic liberalism."[126] Nearly all

Democratic candidates endorsed Humphrey-Hawkins in some form, with the noteworthy exception of Jimmy Carter. Lawrence Klein, coordinator of Carter's economic task force, told *Time* that it could become "an albatross" but that he could "envision no amendments that would make this a good bill." Carter shied away from a firm commitment but told journalists that 3 percent unemployment "as a goal" was "a good one."[127] Questioned directly on Humphrey-Hawkins, Carter dismissed the bill, in its present form, as "too expensive." Humphrey responded with a broad condemnation of opposition to big government as "a disguised new form of racism," which prompted Carter to brand the former presidential nominee a "loser."[128]

In mid-1976, the passage of some form of full-employment legislation seemed increasingly likely. President Ford understood this, telling the Annual Convention of the National Chamber of Commerce in April 1976 that the proposals were "dangerously deceptive" and "a vast election year boondoggle" that would be halted by presidential veto if necessary.[129] With the exception of Senator Edward Brooke of Massachusetts (the only African American in the Senate), the entire Republican congressional caucus was united against it. Similar opposition came from conservative economists. In his testimony at the Chicago hearings, Milton Friedman told the JEC that the nation's economic problems "don't arise from the absence of planning . . . [but] from substituting planning by the visible hand of government for planning by the invisible hand of market." Federal Reserve Board Chairman Arthur Burns told the Senate Banking Committee that the bill was "dangerous and inflationary."[130]

As his presidential prospects diminished, Humphrey explored options to ensure that full employment legislation would remain a priority for the next, almost certainly Democratic, administration. He had set his eyes on the position of Senate majority leader, left vacant by incumbent Mike Mansfield's retirement, which would have given him direct influence over the legislation that reached the Senate floor. However, Humphrey lost that race decisively to West Virginia's Robert C. Byrd. Though Byrd was a conservative southerner—a member of the Ku Klux Klan in his youth who had filibustered the 1964 Civil Rights Act—Senate members were swayed by his reputation as a man who could run the Senate efficiently and deliver favors for his colleagues.[131] Disorganized and usually tardy, Humphrey could not match his rival's service-oriented platform. Moreover, a few months before the election, a cancer-stricken Humphrey underwent major surgery to remove his bladder.[132] Humphrey's defeat also reflected the expectation that a Democratic Congress would follow the policy agenda of the incoming Carter White House rather than chart its own course. With a Democrat in the White House, remarked Gary Hart, the Senate majority leader would likely function as "a hollow log in which both sides leave messages."[133]

Given Carter's wariness, it might be assumed that Humphrey-Hawkins was a pipe dream entertained by a band of aging New Dealers, unable to reconcile themselves to an increasingly conservative electorate. Certainly, Americans were growing more resentful of tax burdens, and inflation alternated with unemployment as the public's principal concern. However, the available polling data reveals a more complicated attitude toward government activism. A *Time*/Yankelovich poll taken in August 1976 showed 56 percent in favor of an indeterminate full employment bill "in which the government guarantees a job to everyone who wants to work." Another poll taken by the same organization in March 1977 showed that support had climbed to 60 percent. A further poll, taken in October 1977 by Cambridge Reports/National Omnibus Survey, showed 54 percent specifically in favor of the Humphrey-Hawkins bill, compared to 29 percent opposed. Even in November 1980, as the Reagan Revolution was supposedly surging to power, an ORC Public Opinion Index poll showed that 78 percent of respondents were in favor of the federal government doing more to provide jobs for all Americans who were able to work during the 1980s.[134] Federal full-employment legislation enjoyed consistently solid public support throughout the 1970s. However, the Carter administration chose to prioritize inflation and balancing the budget over unemployment.

For much of 1977 and 1978, the Carter administration's reluctance to move forward with full-employment legislation created friction with the bill's supporters in Congress, and especially with the Congressional Black Caucus. In March 1977, just two months after Carter's inauguration, special assistant Valerie Pinson reported a fractious meeting with members of the Congressional Black Caucus and supportive groups who wanted "to blast the President because of his lack of support for the bill."[135] "We are sitting on a timebomb here which will explode unless we move quickly," chief domestic policy advisor Stuart Eizenstat wrote in a memo two weeks later.[136] In June, Humphrey and Hawkins wrote to the president noting that they had not yet "obtained a reaffirmation of [his] position on the Bill this year, nor any specific suggestions for further improvements in it from [his] representatives." A "clarification" on those points, they suggested, would be "mutually beneficial to all concerned."[137]

Similar pressure came from African American groups outside the national government. At the sixty-seventh annual meeting of the National Urban League, Executive Director Vernon Jordan criticized the administration for "not living up to the first commandment of politics—help those who help you."[138] In November 1977, Jordan endorsed Humphrey-Hawkins, calling it "a short-term promissory note to be redeemed in jobs."[139] A month earlier, when the NAACP board of directors met with Carter, the issue of jobs was at the top of their eighteen-item agenda.[140] Many black activists had reason to expect, indeed demand, such a commitment from the White House. Carter's narrow victory in 1976 had been made possible by his sweep of the southern states, where newly enfranchised African American voters had often provided his margin of victory. As Walter E. Fauntroy, delegate for the District of Columbia, remarked in 1978, "hands that picked cotton had picked a president."[141]

Carter's concerns over the inflationary impact of the bill and his determination to curtail excessive spending proved the most significant stumbling blocks. The negotiations to agree a "full employment unemployment rate" were some of the most torturous. After initial talks, OMB director Bert Lance reported to Carter that Hawkins regarded "both a very low numerical full employment unemployment rate and a guarantee of government jobs as essential ingredients of any bill he would sponsor." As neither of these was acceptable to Carter, there might "be no version which could be consistent with both moderate principles of economic policy and the true objectives of the sponsors of the bill."[142] House Speaker Tip O'Neill advised Carter's staff "to put in the low unemployment rate as the sponsors want and just not worry about it."[143] Eizenstat urged the importance of "the Administration [being] perceived as having made every effort to reach an accommodation."[144] The administration was unsuccessful in persuading Humphrey and Hawkins to prefix the unemployment goals with the words "about" (i.e., "about 4%"). Though this would have had little practical impact, it would convey "some image of flexibility in the bill to counter conservative and moderate critics." The bill's sponsors rejected this on the same grounds: "They want an image which, to the maximum extent possible, appears to bind the President to hard targets."[145]

In his discomfort with Humphrey-Hawkins, Carter found some allies within Congress. Many of the Watergate Babies, particularly those with suburban constituents, were skeptical of the bill. Gary Hart had singled out the Minnesota senator in his infamous postelection remark summarizing the ideological shift that the class represented: "We're not a bunch of little Hubert Humphreys." These legislators were instinctively suspicious of grand federal schemes and more sympathetic to Carter's liberalism of limits than to the expansive vision of Humphrey-Hawkins. Humphrey was not without insight into that position. He wrote to JEC economist Jerry Jasinowski that he tended "to agree with some of these 'young turks' in the reaction to government control, government regulation, and of course the ever bloated bureaucracy. People do resent this meddling in their lives and activities by government." Nonetheless, he concluded, in "a highly organized corporate society" such as the United States, only "big government" could stand against the destructive force of unregulated capitalism.[146]

The administration's reluctance was also informed by the opposition of business interests. Business antipathy to big government had existed since the New Deal, but by the end of the 1960s, it was encountering a more receptive public.[147] Unlike in the 1930s, there was no widespread sense that the present economic crisis was due largely to the fecklessness of corporate America and the inactivity of the government. The prospect that Humphrey-Hawkins, or legislation like it, would increase federal intervention in the market economy was deeply unsettling for business leaders. Three days after Carter's inauguration, James H. Evans, president and CEO of the Union Pacific Corporation, used a *New York Times* op-ed to dismiss Humphrey-Hawkins as "old fashioned and wrongheaded," a "big brother" scheme that would "eat up" taxes, spur "devastating" inflation, and offer, at best, only temporary respite from unemployment.[148] The Chamber of Commerce, the National Association of Manufacturers, and the Business Roundtable were all flatly opposed to the bill, citing its likely inflationary effects. Along with other business organizations, they mounted a vigorous lobbying effort, "sending executives to pay personal calls to senators, promoting packaged editorials . . . , and mobilizing letter-writing campaigns."[149] Eizenstat had warned Carter that the administration should expect to be "blast[ed] by the business community" regardless of any "substantial revisions" to the bill. Indeed, he wrote, "The term 'Humphrey-Hawkins Bill' has taken on a dynamic of its own and can be seen as a code word for excessive spending."[150]

Some of the most damaging criticisms of the bill came from liberal economists. John Kenneth Galbraith, for instance, begged optimistic Democrats not to succumb to the "wishful economics" of imagining there was "some undiscovered fiscal or monetary magic" that could control both inflation and unemployment.[151] Charles Schultze, the chair of the CEA, was adamantly opposed to the bill in its original form, despite styling himself as a "friendly" critic. Although he eventually supported Humphrey-Hawkins as "a broad and flexible instrument," he cautioned a House subcommittee that it was "unlikely" that a 4 percent unemployment rate could be achieved "without at the same time causing increased inflation."[152] The bill's most forthright defender among economists was Leon Keyserling, a principal drafter of the 1946 Employment Act and the first chair of the CEA.[153] He urged its passage in congressional testimony, on the op-ed pages, and in a flurry of private, often tetchy, letters to his colleagues.[154]

If many economists were lukewarm on the bill, Humphrey and Hawkins could count on vigorous activist support. In early 1975, a coalition of labor unions, religious and civil rights groups, and community organizations established the Full Employment Action Council (FEAC) to lobby legislators to pass the bill, cochaired by Murray H. Finley of the Amalgamated Clothing Makers Union and Coretta Scott King, president of the Martin Luther King Jr. Center and King's widow.[155] Many feminist groups, including the National Organization for Women (NOW), also lined up behind the bill.[156] Their participation reflected the growing strength of feminist activism and the increasing focus of the women's liberation movement on legislative goals alongside consciousness-raising activities. Women's rights groups could point to their success in pressing Congress to pass the Equal Rights Amendment in 1972 as evidence of their increasing clout and skill.[157] NOW cofounder Betty Friedan predicted that to make significant economic gains, the women's movement would have to make alliances "with old people, young people, heart-attack-prone executives, trade unionists, blacks and other minorities."[158] In July 1976, full employment legislation would be one of the demands made by women's groups demonstrating at the Democratic National Convention at New York's Madison Square Garden.[159]

Feminist organizations supported Humphrey-Hawkins despite the fact that, as Robert Self argues, debates over full employment "revealed that neither conservatives nor most liberals had yet abandoned the male-breadwinner model of the economy." One early version of the bill, for instance, placed a cap on the "number of employed persons per household" who could benefit, a provision that would almost certainly have discriminated against women.

Pressure from women's groups meant that the final bill replaced the workers per household limit with one based on household income.[160] In drafting the bill, New Politics groups and old guard Democrats worked to resolve such ideological tensions, contradicting the traditional image of permanent conflict between those factions over mutually irreconcilable visions of liberalism.

In an effort to assuage concerns about its inflationary impact, Humphrey and Hawkins initially incorporated wage and price controls into the bill, before objections from organized labor forced their removal.[161] Similar objections from the AFL-CIO compelled the bill's supporters to remove its most potent enforcement mechanism: the legally enforceable right to a job.[162] The bill was revised numerous times, both to strengthen its anti-inflation provisions and to win the support of the Carter White House. By November 1977, a shaky accord had finally been reached between the forces in favor of the Humphrey-Hawkins bill and the Carter administration. In a joint press release, Humphrey and Hawkins declared themselves "pleased" with the agreement and predicted "favorable" action on the modified bill in the new year.[163] FEAC chairs Coretta King and Murray Finley endorsed the bill, calling it "an essential first step toward full employment" and "an enormous improvement over existing law and policy." In a memo circulated to local coalitions and supporters, Executive Director John Carr announced that the FEAC was "going on the offensive" against those who called the bill "an empty gesture or a costly spur to inflation." Lobbying was intensified, hostile newspapers petitioned, educational conferences organized, and sympathetic legislators recruited.[164]

Humphrey's death in January 1978 was a further impetus for the bill's supporters. Its passage would be, said Labor Secretary Ray Marshall, "as fitting a tribute to Senator Humphrey as this Congress, and this Nation, could pay."[165] Nonetheless, the fate of the bill remained uncertain until its passage. Though the Carter administration had finally thrown its weight behind a revised version of Humphrey-Hawkins, the bill seemed close to expiring on several occasions as it ground its way through Congress. Republican opponents threatened filibusters and sought to hamstring the law with amendments, despite cajolery and public criticism from the White House. The bill's supporters were compelled to dilute it further to appease vocal congressional opposition. Utah's Orrin Hatch, a conservative Republican senator then in his first term, was so influential in shaping the final iteration that some jokingly began referring to the bill as the Humphrey-Hawkins-Hatch Act.[166]

In October 1978, a neutered version of the bill was signed into law. Having been introduced as the Equal Opportunity and Full Employment bill, Humphrey-Hawkins ended its troubled passage through the legislature as the Full Employment and Balanced Growth Act. It was something of a smorgasbord. Alongside the unemployment targets, the act enjoined the government to hold inflation at 3 percent, to balance the federal budget, to keep prices stable, and to produce an international trade surplus. It offered no new mechanisms to enforce any of these goals and only required the president to set nonbinding numerical goals for the economy. The second attempt to enforce full employment legislation since World War II had, it seemed, suffered a similar fate as its predecessor.

At the bill signing in October 1980, flanked by Senator Muriel Humphrey (appointed to fill her husband's seat earlier that year) and Hawkins, Carter offered praise for the bill's drafters and measured remarks for its contents: "Although attaining the unemployment and the inflation goals of this bill will be very difficult, we will do our best to reach them." The president dismissed criticism that the act's provisions were so diluted as to be meaningless, remarking that "if the bill wasn't [substantial], the struggle wouldn't have been so hard." Its supporters were more fulsome. "I think we're on our way," said Hawkins proudly, pronouncing the new act nothing less than "a modern-day Magna Carta of economic rights." FEAC cochair Coretta Scott King suggested that perhaps "history will record that it may be even more significant" than the 1964 Civil Rights Act and 1965 Voting Rights Act because it concerned "the most basic of all human rights, the right to a job."[167]

This praise concealed obvious disappointment with the outcome of this legislative struggle. AFL-CIO lobbyist Ken Young, for instance, conceded only that that act was "a small symbolic step forward" and held that it had been "weakened ... severely" by the Senate.[168] A bill that had been introduced to revolutionize the political economy of the United States had been stripped of its most potent provisions and recast as an aspiration rather than a requirement of federal policy.

The reasons for the bill's ultimate failure are manifold. However much Humphrey hoped that Congress might play a coequal role in national planning, he and his allies discovered that grand visions of a "New New Deal" would go nowhere without forceful presidential leadership. Ford was a roadblock and Carter had little interest in being FDR's second coming. Carter's concern for inflation and budget deficits made him wary of high spending programs like Humphrey-Hawkins, especially as he had promised repeatedly during the 1976 campaign to balance the budget by 1980. But it would be a mistake to characterize these legislative struggles as a case of a predominantly "liberal" Congress continually frustrated by two "conservative" presidents. Carter enjoyed considerable support in his fiscal conservatism from numerous congressional Democrats. For the most part, Democrats who entered Congress in the 1970s were less amenable to grand federal projects. They shared their suburban constituents' dislike of inflation and tax increases and backed Carter's push for budgetary discipline. Michigan congressman Bob Carr recalled that he and many other younger members had "fabulous relationships with the president."[169]

The Humphrey-Hawkins episode reveals a Democratic Party struggling to come to terms with the twin legacies of the New Deal and the 1960s. Democrats like Humphrey and Hawkins were anxious to demonstrate that solutions predicated on vigorous government activism were still relevant in the era of stagflation. By enshrining the "right to a job" in law, they sought to demonstrate that federal power could once again be mobilized to tame the business cycle. They also sought to demonstrate that the New Deal's "universalist" ideology was capacious enough to incorporate once excluded groups who were clamoring for full economic citizenship. In this, they enjoyed the support of many campaigning organizations, most notably African American and feminist groups, who had long understood the connections between questions of economic status and their other objectives. That such groups could be drawn into cohesive political coalitions with, for instance, labor unions seemed to offer the hope for a renewed Democratic majority around traditional pocketbook issues. The fact that such a piece of legislation was politically viable in the 1970s, and indeed commanded such widespread public support, is a standing rebuke to the idea that the crises of the decade were destined to produce a popular swing away from government activism and toward market solutions.

The Humphrey-Hawkins episode also reveals the slow degeneration of the relationship between some factions within the congressional Democratic Party and President Carter. Over the next two years, Democrats who despaired of Carter's supposed failure to show more audacious leadership in the face of the crisis of the 1970s would seek a replacement, settling on several alternatives before finally coalescing behind Senator Ted Kennedy's 1980 primary challenge. That factions of the congressional Democratic Party could entertain thoughts of replacing its president without jeopardizing the White House underlines the extent to which, even by the late 1970s, the party still believed its position as the nation's majority party was secure. To the end of his presidency, Carter's relationship with many of his nominal congressional allies was marked by misunderstanding and missteps. Accepting the nomination at the 1980 convention, the president paid tribute to "a big-hearted man who should have been President and would have been one of the greatest Presidents of all time . . . Hubert Horatio Hornblower!" He swiftly corrected himself to "Humphrey" to audible laughter from delegates.[170]

Persona Non Carter
The Democratic Party Searches
for an Alternative, 1978–1980

"Our turndown list reads like a Who's Who of American politics," remarked DNC staffer Elaine Kamarck.[1] The statement probably should have struck party members as a warning. As the party prepared to head to Memphis, Tennessee, at the end of 1978 for its second midterm convention, Democrats were distinctly less upbeat than they had been four years earlier. As before, the convention had been scheduled for December so as not to overshadow the midterm campaigns. The 1978 elections gave the party far fewer reasons to celebrate, as Democrats sustained a net loss of three seats in the Senate and fifteen in the House. But though they had been reduced, the party's congressional majorities remained substantial. As Adam Clymer noted in his roundup ("Democrats Dominate" ran the headline), if the Republicans' impressive haul of governorships and state legislatures suggested a party building for the future, "most American voters rejected the [GOP]'s arguments of the moment and maintained their identification with the Democratic Party at its recent high level."[2] Democrats could console themselves that they still belonged to the nation's majority party.

President Carter had just pulled off a major foreign policy success with the conclusion of the Camp David Accords in September, which would ultimately lead to the Egypt-Israel Peace Treaty of 1979. However, these achievements encouraged little admiration for the president from within his own party. Democratic legislative ambitions were stalling on a range of fronts, and various party factions were becoming fractious. "We're not gathering here in Memphis to sing a hallelujah chorus to Jimmy Carter," Maryland representative

Barbara A. Mikulski told a women's caucus meeting.[3] "You've got to hand it to the Democrats," noted the *Washington Post* wryly. "Any other political collectivity with that many internal divisions and so ingrained a habit of coming apart the minute it is brought together under a single roof, would be looking for ways to hold fewer conventions, not more."[4]

Senior officials in the Office of White House Communications advised Carter to adopt a "strong, responsible, confident, proud, uplifting, but determined and firm" tone in his speech to the convention, his first at a party-wide gathering since his nomination two years earlier.[5] Carter's aim was to use the convention to mollify the rebels, appearing at a series of workshops to defend the administration and listen patiently while the discontented voiced their frustrations.[6] According to one report, Carter received "sustained" applause from the delegates only once: when he recommitted himself to the passage of the Equal Rights Amendment (ERA). Though the ERA was struggling nationally, thanks to a well-organized anti-ERA campaign, feminist groups were among the biggest winners at the 1978 midterm convention. The convention conceded to their demands for greater representation, including a guarantee of a half-female national convention in 1980 and a commitment to the goal of fifty women elected to Congress by 1980.[7]

By far the biggest draw of the convention was the workshop on health insurance. The president did not appear in person, but the panel did feature the increasingly disgruntled senator from Massachusetts, Edward M. Kennedy. Largely through his campaign for national health insurance, Kennedy had emerged as President Carter's chief rival and the would-be savior of the liberal Democrats. Apart from Kennedy, the panel included UAW president Douglas Fraser and two administration officials: domestic policy adviser Stuart Eizenstat and Secretary of Health, Education, and Welfare Joseph Califano. The chair was the governor-elect of Arkansas, Bill Clinton, the youngest governor in the country and a rising star in the party.

Kennedy's contribution was typically impassioned and elicited the warmest response. Invoking FDR and JFK, Kennedy defended his health-care reforms and warned that Carter's reliance on fiscal restraint to combat inflation should not adulterate the Democratic Party's commitment to the impoverished. Thumping the rostrum, he pledged to continue the fight for "that Democratic platform plank that provides decent quality healthcare, North and South, East and West, for all Americans, as a matter of right and not of privilege." A keen yachtsman, Kennedy concluded his remarks with a metaphor that came to define the primary challenge to the president that he would launch a year later: "Sometimes a party must sail against the wind. We cannot afford to drift or lie at anchor. We cannot heed the call of those who say it is time to furl the sail."[8] By implication, Kennedy contrasted his audacity and conviction against Carter's supposed weakness and indecision. The crowd roared its approval, and Kennedy's speech led that evening's news bulletins. Carter later said that he interpreted the speech as Kennedy "kind of throwing down the gauntlet."[9]

However, when asked about his own ambitions, Kennedy demurred: "I expect the president will run and he'll be re-elected. I intend to support him."[10] Such deflections did not dissuade the media from speculating about Kennedy's future ambitions. Nor did they dissuade Democratic activists who were unhappy with Carter's leadership from fixing on Kennedy as an alternative. In the early hours of one morning during the mini-convention, a Democratic city councilor from Minnesota, George Mische, cornered Hamilton Jordan in a Memphis saloon. Harsh words about Carter's record were exchanged and, reportedly, only the intervention of one of Jordan's companions prevented a fistfight. In June 1979, Mische was among 260 attendees at the first meeting of Minnesotans for a Democratic Alternative, the largest Draft-Kennedy organization up to that point.[11]

The confrontation in Memphis encapsulated the latter years of Carter's presidency, which were marked by profound dissatisfaction with his leadership across the Democratic Party. Dissatisfied activists and party grandees fixed on a variety of plausible alternatives to the president before Senator Ted Kennedy finally emerged as the standard-bearer of the anti-Carter wing by 1980. Most of those alternatives were, like Kennedy, members of Congress with an increasingly dysfunctional relationship with Carter. They also drew their support from different wings of the party who were unified only in their hostility to the president. The diversity of these critiques not only reveals the heterogeneity of the Democratic Party by the end of the 1970s but also underscores a widespread belief that the Democratic political hegemony was fundamentally secure. Such intraparty disputes were not thought to be a serious threat to the Democratic Party's status as the national governing majority, and particularly not to the party's continued control of Congress.

"The Conscience of a Neoconservative":
Pat Moynihan's Minority Report

New York senator Daniel Patrick "Pat" Moynihan was one of the party big-wigs who had declined to attend the convention in Memphis.[12] Though he was in his first term in the Senate, the only elected office he had held to that point, he had already become a recognized figure on Capitol Hill. This was due in part to his eccentric mannerisms ("the herky-jerky Anglo-speech, the bow tie slightly askew, the tweedy caps and professorial rambles," in David Remnick's summary) and in part to his status as one of the leading members of the so-called neoconservative faction within the party.[13]

Neoconservatism was and continues to be a contested idea, and it is doubly problematic in this instance because Moynihan himself always rejected the label. Though later appended to the foreign policy of the George W. Bush administration, originally the term was attached to a group of Democrats who rejected what they saw as the New Politics or McGovernite take-over of the party. To the neoconservatives, McGovernism represented an embrace of moral relativism, countercultural values, and a retreat from the internationalism of Cold War liberalism. This faction began to take shape with the formation of the Coalition for a Democratic Majority (CDM), an ad hoc alliance of labor leaders, party elders, and liberal intellectuals that was created in a hotel room during the 1972 national convention. The CDM announced its existence with an ad that it ran in the *New York Times* and the *Washington Post* in December 1972 headlined "Come Home, Democrats," an echo of McGovern's acceptance speech. "For too long now," declared the ad, "the voices of common-sense liberals have been barely audible in the blare of the New Politics." What was needed was "a robust voice" to reply to the cacophony.[14]

The term "neoconservative" was first applied to this faction by the socialist writer and activist Michael Harrington in a *Dissent* article in 1973.[15] "We finally started calling them 'neoconservatives,'" Harrington said, "because we recognized that they represented something new in American politics."[16] In Harrington's formulation, the "neoconservatives" were liberal intellectuals who had been so disillusioned by the perceived failures of the War on Poverty that they had embraced the conservative critique of social welfare programs as dependency-fostering. It was surely only a matter of time, he reasoned, before they surrendered to a broader critique of the welfare state and made common cause with the New Right.[17]

"Neoconservatives" mostly rejected the label, however, and few more vehemently than Moynihan. As far as they were concerned, they were the defenders of the Democratic Party's New Deal and Cold War traditions. They were the real liberals. According to John Ehrman, it is more accurate, albeit unwieldy, to describe these "neoconservatives" as "veterans of the vital center."[18] Over the course of the 1970s, the "neoconservative" grouping began to fracture, with some moving into Reagan's orbit and others remaining committed to their liberal roots. Moynihan was part of the latter cohort. If there was an abiding theme in Moynihan's political thought, it was the problem of how to make government work, which distinguished him from New Right activists, who viewed federal power as essentially incompetent or malignant. This preoccupation identified him as a Democrat who was prepared to think deeply about the party's historical mission.[19]

Oklahoma-born and New York–bred, Moynihan had had a lengthy career in politics, both Republican and Democratic, before he arrived in the Senate. He served in the Labor Department of the Kennedy and Johnson administrations and was forced to resign from the latter after an internal report he had drafted—*The Negro Family: The Case for National Action*—brought him unwelcome national attention.[20] After a few years at Harvard, Moynihan was recruited by President Nixon to serve on the White House staff as counselor for urban affairs.[21] Like many officials in the Nixon administration, Moynihan was preoccupied with the burgeoning resentment among blue-collar whites, mostly male and often ethnic, toward government welfare programs. While Republican political strategists machinated to peel these voters away from the New Deal coalition, Moynihan worried over the question of what their growing disillusionment would mean for the long-term legitimacy of American government.[22]

It was this concern that led to Moynihan's signature policy preoccupation in this role: the Family Assistance Plan (FAP), a guaranteed income scheme that sought to replace "costly and questionable [social] services" with a system of direct payments to the impoverished. Nixon was initially enthusiastic about the reform (Moynihan told the president that FAP would enable him "to assert with full validity that it was under your Presidency that poverty was abolished in America"), but when it ran into difficulty in Congress, he proved to be a fickle patron.[23] FAP would eventually founder on an unlikely coalition of conservative Republicans and liberal Democrats. Moynihan bitterly regretted the defeat and particularly resented the fierce liberal opposition.[24]

In 1970, another leaked internal memo reopened old wounds. Moynihan had been growing increasingly concerned about intemperate rhetoric on matters of race and fearful of a backlash that might jeopardize black gains. "The issue of race could benefit from a period of 'benign neglect,'" he wrote to Nixon. "The subject has been too much talked about.... We need a period in which Negro progress continues and racial rhetoric fades."[25] When this memo leaked, the most damning phrase was the one that Moynihan had chosen for its eye-catching qualities: "benign neglect." Once again, Moynihan found himself denounced as a racist. For many liberals and African Americans, this confirmed suspicions raised by the 1965 report.[26] Stung by FAP's defeat and fresh accusations of bigotry, Moynihan retreated briefly to Harvard. In 1973, the now embattled Nixon appointed him ambassador to India. Two years later, with Gerald Ford in the White House, Moynihan was appointed ambassador to the United Nations. The cause of Moynihan's appointment was an article he had written for *Commentary* in March 1975, "The United States in Opposition," in which he argued that the United States should "go into opposition" within the United Nations, where it found itself outnumbered by anti-American autocracies.[27]

Though he spent less than a year in the post, at the UN Moynihan established himself as a pugnacious defender of American ideals and interests, courting national popularity for the first time in his career. His most dramatic confrontation was in leading the opposition to UN General Assembly Resolution 3379, which condemned Zionism as "a form of racism and racial discrimination." Israel, claimed Moynihan, was "one of the very few places ... where Western democratic principles survive, and of all such places, currently the most exposed."[28] That the resolution was sponsored principally by authoritarian Arab and Third World states, and apparently the product of Soviet machinations, was evidence enough for Moynihan of a totalitarian assault on democracy. Despite a determined effort to defeat the resolution, in the end Moynihan could offer only symbolic acts of resistance. When the General Assembly passed the resolution, a furious Moynihan rose to declare that the United States "does not acknowledge, it will not abide by, it will never acquiesce in this infamous act."[29]

Ambassador Moynihan infuriated both fellow diplomats and his State Department superiors. However, growing admiration of his style among the

American public offered some insulation. By January 1976, the US mission to the UN had received more than 28,000 pieces of mail relating to Moynihan's performance, fewer than two hundred of which were critical. Praise even came from former California governor Ronald Reagan, then challenging Gerald Ford for the Republican presidential nomination. Moynihan was a pioneer of what Gil Troy has defined as "the politics of patriotic indignation," which Reagan would use to great effect in his 1980 campaign.[30] Months after the fall of Saigon and the communist takeover of Cambodia, at a moment of intense crisis for the United States, the fact that one of its representatives was mounting a noisy defense of its values proved immensely popular. One poll found that 70 percent of respondents wanted Moynihan to continue speaking out "frankly and forthrightly" even at the expense of "tact and diplomacy."[31]

Moynihan's rhetorical pyrotechnics as UN ambassador led more than one observer to wonder at his career plans. Speculation began to rise that he might run for one of New York's Senate seats. The chatter rose to such a distracting level that in October 1975, appearing on *Face the Nation* in the midst of the "Zionism is racism" fight, Moynihan was asked outright about his political ambitions. He was initially unequivocal in his denials, saying he would "consider it dishonorable" to leave the UN to run for office.[32] Some hoped that Moynihan would vanish quietly into academia after his tenure at the UN ended. In particular, many liberals cast a jaundiced eye over Moynihan's career trajectory. "Will we ever be free of the Moynihan phenomenon?" lamented a *Nation* editorial in February 1976. "Is it possible still to think of this ponderous lightweight as a Democrat?"[33]

Despite liberal skepticism, Moynihan's newfound fame made a bid for a New York Senate seat in 1976 a plausible next step. The incumbent senator, James Buckley, had made himself unpopular by opposing a federal bailout of New York City, then in the grips of a terrible fiscal crisis.[34] Buckley had the support of Republican president Gerald Ford, who had rejected New York's appeals for federal aid and urged the city to pursue stringent cost-cutting measures instead. The Ford administration argued that any bailout would only encourage further profligacy on the part of the municipal authorities. The president may have imagined he was administering some tough love, but the people of New York settled on a less generous interpretation. The *Daily News* distilled the resentment when it ran the notorious headline, "Ford to City: Drop Dead."[35] Buckley—the elder brother of *National Review* founder William F. Buckley Jr. and who had originally won the seat in 1970 as the nominee of the Conservative Party—may have been committed to his principles, but they were politically toxic as the city's financial condition worsened and left him acutely vulnerable to a Democratic challenge.

After several months of indecision, Moynihan committed himself to the Senate race in June 1976.[36] Though one of five candidates, Moynihan's principal opponent in the primary was Bella Abzug. A native New Yorker, Abzug started out as a lawyer; her early cases included defending civil rights activists in the Deep South. She was one of the few women in her profession when she began practicing in the 1940s, and to ensure that she would not be mistaken for a secretary, she took to wearing large, wide-brimmed hats, an affectation that would become a political trademark. In 1970, she won a congressional seat on Manhattan's solidly liberal West Side, defeating a seven-term incumbent in the Democratic primary. "A Woman's Place Is in the House," ran her campaign slogan, "And the Senate."[37] She cofounded the National Women's Political Caucus with Gloria Steinem and Betty Friedan and championed the Equal Rights Amendment. A fierce opponent of the Vietnam War, Abzug's uncompromising liberalism won her a spot on Richard Nixon's enemies list.[38]

Abzug had credibility with liberals the like of which Moynihan could only dream. Nonetheless, Moynihan brought considerable advantages. He was the favored candidate of both organized labor and the Jewish community. Al Barkan, the head of the AFL-CIO's political action committee, and Lane Kirkland, secretary treasurer of the AFL-CIO, gave Moynihan private undertakings that his campaign could expect $100,000 in union contributions.[39] Moynihan's robust defense of Israel at the UN meant that he could expect considerable goodwill from Jewish voters, who made up almost one-third of the Democratic primary electorate.[40] Moynihan's campaign manager, Sandy Frucher, fearing that the campaign would be undermined if the candidate ended up on the wrong side of a liberal versus conservative primary fight, sought to downplay the ideological differences between Moynihan and his rivals. "There are no issues of substance in this campaign," he told the *New Republic*, "the only issue is the character of the candidates and in both cases that is pretty well defined."[41]

Nonetheless, Moynihan's campaign did rest on substantive foundations, and Moynihan outlined those in four speeches delivered in late August and early September.[42] Each took a different unit as its focus: the nation, the Democratic Party (or the "liberal tradition"), New York City, and the family. He restated the liberal internationalism that had distinguished his tenure at the UN and called for "a strong and resolute America" to stand against the relentless onslaught of totalitarianism. He situated himself in what he defined as the reformist liberal tradition of the New York Democratic Party: "I stand for the liberalism of Al Smith and the Democratic Party tradition that says never promise anything you can't deliver." He announced his opposition to "the politics of racial polarization and reverse discrimination" and argued for social policies founded in universalist ideas. Finally, he attacked the welfare system for actively encouraging the disintegration of the American family and pressed for the federal government to assume the costs of New York's welfare system.

This quartet offered a vision of liberalism that he had been defending throughout his career in public life: a liberalism that was patriotic, internationalist, and anticommunist in foreign policy, opposed to utopian schemes in public policy, and wary of reforms that weakened a party's ability to deliver for its constituents, and that situated itself within the liberal tradition of New York, the state that had given birth to the New Deal. His foils in these speeches were those who thought America "so immoral a nation that the best thing we can do for the rest of the world is withdraw and concentrate all our attention on cleansing ourselves of sin." They were "usurpers" who had "made off with [liberalism's] banner and corrupted its language" and who maintained "that the American political system is sick and that only radical surgery can save it, if indeed it can be saved at all." They were "a certain kind of 'liberal' . . . [who] would rather protect what he considers the good name of the poor than do something about poverty." They were, though unnamed as such, New Politics liberals. Liberalism's real enemies, as far as Moynihan was concerned, came not from a resurgent conservatism but from within its own house.[43]

On primary day, September 15, Moynihan beat Abzug by 10,000 votes, a razor-thin margin of 0.1 percent. The next day, at a press conference at his campaign headquarters, Moynihan announced, "I believe we are seeing a rebirth of the Democratic majority in New York." One journalist asked whether he would be taking steps to make peace with the liberals. "We were the liberals in the race," he replied with a grin.[44]

The general election contest was considerably more lopsided in Moynihan's favor than the primary had been. The most influential issue in the contest was New York's continued economic weakness and the extension of federally backed loans to keep the city solvent. An opponent of federal support,

Buckley sought to exploit cultural resentments, addressing Moynihan as "Professor" throughout the race.[45] Moynihan responded by characterizing Buckley as "a radical of the Right" who had never reconciled himself to the New Deal. "My opponent keeps saying he wants to get Washington off our backs," Moynihan told one labor group. "I say I want to get Washington on our side." Though he opposed any federal role in a municipal rescue package, Buckley was unable to offer a convincing alternative. "That was how I got elected," Moynihan said later.[46]

The result was not even close. Moynihan won a decisive victory, with 2,913,200 votes to Buckley's 2,517,292 (54.1 to 44.9 percent). Statewide, Moynihan ran approximately 33,000 votes ahead of Jimmy Carter.[47] This was by no means a unique occurrence in the industrial Northeast and Midwest, where Carter was the beneficiary of a reverse coattails effect and formidable union mobilization.[48] This fact would color Moynihan's turbulent relationship with the president. Months earlier, journalist Michael Novak had written that if Moynihan won, there would at last be a senator "in touch with the generous, liberal, and realistic attitudes of a great majority of Americans. We will have a model for the future."[49] New York Democratic committee chair Joseph Crangle had predicted that Moynihan's election "would place the moderate-center philosophy in the forefront of the national Democratic Party."[50] Now, Moynihan had a platform to fight for that "moderate-center" philosophy. Of all the CDM's putative leaders, he seemed best placed to exploit that platform.

In January 1977, Moynihan entered what historian Ira Shapiro has described as "the last great Senate."[51] He became a reliably, and calculatedly, idiosyncratic figure. He responded to his name in the caucus roll call with the naval cry "Yo" and opened his regular constituent newsletters with the quaint archaism "Dear Yorker."[52] Newspaper and magazine profiles of this exotic addition to the Senate soon began to proliferate. "Like John Wayne walking into a Wild West saloon," ran one, New York's junior senator "attracts immediate attention [when] he rises to address the Senate or a public gathering."[53]

During the primary, Moynihan had been asked which of the Senate's major committees he would seek to join if elected. "Finance," he replied without hesitation, because "that's where the money is."[54] Most importantly, legislation pertaining to any future refinancing of New York would pass through that committee. No New Yorker had served on it since Reconstruction, and Moynihan delighted in reminding people that his predecessor had placed Samuel Tilden's name in nomination at the national convention.[55] Moynihan also sought appointment to the Public Works Committee, traditionally responsible for doling out pork in the form of valuable infrastructure projects. With these placements, Moynihan was signaling his intent to focus on domestic issues during his first term. This was hardly surprising. After all, he had claimed that his support for federal aid had won him his Senate seat. New York's condition remained precarious and the state would require a second federally backed refinancing in 1978. Moynihan's first term would be dominated by an effort to secure New York's finances permanently by redressing the supposed imbalances in the state's fiscal relationship with the federal government. This would bring him into frequent conflict with President Carter.

During the campaign, Carter had stressed that he would be far more sympathetic to New York's plight than Ford had been. He pledged a federal guarantee of the state's bonds and promised to meet with Governor Hugh Carey and Mayor Abraham Beame before his inauguration to work out a plan for New York's future.[56] Carter and Moynihan had campaigned together in the conservative upstate counties, and photographs of Carter and Mondale were included on Moynihan's campaign literature under the slogan, "They'll Never Say 'Drop Dead' to New York City."[57] In the days after Carter's election, it seemed the president was gearing up to honor these pledges. "In the 1930s we had a President from the Northeast who was particularly sympathetic to the problems of poverty in the rural South," remarked White House press secretary Jody Powell. "The President-elect hopes to reciprocate some of the concern and aid that Roosevelt provided to the South."[58]

At his first postelection press conference, days after his victory, Moynihan told the assembled journalists that he was "confident" that the Carter administration would respect its "contract with the people" by redeeming the urban policy planks of the party's platform. He reiterated an argument made on the campaign trail and to which he would soon give more empirical heft: that it was time to redress the regional imbalance that had come from disproportionate federal aid to the booming Southwest. This would offer those states, he added archly, "a new experience—the joy of benevolence toward others."[59] During his campaign, Moynihan said that the most serious question the next senator from New York would face was "what the federal government can and should do to help."[60] This would depend on Moynihan's ability to persuade the Carter White House to embrace his analysis and recalibrate federal policies accordingly. Unfortunately, Moynihan's personal relationship with Carter was tense from the outset. The senator never quite discarded the conceit that his candidacy had delivered New York, and thus the presidency, to Carter. For his part, Carter never warmed to Moynihan. In July 1977, one anonymous presidential aide leaked that "the President just doesn't care very much for Pat. He's too Northern, too much New York, too much Harvard."[61]

The first clash between Moynihan and the Carter White House over an issue of substance centered not on federalism, however, but on foreign policy. That episode illuminated a widening split in the Democratic Party—one that would drive many neoconservative Democrats into Reagan's coalition in 1980—and also reaffirmed Moynihan's gift for antagonizing his nominal allies. Throughout his Senate career, Moynihan remained determined to inculcate US foreign policy with the confrontational patriotism he had promoted at the UN. Initial efforts yielded disappointing results. By now a cochair of CDM, Moynihan, along with Washington senator Henry "Scoop" Jackson, presented Carter with a list of fifty-three candidates for national security and foreign service positions. Only two ultimately received appointments and then only in minor roles.[62] Brewing tensions between the Carter White House and the Moynihan-Jackson faction came to a head over the nomination of Paul Warnke as chief negotiator for the second round of bilateral Strategic Arms Limitation Talks with the Soviet Union.

Warnke was an established liberal lawyer and public servant who had founded his own Washington-based law firm with former Johnson administration official Clark Clifford as partner. He had served in the Defense Department under LBJ and, briefly, Nixon, where he had been a critic of the Vietnam War, and then as an adviser to George McGovern. In 1975, he contributed an article to *Foreign Policy*, in which he had argued that the United States should undertake unilateral acts of disarmament in the hope that the Soviet Union would respond with "reciprocal restraint."[63] To his critics, this revealed Warnke's dangerous naivete about Soviet ambitions. The CDM lobbied vigorously against his nomination, circulating an anonymous memorandum, part of which had been drafted by one of Moynihan's staffers.[64]

While affirming his support for Carter's broader approach to the Strategic Arms Limitation Talks, Moynihan announced his opposition to Warnke's appointment. Warnke, he declared on the Senate floor, had been "so shaken by the failure of American strategic and military power in Vietnam that he came to feel it must equally fail, that it must prove equally futile, in other circumstances and other places." He was, continued Moynihan, essentially content to accept a decline in America's international standing and to seek an unacceptable "accommodation" with the Soviet Union. "I cannot support, as SALT negotiator, a nominee who minimizes or dismisses the profound differences in the arms control motives and objectives of the Soviet Union and the United States."[65] Warnke was confirmed but by the relatively close margin of 58–40. Moynihan joined with eleven rebel Democrats and twenty-eight Republicans in opposition.

With this intervention, Moynihan alienated those who had expected that, once in the Senate, he would swiftly reveal himself as a more conventional northeastern liberal.[66] In his first major issue statement, he had placed himself on the side of Republican conservatives such as Jesse Helms and Strom Thurmond and against Ted Kennedy, Frank Church, and George McGovern. One major Democratic donor (a "liberal business tycoon") reportedly complained that he wished he could retrieve his "substantial" contribution to Moynihan's Senate campaign.[67]

The Warnke clash briefly reinvigorated the CDM. It embarked on a fund-raising drive shortly afterward and raised $25,000 in a matter of weeks.[68] Despite efforts to broaden its portfolio, however, it remained largely a vehicle for those dissatisfied with Carter's supposedly misguided foreign policy. It was an increasingly marginalized force in domestic politics, perhaps inevitable given its character as an elite lobbying group with no meaningful grassroots presence. Moynihan's opinion of the Soviet menace would mellow in the ensuing years, straining relations with those former allies who would be drawn to Reagan's bellicose defense buildup. Moreover, the CDM had little interest in the issue that was to dominate Moynihan's first term: the continued fiscal disadvantages faced by New York State.

Moynihan's determination to shape the national conversation on New York and its fiscal relationship to the federal government led his Senate office to start publishing an annual report that purportedly confirmed the imbalance. These statements, commonly known as the Fisc. reports (a typically esoteric borrowing of the term used for the taxes collected by the Merovingian and Carolingian royal households from their feudal territories), marshaled reams of data to demonstrate the disadvantageous "balance of payments" that existed between New York and the federal government. The first was released in June 1977. "I have come to the conclusion," Moynihan wrote in the cover letter to the president, "that the Federal government is very much more responsible for [New York's] decline than any of us have quite realized."[69]

The most distorting items in the ledger, concluded the first Fisc., were those that were erroneously counted as expenditures for the state simply because they were processed through New York–based banks. For instance, New York was on record as receiving 51 percent of interest on the federal debt and 44 percent of foreign aid.[70] New York also received most of its payments in what Moynihan called "soft" expenditures—Medicaid, welfare, and so on—rather than "hard" expenditures of infrastructure and defense contracts, which southern and western states received. "We get food stamps; they get infrastructure," as he put it later.[71] As a result, New York (along with other northeastern and midwestern states) was effectively subsidizing the booming economies of the South and the West. However necessary this arrangement had been when the Sunbelt renaissance had been a glint in the eye of federal developers, as the Frostbelt struggled to cope with accelerating deindustrialization, the imbalance was intolerable. Moynihan called on the federal government to end "a policy of further weakening the weakest economy in the nation."[72]

It was mid-September before Moynihan received an official acknowledgment of the report from the president. In the meantime, he had convened a press conference to angrily denounce the federal bureaucracy as a "peabrained dinosaur" without the competence to develop long-range solutions. While Carter's reply was cool, he directed OMB director Charles Schultze and Stuart Eizenstat to prepare an administration review of Moynihan's statement.[73] Their response, released two weeks later, conceded to Moynihan's analysis "in certain respects" but disputed the senator's principal contention and argued that the balance of payments was "not an appropriate measure" of "the federal impact on individual states." Publicly, Moynihan was quick to declare victory: "It's taken a long time for this argument to sink in with the Federal Government. Now, suddenly things become possible."[74]

But Carter remained unsympathetic to Moynihan's efforts. The president viewed Moynihan in the context of what he perceived as a parochial, self-interested Congress whose members jostled to defend their pet stipends while he struggled to balance national commitments amid encroaching austerity. This impression was only confirmed when Moynihan joined with southern and western members to oppose the president in the water projects controversy, explaining that he had anticipated legislative "trade-offs" in his defense of the Northeast. "If they voted for us, I let them know they can expect me to be a friend."[75] By mid-1978, Carter was writing in his journal that he was "discouraged" by the pressure from Congress to increase spending "almost across the board." The president noted that he felt "more at home with the conservative Democratic and Republican members of Congress than I do the others, although the liberals vote with me more often."[76]

Moynihan had limited success in squeezing concessions out of the Carter administration. Though the Fisc. project may have been, as Godfrey Hodgson has suggested, "a fairly successful" venture "to change the way people thought about New York and its economy," it yielded few tangible policy successes in the late 1970s. Moynihan's greatest triumph in this may have been his role, in concert with New York's senior senator Jacob Javits, a Republican, steering a bill through the Senate in 1978 that authorized a federal loan of $2 billion to New York City. This was the first recapitalization of the troubled city since 1976, and it passed amid a climate of increasing hostility toward any New York "bailout."[77] While the bill was making its way through Congress, California voters passed Proposition 13, a ballot initiative that drastically cut California's property tax rates, touching off a wave of taxpayer revolts that cautioned legislators against appearing too loose with the public purse.[78] Such isolated successes aside, however, a more significant reorientation of federal priorities proved elusive.

Moynihan's sparring with Carter marked him out as one of the president's regular and most colorful critics. As Carter's approval ratings sank, Moynihan's name was being floated as a possible primary challenger. "If there is not yet a Moynihan campaign," wrote Morton Kondracke, "there is a Moynihan movement and a Moynihan logic."[79] Support came largely from his old neoconservative allies. "If I had to invent a candidate to suit the political mood of the country," said Norman Podhoretz, "it would be somebody like Moynihan."[80] Confirming liberal suspicions, Moynihan also received support from the Right. While stopping short of an endorsement, William F. Buckley wrote warmly about his putative candidacy.[81]

The expectation was that Moynihan would leap into the race as the champion of the CDM-inclined faction. By 1980, Scoop Jackson, the other most prominent CDM-associated Democrat, already had two unsuccessful and unremarkable presidential campaigns behind him and was unlikely to tilt at the windmill a third time. For a neoconservative who still identified as a Democrat, Moynihan was the only game in town. The *Nation* was sufficiently disquieted by the quickening drumbeat around Moynihan's presidential prospects to devote an entire special issue to the senator, under the heading "The Conscience of a Neoconservative." "Why is this man on our cover?" asked the editorial. Moynihan, it explained, "is the point man for an increasingly visible, vocal and . . . powerful intellectual movement: the neoconservatives, who cloak conservative conclusions in the language of liberalism." Contributors dissected Moynihan's positions, and by extension the neoconservative platform, on welfare, foreign affairs, race relations, and the use (or misuse) of social science in answering questions of public policy.[82]

Eventually, Moynihan backed away from running against Carter, if he had ever seriously considered it. In private, he was among those who urged Ted Kennedy to challenge the president, though in public he remained scrupulously neutral.[83] Podhoretz wrote later that it was Moynihan's decision not to launch a campaign that freed him to vote for Reagan.[84] By 1980, Moynihan was already in the process of politically detaching himself, in subtle but distinct ways, from his neoconservative networks. He had never accepted the label and frequently corresponded with newspapers and magazines to assert his preferred nomenclature. In 1979, for instance, he wrote to the journalist Peter Steinfels, protesting the label's use in a recent profile Steinfels had written for *Esquire* magazine. This mischaracterization, wrote Moynihan with typical modesty, would mean that a "good many persons of open mind and friendly mien will simply learn that the smartest people these days are something called neo-conservatives, and adapt their own disposition accordingly. Is it a service to liberalism to encourage this?" The so-called neo-conservatives were, he continued, "liberals much as John F. Kennedy was a liberal. A bit more so."[85]

"A Matter of Right and Not of Privilege": Health-Care Reform and the Kennedy Challenge

If Democratic liberals had a king-over-the-water in the 1970s, it was surely Ted Kennedy. The senator from Massachusetts had been the acknowledged front-runner for the Democratic presidential nomination in both the 1972 and 1976 cycles, though on both occasions he backed away from announcing his candidacy. Kennedy would eventually be induced to seek the presidency in 1980, in a quixotic bid to unseat Jimmy Carter, with whom he had become increasingly disillusioned since 1976. The proximate cause of his disillusionment was Carter's reluctance to support a national health insurance (NHI) scheme, the defining policy goal of Kennedy's long political career. Much like the Humphrey-Hawkins episode, the failure to pass NHI would underscore for congressional liberals Carter's lack of policy ambition and unwillingness to expend political capital on transformative legislation. The major difference is that a diluted full employment law was enacted, which was not true for health-care reform. Kennedy became a rallying point for unhappy liberals hoping to replace Carter with a more dynamic executive. Although other possible contenders had their moments in the limelight, no other candidate could match Kennedy's mystique or the depth of his support in the party.

The youngest scion of the Kennedy family, Edward Moore Kennedy had first been elected to the Senate from Massachusetts in 1962. With his brothers occupying the White House and the Attorney General's office, it seemed that the first family had bestowed a sinecure on a rather louche and irresponsible younger brother. Ted had held no elective office prior to his election to fill his brother's Senate seat, nor for that matter had he held down a proper job. A child of privilege, Kennedy had been educated at Harvard, where he had distinguished himself on the college football team and by being temporarily expelled for cheating on a Spanish exam. His first experience of politics was in 1958, when he managed his eldest brother's Senate reelection campaign, and he oversaw the Kennedy campaign in the West when John sought the presidency two years later. After JFK left the Senate in December 1960, Kennedy's father ensured that a placeholder was appointed until Ted turned thirty (in 1962) and became constitutionally eligible to occupy the seat. The casual observer might assume that Ted was a prototypical younger son of a grand family: sheltered, unambitious, and feckless. Indeed, during the 1962 special election, Kennedy's opponent famously remarked that "if his name was Edward Moore, his candidacy would be a joke."[86]

Nonetheless, despite some hedonistic tendencies, Kennedy proved an effective senator, with a high tolerance for the drudgery that made up much of a legislator's work.[87] His early years in office were punctuated by tragedy, however. His two elder brothers were felled by assassins' bullets, and in 1964 a near-fatal plane crash left him with chronic back pain for the rest of his life. Then, in July 1969, came the event that would loom over the rest of his career. Returning from a party on Chappaquiddick Island, adjacent to Martha's Vineyard, accompanied by Mary Jo Kopechne, a twenty-eight-year-old former secretary to RFK, Kennedy's Oldsmobile plunged off a bridge into the Poucha Pond. He escaped; she did not. Kennedy claimed that he dove repeatedly in a vain attempt to rescue Kopechne. But he failed to report the accident until the next morning.[88] For the rest of his life, Chappaquiddick would be cited as evidence of Kennedy's moral deficiency.

Politically, whereas John Kennedy had maintained clear ideological distance from the party's New Deal legacy, Ted was situated more squarely in the Roosevelt tradition. Kennedy, wrote Burton Hersh, was "an heir to the aspirations of the New Deal Left" and "not nearly as squeamish at being labeled a man of the left as Jack or the early Bobby."[89] Like his colleague Hubert Humphrey, he had fewer neuroses about being perceived as a big-spending liberal than many other Democrats. Also like Humphrey, Kennedy had an appeal to white blue-collar voters that was rare among avowed liberals. *Time* magazine reported an incident when Kennedy, marching in an anti–Vietnam War parade, had been cheered by a counter-demonstration of construction workers wielding "Back Our Boys in Vietnam" signs.[90] However, Kennedy was not immune from the white working-class backlash, as was made painfully clear when he confronted Boston's antibusing protests. As the protests reached their rowdy climax in September 1974, Kennedy had appeared at a rally of some 10,000 angry parents, at the invitation of the sponsor organization Restore Our Alienated Rights (ROAR), to appeal to the protestors to obey the court orders. He was drowned out by jeering and choruses of "God Bless America," until he was escorted off the speaker's platform by the police.[91] Kennedy was troubled by this evidence of white blue-collar alienation, especially given his own presidential ambitions, and he resolved to take steps to combat it.

In 1973, Kennedy had appeared onstage with George Wallace at a "nonpolitical" July fourth event, at which he had hailed the Alabama governor as a fellow populist critic of the Nixon administration who used "the people's power" to "strike at the rights of the people."[92] Kennedy's policy priorities also reflected his sensitivity to the backlash. On law and order issues, Kennedy became increasingly hawkish. He sponsored a bill (ultimately defeated in the House) to broaden federal prosecutorial powers and institute mandatory minimum penal sentences for certain crimes, as well as another, successfully enacted, bill to give the federal government new wiretapping powers. Such measures drew criticism from civil libertarians and antagonized the liberal portions of Kennedy's coalition.[93] It was far safer to pursue universalist policies, such as NHI, in the hope that they would smother tensions exacerbated by disagreements over issues of race and culture.

As a policy goal, national health insurance shared many features with the Humphrey-Hawkins bill. Like full employment, NHI had been part of FDR's "Second Bill of Rights," a central component of Truman's frustrated Fair Deal, and then a Democratic preoccupation in the ensuing decades. By the 1970s, spiraling health-care costs were being identified by analysts as a leading driver of inflation, which encouraged reformers to believe that they might be able to pass a far-reaching NHI plan. Reform of the health-care system, argued many liberals, was a means to lessen the financial burden on beleaguered middle-class families and the urban poor. In 1977, *U.S. News & World Report* calculated that health care cost an average of $650 per person, or $2,600 for a family of four, almost 11 percent of the typical American's annual income.[94] A few months later, journalist Eliot Marshall wrote that health-care inflation was running at such an alarming rate "that economists and budget planners now regard it as a kind of good soldier gone berserk."[95]

None were more zealous in their efforts to tackle the berserker than Kennedy. His commitment to NHI was both philosophical and personal. Like full employment, national health insurance was a means of extending rights-consciousness into the Democratic Party's traditional economic agenda, a way to give "white middle-class voters a stake in the Great Society."[96] Inevitably, this put Kennedy and his supporters on a collision course with the fiscally cautious administrations, both Republican and Democratic, of the 1970s. Rights had to be observed, said Kennedy, regardless of the economic or political climate. In any case, as far as the supporters of NHI were concerned, the political climate was propitious. As he later recalled, Kennedy believed that the Democratic victories in 1976 "called for bold leadership and swift action built around a single piece of legislation."[97] He wanted NHI to be that legislation. But the audacity that Kennedy expected from the White House would not materialize. Nonetheless, exploiting the recent congressional reforms and the changing media context, Kennedy was able to provide that policy leadership himself from within the Senate, emerging as a kind of "shadow president" by the end of the decade.[98] Though not occupying any leadership position, Kennedy was able to make use of his chairmanship of the Subcommittee on Health and Scientific Research to champion NHI.[99]

Kennedy also had a well-organized and well-financed pressure group to lead, the Committee for National Health Insurance (CNHI). The CNHI had been founded in 1969 as a joint venture between the UAW and the AFL-CIO. At the instigation of the CNHI, Kennedy introduced several health-care reform bills over the course of the 1970s, first with Wilbur Mills as co-sponsor in 1973, and, after Mills left Congress in disgrace, with Rep. James Corman of California. These bills would have introduced a single-payer, not-for-profit national health insurance scheme, which would cover all Americans regardless of income, employment status, or preexisting conditions. Kennedy made some headway toward securing White House cooperation. Between 1974 and 1976, for example, he came maddeningly close to reaching a compromise deal with the Ford administration. Ultimately, he was forced to disown the resulting legislation, largely because of the objections of the CNHI, which had no intention of settling for a Republican-diluted bill when all signs pointed to a Democratic landslide in 1976. In this way, as Timothy Stanley argues, Kennedy was "a hostage to his own constituency . . . as much a product of his own movement as its steward."[100] That the CNHI would reject a compromise reform, confident that something more robust would be possible soon, reveals how secure key Democratic constituencies believed the party's hegemony to be.

President Carter, however, was unenthusiastic about the prospect of reforming the American health-care system. Though by no means indifferent to its iniquities, it was simply not high on his list of priorities. Technocratic and averse to grand schemes, he seemed less concerned about extending insurance coverage than with correcting inefficiencies and abuses within the existing system. As Peter Bourne, the president's special assistant on health issues, explained, Carter "preferred to talk movingly of his deep and genuine sympathy for those who suffered for lack of health care, as though the depth of his compassion could be a substitute for embracing a major new and expensive government solution for the problem."[101] He stood firm only on the need for stringent cost-containment measures, which he insisted should be implemented before broader reform could be undertaken. During the campaign, Carter had made a vague commitment to health-care reform, while the more ambitious party platform had called for "a comprehensive national health insurance system with universal and mandatory coverage."[102] Even Carter's tepid pledge had been grudgingly extracted, largely to win the support of the UAW.[103]

The growing realization that Carter's cost-containment proposals were a substitute for, rather than a precursor to, NHI prompted a swift and angry response from liberals. It would fall to Kennedy to lead the charge. However, both had been anxious to avoid a public confrontation. In June 1977, Peter

Bourne, the administration official most sympathetic to Kennedy's position, recommended unsuccessfully to Hamilton Jordan that they should quietly begin working with the senator. "He has, I think, tried to demonstrate restraint by holding back on criticizing our slow start on this issue, but National Health Insurance is the most important thing in his career at the present time, and he feels that his own credibility will be in jeopardy if he goes too long without saying something." Without "evidence of a major move on this issue" in the near future, Kennedy would likely be obliged to "drop a bomb" on the administration to preserve his own credibility.[104] Bourne was among those urging Carter to adopt a more radical plan, arguing in a December 1977 memo that "opposition to a conservative, limited plan will be almost as great as opposition to a more comprehensive program. On the other hand the intensity of support will be tied directly to comprehensiveness."[105]

The White House's position was further complicated by its strained relationship with the Department of Health, Education, and Welfare (HEW), then under the direction of Joseph Califano. Califano had spent nearly his entire career in Washington, including stints as a special assistant to LBJ and in various roles for the DNC. In many respects, Carter and Califano had overlapping political priorities ("I saw it as my job to prove that these programs could be run with competence and integrity, to convince taxpayers that they were getting full value for the dollars they were investing in HEW," Califano writes in his memoirs).[106] Nonetheless, Califano resented White House intrusion in the working of his department and resisted attempts to move faster on developing legislation. This bureaucratic infighting obstructed progress on any bill. Within six months of Carter's inauguration, Bourne was complaining about HEW's stalling on NHI proposals and was unsure "whether he [Califano] [was] unaware of the lack of movement or whether he [was] just trying to keep us off his back."[107] As early as September, Eizenstat's staffers were reporting to him that the "spirit of detente with HEW seem[ed] to have broken down."[108]

Though he initially shrank from frontal assaults on Carter, Kennedy was not averse to chiding the administration in public for its irresolution on NHI. In May 1977, 116 days after Carter's inauguration, Kennedy used an address to the UAW to warn that health-care reform was "in danger of becoming the missing promise in the Administration's plans."[109] In August, Bourne reported that Kennedy was planning "a multi-city blitz in the fall to push National Health Insurance, not necessarily [for] his legislation, but [which] will inevitably focus on our failures of which he is extremely aware."[110] The senator continued to push for the administration to adopt his bill, while Carter remained disdainful of Kennedy's proposals, dismissing them as too expensive.

The president's qualms only intensified as the economy worsened and he doggedly insisted that inflationary costs must be brought under control before further reform could be countenanced. For Kennedy, who believed that every American citizen had a right to good-quality health care, such preconditions were irrelevant.[111] By early 1978, Kennedy and the CNHI were pressing the administration to commit to comprehensive reform proposals that could be used as a Democratic platform in that year's midterm elections. The Carter administration hoped to avoid any serious moves on health care until 1979. Eizenstat counseled Carter against releasing any detailed plan before the midterms that might damage Democratic candidates by affixing the "big spender" label to them: "When the history of NHI is written, whether the plan came before or after the election will be irrelevant."[112] As well as fencing with dyspeptic liberals, Carter was forced to contend with pressure from conservative Democrats, who began to mobilize to oppose such legislation, citing their concerns about limited available revenues for such a dramatic expansion of government responsibility.[113] Both sides were keen to secure commitments from any incoming Democrats, or those facing reelection, in preparation for a potentially divisive legislative battle.

As liberal dissatisfaction with Carter intensified, Kennedy became a rallying point for the disillusioned and NHI his battle standard. Attorney General Griffin Bell told the *Boston Globe* in 1978, "The President . . . asked me the other day if I thought Senator Kennedy would accept an appointment to the Supreme Court. I replied that I did not believe he would want to give up being co-president."[114] The situation came to a head at the midterm convention in Memphis, where Kennedy exhorted the party to "sail against the wind" and pledged to continue the fight for "decent quality healthcare, North and South, East and West, for all Americans, as a matter of right and not of privilege."

From that point onward, efforts to pass NHI became snarled up in the Carter-Kennedy psychodrama. Republican gains in the congressional elections of 1978 only confirmed Carter's conviction that he had been elected to "bring fiscal responsibility to the federal government."[115] Greg Schneiders, deputy assistant to the president for communications, suggested that they stop underplaying the split with Kennedy on NHI. The administration was "in a position to look 'conservative' whenever we discuss the issue. Therefore, the more columnists and others write about it now, the better." It should be stressed, argued Communications Director Gerald Rafshoon, that Carter was on the right side of the issue, both politically and substantively, and that his "taking on" of Kennedy was an indication of the new spirit of "toughness."[116]

In January 1979, as the new Congress convened, the Carter administration decided to propose a modest catastrophic insurance plan together with reforms to Medicare and Medicaid. Alongside catastrophic insurance, the Carter plan mandated employers to cover workers, introduced a new federal insurance plan for the elderly, poor, and uninsured (which would absorb both Medicare and Medicaid), and introduced further systemic reforms such as the promotion of Health Maintenance Organizations (HMOs) and the constraining of hospital and physician fees.[117] As with Carter's other proposals, the focus was on cost containment rather than on coverage for the uninsured. Appearing on NBC's Today Show the day after Carter's plan was revealed, Kennedy announced his opposition to the plans and called for a fundamental rethinking of American health care. He told Tom Brokaw that the nation could not simply "add more benefits to the health care system." It was essential, he said, to follow other nations and pursue "prospective budgeting": "To establish a budget [for health care], as we do for national defense, as we do for education, as we do in fighting crime . . . and then see the distribution of benefits underneath."[118]

Carter's response to Kennedy's objections, as outlined by Press Secretary Jody Powell, stressed that the proposals were "fiscally responsible" and "a first step in a national insurance plan." Kennedy was dismissed as the representative of those who had raised NHI into "a semi-sacred ideological principle."[119] This strategy fell flat, however, and the Carter-backed bill expired in the House. By September 1979, despairing of the apparently terminally unambitious Carter administration, Kennedy decided to push forward with his own bold initiative. Joining with California representative Henry Waxman, Kennedy introduced the "Health Care for All Americans" bill. To placate the deficit-averse White House, the Kennedy-Waxman bill included a heavy cost-sharing component and employed private insurers as fiscal intermediaries. Kennedy's onetime cosponsor, James Corman, condemned the bill for its reliance on the private insurance sector.[120] The Kennedy-Waxman bill failed, despite its moderated provisions, as all NHI bills were to fail in the 1970s.

Carter was convinced that his reforms had been the victim of Kennedy's overweening ambition. The overprivileged Massachusetts senator had set his covetous eyes on the White House and was apparently prepared to undermine a cause to which he was passionately committed so long as Carter would be denied a victory. In a postscript to his published White House diary, Carter acidly concluded that he could have done little to forestall a challenge from the Massachusetts senator "to remove me for the political office that he considered his justifiable family heritage."[121]

However, Kennedy's bid for the presidency was grounded in more than his own ambition. In his autobiography, Kennedy claimed that it was the notorious "crisis of confidence" speech, which Carter delivered in July 1979, that first prompted him to consider mounting a primary challenge. In this televised address, unfairly remembered as Carter's "malaise" speech, the president diagnosed a spiritual crisis afflicting the nation and called on the support of Americans to fight against it.[122] Kennedy recalled watching the talk "with mounting incredulousness and outrage. . . . This message was contrary to—it was in conflict with—all the ideals of the Democratic Party that I cherished."[123] Kennedy's disgust exposes a principal cause of the bitter rift between him and Carter: a fundamental disagreement about the proper handling of the presidency. For Carter, a crisis was an opportunity for reflection; for Kennedy, such moments demanded audacity. This differing conception of presidential power, and of the future of the Democratic Party, was sublimated into the clash over health-care reform. "Kennedy and his supporters saw a deep human need for protection against the cost of illness. Carter saw a broken, inefficient healthcare system to be reengineered."[124] Ultimately, it would find expression in Kennedy's 1980 campaign, a rebellion of Democratic liberals against Carter's post–New Deal politics of lowered expectations.

"Dr. Udall's Patented Unity Medicine": Mo Udall, Peacemaker

"We are getting a lot of letters complaining about Carter, particularly from liberals." So began an internal memorandum from Arizona congressman Mo Udall to his staff, dated June 1977. Udall noted that he was increasingly being asked to evaluate the president's record, and so the memo was an effort to clarify his impressions of Carter, and reflect on liberal criticisms, with an eye to drafting a response, in the form of either a letter or a speech. His conclusions were measured. The Carter administration, Udall noted, had been "pretty good for liberals in many respects." He cited consumer protections, the amnesty for draft resisters, and skepticism of nuclear power. "The common denominator of all of this is that none of them costs much money. Liberals should understand that he will give them some things, but money will not be among them." On other, more expensive, Democratic ambitions, he predicted continued disappointment. He was "dubious" that a health-care reform bill would pass, and though it was "tragic" that its supporters would have to wait at least four years, liberals had to accept that Carter had not prioritized it. On environmental issues, Udall noted that while Carter was prepared to "do unpopular things" (particularly, as the water projects confrontation had shown, where the Army Corps of Engineers was concerned) and his appointments were "first-rate," it was still unclear whether he would "spend money . . . for environmental goals."[125]

That Udall had become the focus for liberals venting their frustrations with Carter reflected his growing stature in the party and his role as one of the de facto leaders of its liberal wing. His reputation had been enhanced by his presidential campaign, and he had by no means abandoned his ambitions for higher office.[126] On the day of the election 1976, legislative aide Terry Bracy had sent Udall a memo speculating on how he might maintain and cultivate his political profile. Udall, claimed Bracy, was now "one of the top five Democrats in the country" and he ought to take steps to consolidate and expand that status. "You are now in a position to become, at the very least, perhaps the conscience of the Democratic Party, a man who would have the kind of clout that Goldwater does in GOP circles." Bracy suggested that Udall could follow the "HHH and Ted Kennedy models" of wielding influence without being a "formal leader" by being "known, hav[ing] large and effective staffs, and work[ing] the press hard."[127]

Over the course of Carter's term, Udall established himself as an informal leader within Congress and a plausible replacement for the increasingly unpopular Carter. In the midst of the Kennedy challenge, however, Udall emerged as a mediator between the hostile factions. With the party in a bitter and recriminatory mood as the 1980 elections approached, the avuncular Udall took on the unenviable task of trying to heal the party's divides.

Udall's stature was due in no small part to his leadership on environmental issues and, in this period in particular, his vital role in the campaign to preserve huge swathes of Alaska's wilderness. That campaign reveals not only the policy bona fides that endeared him to liberal Democrats but also his complex and often fruitful working relationship with the Carter White House, which gave him credibility as a peacemaker. Udall oversaw the Alaska Lands effort as chairman of the House Committee on Interior and Insular Affairs, to which he acceded in 1977.[128] The legislative fight would land him in the middle of a controversy roiling the western states and adding to the Carter administration's various headaches, the Sagebrush Rebellion, a movement that sought a fundamental restructuring of federal-state relations in the area of land policy.

In most western states, the federal government was the largest landowner. In the late 1970s, it held in trust 87 percent of Nevada, 66 percent of Utah, 45 percent of California, and 42 percent of Arizona. By contrast, no more than 12 percent of any state outside the West was under federal control.[129] Most of these lands were managed by the Bureau of Land Management (BLM) and the US Forest Service, agencies in the Department of the Interior and the Department of Agriculture, respectively. The federal presence had always been a cause of simmering grievance, but this was given fresh impetus by the passage, in 1976, of the Federal Land Policy and Management Act, which stated that it would be the policy of the United States government that "the public lands be retained in federal ownership, unless . . . it is determined that disposal of a particular parcel will serve the national interest."[130]

This clarification of federal policy toward the public lands was the culmination of a significant shift in focus away from resource development and toward conservation, which had been underway since the early 1960s. Western interests had been used to a favorable reception from policy-makers. Indeed, the BLM was often dismissed by environmentalists as the Bureau of Livestock and Mining.[131] By the 1970s, this was no longer the case. The change, which reflected the growing influence of the environmental movement, had begun with the 1964 Wilderness Act, which extended regulation of federal lands in the West. The act created a National Wilderness Preservation System, which outlawed a plethora of destructive activities—including logging, grazing, and mining—in areas designated as "wilderness."[132] Over the next decade, BLM regulation of federal lands became more extensive, and many westerners—particularly the aforementioned mining, logging, and grazing interests—became increasingly disgruntled. "By the late 1970s," wrote one historian, "the West was a political tinderbox, and nowhere was the tinder drier than on the lands managed by the BLM."[133] For many westerners, their intrusive landlord had become an intolerable burden. By 1979, this would bubble over into a full-blown political campaign to take control of the lands under federal stewardship.

In early 1978, the Carter administration was trying to negotiate a cease-fire in the "War on the West" that it had unknowingly declared in pursuit of water resource reform. Carter himself had toured the West in late 1977 to express his "sincere concern about Western problems."[134] In January, Vice President Walter Mondale was dispatched on a week-long trip through the western states with an olive branch. Reporting on the trip, Lou Cannon noted that Mondale's "relaxed good-humored manner" had proved a hit with western-ers. Not everyone was placated, however. "We want a real partnership with the West," Mondale told one audience. "How about just diplomatic recogni-tion," a young politician reportedly muttered from the back of the room.[135] Such solicitations did not solve the administration's problems. There were no significant revisions of those policies that western opponents of the admin-istration found most offensive. Carter remained committed throughout his presidency to defunding water projects he deemed wasteful. Furthermore, the administration pressed ahead with a series of new wilderness reviews that had been initiated by the Federal Land Policy and Management Act, which a 1978 article in the *Conservative Digest* derisively christened "The Big Federal Land Grab."[136] A *New York Times* report from March 1979 found that the West had "replaced the South as the region that feels itself most abused by the Fed-eral Government and least understood by the rest of the nation, the area that believes itself to have the most peculiar problems."[137]

The Sagebrush Rebellion broke out in July 1979 when the Nevada state leg-islature passed a bill asserting its rights over approximately 49 million acres of land then in federal hands.[138] "We're tired of being pistol-whipped by the bureaucrats and ambushed and dry-gulched by federal regulations," declared the author of the legislation, Nevada state senator and Elko cattle rancher Norman Glaser.[139] By 1981, similar legislation had been passed in all remain-ing western states. *National Journal* saw more bluster than menace in the uprising. "The sagebrush rebellion rhetoric may be merely a satisfying way to vent frustration over the complicated regulations that accompany a more complicated society."[140] Nonetheless, the Carter administration believed it had to take the resistance seriously and endeavored to reach out to the region. In an August 1979 message to Congress, a month before the Reno conference,

Carter used a restatement of the administration's environmental priorities to offer several concessions to the malcontents. The federal government, he said, must not only endeavor to be "a good steward" of the 417 million acres then under its control but also "a good neighbor," sensitive to those affected by federal management decisions, particularly in the western states.[141]

Even many western Democrats, and especially governors given their political contexts, felt the need to genuflect to the growing antifederal sentiment. One such example was Governor Scott Matheson of Utah, so far the last Democrat to serve in that post, who made a positive hobby of clashing with the federal government. Elected in 1976, in his first three years in office, Matheson locked horns with the federal bureaucracy over water and federal land rights, the movement of "weteye" nerve gas bombs from Denver to his state, the deployment of MX missiles in Utah's western desert, and radioactive fallout from nuclear tests decades previously. "It's up to the states to aggressively take after the federal government and put them back in their historical posture of federalism," he told the *Christian Science Monitor* in March 1980. "They are not going to give up anything without a fight."[142]

Another Democrat with rebel sympathies was Richard Lamm, the governor of Colorado and elected in the same sweep that brought Gary Hart to office. Lamm became an occasional contributor to the *New York Times*, bringing a western liberal perspective to its op-ed page. In one 1976 piece, he had cautioned his party against complacency in the face of recent triumphs and castigated it for its overreliance on the proliferation of federal programs in an era of increasingly scarce resources and public mistrust of government. "The Democratic Party would make a great mistake to allow another party to capture the public feeling against our overcentralized bureaucracy, red tape and the illusion in Washington that passing a law is tantamount to solving a problem." By 1980, Lamm was using his column to throw in his lot with the Sagebrush Rebels. "When Colorado Springs wants to be able to store a little water, it has to play 'Mother, May I?' with a thousand high-level bureaucrats in Washington."[143]

Udall was unusual among western politicians in terms of the force with which he pushed back against the perception that the West was being shortchanged. In a newsletter to his constituents, he dismissed the gripes: "The West, in fact, is the only region in the country with its 'own' Cabinet agency— the Department of the Interior."[144] Nonetheless, Udall was well-liked by other politicians in the region and generally enjoyed good relationships with most of them. "He thinks as a westerner," observed Republican congressman Richard Cheney of Wyoming in 1985. "Nobody would call me an environmentalist but Mo and I see eye-to-eye on some legislation involving the land and the water."[145]

While the Sagebrush Rebellion raged around him, Udall oversaw the negotiations to settle the question of land ownership in the comparatively new state of Alaska. This fraught and ponderous legislative debate would result in the doubling in size of the US national parks system. The controversy over the apportionment of Alaska's lands dated back to the territory's incorporation into the Union as a state in January 1959. As with most of the states west of the one hundredth meridian, the federal government was the major landowner, and Congress authorized the state government to select, over twenty-five years, some 104 million acres of land to be returned. In 1971, with Alaska yet to complete its land selection, Congress passed the Alaska Native Claims Settlement Act, which appropriated $942 million and 44 million acres for distribution among various indigenous peoples. Udall, along with Republican congressman John P. Saylor of Pennsylvania, proposed an amendment that would be incorporated into the act empowering the interior secretary to select 80 million acres of Alaskan land for national parks, wildlife refuges, and national forests. The amendment set a deadline on this appropriation, requiring Congress to pass legislation protecting the chosen land by December 18, 1978.[146] The Sagebrush Rebellion exploded into life while the torturous congressional debate over successive Alaska Lands Bills neared completion. The rebellion made Udall and his conservationist allies ever more determined to pass legislation protecting the land.

As the new Interior and Insular Affairs Committee chairman, Udall was able to become a central influence in the endgame of the Alaskan lands dispute. Only the congressional reforms of the early 1970s made this possible. Decades earlier it would have been unlikely for a politician who had so antagonized the House Democratic leadership to be able to exercise such responsibility. Denied the opportunity to ascend the party hierarchy, Udall wielded power instead as a committee chair, becoming a key actor in the passage of one of the most significant acts of conservation in American history. Before joining that effort, Udall had never even visited Alaska; he made his first trip there in 1977. When his National Guard helicopter touched down on a plateau in the snow-topped Wrangell Mountains, Udall bounded out and exclaimed, to the laughter of his traveling companions, "I want it all!"[147] To opponents of the plans, Udall represented everything that was wrong with modern liberalism's attitude toward the states. For them, he was a meddlesome big government type from a desert state thousands of miles away scheming to appropriate a huge tranche of Alaska's lands to save some caribou and a vista that could be seen only by Americans who subscribed to *National Geographic*. Signs sprang up demanding "States Rights!" and declaring, "Alaskans Can Manage Alaskan Land."[148]

Udall was supported in his efforts by a federation of environmental groups, the Alaska Coalition, which maintained continuous pressure on lawmakers throughout the dispute. The coalition had been formed in 1970 and included more than fifty environmental groups, such as the Sierra Club, the Wilderness Society, the National Audubon Society, the League of Conservation Voters, and the National Wildlife Federation. This coalition drew on a vast network of environmental activists across the nation and applied insistent and targeted pressure to waverers and opponents of the various incarnations of the Alaska Lands bill in Congress. "We did the ultimate kind of civics and lobbying jobs that you read about in the textbooks," Udall would later boast.[149]

Udall found an ally in Carter over the Alaska issue, although their relationship since the 1976 campaign had not always been easy. Cecil Andrus, Carter's interior secretary, confided to Udall in April 1977 of the president's "continuing hostility" toward him. Udall noted in his file memo of that conversation that "obviously the campaign had left some scars and that Carter privately has little good to say about me."[150] They also clashed over the Central Arizona Project (CAP), a long-running scheme to construct an aqueduct to divert water from the Colorado River to Arizona and which Carter identified as another wasteful water project (though Udall did not think Carter's antipathy to the Central Arizona Project was "an anti–Mo Udall thing").[151] Nonetheless, Carter and Udall made common cause over Alaska. In January 1978, Udall had a lunch meeting with Carter at which he gave the president his "stock pitch about Alaska, the largest conservation decision since Theodore Roosevelt and the national forests. The need to be wise and far-sighted, etc." Udall was positive about their discussions on the issue: "I think I really got to him on this and he promised support."[152]

The passage of the Alaska National Interest Lands Conservation Act followed a complex and arduous struggle, stretching over three years.[153] After considerable wrangling within Congress, the bill was finally signed into law on December 2, 1980. At the signing ceremony, Carter declared that it was "without a doubt . . . one of the most important pieces of conservation legislation ever passed in this Nation. . . . Never before have we seized the opportunity to preserve so much of America's natural and cultural heritage on so grand a scale."[154] "For environmentalists, it was little short of glorious," wrote Udall's biographers.[155] History, said fellow westerner Gary Hart, would "count [Udall] as one of the great environmentalists."[156]

As the Alaska bill was wending its way through Congress, Udall's name had been added to the list of Democrats being touted as a possible primary challenger to President Carter. He demurred, however, in characteristic fashion. "If nominated, I'll run to the Mexican border," he said. "If elected, I'll fight extradition."[157] However, he withheld his own endorsement of the president without explicitly rejecting him. Notwithstanding their alliance on Alaskan conservation, Udall's opinion of Carter's leadership abilities had continued to deteriorate, and in December 1979, he endorsed Kennedy for the presidency, describing the Massachusetts senator as "a gifted, exceptional leader with a proven ability to put together a consensus behind which all Democrats can unite."[158] (Soon after Udall endorsed Kennedy, officials from the Carter White House reportedly leaked that Department of Justice lawyers had discovered an error in the 1853 Gadsden Purchase that meant that most of Southern Arizona, including Udall's district, was rightfully Mexican territory. Udall put out a jokey statement in response declaring that he did not believe that the administration had acted "vindictively" and that the impact would likely be "minimal"—especially, he added, "if all my constituents adopt Spanish surnames and attempt to smuggle themselves into the United States, which now begins somewhere north of Casa Grande.")[159]

Kennedy's challenge to Carter fizzled with unusual speed, and despite winning a number of key primaries, he was never as significant a threat to Carter as he had been prior to declaring his candidacy.[160] The apotheosis of Kennedy's campaign came some months after it was clear that it was over, in August 1980, at the Democratic National Convention in Madison Square Garden, New York. It was there that Kennedy delivered perhaps the most memorable speech of his career. Kennedy made only one fleeting reference to Carter, congratulating him but stopping short of a full endorsement. Instead, Kennedy expressed his confidence that "the Democratic party will reunite on the basis of Democratic principles, and that together we will march towards a Democratic victory in November." He ended with a stirring call to arms, telling the hall, "The work goes on, the cause endures, the hope still lives, and the dream shall never die."[161] It was a rousing and defiant distillation of Kennedy's liberalism that harkened back to his fiery speech in Memphis and became the symbol of a road not taken in Democratic politics.

At the same convention, Udall had the rather more delicate task of reunifying the fractious party. Though known as a Kennedy supporter, Udall had been chosen by Carter as the convention's keynote speaker, an indication of the esteem he was held in across the party. It marked, said one commentator, Udall's transition from "reformist Young Turk" to "paternal sage unifier."[162] He had served a similar role in 1976, though it was in the aftermath of his own presidential candidacy then, telling the convention delegates that year that he was "enlisting as a soldier" in Jimmy Carter's push for the White House.[163]

The speech was classic Udall, laden with jokes and tenuously relevant humorous anecdotes, from Al Smith sending a telegram to the Pope on election night in 1928 to the 1930s "tycoon" who would buy a newspaper each morning and throw it away when Franklin Roosevelt's obituary was not on the front page. He defended the record of the Carter administration and attacked the Republican Party, which he characterized as narrow, unrepresentative, and dominated by the "radical right." But the most significant theme of his speech was unity. He even suggested that the divisions within the party were indicative of its essential strength. "We do have fights and we kick and yell and scream and maybe even scratch a bit . . . but we fight because we're a diverse party and because we've always tried to listen up . . . to new ideas." Nonetheless, he urged the assembled Democrats to choose "the path of forgiveness and magnanimity" and to remember that "the real fight" would come in November. For those delegates who still resisted the spirit of unity, he recommended "Dr. Udall's Patented Unity Medicine. Take one tablespoon, close your eyes and repeat: *President Ronald Reagan.*"[164]

5

Marauders at the Gates
The Democratic Congress Defends
the New Deal State, 1980–1984

"You guys came in like a bunch of jerks, and I see you're going out the same way."[1] Tip O'Neill was furious. Though polls had yet to close on the West Coast, Jimmy Carter had already conceded defeat to his Republican opponent, Ronald Reagan. But if the White House was already lost, O'Neill hoped that the Democrats might yet hold the other House. Carter's early concession made it less likely that Democratic voters in western states would turn out to cast votes for down-ballot candidates and so imperiled O'Neill's majority. O'Neill's barked complaint that night, made over the phone to congressional liaison Frank Moore, represented the culmination of four years of deteriorating relations between Congress and the Carter administration.

It was perhaps understandable that Carter would not want to prolong the moment of his concession. He had just become the first incumbent Democratic president to lose his reelection bid since Grover Cleveland in 1888. In Alaska, Arizona, California, Connecticut, Colorado, Idaho, Iowa, Massachusetts, Montana, Nebraska, New Hampshire, Nevada, both Dakotas, Oregon, Utah, Wisconsin, and Wyoming, he received a smaller popular vote percentage than had McGovern eight years earlier. Carter also resembled McGovern in the coalition partners that he lost. As well as falling back among traditionally Republican-leaning groups, where he had once shown atypical strength (white evangelical Protestants, for instance), Carter lost crucial New Deal constituencies to Reagan.[2] He was deserted by Roman Catholics and southerners, maintained an anemic five-point edge in union households (49–44 percent), and managed only the plurality of Jewish voters (47 percent; McGovern had won 66 percent eight years earlier).[3]

Even beyond the presidential level, the 1980 elections represented the Democratic Party's worst defeat in a generation. Whereas in 1972 Democrats could draw comfort from their continued hold on Congress, there was no such consolation in 1980. "Quite a few savvy folks . . . seemed simply to assume that some earlier Act of Tenure authorized Democratic control of Congress in perpetuity," editorialized the *Washington Post*.[4] Such assumptions were swept aside with Reagan's election. The Republicans gained control of the Senate, picking up twelve seats, the largest swing in their favor in that chamber since 1946. In the process, Republican challengers unseated numerous high-profile Senate liberals, a series of decapitations that seemed to symbolize the American people's repudiation of Democratic liberalism. Among the casualties were Gaylord Nelson, Warren G. Magnuson, Frank Church, John Culver, and McGovern himself. "You cannot look at the defeat of such stalwart liberals," reflected the *Washington Post*'s David Broder, "and not get the [ideological] message."[5] The mood was despondent. An aide to Senator John Culver greeted one visitor by asking, "Can we offer you a cup of tea? A broken beer bottle?" Another senator had reportedly queried his staff, "How's a minority supposed to act?"[6]

The outlook was rosier in the House but only comparatively. Two months before the election, O'Neill was predicting a net loss of ten to eighteen seats and boasting of a $100 bet he had made with the House minority whip that no more than a dozen incumbent Democrats would be defeated.[7] In fact, the Republicans won thirty-four seats. That this was still far short of the sixty they needed to take control was some consolation. Nominally, the Democrats maintained a comfortable advantage (243 seats to the Republicans' 192) that was insulated by the bumper majorities they had consolidated in the previous decade. Nonetheless, the halving of an opposition party's considerable majority in one cycle was a significant achievement for the GOP. In only four instances did Democrats gain seats that had previously been in Republican hands. By contrast, thirty-seven elections saw the opposite outcome: Democratic seats won by Republican challengers. For the first time since Reconstruction, the GOP won the majority of representatives in the congressional delegation of a Deep South state: South Carolina. As in the Senate, several prominent Democrats were ejected, including Ways and Means chairman Al Ullman, DCCC chairman James Corman, and party whip John Brademas.[8]

Other indicators seemed to suggest that the Republicans would take the House soon enough and cement control of the national government. Demographic trends, for instance, were running in favor of the GOP. In the 1980 census, the states of the Republican-leaning Sunbelt gained fifteen Electoral College votes and congressional seats, at the expense of northeastern and midwestern states, which lost sixteen. The biggest loser was New York, which saw its share of the Electoral College and its congressional delegation decrease by five. Some commentators began to talk of a Republican "lock" on the presidency, with some twenty-nine states (that between them would award 295 Electoral College votes in 1984) having voted for the Republican candidate in six of the previous eight elections.[9] "Eisenhower took the West away from the Democrats, and Goldwater and Nixon took away the South," said Horace Busby, former aide to LBJ.[10] "It has come to pass that the electoral *base* of the [Democratic] party is now in the East," wrote Senator Pat Moynihan the following January.[11] If so, that base was shrinking.

Even more troubling than these looming structural disadvantages was the rusting of the once formidable party machinery. The results of the 1980 elections, wrote consultant Sheryl Losser to new DNC chairman Charles Manatt, revealed "the underlying problem of a deteriorating base of support at a grassroots level." In recent years, reported Losser, the party had been neglecting races at the precinct and ward level (state legislative, city council, and county commissioner seats).[12] Consequently, in 1980, Democratic Party officials had been comprehensively out-organized and out-fund-raised by their Republican counterparts. The RNC, nearly bankrupt in the mid-1970s, had, under chairman Bill Brock, devoted the years leading up to 1980 to rebuilding the national Republican Party from the ground up, seeking out new contributors to replenish the party coffers and focusing efforts to an unprecedented extent on local and state races.[13] Democrats had been caught on the hop by this unexpected organizational challenge. "The Democratic Party has been suffering from slow erosion," wrote Pamela Harriman. "An erosion without a rallying point to prevent it."[14]

All observers agreed that the elections of 1980 represented a watershed moment, and insofar as there was a consensus on the character of that watershed, it was that America was swinging away from Democratic liberalism toward Republican conservatism. "This could be the breakpoint election in bringing about a party realignment," boasted Bill Brock.[15] The pundit Hedrick Smith summarized his profession's conventional wisdom when he wrote that the new president, Ronald Reagan, had "won the opportunity . . . to lead a conservative reformation that seeks to redirect the role of government in American life and perhaps to reshape the national political landscape for the rest of the century."[16] David Broder was emphatic about Reagan's mandate. "You had to be very shrewd to discern the shape of the New Deal in the rhetoric of FDR's [1932] campaign," he wrote. "But you had to be dense to miss the message of Reagan's campaign: a flat-out repudiation of basic economic, diplomatic and social policies of the reigning Democratic liberalism."[17] Massachusetts senator and Watergate Baby Paul Tsongas offered an even blunter assessment: "Basically, the New Deal died yesterday."[18]

This interpretation was certainly shared by the incoming Reagan administration. In the days after his election, Godfrey Hodgson writes, Reagan acted "as though he did indeed carry the mandate of heaven."[19] On January 20, 1981, Democrats had to watch as a president many of them had dismissed as either an extremist or a clown pronounced the last rites over a central tenet of the liberal faith: activist government as an ameliorator of social and economic ills. From the podium on that bright winter day, Reagan attacked the hubris and profligacy of governmental power. "For decades we have piled deficit upon deficit, mortgaging our future and our children's future for the temporary convenience of the present. To continue this long trend is to guarantee tremendous social, cultural, political, and economic upheavals." In the inaugural address's best-known sentence, Reagan laid the calamities of the 1970s at the feet of government excess. "In this present crisis, government is not the solution to our problem; government is the problem."[20]

More circumspect observers declined to be swept along in the heady—and often self-serving—talk of revolution. They pointed to the fact that Reagan had won a bare majority of the popular vote (50.8 percent). His nearly ten-point margin over Carter was due in large part to the third-party candidacy of John Anderson, a moderate Republican congressman from Illinois who had remade himself as the option for liberal voters disillusioned with Carter. The New Republic had endorsed Anderson for president, and many prominent liberals lent him their support.[21] The presidential election could thus be construed as an anti-Carter, rather than a pro-Reagan, landslide. This was the conclusion of Democratic pollster Peter Hart. The election, according to his postmortem report, was not a "strictly ideological" win for Reagan. "Voters perceived that the status quo—on economics, defence, and foreign policy—was failing and the non-incumbents were the beneficiaries of this dissatisfaction."[22] Morton Kondracke crystallized liberal hopes when he wrote that "political dominance" was "still up for grabs." "The Republicans certainly have a great opportunity now to become the country's dominant party. But the GOP has had the opportunity before and has blown it."[23]

If the Democrats were to ensure that the Republican Party blew that second opportunity, they would need a platform. As Reagan-dominated Washington was to be the front line of the conservative legislative revolution, Congress, one chamber of which was still in grateful Democratic hands, presented the likeliest base from which to coordinate the resistance. This had certainly been the conclusion of the *New Republic* when it had endorsed "Democrats for Congress" the previous October. Declining to endorse Carter, whom it dismissed as "a tinkerer and a muddler, an ideological wanderer," the editorial concluded that for the Democratic Party to rebuild, "it must retain a strong congressional base, a locus of power and also of debate."[24] Badly battered by recent events, that base was still standing—just about. The *Washington Post* noted that "the House will become the national Democratic Party to the extent that it exists as a combat force."[25] For some liberals, this outcome was even preferable to a continuation of the status quo. Before the election, Arthur Schlesinger had mused in his diary, "Reagan, contained by a Democratic Congress, would be no worse than Carter compromising and confusing a Democratic Congress."[26]

After a faltering start, the Democratic Party would prove surprisingly adept at using Congress to contain the Reagan administration during the early 1980s. Under Speaker Tip O'Neill, the House in particular was able to resist successfully the Reaganites' drive to reduce the scope of the welfare state dramatically. This counteroffensive would lead to an impressive Democratic recovery in the midterm elections of 1982 that seemed, for a time, to imperil Reagan's reelection prospects.

O'Neill had never wanted to be the public face of his party. For most of his career, his highest ambition had been to become Speaker and serve alongside a Democratic president as a legislative mechanic. However, he was well-matched to the moment. A tactician rather than a strategist, he was a good leader for a liberal rearguard action against the Reagan Revolution. This would climax in the Democratic Congress's successful defense of Social Security against an ambitious Reagan-backed reform package, a confrontation in which New York senator Pat Moynihan would play a major role. Despite initial factional squabbling, the Reagan presidency would ultimately have a unifying effect on the congressional Democratic Party. Confrontations like that over Social Security reminded Democrats of what they stood against. The question of what they stood *for* was a trickier one.

Divided and Punch-Drunk

Congress at the beginning of the 1980s was a very different beast to that of even a decade earlier. The reforms of the 1970s had, paradoxically, diffused and centralized power. The vesting of power in the party caucuses, particularly in the House, had strengthened the prerogatives of the congressional leadership at the expense of committee chairs. At the same time, the reforms had created an expanding constellation of committees and subcommittees, each laying claim to fragmenting areas of policy jurisdiction. By 1984, there were some 326 committee or subcommittee chairmanships available to members. That year, the *Atlantic Monthly* calculated that, allowing for those who occupied more than one chair, 202 of the 535 members of Congress (or 38 percent) were "in charge of something."[27] This had been accompanied by a dramatic expansion of resources and staff members for both individual representatives and committee members. It was estimated that some 1,000 Democrats, belonging to personal congressional and committee staffs, lost their jobs as a result of the 1980 elections.[28] The new positions and resources had been enthusiastically seized upon by the ambitious Watergate Babies, and their successor classes, as a means of cultivating their own profiles and policy concerns. "You begin to see Tim Wirth taking on the telecommunications industry," reflected Pennsylvania's Bob Edgar in 1984. "You see Jim Florio [of New Jersey] making an imprint on superfund legislation. Henry Waxman plays a role on health policy and clean air. We've each taken on a specialty area."[29]

Furthermore, Congress existed in a transformed media environment. Legislators found themselves under greater scrutiny, and with more avenues for self-promotion, than ever before. In 1964, there were 1,649 journalists accredited to cover Congress. By December 1984 that figure had more than doubled, to 3,748—approximately seven journalists for each congressperson.[30] The Cable-Satellite Public Affairs Network (C-SPAN), a nonprofit cable network broadcasting "gavel-to-gavel" coverage of proceedings in the House, had launched in 1979. The Senate followed suit in 1986 and a second channel, C-SPAN2, was born. C-SPAN was a modest operation to begin with;

initially its programming alternated with a wrestling channel and it hoped
to reach some five million homes. The House also maintained considerable
control over the broadcasts. It could ensure that the unflattering shots of, for
instance, members dozing at their desks never made it to air. Nonetheless,
it represented a watershed in the American public's relationship with their
legislature.[31]

If the House was to become the vanguard of the Democratic resistance,
then the most obvious leader was the senior official of that body: Speaker
Tip O'Neill. Indeed, days after the election, aide Burt Hoffman had written to
O'Neill, "Until such time as we nominate a new presidential candidate, you
are the leader of the Democratic Party, as well as the highest public official
of that party." Hoffman advised the Speaker to take "a major role in rebuilding party strength," working with the Campaign Committee and the DNC
to devise a legislative program.[32] The quintessential Boston ward heeler, an
unabashed relic of New Deal machine politics, O'Neill was an improbable
leader for the new Democratic Party. Since his election as Speaker in 1976,
his political fortunes had fluctuated, often wildly. He had proven himself a
gifted legislative tactician in shepherding Carter's agenda through Congress.
One 1978 profile dubbed him "the least likely cult hero of Carter-era Washington" enjoying "a protective press, an image of integrity and an awesome
reputation for competence."[33] He had better relations with younger members
than many others in the congressional leadership, having come out early as
an opponent of the Vietnam War. Nonetheless, he was also known to greet
deputations of Watergate Babies entering his office with the question, "What
do you sons-of-bitches want now?"[34]

However, O'Neill had been tainted by a succession of grubby scandals,
most notably "Koreagate" (a byzantine affair involving South Korean officials
allegedly seeking to influence Democratic politicians through businessman
Tongsun Park; O'Neill was eventually exonerated of corruption charges).
Concerns also mounted over his image as the representative of an earlier,
tainted era. Some members worried that he was too attractive a punching bag
for Republicans. He had been the principal target of a $5 million ad campaign
mounted by the RNC in 1980. One ad had featured an obvious O'Neill look-
alike driving a black Lincoln along a highway, past several conveniently sited
gas stations, cheerfully dismissing his passenger's warnings about the low fuel
gauge. The ad concluded with the car sputtering to a halt while the O'Neill
character exclaimed, "Hey, we're out of gas!"[35] O'Neill was, in the words of

Republican congressman John LeBoutillier of New York, "big, fat and out of control—just like the federal government."[36] Nonetheless, O'Neill was a prodigiously talented legislative tactician, and, in defiance of low expectations, he would become perhaps Reagan's most formidable Democratic adversary.

Alongside disquiet about his abilities, O'Neill had to contend with an increasingly disgruntled conservative faction in his caucus. A Conservative Democratic Forum was established within the House in early 1981 and boasted some thirty-four members by the end of November. The group's leader, Rep. Charles W. Stenholm of Texas, announced that conservatives had been "ignored for too long" and that they intended "to moderate the liberal leanings of the House leadership."[37] These representatives, mostly drawn from the West and the South (the latter came to be known as the "boll weevils," after the crop-destroying pest, a nickname that had intermittently been applied to conservative southern Democrats since the New Deal), would habitually turn against their party leadership over the next few years, often giving Reagan a "philosophical majority" in the lower house. Indeed, in March 1981, a delegation of conservative Democrats, led by Congressman Stenholm, requested an additional $11.2 billion in spending cuts from the administration at a breakfast meeting with the president. In response, a delighted Reagan quipped, "I might consider becoming a Democrat again."[38]

With the Reagan administration exultant, with the congressional Democratic Party in disarray, and with the conventional wisdom proclaiming the arrival of a conservative revolution, the question had to be asked: What was the place of the Democrats in Reagan's America? What should the Democratic Party stand for in the 1980s? Asked that question by a reporter for *U.S. News & World Report*, the Iowa state party chairman replied, "I imagine most Democrats mumble to themselves when you ask that."[39] Should the party accept repudiation and prepare to adapt to a post-Reagan policy context, much as the Republicans had to adapt to the New Deal, and even to the Great Society? Or should it engage in a policy of scorched-earth resistance to the new president—obstruct, harass, and sabotage—in an effort to rescue a liberal order that had seemingly failed to address the problems of the 1970s?

Most Democrats, O'Neill principal among them, agreed that Reagan should be given an opportunity to test his policy agenda. Even if one believed that the Republicans had not won an ideological mandate, there was little doubt that the Democrats had lost one. "The American people wanted to give Reagan a chance . . . and they had voted for a change," recalled the

Speaker's aide Kirk O'Donnell. "There had been a strong repudiation of Democratic leadership."[40] Indeed, some were relieved that responsibility had devolved away from them for a spell. "I feel psychologically lighter than I have in years," said Representative Gillis Long of Louisiana.[41] The saber-rattling of the conservatives in their own caucus was also a powerful inducement to cooperate with the administration, at least temporarily. When the political context made resistance a more viable strategy, the Democrats rediscovered a degree of cohesion and common identity that they had rarely displayed in the 1970s, when many still assumed that they belonged to the nation's majority party. First, though, came a period of defeat and disorientation.

The Reagan administration seized the initiative with a speed and an adroitness that stunned its political opponents and the Washington press corps. In the previous decade, several scholars, faced with the Nixon-Ford-Carter trifecta, had mused that perhaps the presidency itself was somehow constitutionally hardwired to fail.[42] Reagan's first months in office were a decisive rejoinder to such thinking. Unlike Carter, whose administration had devoted itself to a plethora of worthy legislation, the Reagan administration made the economy its sole focus, delivering a budget to Congress in record time. Reagan's goal was twofold: to reduce both the tax burden and federal government spending. The American taxpayer, he had declared in 1973, had "become the pawn in a deadly game of government monopoly whose only purpose is to serve the confiscatory appetites of runaway government spending." That monopoly was maintained by the selfishness and greed of legislators, bureaucrats, and special-interest groups. Speed, the White House reasoned, was essential for preventing those interests from mobilizing against the Reagan agenda.[43]

In 1980, the political scientists Joseph White and Aaron Wildavsky wrote that Americans were living "in the era of the budget. The budget has been to our era what civil rights, communism, the depression, industrialization, and slavery were at other times."[44] In the Reagan years, the budget process would become an arena in which conservatism and liberalism contested the future of the nation. The initial skirmishes were not promising for the Democrats. On issues of taxing and spending, Reagan seemed to have the wind at his back.[45] On February 18, 1981, Reagan used a nationally televised address to unveil his economic program, a mixture of tax and spending cuts aimed at turning the $55 billion budget deficit into a surplus by 1984.[46] The first component of that program, tax reduction, proved comparatively straightforward to achieve.

The unsurprisingly popular Economic Recovery Tax Act (ERTA), a universal reduction in marginal income tax rates, was signed into law in August 1981. With the assistance of the "boll weevil" Democrats, the White House was able to engineer the passage of the ERTA. The pernicious "bracket creep" created by inflation had been squeezing the American taxpayer for much of the 1970s and some form of relief was long overdue. The tax cut's brother, the Omnibus Budget Reconciliation Act, had a stormier passage through Congress. Nonetheless, the bill passed, reducing funding to more than two hundred domestic programs that amounted to $35 billion in spending cuts, with only the defense budget explicitly protected.[47] Before long, many congressional Democrats were complaining at the lack of a coordinated response to Reagan's juggernaut. "It's as if Reagan has slipped tranquilizers into the water," despaired one.[48]

Few emerged from that first budget scrap with a worse reputation than O'Neill. The Speaker had unwisely opted to head out on a junket to the South Seas while the president had rounded up votes.[49] O'Neill was, Wisconsin Democrat Les Aspin wrote to his constituents, "reeling on the ropes . . . he's not part of what is happening, and has no idea of where to go."[50] One Melville-inspired cartoon portrayed O'Neill as a fed-up "great white whale" speared by the mariners on the good ship "Reagan Budget."[51] By March, there was press speculation that O'Neill might not stand for reelection in 1982.[52] Embattled as he was, the Speaker remained confident that the budget cutbacks would prove the Reagan Revolution's undoing. "Wait till Middle America realizes what's happened with these budget cuts," O'Neill told *Time*. "Am I going to get some Republican scalps down the road? You bet I am."[53]

The Reagan economic program—a mix of supply-side tax cuts, deregulation, and retrenchment of social programs—was supposed to initiate a resurgence of growth within the US economy. In fact, the first years of Reagan's presidency were marred by the deepest and sharpest recession since the 1930s. The unemployment rate reached 10.8 percent at the nadir and the recession "destroyed the harvest of new revenues that economic growth was supposed to deliver with the tax cut fertilizer."[54] As tax revenues collapsed, the budget deficit exploded. The administration had initially projected a deficit of $45 billion for fiscal year 1982. In fact, by fiscal year 1984, when the administration had pledged to deliver a balanced budget, the deficit would reach $127.9 billion.[55] The recession itself was less Reagan's fault than it was the Federal Reserve's, whose chairman, Paul Volcker, was determined to administer a dose of "monetary castor oil" to finally douse the inflation that had bedeviled the American economy for a decade. Nonetheless, it badly damaged the Reagan White House's reputation for near-supernatural political skill, and the president's personal ratings went into free fall.

The worsening economic climate, and the concomitant souring of the public mood, afforded congressional Democrats their first real opportunity to frustrate the Republican agenda. "The struggle has entered a new and confusing phase," wrote pollster Pat Caddell. "The moment is laden with grand opportunities for the Democrats if they are capable of seizing the initiative."[56] The New Deal might have expired, but liberals could at least prevent conservative revolutionaries from dismantling the welfare state that stood as its monument. There were few liberals better able to lead such a charge than Speaker O'Neill. Though arguably unsuited for the intellectual thrust-and-parry work required to redefine the Democratic agenda, he was more than qualified to fill the role of, as his biographer puts it, "a Travis for their Alamo, a Kutuzov to lure Napoléon into a Russian winter, a Horatius at the bridge."[57]

O'Neill's staff had been planning a public relations counteroffensive since the Speaker's flat-footed response to Reagan's first budget. Advisor and former television producer Jerry Colbert urged O'Neill to use a TV-centric strategy to push back against Reagan. "Television is being used as the main battleground for the Administration in its attempt to convert the American people to his Republican philosophy," Colbert told O'Neill. The Democratic Congress's response was woeful by contrast, an especially dangerous situation when one reflected that Americans now received some 70 percent of their news from television.[58] In June 1981, O'Neill made his first appearance on a network interview show in three years as a guest on ABC's *Issues and Answers*. He let Reagan have it with both barrels. The president, he declared, had "no concern, no regard, no care for the little man of America. . . . Because of his lifestyle, he never meets those people." While denying that he thought the president personally "callous" ("I've never met a finer fellow"), O'Neill argued that he had surrounded himself with "very, very selfish people . . . those who have made it along the line and forgotten from where they've come."[59] The image of Reagan as a complacent elitist cosseted with his clueless rich friends was one to which O'Neill would return frequently, to the president's mounting frustration.

Like Reagan's, O'Neill's political principles were clear and straightforward, underpinned by an unshakeable faith in the ameliorative powers of government. This made him a powerful media performer. O'Neill's staff also fashioned a template for this new media management strategy: identify the "real world" impact of any government cuts and fashion it into a cudgel to beat the administration. A little over six months after Reagan's inauguration, they were strategizing to use the House committee system to undermine Republican ambitions. "Committees must travel out of Washington to listen to real people with real concerns," Kirk O'Donnell wrote to O'Neill. "For example we cannot assume the cuts will be felt. . . . We must identify where they are going to occur and who is going to be hurt. In short the House, through its Committees and hearings, must inform Americans about what is happening. . . . With control of the House the Administration's failures and misguided policies can be exposed in a forum we control and they have no choice but to respond to."[60] Another nautically themed cartoon, published in the conservative *Chicago Tribune*, depicted O'Neill as a grimly determined saboteur in a small, wooden rowing boat dropping sea mines in the path of Reagan's warship, the "U.S.S. Mandate."[61] But the biggest sea mine that the Reagan administration collided with during Reagan's first term was one that they had dropped into the water themselves: the attempted reform of Social Security. This assault on the linchpin of the New Deal welfare state would reassemble the fractious congressional Democratic Party and deliver them a much-needed policy and public relations win.

On the Barricades: Social Security Reform

In March 1981, with Reagan in full pomp and the Democrats in disarray, Senator Daniel Patrick Moynihan gave one of the keynote speeches to the first Gridiron Club dinner of the new administration. A lighthearted, white-tie affair held at the Capital Hilton in Washington, DC, the dinner traditionally featured a bipartisan pair of speakers delivering a humorous talk each, alongside songs and sketches. It was, wrote one journalist, "a cozy evening of high-powered, off-the-record high jinks" for Washington's political establishment.[62] That year, Moynihan was the Democratic speaker, with newly appointed OMB director David Stockman representing the GOP. Moynihan began by joking that Reagan was a mole planted to destroy the Republican Party from within: "Mr. President, you've been perfect, and by the time *you're through*, we Democrats will be all set for yet another half century." But his speech ended on a more serious note, with a full-throated defense of the "great idea" at the heart of the Democratic tradition: "that an elected government can be the instrument of the common purpose of a free people; that government can embrace great causes; and do great things." It was a deliberate counterpoint to Reagan's inaugural address. Moynihan cast himself and his fellow Democrats as guardians of a faith whose day would come again. "We *believe* in American government and we fully expect that those who now denigrate it, and even despise it, will sooner or later find themselves turning to it in necessity, even desperation. When they do, they will find the Democratic party on hand to help."[63]

Few ordinary Americans may have taken note of the remarks of one middle-aged senator at a backslapping Washington gala. Nevertheless, it was rare to find a high-profile liberal in those months making such a forthright defense of government. Unsurprisingly, Moynihan thought highly of the speech. "Somewhere in those last few paragraphs," he wrote to journalist Theodore White, "the audience seemed to sense that the Democrats still had something to say."[64] With this speech, Moynihan arguably made the decisive break with the neoconservative movement with which he had been associated since the previous decade.[65] Reagan's confrontational antigovernment populism now defined Washington politics, and Moynihan was coming down on the opposing side to many old allies. Within a matter of months, Republicans would discover the limits of that antigovernment credo and Democrats would find an issue that gave their faltering coalition new impetus.

It was fitting that Moynihan's fellow speaker at that Gridiron dinner was David Stockman, perhaps the most impassioned revolutionary in Reagan's cadre. Born into a conservative Republican farm family in central Texas, Stockman had drifted into the New Left while at Michigan State University, becoming "a full-fledged (if half-baked) neo-Marxist." In 1968, he embarked on both graduate studies at Harvard Divinity School and his long trek from New Left radical to supply-side crusader. Stockman and Moynihan had a longstanding friendship. As an ambitious student, Stockman had developed a fascination with Moynihan, who was then dividing his time between Cambridge and the Nixon White House. Hoping to advance his political ambitions by proximity to a "Washington-connected rabbi," Stockman obtained a place as the Moynihans' live-in babysitter. His association with Moynihan led to a position on the staff of liberal Republican John Anderson. From there,

Stockman moved deeper into Republican politics. In 1976, he was elected as the Republican congressman from Michigan's fourth district and would remain there until poached by the Reagan campaign.[66]

Stockman's legislative experiences transformed his politics. By the end of the 1970s, Stockman had concluded that "the politicians were wrecking American capitalism. They were turning democratic government into a lavish giveaway auction. They were saddling workers and entrepreneurs with punitive taxation and demoralizing and wasteful regulation."[67] In 1980, he was enlisted by Reagan campaign officials to act as a debate rehearsal stand-in for third-party candidate John Anderson, Stockman's former boss. Impressed by his talent and ideological commitment, Reagan offered him a cabinet-level post after the election. Thus, at age thirty-four, Stockman found himself director of the Office of Management and Budget, the youngest person ever to hold that post. Youthful, wholesome, and self-confident, Stockman made an immediate impression with the political media. Newspaper profiles soon began to appear, and Stockman was the first administration official featured on the cover of *Newsweek.*[68]

Few could match Stockman for tax-cutting or state-slashing zeal. During the transition, he recommended that Reagan declare an economic state of emergency and push through a package of measures akin to the reforms of FDR's Hundred Days. He warned the president that the nation would face an "economic Dunkirk" without swift and decisive action. Part of the sweeping package of cuts he recommended included $260 billion to be taken from Social Security.[69] In May, the administration sent proposals to Congress to sharply reduce Social Security benefits for those who retired before age sixty-five.

From the leadership down, the congressional Democrats were energized by these proposals. Senate Minority Leader Robert Byrd denounced them as "precipitous, harsh and very unfair." O'Neill said the proposed reforms were "despicable" and a "breach of faith" given Reagan's campaign promises. It was, he added, "a rotten thing to do." Asked whether the proposals would command significant support in Congress, O'Neill replied that he doubted many members were "stone-hearted enough" to vote for them.[70] Moynihan's position as ranking Democratic member on the Finance Committee's Social Security subcommittee made this his opportunity. Moynihan had shared with many of his colleagues the belief that Reagan should be given space to govern. He was one of a clutch of Senate Democrats who had voted for the president's tax cut. Social Security was different. He claimed later that Social Security represented the Democratic Party's "best issue with the new president. . . . This was my responsibility and our moment." At a press conference in Rochester, New York, Moynihan condemned the proposed reforms as "a breach of contract, startling in magnitude as well as content." With his chivvying, the Republican-dominated Senate voted to reject the proposals in their entirety, 96–0. The House rejected the proposals by the equally overwhelming margin of 405–13.[71] Even congressional Republicans recognized the inherent danger in a drastic restructuring of a popular entitlement program.

While Democrats opposed Reagan's proposed cuts to Social Security benefits, they did belong to a consensus that acknowledged that some reform was vital. The stagflationary economy of the 1970s had exacerbated a terrible convergence of crises for Social Security. Obstinately high unemployment meant that able would-be workers were not contributing, while the pool of scheduled retirees continued to expand, placing more pressure on the program. Congress had worsened the situation by enacting popular, but fiscally unsustainable, increases to the program's benefits. After automatic cost-of-living adjustments (COLAs) were instituted in 1975, for instance, runaway inflation caused benefit payments to grow precipitously. The program began to record its first deficits since its creation.[72] A 1980 report by the trustees warned that without congressional intervention, the Social Security trust fund would be insolvent by early 1982 at the latest.[73]

Since its enactment, Social Security had been woven into the national fabric. Even as other components of the New Deal settlement came in for increased criticism, Social Security remained "the Democrats' ace in the hole at election time."[74] In some conservative quarters, skepticism about the program had grown since 1970. However, such opposition remained outside mainstream political discourse, and those politicians who aspired to a national stage embraced the program. During the 1980 campaign, Reagan had promised to "support and defend" Social Security. The system would be "strong and reliable and protected under a Reagan Administration."[75] Nonetheless, as early as 1964, Reagan had expressed his opposition to "forcing all citizens, regardless of need, into a compulsory government program" and suggested introducing "voluntary features" for those that sought to opt out.[76] It was therefore hardly surprising that in the early years of the Reagan administration Social Security emerged as "a leading fault line of partisan politics" in a way it had not been since its creation.[77]

In advancing a controversial reform so early, the Reagan White House had hoped to make the most of its political capital. However, it had over-reached badly, and the stumble played into Democratic hands. The hasty and far-reaching nature of the reforms and the lack of initial congressional consultation doomed the proposals. Many Republicans resented the fact that the administration had dropped the putative benefit reductions upon them without warning. Stockman, who had been principally responsible for devising the reforms, claimed later that he had "screwed up."[78] Democrats were gifted a popular issue that they exploited ruthlessly. Liberals, Moynihan among them, contended that the program's funding crisis was a temporary aberration brought about by the exigencies of the moment. They pointed to predictions that Social Security was expected to go into surplus around 1990 to prove that radical reform was unnecessary.[79]

Opposition came from without Congress as well as from within. Like all distributional government programs, Social Security had developed its own special-interest faction, dubbed the "gray lobby." It comprised several dozen organizations, among them the National Council on the Aging, the American Association of Retired Persons, and the National Black Caucus on Aging. Moreover, older citizens had higher political participation rates than did other demographic segments. They voted and petitioned their representatives. Older voters were also concentrated in Sunbelt states, giving them considerable leverage over significant portions of the GOP.

The latter years of the Carter administration had seen the formation of Save Our Security (SOS), in response to an earlier push for reform. Led by Wilbur Cohen, a civil servant nicknamed "Mr. Social Security" who had been involved in the program since its creation, the coalition drew on the support of some 115 groups. Alongside those mentioned above, backers included AFL-CIO president Lane Kirkland, UAW president Douglas Fraser, social welfare expert Elizabeth Wickenden, retired congressman Wilbur Mills, the National Conference of Catholic Charities, and Disabled American Veterans. In early 1981, members of the dormant coalition began flexing their muscles again.[80] When the proposed cuts were revealed, SOS convened an emergency meeting to plan a major lobbying campaign. Cohen denounced the proposals as "a calamity, a tragedy and a catastrophe."[81]

From his perch on the Social Security subcommittee, Moynihan was particularly zealous in pushing back against the White House. In early July, when hearings began, Moynihan went on the attack again. He condemned the administration's tactics as "political terrorism," arguing that the true purpose was to balance the budget by 1984, not to safeguard the program.[82] Despite initial setbacks, Reagan did not abandon the issue. The president intended to defend his plans in a nationally televised speech scheduled for July 27, 1981, and Moynihan was chosen to deliver the official response. It was a potent symbol of his having been welcomed back into the Democratic fold. Ultimately, Reagan yielded to appeals from the harried Republican congressional leaders and avoided the issue in the speech, in favor of the tax cut package then making its way through Congress.[83]

Under a fierce onslaught from Democrats, Republicans, and an assortment of extra congressional advocacy groups, the White House sought a way out of the melee. In an effort to calm the situation, on December 16, Reagan created a presidential commission.[84] The National Commission on Social Security Reform was chaired by economist Alan Greenspan—who had been chairman of Gerald Ford's Council of Economic Advisors—and its membership was chosen by the president and the congressional leadership of both parties. Moynihan was one of the commissioners, serving alongside Senator Robert Dole, chairman of the Finance Committee, Congressman Claude Pepper, chair of the House Select Committee on Aging and a leading spokesman for the elderly, and Robert Ball, the former commissioner of Social Security who had been helping to husband the program since the 1930s.[85] Due to report in December 1982, the commission offered if nothing else the president and Republicans a face-saving way to avoid answering questions on the administration's plans for Social Security until after the midterm congressional elections.

Though the Democrats could be justly proud of a successful counteroffensive, the problem of Social Security's solvency remained pressing. The potential bankruptcy of the program took on greater urgency as the scale of the federal budget deficit became apparent. Despite the rosy projections of Stockman's OMB, the 1981 tax cut did not yield a booming economy and endless budget surpluses. In fact, 1982–1983 saw the worst recession since the 1930s and ballooning deficits.[86] Moynihan's principal concern was the impact that the deficits would have on the options available to policy-makers. "The politics of the next decade," Moynihan wrote in a 1981 newsletter, "risk becoming an endless, joyless, pointless squabble about how big the budget cuts must be in order that the budget not be even bigger."[87]

Moynihan blasted the Reagan administration for failing to grapple with the deficit, accusing the president of neglecting the duties of his office: "He wanted the job, and he ought to do the hard part as well as the fun part."[88] He became increasingly convinced that this fiscal incontinence had been a calculated strategy on the part of the supply-siders and in particular of his old protégé, Stockman. These deficits had been "purposeful" and the result of "a hidden agenda" to create a fiscal crisis that would force the retrenchment of social spending.[89] This suspicion was confirmed by an infamous profile of Stockman published in the *Atlantic Monthly* in December 1981, in which, among other incendiary quotations, he had described the ERTA as "a Trojan horse."[90]

Amid these battles, newspapers began to describe Moynihan as a "liberal" again, or sometimes as a "neo-liberal," much to his delight. He forwarded one clipping from the *New York Times* to its publisher and his friend, Arthur Sulzberger, exulting, "A Neo-Conservative no more! Never underestimate the power of the Reagan administration!"[91] In October 1981, the senator from New York was featured on the cover of the *New Republic*, smiling benignly under the headline "Pat Moynihan, Neo-Liberal."[92]

Some who had once counted Moynihan as an ally were disappointed. The *National Review*, which had named Moynihan "Man of the Year" in 1975, declared him "a national disaster" in 1983. "Since his election to the Senate," huffed its editorial, "Mr. Moynihan would be a suitable subject for a series of engravings by William Hogarth: 'The Decline of a Politician.'"[93] Checker Finn concluded that Moynihan had "gradually moved leftward" on several issues in preparation for his 1982 reelection bid, reinforced by the "shrewd counsel" of his aide Tim Russert. Moreover, the recalibration "suited his countercyclical tendencies, given that Reaganism had replaced Carterism as Washington's conventional wisdom."[94] Stockman was inclined to make a similar interpretation, telling presidential aide Dick Darman, "Moynihan's got a problem. He went off and got himself elected Senator from New York. He just can't get away with holding a sound view of economic policy. New York *is* the welfare state."[95] Undoubtedly, Moynihan had undergone a shift of sorts. However, it would be too crude to dismiss this as solely the product of calculation or contrarianism. Arguably, Moynihan's shift was one of emphasis rather than essence. He had always protested to doubters, with varying degrees of success, that he was a liberal Democrat, and the polarized context of the early 1980s had sharpened his political identity.

Moynihan's growing reputation as one of Reagan's most effective liberal critics led to his being targeted for defeat by the same conservative advocacy groups that had enjoyed such success toppling liberal senators in 1980. The National Conservative Political Action Committee (NCPAC) launched a campaign of radio advertisements denouncing Moynihan as "the most liberal United States Senator." A local branch of NCPAC, New York State Taxpayers Fed Up with Daniel Moynihan, sprang into life. NCPAC had targeted Democratic senators in 1980—including McGovern, Church, and Bayh—and Moynihan joined its list of senators to be unseated in 1982.[96] For his part, Moynihan hoped to use his reelection campaign to demonstrate that the New Right could be stopped electorally, just as it had been obstructed in Congress. He held groups such as NCPAC in particular contempt. "They're the bane of a good strong party-system," he had told NBC, when interviewed soon after the 1980 election. "You just have to fight them off, that's all. . . . You beat 'em." But, prompted the interviewer, he conceded that they had been winning. "Wait'll they get to New York," replied the senator with a wink.[97]

His Republican opponent was Florence M. Sullivan, a state assemblywoman from the Bay Ridge area of Brooklyn with little statewide profile. Sullivan was a Roman Catholic widow with a law degree from St. John's University, which she had earned as a mature student. She had come to politics late, winning her assembly seat in 1978 after friends commended her to a local Republican leader.[98] Sullivan had run an underdog campaign in the primary, with a budget of around $42,000, significantly less than both of her better-financed opponents. Nonetheless, she carved out a clear niche for herself as the most conservative candidate. She positioned herself alongside Reagan—a bold move considering the president's sinking popularity—and described her own candidacy as the "final conflict between what's left of the old Rockefeller-Javits segment of the G.O.P. and the new team of Reaganites." Sullivan won the endorsements of the Conservative and Right to Life Parties months before the primary and so was able to style herself not only as the most conservative but also as the "unity" candidate. The strategy paid handsome dividends, and on primary day, Sullivan took 42 percent of the vote to the 29 percent apiece taken by her opponents.[99]

With the Greenspan commission scheduled to report on December 31, the specter of Social Security reform loomed over the election. At a *Times-*

organized candidate debate, Sullivan hailed Reagan's "courageous" reform efforts and condemned Moynihan for "trying to scare the life out of senior citizens." "There should be actuarial policies followed that have not been followed," she added, "that have succeeded in insurance business." Leaning forward and frowning over the top of his reading glasses, Moynihan replied, "What are you talking about? . . . This is not the Prudential Life Insurance Company. This is the United States Government."[100] A few weeks later, the Moynihan campaign obtained several "ballot cards" circulated with Republican fund-raising letters that invited contributors to indicate what reforms to Social Security that they would favor; one of the possible reforms was to transform it into a "voluntary" program. Moynihan denounced the suggestion as "an outrage" and, despite protestations from the RCCC that the letter did not represent settled policy, asserted that it reflected the views of "a surprising number of people in the party."[101]

When Election Day came, with the Reagan administration fighting to shed the blame for supposedly causing the worst downturn since the Depression, NCPAC found itself unable to replicate the successes of 1980. Not one of the senators it had targeted was defeated in 1982. Of the Democratic incumbents targeted, only one failed to win by more than 60 percent of the vote in the general election. Moynihan defeated Sullivan by a thumping one million vote margin, the biggest majority ever recorded in a New York Senate race. "I'm one of the five millionaires of the Senate," he boasted in his victory speech.[102] Returned to the Senate, Moynihan was facing the prospect of a final showdown over Social Security.

For most of 1982, the Greenspan commission had deadlocked, "too riven by partisan and ideological differences to produce a plan."[103] To Moynihan's dismay, in the vacuum created by inaction, even some Democrats began to embrace radical reforms to the program. At a "working" Washington breakfast with a group of political journalists in August 1982, aspiring presidential candidate John Glenn idly floated the idea that consideration be given to a voluntary "quasi-private" alternative to Social Security for younger Americans.[104] "When a candidate seeking the Democratic nomination for President," Moynihan wrote despondently to Lane Kirkland, "proposes that Social Security be made voluntary (Ronald Reagan circa 1960), you can be sure we're losing the argument."[105]

By the end of the year, it seemed plausible that the Greenspan commission would simply fizzle out. "I'm afraid our bipartisan commission has failed us," Reagan noted gloomily in his diary.[106] Badly burned by the poor Republican showing in the midterms and fearing a debacle if the commission failed to produce something workable, the White House began liaising with Moynihan and Robert Ball. Now anointed as the administration's Democratic conduit to Congress, Moynihan enlisted Finance Committee chairman Robert Dole on the Senate floor. With Republican congressman Barber Conable of New York, these four formed a micro-commission that began meeting secretly with White House representatives, among them Stockman. Moving swiftly, the micro-commission accepted the liberal Democratic interpretation of the crisis and concentrated on formulating a stopgap measure that would keep Social Security solvent until 1990, "when relief would come from demography." The commission deadline was extended to January 20 and a hastily designed reform package was presented to Congress. Among other provisions, the commission recommended delaying several COLAs and moving up certain tax increases, with an additional amount being made up by unprecedented new taxes on the benefits of high-income earners.[107]

In April 1983, the Greenspan commission's reform proposals were finally passed by Congress, which also shocked many observers by passing later amendments to raise the retirement age to sixty-seven to tackle the program's longer term deficit. The general response to the commission's recommendations was positive. The *Washington Post* editorialized that the reforms were "as close to absolute fairness as any Social Security revision can ever be."[108] Moynihan claimed to see a different, deeper moral. The real lesson of the compromise, he argued, went beyond a patch-up of a threatened welfare program. It was a rebuke to the idea "that there are fundamental issues that our system cannot resolve. . . . There is a center in American politics. It can govern."[109]

Moynihan had been deeply troubled by what he perceived as the sclerosis afflicting the workings of American government. This was partly due to the limiting of policy options brought about by recession and budget deficits, but it was also due to the unintended consequences of attempts to expand the capacities of the legislative and executive branches. "The Congress is in awful shape," Moynihan had written to James Reston in late 1982. "Each new increment of staff raises the level of entropy, as they say in thermodynamics. The White House is worse. The President spends his time managing his staff, which spends its time trying to manage him, and you have the institutional equivalent of the dog chasing its tail."[110] For Moynihan, this reform demonstrated that, albeit imperfectly, the system could be made to work. Reform had been enacted and a welfare service that millions of Americans relied upon had been secured for decades. This was a somewhat optimistic gloss on the result. In fact, in an important sense, the system had *failed* to work. A crisis had been resolved only by the creation of an ad hoc presidential commission that had very nearly produced no solution. Nonetheless, if the episode underscored Congress's remarkable facility for obstructing action, this was at least an occasion when that worked in favor of the Democrats.

David Stockman was in no doubt as to the significance of the outcome. "The centrepiece of the American welfare state had now been overwhelmingly ratified and affirmed in the white heat of political confrontation," he wrote in his memoirs.[111] Surveying the aftermath, Stockman placed much of the blame with the president. "The Reagan Revolution," as he understood it, "required a frontal assault on the American welfare state. . . . Forty years' worth of promises, subventions, entitlements, and safety nets issued by the federal government to every component and stratum of American society would have to be scrapped or drastically modified." It needed "an iron chancellor" and Reagan "wasn't that by a long shot."[112] Stockman's critique has some merit, but it drastically overstates the sort of power any president can wield. Without a cooperative Congress, even the most determined and politically astute president would struggle to pass a controversial reform.

Moreover, the nature of Reagan's victory in 1980, and the myth-making that followed it, has obscured the extent to which many components of his political agenda lacked a popular mandate. Many Americans resented what they saw as a profligate, deadbeat-coddling government in the abstract, but when the question became which benefits should be cut or which services withdrawn, antistatism tended to wither. Moynihan understood this political reality. "The problem, of course, lay in [Reagan's] simple misunderstanding of what is *in* the budget," he reflected in 1984. "There is no line item for $270 billion worth of waste, fraud, and abuse. It is filled with programs which, whatever their merits, have their reasons and their constituencies."[113]

With the Reagan administration at its strongest, the failure to enact such a publicly significant cut to the welfare state was striking. For all the administration's protests, a concerted effort spearheaded by liberal Democrats had prevented a more serious restructuring of the program. Social Security became a stick that Democrats could beat Republicans with for decades to come. Tip O'Neill took to referring to Social Security as the "third rail" of

American politics. You touch it, you die.[114] Even under the administration of George W. Bush, when one might have assumed a more deeply solidified conservative hegemony, a Republican attempt to reform the program would founder on a similar alliance led by Democrats and dependent pressure groups.[115] In this, the durability of the New Deal settlement was manifest, even after the chaos and crises of the 1970s.

The clash over Social Security reform exemplifies the limits of the Reagan Revolution. Reagan's pursuit of Social Security cuts was one of the most catastrophic political missteps of his administration. The same inertial forces and institutional shortcomings that frustrated the efforts of congressional Democrats to create a public philosophy for the post–New Deal order also enabled the Democrats to fight in defense of the legacy of the New Deal and Great Society. Democrats would experience surprising success when beating back a Reaganite onslaught on existing government programs, in particular middle-class entitlements.

Brotherly Love: The 1982 Midterm Convention

When the Democratic Party assembled in Philadelphia for its third midterm convention, in June 1982, it was in considerably better humor than it had been two years earlier. For the first time, the convention was scheduled before that year's elections, affording the party an opportunity to capitalize on the mounting unpopularity of the Reagan administration and on their own successes in blocking the president's agenda. However, after the scarring experience of the 1978 convention, when the Carter White House had to mount an all-fronts offensive to prevent the delegates from repudiating the administration, the DNC had been machinating to establish greater control over the gathering.

Most notably, a year earlier, the DNC had passed a resolution overruling a motion at the 1980 national convention that had mandated that two-thirds of the delegates be elected by grassroots party members. Instead, the number of convention delegates was halved and the majority of the remaining seats were allocated to party and elected officials. Although new DNC chairman Charles Manatt denied that Democratic officials were "in any way turning their backs on the participatory process," this was clearly a repudiation of the democratic spirit in which the midterm conventions had been established in

1972. Defending the changes, Maryland senator Barbara Mikulski, who had chaired one of the party's post–McGovern-Fraser reform commissions, said, "We're a political party, not a think-tank. We have to concentrate on issues that help win us votes."[116]

Much like his predecessor Robert Strauss eight years earlier, Charles T. Manatt was principally concerned with presenting a united front to the American people. "This is a single party, not a collection of squabbling interests," he told the delegates when he had been elected chairman the year before.[117] Though born in Chicago, Manatt was the scion of an Iowa farming family who got his political start in California after a stint as a banker and lawyer. From 1969, he served as chairman of the California Democratic Party, facing Reagan in the governor's mansion. "As far as understanding the Reagan crowd, we have had them around California, forever," he remarked shortly after his election. "We know them well." As the DNC's finance chairman and then chairman, he promised to revitalize a party that had been "out-conceptualized, out-organized, out-televised, out-coordinated, out-financed and out-worked." Manatt maintained a large and sophisticated political network through a mixture of bonhomie and hard-nosed wheeling and dealing. As party chairman, he took a debt-ridden party using broken typewriters in rented office space and transformed it into an efficient fund-raising machine with $6 million custom-built headquarters on Capitol Hill.[118] His campaign for the party chairmanship alone was rumored to have cost $100,000, more than ten times what Strauss had spent less than ten years earlier.

The convention over which Manatt presided lacked the high drama of four years earlier. Instead, according to one account, it was "a deliberately ingrown affair insulated from the public by special credential checkpoints and a special system of borrowed buses." This insularity gave the rhetoric "all the force of shadow-boxing."[119] *Rolling Stone*'s correspondent was even more vituperative, calling it both "dull" and "fraudulent": "The Democrats do not have their act together. They are not unified. They seem like a dead circus whose weary performers suddenly see the crowds streaming back into their tent and are not sure how to react."[120]

Without any real role as a rule-making or policy-formulating body, the convention swiftly became little more than a forum for would-be presidential candidates to court party factions and bid for media attention. The gathering began with a succession of receptions—or rather "one behemoth movable cocktail party"—at which aspirant presidential candidates mingled with party grandees.[121] One reception offered two lard sculptures of a bald eagle and the Liberty Bell. The biggest event on the first night was the bash thrown by former vice president Walter Mondale on the nineteenth floor of the Bellevue-Stratford Hotel. For some unexplained reason, the elevators insisted on stopping at every floor on the way up, to the frustration of the delegates packed inside. "Wherever Democrats convene," wrote *Rolling Stone*, "the hotel elevators do not work, nor does the air conditioning."[122]

Hollow as it may have been, the Philadelphia convention did little to derail the Democratic momentum as the midterm elections approached. That November, the Democrats regained much of the ground they had lost in the House of Representatives, winning 26 seats and increasing their majority to 102. Majority Leader Jim Wright exulted that these new members were "real Democrats—not your boll weevil types," and *Newsweek* declared Reagan had lost his "philosophical majority" in the House.[123] Of particular satisfaction was the defeat of Republican congressman John LeBoutillier, who had so memorably analogized O'Neill to the bloated leviathan state and had gone on to personally finance a "Repeal O'Neill" campaign.[124] Though the Republicans maintained their edge in the Senate, the Democrats made an admittedly modest net gain of one seat. One poll conducted a month before the election showed that a clear plurality of respondents (36–28 percent) preferred to see the Democrats win "the majority in Congress" in the upcoming elections. Perhaps the more revealing statistic, however, was the 29 percent who replied, "Don't care which party gains the majority."[125] After two years of fierce partisan confrontation in Washington, in which each side had denounced the other in urgent and melodramatic terms, close to one-third of the electorate felt no investment in the outcome of the elections.

The former Nixon staffer Kevin Phillips warned the Democrats not to let the advances go to their heads. The available evidence, he argued, indicated that "American politics are undergoing a watershed transformation because of the inadequacy of both 1970's liberalism and the conservatism of 1981–82." If that was the case, then an "inept Democratic regime" might be even more disastrous to the cause of liberalism than Reagan's "triumphant" reelection. "If the Carter administration led to Ronald Reagan, what would a second Carter-type Administration produce?"[126]

This was the question that confronted the Democrats as the post-midterm celebrations died away. The first two years of the Reagan administration had demonstrated that Democrats were surprisingly adept at obstructing the antistatist ambitions of the Reagan revolutionaries. What they had yet to demonstrate was that they could defined a public philosophy that could incorporate or counteract widespread *ideological* dissatisfaction with the federal government. Although Reagan struggled to reduce the size of the federal government, the skeptical, anti-government currents that had swept him into office in 1980 did not dissipate. If anything, they continued to intensify over the course of the decade. The ideology that some Democrats began advocating as a response—neoliberalism—would struggle to gain traction both within the party and among the general public, dogged by accusations of vacuity and callousness.

In adapting to the ideological currents of the 1980s, the Democrats would find themselves with one less forum for the resolution of intraparty tensions. By 1985, Manatt's replacement as DNC chair, Paul Kirk, had concluded that the quadrennial midterm conventions were "a place for mischief" and a costly nuisance that forced party leaders to devote finite energies to papering over divisions. "I just think it's wrong to spend a lot of money on . . . what becomes an exercise in damage control." He also said that they were increasingly dominated by the presidential candidates and that the party should not spend the $1 million to "construct a stage" for the candidates to strut. In June 1985, at Kirk's instigation, the DNC voted to discontinue the midterm conventions.[127]

6

"Reaganism with a Human Face"?
The Rise of the Neoliberals, 1980–1992

In June 1980, the junior senator from Massachusetts, Paul Tsongas, delivered the keynote address at the annual convention of Americans for Democratic Action (ADA). The forum was a significant one. The ADA had been founded in 1947 by an alliance of Democratic legislators, labor leaders, and liberal intellectuals as a forum for the definition and defense of liberalism. The ideology that the ADA promoted—pro-government action to address social and economic problems, pro–civil rights, internationalist, and anticommunist—dubbed "Vital Center" liberalism by one of the organization's founders, Arthur Schlesinger Jr., defined it over the next several decades as the most important vehicle for moderate Democrats and as a bulwark against perceived extremism.[1] Though the ADA was long past its heyday as a broker in intraparty debates, there was considerable symbolism in Tsongas using a speech at the organization to reflect on the future of liberalism.

In the years since arriving in the House, Tsongas had been cultivating his status within the party. He had made the jump from the House to the Senate in the 1978 midterms, defeating Republican Edward Brooke (the only African American in the upper chamber at the time). Tsongas's victory was one of the Democratic Party's few pickups in a generally Republican year. In the aftermath, Tsongas had sought to maintain his outsider's aura. "There's somehow a chemistry in the Senate that is not healthy," he told reporters. "I hope not to fall prey to it."[2] As both a House and a Senate member, Tsongas had distinguished himself as a dogged policy entrepreneur, with a portfolio that covered energy, urban affairs, and US-Africa relations, a legacy of his days in the Peace Corps. The immersive political scientist Richard Fenno wrote that Tsongas was "the most issue-oriented, issue-driven senator of all those with whom I traveled."[3] He also compiled a consistently liberal voting record. He received several perfect 100s in the ADA's legislative rating system.[4] But when he appeared at the ADA's convention that summer, months before Carter lost reelection to Ronald Reagan, it was as a critic of orthodox liberalism.

Tsongas was not the star attraction at the ADA's convention. That honor went to Tsongas's fellow Massachusetts senator Ted Kennedy, then reaching the end of his quixotic primary challenge to President Carter and fueled by partisan fire in the dog days of his campaign. Kennedy appealed to the cherished beliefs of the ADA members in attendance; he "spoke their minds, freeing them from the nagging realities of Ronald Reagan's and Jimmy Carter's delegate totals." To cheering and brandished "Kennedy All the Way" signs, the candidate promised continued desegregation, health care, and regulation of the oil industry. A spontaneous chant of "We Want Ted!" broke out when Kennedy denounced the pursuit of "phantom policies" to achieve a balanced budget. "It was their kind of liberalism," noted the Washington Post's correspondent.[5]

Tsongas, by contrast, came not to praise liberalism but to criticize it. Liberalism, he argued, was failing to adapt to a changing political environment and a changing electorate. It had to appeal to a younger generation who had "never known the anger that fed the liberal cause. They have not grown up reading about hungry, poor people; they have grown up reading about abuses in the food stamp program."[6] Tsongas's speech to the ADA—delivered months before Carter's defeat—was of a piece with his desire to be ahead of the curve. He castigated liberals in Congress for rejecting Carter's proposals to increase gasoline taxes, for coddling unions, and for leaving "the cause of Afghan freedom fighters" to conservatives. Liberals were revealing themselves as unfit to govern, he said, by clinging to dogmas at the expense of new realities.[7] Liberalism, Tsongas concluded, was "at a crossroads. It will either evolve to meet the issues of the 1980s or it will be reduced to an interesting topic for PhD-writing historians."[8]

The Washington Post called the speech "a doomsday denunciation of orthodox LBJ liberalism."[9] The ADA's leadership, like Kennedy, was in a more defiant mood. The organization's president, Patsy T. Mink, boasted that "liberalism is alive and kicking." Executive Director Leon Shull (a proudly self-described "old-fashioned, knee-jerk liberal") suggested that any difficulties liberalism currently faced were a consequence of its own success: "Basically, liberalism has won. . . . But the intense work of past decades has really tired people." When Shull asserted that the "essence of liberalism" was "the use of government to intervene on behalf of people," Tsongas demurred. "I don't think the government is where it's at," he remarked. "The Johnson-Humphrey Great Society approach is that government does work, but I think government has a deadening impact."[10] Democrats, suggested Tsongas, had to win over the voters who were defecting to the independent candidate John Anderson in the 1980 presidential election, voters who political analyst John Baron dismissed as "suburbanites in their Volvos."[11] Tsongas was dismissive of "traditional" liberals: "I feel they're mired in yesterday's truisms. Listening to them is like going to an old movie."[12]

Tsongas said later that the speech was "the most important thing I've ever done and the thing I'm proudest of."[13] Though Tsongas did not give a label to his critique, it soon acquired one: "neoliberalism." Randall Rothenberg later described Tsongas's speech as "the first salvo in the neoliberals' war for the soul of the Democratic party."[14] Neoliberalism was one of the most high-profile ideological alternatives to Reaganism to emerge within the Democratic Party during the 1980s. Driven largely by former Watergate Babies, it was an ideological tendency that attracted a great deal of media comment and criticism throughout the decade and found initial expression in the presidential campaigns of Gary Hart in 1984 and 1988. It would also feed into the Democratic Leadership Council (DLC), a similarly revisionist organization that took credit for devising the "New Democratic" public philosophy that would see former Arkansas governor Bill Clinton elected to the presidency in 1992, ending the Democrats' long exile from the White House.[15] It was, however, distinctive from the DLC, as demonstrated by the fact that Tsongas, one of the defining figures of the neoliberal tendency, became one of Clinton's principal rivals for the Democratic presidential nomination in 1992.

It was significant that Tsongas gave his speech months before the election of 1980, when Reagan's victory was by no means a foregone conclusion and in fact the reelection of President Carter seemed a plausible outcome. Neoliberalism was not simply a reaction to the election of Reagan, although this traumatic event confirmed the neoliberal analysis for many of its adherents. Instead, it was a critique that had been developing over the course of the 1970s and that had been shaped and reinforced by the Democratic experience of governing during that decade's crises. It was deeply rooted in the cultural, ideological, and coalitional peculiarities that the Watergate Babies had brought with them to Congress. It was defined by the increasingly suburban tilt of the Democratic Party's base and by the skeptical antigovernment turn of the country at large, something that suffused the political consciousness of most of the class of 1974.

However, neoliberalism was only one interpretation of the Democratic Party's recent history competing to determine its future. The newly elected chairman of the House Democratic Caucus, Gillis Long, would endeavor to coordinate the debate on the party's future through his newly formed Committee on Party Effectiveness. But this body would only underscore the difficulties of using Congress as a venue for reorienting the public philosophy of the party. Increasingly, the Democrats' search for a popular alternative to Reaganism would turn to extra-congressional vehicles after the 1984 elections, the most notable of which was the DLC. Although the two most prominent neoliberals—Tsongas and Hart—were members of Congress, neither saw the legislative branch as the best platform for their brand of politics. Both ultimately saw the White House as the catalytic institution in the remaking of the Democratic Party. The neoliberal critique, and its ultimate failure to defeat Reagan or Reaganism in the 1980s, illuminates the difficulties that Democrats encountered when they tried to make the case for a progovernment philosophy (even a qualified one) at a moment when faith in the institutions of government was in apparently terminal decline.

It was comparatively straightforward to defend existing programs like Social Security, particularly if those programs offered popular middle-class benefits. It was, however, harder to make the case for further interventions while trying to dodge accusations of being tax-hiking big spenders, a caricature that obsessed many Democrats in the 1980s. Prior to 1984, the Democrats seemed to have discovered a unifying and popular issue in "fairness," which, amid the recession of 1981–1982, helped the party make up some ground in that year's midterms. As the economy improved, however, many Democrats endeavored to recast themselves as deficit hawks, leaving the party with a gloomy message for the 1984 election that was overwhelmed by the fuzzy optimism of the Reagan campaign. By joining Republicans in denouncing the deficit as an urgent threat to the country's prosperity, Democrats hemmed themselves in politically and allowed conservative antistatism to define the terms of the national debate throughout the decade.

Neo Thinking

The defeat of 1980 prompted considerable soul-searching by the Democratic Party, both publicly and privately. A postmortem feature for NBC News focused on the Senate, which was in Republican hands for the first time since the 1950s. As reporter Jessica Savitch roamed the hallways of the Senate office buildings, filming despondent Democratic staffers packing up offices, she found a party asking itself "What went wrong?" and "What to do?" Savitch's report identified three senators as national spokespersons among the remaining party members: Tsongas, Hart, and Pat Moynihan. According to Tsongas, the Democrats needed to do three things: "One, give Reagan running room, so that he may indeed show what he can and cannot do. Secondly, arrive at our own agenda, and do that rather quickly. And thirdly, importantly, do the same kind of organizational and fund-raising things the Republicans did so well." Identifying the problems was "not that difficult," added Tsongas (he cited energy, the Soviets, the environment, the economy). Hart returned to a theme he had been emphasizing since his first Senate run: "We don't abandon our principles . . . what we do is probably abandon the programmatic or bureaucratic approach to solving those problems. There are other ways to help senior citizens, to help poor people, to help unemployed people, than creating an agency and throwing dollars at that problem." Of the three interviewed, Moynihan was more upbeat, though he acknowledged that the party would likely be "out of power here for the rest of this decade . . . unless we pay attention to what the Republicans did." Nonetheless, he thought the party had some reasons for optimism: "We're not short of leaders. We're short of followers, for the moment. But we're still the majority party, and we don't have an agenda for the 1980s. So, we'll produce one."[16]

Nonetheless, if Moynihan was bullish on camera, he was under no illusions about the magnitude of the task ahead. "It occurred to me," he wrote to columnist Tom Wicker in early 1980, "that the Republicans, dammit, have become a party of ideas without the rest of us in the least noticing."[17] Wicker would expand on this, citing Moynihan's observation in an op-ed published days after Reagan's inauguration a year later. The Democrats' "basic approach—big and costly Government programs of benevolent intent but mixed results—has fallen in to disrepute with inflation-conscious voters." Some Democrats, Wicker continued, believed the party needed:

a new kind of instrument . . . to help develop and publicize what has been most lacking—new ideas about governing and new means of pursuing the traditional Democratic goals of social and economic justice, and economic opportunity for all, without bankrupting or alienating the middle class. Such a revitalization is overdue for a party that has let itself become the proponent of political ortho- doxy and elephantine bureaucracy.[18]

Reagan's early successes, and the apparent inability of establishment lib- erals to resist them, created a space for revisionist thinkers within the Dem- ocratic ranks to make their case. By the end of February 1981, a group of liberal Democrats had established the Center for Democratic Policy (CDP) to develop new policy ideas to counter the party's "crisis of confidence."[19] The center had an operating budget of some $500,000 for the first year of its existence, rising to $1.5 million in 1982.[20] Along with Moynihan, many other Democrats were astonished to discover that the Republicans had become the "party of ideas." The center's purpose, as its president Ted Van Dyk put it, was "to plant many seeds among which some will undoubtedly grow and some won't."[21] The first sowing came in October, with the release by the CDP of three studies of strategies to combat inflation. Each paper was styled as a "counterpoint" to the work of one of the leading conservative think tanks, the American Enterprise Institute, inadvertently underlining the game of in- tellectual and institutional catch-up that the Democratic establishment was being forced to play.[22]

A similar grasping for a new direction was underway within Congress it- self. At the head of these efforts were veterans of the class of 1974, particu- larly Tsongas and Hart. Tsongas's speech to the ADA, though not particularly well-received in the hall at the time, acquired new relevance after the elec- tions of 1980. Hart had embraced a similar critique of orthodox liberalism as Tsongas, and soon the two would find their names frequently invoked as leading lights of the "neoliberal" movement. Though their personal relation- ship was never particularly close, they shared many of the same enthusiasms and antipathies.

From his first election, Hart was determined to help his party rediscover "the experimental pragmatism that had defined Franklin Roosevelt's presi- dency."[23] Like Tsongas, he showed himself as an adept policy entrepreneur, serving as a fiscally hawkish member of the Budget Committee, an enthu- siastic environmentalist on the Environment and Public Works Committee, and a champion of military reform on the Armed Services Committee. At the same time, his office strove to build his national profile. In 1979, for instance, one Hart advisor, having discovered that NBC was looking for stories for a new show it was creating to rival CBS's *60 Minutes*, recommended to Hart that they "suggest the story of a Western senator who is being forced by circumstances and talent to take on the issues of the 80's" or a story about "the frustrations of pragmatism in Washington and the attempts of several members to deal with it, with the focus on [Hart]."[24]

In 1980, facing reelection, Hart found himself, with other Senate liberals, targeted by a cadre of New Right groups. Hart's opponent was Colorado secretary of state Mary Estill Buchanan, a relatively moderate Republican who had supported both the Equal Rights Amendment and federal funding for abortions for impoverished women. Fending off Buchanan's charge that he talked like a conservative and voted like a liberal, Hart stressed his fiscal conservatism and his support for a balanced budget and accused Buchanan of being the puppet of sinister national conservative organizations.[25] Unlike many of his Senate colleagues, Hart would survive this challenge, and both the fact and the narrowness of his victory confirmed, to him, the rightness of his course. Hart understood the redefinition of the Democratic Party to be an essentially intellectual, rather than an institutional, exercise. Political leadership in the 1980s, he told a journalist soon after his reelection, "will come more from a person's mind than from traditional organization."[26] The day after the election, Morton Kondracke, the *New Republic*'s executive editor, appearing on PBS's *MacNeil-Lehrer Report*, said Hart's political survival "was a very important event in the Democratic Party." If, Kondracke explained, the party was to redefine itself around a "neoliberal" ideology, it needed iconoclasts like Hart in the Senate.[27]

The neoliberal ideology as it existed in this period can be difficult to define. The fact that most neoliberals celebrated pragmatism and used "ideologue" as an epithet (usually one directed at other Democrats) meant that efforts to codify their thinking often ran into difficulties. Nevertheless, it is possible to identify certain pillars of the neoliberal ethos. At the heart of their thinking was a commitment to pro-growth, pro-business economics, as opposed to the redistributive thinking that had undergirded, for instance, such initiatives as the Humphrey-Hawkins Full Employment Act. "If you have an expanding economic pie there is room for generosity," said Tsongas. "There is room, if you will, for liberalism."[28] They castigated fellow Democrats for a supposedly reflexive opposition to business and for being excessively fond of regulations that stifled economic activity. Tsongas would often cite his efforts as a city councilor in regenerating the Massachusetts town of Lowell, a victim of the decline of the textile industry. Dissatisfied with his first move, the creation of a national park that would protect the town's historic architecture ("It became obvious that we would end up with a national park—five restored buildings—in the middle of decay"), Tsongas had devised the Lowell Plan, which aimed to involve local business concerns in the long-term development of the city.[29]

Allied to this, the neoliberals expressed faith in technological advancements as the key to enduring economic success and spoke excitedly of the transition to a "post-industrial economy." They were far more sanguine than many older Rustbelt Democrats about the costs of deindustrialization. As Gary Hart wrote later, "Let the Japanese and Germans compete in our automobile markets. We would build their telecommunication systems."[30] Tsongas declared that the federal government had to "set the agenda and establish the framework for igniting the individual initiative and enterprise" to "meet the challenges of the new technological era."[31] The more enthusiastic technophiles in the neoliberal ranks, who advocated government support of high-tech industries as a spur to economic growth, were nicknamed "Atari Democrats," after the widely known consumer electronics business.[32]

The neoliberals also sought to shift their party's position on foreign affairs, but this was only in part because they believed that Democrats were open to the charge of naivete in the face of the challenges of the 1980s. The quagmire of Vietnam had been as influential in molding the Watergate Babies as any other event, and many understood it as yet another manifestation of liberal hubris and overreach. To that extent, they were offering an overarching critique of Cold War liberalism as it was applied in the domestic and foreign arena. This sentiment animated Hart's commitment to transforming US defense policy. His vision focused on "maneuver warfare," advocating technologies and tactics to make the US armed forces more mobile and adaptable and to make weaponry simpler and more effective.[33] Hart's interest in reforming the US Navy in particular was so pronounced that some wags nicknamed him "the admiral from Colorado."[34]

In opposing Reagan's foreign policy, Democrats were on safe political ground, as Reagan's bellicose anticommunism proved consistently unpopular with the public.[35] Neoliberals, for instance, took the lead in opposition to the Reagan administration's policies in Central and South America, where the White House sought to enact the "Reagan Doctrine" to give covert US assistance to anti-communist resistance groups. In 1982, Tsongas cosponsored legislation to require congressional approval for any US military or intelligence operations in the region.[36] Neoliberal Democrats offered similar support for the Boland Amendments, the first of which was passed the same year, named for Representative Edward Boland (a former colleague of Tsongas in the Massachusetts delegation), which outlawed US assistance to the Contras, anticommunist paramilitaries resisting the socialist Sandinista government of Nicaragua. Gary Hart, who supported the Boland Amendments, later tried to introduce stricter language that would prohibit aid for any group whose "professed aim" was the overthrow of the Nicaraguan government.[37] Asked in 1982 about US policy in Central America, Hart invoked what he understood to be JFK's position on South Vietnam: "It's their war and they'll have to win it." Nonetheless, he did support some military and economic support for American allies in the region.[38] In this way, many neoliberals self-consciously sought a "pragmatic" middle course between uncompromising opposition to and support for the Reagan administration's foreign policy.

However, like many doctrines, neoliberalism was better defined by what it was *not* than by what it was. It was not ideological, it was not inflexible, and it was not unfeeling. It was, instead, pragmatic, realistic, and compassionate. To this extent, it positioned itself in opposition to the heartless extremism of Reagan and the reflexive liberal defense of the leviathan state. "Compassion is not just getting red in the face and waving the arms," protested Hart. "Compassion is solving problems."[39] This kind of sleeves-rolled-up pragmatism appealed to those Watergate Babies who had always constructed their political identities around an explicitly nonideological stance.

The neoliberals could count on the support of a sympathetic newsmagazine, the *Washington Monthly*. This periodical, launched in July 1969, was the creation of Charles A. Peters, a West Virginia native who had been educated at Columbia University, chaired a West Virginia county organization for JFK's 1960 presidential campaign, and then become a director of evaluations in the Peace Corps. He left government service in 1968 to establish his magazine, raising seed money for the enterprise from friends. He had founded the *Washington Monthly*, he said, to "explore the culture of the Washington bureaucracy." It was a small publication—with a circulation of around 34,000 by 1982—but well known in Washington circles.[40] Initially, the magazine was a combination of explainer and muckraker; articles that detailed a senator's daily life sat alongside exposés on waste, failure, and corruption in the federal government. In 1980, Peters published a book, *How Washington Really Works* ("it didn't" was the central insight).[41] He wrote a regular column for his magazine, "Tilting at Windmills," which was syndicated in the *Washington Post.* In one such column, published in December 1980, he reflected, in distinctly Tsongas-esque terms, that that year's election was "anti-conventional liberal": "Look at the Democratic senators who bit the dust. Mostly good men, but mostly unoriginal men."[42] He was intellectually receptive to the neoliberal case.

By the early 1980s, as the magazine's editor in chief, he was being hailed as the "godfather" or "spiritual guru" of the neoliberal movement (though he thought the name "terrible" because it carried elitist connotations). To Peters, neoliberals were liberals who took "a critical look at liberalism . . . and decided to retain our goals but to abandon our prejudices."[43] In fall 1983, the *Washington Monthly* sponsored a conference on neoliberalism, bringing together a range of political figures, including journalist James Fallows, South Carolina senator Ernest "Fritz" Hollings, sociologist Amitai Etzioni, Arizona governor Bruce Babbitt, and Donald Burr, the president of the airline People Express. Some of the ideas floated at that event included means-testing Social Security payments, some form of draft or national service, the relaxing of liberal opposition to school prayer, and the elimination of bail for those accused of violent crimes.[44] Peters arranged for the contributions to the conference to be published in 1985 as an edited collection, *The New Road for America: The Neoliberal Movement.* One review by political scientist Theodore J. Lowi, written in the form of a letter to Peters, contended, "You and your colleagues just don't offer enough neo to bring liberalism into the 21st century." Lowi also noted the "revealing" absence of "women, blacks and minorities" from the contributors or any panels on civil rights (Peters replied that the panels were "devoted to subjects on which neoliberals tend to disagree with conventional liberals. On civil rights, we not only agree with them, we are proud of the record").[45]

Critics wondered how distinct the "neoliberals" were from orthodox liberals, apart from in their rhetorical positioning. Tsongas, after all, had endorsed Ted Kennedy in the 1980 primaries. Indeed, he had publicly toyed with the idea of entering the Massachusetts primary as "a stand-in or 'stalking horse'" for Kennedy.[46] Such questions, in turn, gave rise to the most potent criticism of neoliberalism: that it was essentially vacuous, "a bloodless, technocratic type of politics." Michael Scully, the editor of the American Enterprise Institute's house journal, *Public Opinion*, scoffed that "if neoconservatives are liberals who got mugged by reality, then neoliberals are liberals who got mugged by reality but refused to press charges." The journalist Robert Kaus dubbed it "Reaganism with a Human Face" in his review of Tsongas's 1981 mission statement, *The Road from Here: Liberalism and Realities in the 1980s.* Tsongas, wrote Kaus, had "abandoned ideology altogether, replacing it with a bland futurism." For all the senator's reliance on "compassion" (one of "the two workhorses of his vocabulary," the other being "realism"), "there would not be much difference between a rational [i.e., nonideological] Ronald Reagan and the Democrats as Tsongas would remake them."[47] Arthur Schlesinger Jr. wrote that neoliberalism reminded him of "the old Chinese proverb: There is a lot of noise on the stairs, but no one enters the room."[48]

The Committee on Party Effectiveness

In their efforts to remake the party, the neoliberals found an ally in Congressman Gillis Long, the new chairman of the House Democratic Caucus. Long belonged to one of Louisiana's most-feted political families, counting among his relations both the populist firebrand governor Huey Long and the courtly ex-chairman of the Senate Finance Committee Russell Long. Originally elected to the House in 1962, Long had lost his primary two years later, to another cousin, who accused him of inconsistent opposition to civil rights (though Long, like the entire Louisiana delegation, had opposed the Civil Rights Act, he had supported the expansion of the Rules Committee that eased its passage). In 1972, after a brief spell fighting the War on Poverty in LBJ's Office of Economic Opportunity (OEO) and a failed bid for the Louisiana governorship, Long reclaimed his seat. Hardworking and conciliatory, Long commanded much respect in the House. When, in 1979, he decided not to resign his seat for another tilt at the governorship, some fifty of his colleagues took the unusual step of paying public tribute, either on the floor or in the *Congressional Record*, to his decision to remain.[49]

Without the preternaturally energetic Phillip Burton at the helm, and with a Democratic president setting the legislative agenda, the caucus had become largely moribund as an instrument of policy formation. This decline reached a surreal nadir on August 20, 1980, when the caucus convened at 9:04 A.M. before being adjourned at 9:05 A.M. when the chairman, Thomas Foley, explained that the meeting was a pro forma affair without any agenda.[50] Though Long lacked Burton's legislative ambitions, he did not intend to preside over further decay. This was reflected in his appointee to the post of executive director, Al From. An Indiana native who had trained in journalism in Northwestern University, From had served, like Long, in the OEO from 1966 to 1969. Afterward he moved to the Capitol, working for Senator Edmund Muskie on the Subcommittee on Intergovernmental Relations. In that role, From had been instrumental in drafting the 1974 Congressional Budget and Impoundment Control Act. Before his appointment as director, From served for two years as deputy advisor on inflation to President Carter. Thought physically unprepossessing, From possessed a sharp political mind and considerable initiative. From recalled that on his first visit to the caucus office, he "found a windowless room on the seventh floor of the Longworth Building with nothing but a pile of rubble—telephones, telephone wires, and other junk—in the middle of the floor." He had it cleaned out and commandeered a conference table from a Republican neighbor.[51]

The new chairman aimed to provide a talking shop for the discussion of issues and the resolution of disputes. One of his first acts was to close caucus meetings to the media and the public, the better to facilitate free and open debate. However, Long showed little interest in directly influencing the party's legislative agenda. "Gillis is an *inclusive* politician, one who reaches out to his colleagues, invites them to participate . . . a conciliator in a party of diversity," said New York congressman Matthew McHugh.[52] Maintaining caucus unity and minimizing "boll weevil" defections ranked high on his list of priorities. Long's own defeat in 1964 had made him sympathetic to the plight of members in conservative districts who, on occasion, had to run against their party to survive.

Long did have an ambitious project for the caucus, but it involved increasing the representation of elected officials in the affairs of the national party. As the journalist Adam Clymer wrote, "the issue of who is in charge never plagued the [Democratic] party so much as it has in recent Presidential campaigns. The so-called reforms that followed the 1968, 1972, and 1976 elections have, in sum, opened the party to activists and often made the nomination process and party platforms independent of the needs and desires of office-holders."[53] Long and From shared this critique. As far as they were concerned, activist groups were not subject to the imperatives of electoral politics or the need to balance often contradictory interests to maintain coalitions. This made them absolutist and myopic as party members, liable to fragment the presidential primary process and demand unworkable pledges from candidates as the price of support. Increasing the influence of elected officials would have a stabilizing effect on the party, reasoned Long and From, giving a decisive edge to those who, theoretically, would be inclined to take a broader and more mature view of the party.

As part of this effort, Long established the Committee on Party Effectiveness (CPE). The CPE was an outgrowth of a conference held by a group of reform-minded younger Democrats—among them Tim Wirth, Geraldine Ferraro of New York, Al Gore of Tennessee, and Richard Gephardt of Missouri—in January 1981. Long hoped that the CPE would engender "general consensus positions on the most important national issues that form the thread that gives our party meaning."[54] The CPE enjoyed broad support from the caucus, drawing members from the Democratic Study Group, the Congressional Black Caucus, and the Conservative Democratic Forum.[55] In general, its membership skewed young. Of the thirty-seven members of the CPE, only eleven had been first elected before 1974 and only five before 1970. A little over a quarter were in their first or second terms in the House. The Committee would meet weekly, and later biweekly, during Long's chairmanship to plan and strategize.

The CPE's first intervention into the public discourse came in April 1981, when it issued the "Statement of Democratic Economic Principles," in the midst of the congressional debate over Reagan's budget proposals. The statement touched on some familiar Democratic themes. It condemned the "Kemp-Roth" tax cut as "the fiscal equivalent of a free lunch," rebuffed the idea that government excess was the principal cause of inflation, and condemned high interest rates for exacerbating economic hardship. However, it also doubled down on the Reagan administration's determination to cut spending, calling for "a lean federal budget—which puts us on the path to balancing the budget and provides for the human needs of our people."[56] The ideas of the statement would be elaborated upon with the publication, in September 1982, of a collection of position papers under the title *Rebuilding the Road to Opportunity: A Democratic Direction for the 1980s*, sometimes nicknamed the Yellow Book.[57] Columnist Joseph Kraft hailed the Yellow Book as "the muddy expression" of a new spirit of "economic realism" in a party where "the belief in throwing government programs at problems still predominates."[58]

Later that year, Long proposed to Speaker O'Neill that Caucus Task Forces (on, respectively, long-term economic policy, housing, crime, the environment, small business, and women's issues) be established to develop "attractive Democratic alternatives" to Reaganism. The task forces would conclude their draft policy statements by February 1982. The statements would be approved by the caucus as a whole, via the CPE and the Steering and Policy Committee, and used as a platform for Democrats throughout the country before being presented to the midterm convention.[59] Through the caucus and the CPE, Gillis Long and Al From were laying the foundations of what would later become the DLC. Indeed, From wrote in his memoirs that he considered Long "in many ways, the godfather of the New Democrat movement."[60]

The Limits of Deficit Politics

As they tried to develop their draft policy statements, the members of the CPE could be confident that the political environment was becoming increasingly friendly to Democratic alternatives. Only two years into his first term, Reagan had reached the lowest point of his presidency. His approval ratings had fallen sharply and, given his advanced years, it was by no means clear that he would even seek a second term.[61] For one brief moment, it appeared to many Democrats that the GOP might once again have squandered the opportunity to consolidate their majority, only this time with economic mismanagement rather than political skulduggery. However, as the economy began to improve steadily from 1983 onward, and with it Reagan's poll ratings, the Democrats were left with a dilemma. "Fairness" had been an effective issue in a climate of widespread economic insecurity, but it began to lose its potency as distress lessened. Moreover, the Democrats had never succeeded in resolving the question of how to offer an alternative to Reagan's "unfair" agenda without risking accusations that they had returned to their big spending ways. With tax revolts fresh in their memory and mounting public mistrust of the government's bookkeeping abilities, Democrats were anxious to demonstrate not only compassion but also fiscal responsibility.

In an effort to square that particular circle, leading Democrats seized on the issue of the deficit. The unrestrained budget deficits, they charged, were inflationary, and they prolonged economic misery by "crowding out" private investment. If the precise causal relationship between the deficit and those economic outcomes was hard to prove, the deficit itself was the most glaring example of Reagan's fiscal mismanagement. After all, at the beginning of his term, Reagan had assured the nation, with the economy primed by tax cuts, that the deficit would fall to $45 billion by 1982, leading to a balanced budget in 1984.[62] Some Democrats, most notably Pat Moynihan, feared that a structural deficit would straitjacket the nation's politics and cripple social welfare policy for decades. Hart called the deficit "this Administration's Vietnam," while Tsongas accused the administration of a having "devil-may-care attitude" and called upon the president to "convene a summit of political and business leaders to hammer out a compromise solution."[63] The preferred Democratic remedy, insofar as one was ever settled, relied heavily on tax increases, especially on high incomes, and significant cuts to defence expenditures.[64]

Reagan disavowed responsibility for the deficits, blaming Democratic "profligacy." He called for bipartisan cooperation on a deficit reduction plan and endorsed a balanced-budget amendment to the constitution.[65] Despite solid support among the public, such an amendment drew widespread opposition from elite opinion formers. Both Jude Wanniski, a conservative and the coiner of the term "supply-side economics," and Alice Rivlin, a centrist Democrat and the director of the Congressional Budget Office, opposed it, and the New York Times denounced it as "ignorant economics, foolish administration and cynical politics."[66] The Democratic congressional caucuses were largely opposed, and leading Democrats preferred to noisily outbid Reagan's budget-cutting proposals. When, in early 1984, the president proposed bipartisan negotiations to find $100 billion worth of cuts, House Majority Leader Jim Wright dismissed them as "cosmetic" and revealed that he was leading a group that planned to present a package of some $200 billion in reductions.[67]

Bellicosity over the deficit proved to be a political cul-de-sac for the Democrats, however. The deleterious economic consequences, at least in the short term, did not materialize. The economy and the deficit grew quite happily alongside one another from early 1983 onward, and the Federal Reserve's tight monetary policy choked off inflation.[68] The size of the deficit just had too slight an impact on the daily life of the average American citizen to resonate in political terms. As one party worker, interviewed at a conference in St. Louis, put it, "If people are back to work, they won't care about the deficits."[69] Moreover, as political scientist James D. Savage argued in 1988, excessive concentration on the deficit had the effect of further undermining the Keynesianism that had underpinned Democratic economics since the New Deal and of solidifying an effective agreement on the limits of policy in Washington. It created a bipartisan consensus around the idea that calling for unnecessary spending cuts was the cornerstone of responsible politics. Consequently, "without a measure that distinguished good from bad deficits, the Democrats lacked a macroeconomic explanation for opposing either the president's efforts to add a balancing-budget [sic] amendment to the Constitution or to cut social spending when the budget was unbalanced."[70]

"Where's the Beef?":
The Neoliberals Seek the Presidency

These developments suggested that debate within the Democratic Party, or at least the congressional party, was trending in the direction of the neoliberals—for good and for ill. In a speech to the National Press Club in October 1982, as the Democrats rumbled toward midterm victories on the back of recession and their uncompromising defense of Social Security, Paul Tsongas declared that the Democrats had two options for 1984. The first was to "fire up the old coalition" and rely on the party's traditional themes and constituencies to retake the White House. That strategy contained the seeds of its own destruction, however. "A Democratic President in '85 will go the same route as Ronald Reagan. Great expectations, little follow-through, [and] a disillusioned electorate." The alternative was to look at Reagan "objectively" and "take the best of what he did and embrace that without [embarrassment] and discard the things he did wrong and discard those without arrogance." The Democrats needed to embrace "cleansing realism" before they could truly defeat Reaganism. Not all spending cuts would be restored and not all corporate tax breaks would be reversed. Asked in the post-speech Q&A whether he would seek the presidency, Tsongas replied, "I would like to be President of the United States if I did not have to run for it. My kind of politics is just not exciting. Pragmatism can never compete with those who would raise a more exciting . . . visceral kind of campaign . . . I see my role as really one of providing the ideas."[71]

In the 1984 Democratic primaries, the neoliberal standard would instead be carried by Gary Hart. Those primaries would be conducted in an institutional context in which party officials wielded more power than they had since the 1960s. The dreams of the reformist Democrats who made up the CPE and its allies, of bringing elected officials into the candidate selection process, had been largely fulfilled. The 1980 national convention had established a Commission on Presidential Nominations—or the Hunt Commission, for its chairman North Carolina governor Jim Hunt—which had reported in early 1982. The commission proposed shortening the primary season, strengthening the convention's decision-making powers, and increasing the number of party officials serving as unpledged convention delegates. This final recommendation would prove the most consequential, leading to the creation of the "super delegates," unpledged delegate seats that would be filled by members of Congress and the state parties.[72]

Party leaders sought to make their presence felt in less formal ways. For the first time, each of the major candidates was invited to make his case and take questions before a House Caucus meeting. Mondale, Hart, civil rights leader Rev. Jesse Jackson, Florida governor Reubin Askew, South Carolina senator Fritz Hollings, and Ohio senator John Glenn all made an appearance.[73] The reformers had hoped that officials would provide a stabilizing influence on the party, bringing a party-wide, and indeed nationwide, perspective to a process that had become too dominated by special interests and single-issue activists. It must therefore have been something of a nasty surprise when the majority of those unpledged delegates came out in support of Walter Mondale, whom Hart was assailing as the prisoner of the special interests. As a former senator and vice president, and often an unofficial legislative liaison for the Carter White House, Mondale could rely on long-established relationships with Capitol Hill lawmakers. Hart, by contrast, had marked himself out as a "loner" early on. Though a talented policy entrepreneur, Hart had never cultivated particularly enduring bonds with his colleagues, and he paid for it as the campaigns pursued delegates.[74]

The 1984 Hart-Mondale contest was, in some senses, a rerun of the McGovern-Humphrey fight of twelve years earlier, another iteration of the struggle that party factions had been engaged in since the 1960s. (Though in many respects it was the candidacy of the only nonofficial in the primaries, Jesse Jackson, leading a "Rainbow Coalition" of disadvantaged voters, that would catalyze some of the most significant transformations of the party's voter base.)[75] Mondale had been a protégé of Humphrey's as Hart had been of McGovern's. Mondale represented the traditional Democratic coalition, augmented by growing minority groups, with organized labor at the bedrock. Fearful of its diminishing influence within the party, the AFL-CIO had announced after the 1982 midterms (in which its favored candidates had done surprisingly well) that it intended to take the unprecedented step of endorsing a presidential candidate before primary season was underway.[76] Mondale thus became the first Democratic presidential candidate to receive explicit AFL-CIO support before receiving the nomination.

Hart's coalition reflected some of the demographic shifts that the nation had undergone in the preceding decades and relied on the atypical Democratic voters who had delivered the party its landslide in 1974. As Hart's Colorado colleague Tim Wirth reflected, "Our constituents are changing. . . . [They] used to be labor, blue-collar and minority-oriented. Now, as in my case, they are suburban, with two working parents—a college-educated, information-age constituency."[77] Beyond the party, this gave Hart an appeal that Mondale could not match. In March 1984, pollster Bill Hamilton reported to Tip O'Neill and Tony Coelho that hypothetical matchups showed Hart leading Reagan 47–44, while Mondale lost to the president 55–37 (eerily close to the eventual result). Hart's secret, argued Hamilton, was his appeal to *the more independent, affluent in our society*—those malleable voters Democrats needed to win most elections."[78]

The hope of the Hart campaign, and of the neoliberals more broadly, was that he could upset the substantially stronger and establishment-favored Mondale campaign through the primaries. When Hart won a surprising upset in the New Hampshire primary at the end of February, beating Mondale by ten points, it seemed as though that strategy might pay dividends. "This campaign just begins tonight," Hart told his supporters as the result was declared.[79] Hart based that campaign on a pitch of "new ideas," most of which were of neoliberal vintage. In the most notorious incident of the primary, Mondale mocked Hart's appeal for new ideas by invoking the catchphrase from a popular advertising campaign by the fast food outlet Wendy's. "When I hear your new ideas," he told Hart at a candidate debate, "I'm reminded of that ad, 'Where's the beef?'"[80] Though Hart ultimately won more contests than Mondale, most of these were in western states that (with the exception of California) netted him fewer delegates that Mondale won in the more populous Northeast and Midwest. Charles Peters declared afterward that Hart had made himself a "hero" to the neoliberals, although he felt that Hart had "got so careful [as a candidate] that he couldn't be bold." Although Tsongas wound up endorsing John Glenn in the primaries, he too was sympathetic to Hart. "As a Democrat, Hart was probably between a rock and a hard place," said his spokesperson, Mary Helen Thompson. "The neoliberal stuff is a lot harder to campaign on."[81]

To reach out to the affluent, suburban voters that Hart was so attuned with, Mondale sought to counterbalance his image as a liberal big spender by returning to the issue that had defined Democratic politics throughout Reagan's first term: deficit reduction. His rhetoric incorporated many neoliberal themes. Mondale's acceptance speech at the party's national convention in New York promised the American people a "new realism." "We are living on borrowed money and borrowed time," said Mondale, inadvertently echoing Reagan's inaugural address. "These deficits hike interest rates, clobber exports, stunt investment, kill jobs, undermine growth, cheat our kids, and shrink our future." By the end of his first term, he promised, the "Reagan budget deficit" would have been reduced by two-thirds. Given the size of the deficit, that was an ambitious goal, and Mondale needed a dramatic gesture to demonstrate his seriousness. "Mr Reagan will raise taxes, and so will I," the nominee told the delegates. "He won't tell you. I just did." This pledge overshadowed all the others in Mondale's speech.[82] Mondale's honesty, though admirable, was hardly good politics. The administration restated its commitment to tax reduction and privately Reagan's senior officials were jubilant ("I haven't seen even a mayor get elected that way," said one).[83]

With the economy recovering, Mondale's "somber Norwegian mien" proved entirely out of step with the spirit of the nation in 1984.[84] That was best embodied by the incumbent. As Gil Troy put it, in 1984 Reagan was "the Wizard of America's Id," a leader who "wanted Americans to feel good, not think too hard."[85] The most memorable ad of the 1984 campaign, for instance, was that which proclaimed it to be "morning again in America," a soft-focus vision of the wholesome prosperity and stability that a Reagan presidency had brought to the nation.[86] This campaign had been the result of a conscious decision on the part of its managers, Chief of Staff James Baker in particular.[87] Many conservatives resented the Reagan campaign's unwillingness to seek a clear ideological mandate (activist Richard Viguerie accused the staffers of having "double-crossed" lower-level Republican candidates), but it was effective.[88] While the president campaigned on a platform of America resurgent and the promise of sacrifice-free boom times, the Democratic challenger promised cold showers and hardship. It was the reappearance of Jimmy Carter's liberalism of limits, and the American people had no stomach for another crisis manager in the White House. However, the consequence of this, as Troy argues, was that Reagan earned a "mushy mandate for peace and prosperity" that effectively doomed his second-term agenda.[89]

Mushy though it may have been, that mandate was undoubtedly emphatic. With 525 electoral votes, Reagan amassed the largest Electoral College total in history. While his 18.2 percentage point margin of victory over Mondale was lower than Nixon's 23.2 percent in 1972 or LBJ's 22.6 percent in 1964, it still represented a comprehensive rout. It was, editorialized the *Washington Post*, "an awesome victory" for Reagan and a "Dunkirk" for the Democrats. The president "told the nation what he hoped to do, and the nation said Yes—in a very big and wholly convincing way."[90] "All indications are that it is no longer possible to think of the Democrats as the nation's normal majority party," wrote the *National Journal*.[91]

There were some signs that the Democrats could turn to for comfort. The party held its House majority (253–182) and had hopes of retaking the Senate in 1986. They held a 34–16 lead in governorships and controlled more than two-thirds of the state legislatures, facts that augured well for the redrawing of constituency boundaries after the 1990 census. Kevin Phillips wrote that no Republican president had ever taken office with his party controlling so few House seats, governorships, and state legislatures. Moreover, according to Gallup, Democrats still held a decisive party identification advantage over Republicans of 40–31 percent.[92] According to a Harris Survey, only 40 percent were enthused by the prospect of the GOP becoming the nation's majority party, while 51 percent were opposed.[93] As political scientist James Q. Wilson argued in the aftermath, perhaps 1984 was "a perfectly ordinary election."[94] Albert R. Hunt echoed that conclusion: "One simple maxim of American political history is that when an incumbent president enjoys party unity, prosperity, and peace, he wins reelection."[95]

Bruised Democrats were inclined to interpret Reagan's victory, publicly at least, in personal terms. The president, they suggested, was just too charismatic and too good on TV. However well considered his policy prescriptions, the worthy yet colorless Mondale simply could not compete. Despite shattering a glass ceiling by putting New York congresswoman Geraldine Ferraro on the ticket—the first female vice presidential candidate in US history—Mondale could not generate enough excitement for his candidacy to overcome the Reagan mystique.[96] The conclusion of some, therefore, was that the party should hold tight and wait for the administration to run into difficulties again. After all, Reagan's name would not feature on the ballot in 1988. Robert Strauss, whose paramount concern as DNC chair had been unity, argued that the party should cease navel-gazing: "If Democrats continue to paint themselves as politically and ideologically bankrupt, this perception could become reality: people will begin to believe that something is fatally wrong with the party."[97]

Nonetheless, many remained convinced that something *was* fatally wrong with the party, and Mondale's defeat had only reinforced that conclusion. Not only had the Democrats lost four of the last five presidential elections, but in two of those it had been able to carry only one state. In only one of them had the Democrat won more than thirteen states. After 1980, the Democratic Party had anticipated that the implosion of Reaganism would return them to power, and it had not come to pass then. Fred Barnes dismissed those Democrats waiting for Reagan to retire or screw up as the victims of a "majority complex, the notion that they are, now and forever, the true and only representatives of the people."[98] A more rigorous accounting of the party's flaws was in order.

There was no shortage of diagnosticians. The most commonly advanced explanation for the party's travails had been in circulation since before the Reagan presidency: that Democratic leaders were in hock to narrowly focused interest groups who undermined party appeals to the American people as a whole. This was the contention of the neoliberals. As the *New Republic* put it, days after Mondale's defeat,

the Democratic Party thinks it cannot stand for equal rights for blacks unless it meets the specific demands of black leaders—this year, the Congressional Black Caucus and next year, perhaps, the Reverend Jesse Jackson. To be for women's equality means it must dance to the tune played by the National Organization for Women. Being for the interests of working people requires obeying the A.F.L.-C.I.O., being for education means following the N.E.A., being against discrimination against gays means adopting the affirmative action agenda of the National Gay Rights Task Force, etc., etc.

The party, it concluded, had become unbalanced. Though some voices had objected to the increased presence of elected officials in the nominating process, the *New Republic* was largely supportive, suggesting they offered a "keel." In fact, the editorial hoped that another class of official would be given more influence in shaping the party's future: "If any one group ought to be elevated in influence, it is the party's governors, who have shown a remarkable ability to win elections while national and Congressional candidates have been losing."[99]

Mo Udall may have thought that Jimmy Carter had "poisoned the well for governors for the next 200 years," but he was in the minority.[100] In institutional terms, governors had some advantages over members of Congress when it came to the business of recasting the party's public philosophy. Their governing agendas were necessarily broad rather than specialized; they were required to manage the demands of competing interest groups to reach workable consensuses; and they had a far easier time embodying the rising anti-Washington animus around the nation. There were, said pollster Peter Hart, "so many good stories coming out of the gubernatorial mansions." If Republicans were running rampant in Washington, Democrats could point to Mario Cuomo in New York or Michael Dukakis in Massachusetts or the baby of the governors' conference, thirty-eight-year-old Bill Clinton of Arkansas. Both of the nation's female governors—Martha Layne Collins of Kentucky and Madeleine M. Kunin of Vermont—were Democrats, as was the only Hispanic governor, New Mexico's Toney Anaya.[101] By early 1985, Arizona governor Bruce Babbitt was being frequently cited in the national press as one of the most exciting prospects for the party. Babbitt, who as governor had lowered state spending as a percentage of personal income, advanced workfare programs, and pegged teachers' salaries to performance, was not shy about recommending his example as a template for the national party. Others were skeptical about the usefulness of Babbitt as a template. "There are no lessons that I can see," said Babbitt ally Donald B. Mathis. "I think Arizona is unique."[102]

The gubernatorial publicity boomlet revealed growing disillusionment among many Democrats with Congress as an arena for the discussion and refinement of a post–New Deal Democratic agenda. The surprising resilience of the party's congressional presence had ensured that it was so far able to deny a final victory to conservatism. However, it had been of little use for those with ambitions to redefine the party. It was with that goal in mind that a group of moderate Democrats created the DLC in 1985, a vehicle independent of traditional party structures to coordinate their reform efforts. Nearly all the forty founding members were from southern and western states. Only four had constituencies in the industrial North. Almost every member was white and male. There were two black members—House Budget Committee chairman William H. Gray III of Pennsylvania and Representative Alan D. Wheat of Missouri—but the only woman on the roster, Ohio representative Mary Rose Oaker, quickly disassociated herself from the council, claiming that her inclusion had been a mistake.[103] This seeming air of privilege would rebound on the organization (Jesse Jackson memorably lampooned them as "Democrats for the Leisure Class").[104] An outgrowth of the Committee on Party Effectiveness, the DLC raised hackles almost immediately. Its highest profile detractor was the newly elected DNC chairman Paul G. Kirk, who had already begun to establish his own Democratic National Policy Group and was suspicious of an alternative power base developing within the party. Cofounder Richard Gephardt countered that the DLC was "not [conceived] as a rival to any other party entity but as a way station or bridge back into the party for elected Democrats."[105] This was disingenuous, however, and for the next decade, the DLC slowly became the group against which other contenders for the party's future would define themselves.[106]

The neoliberals arguably got their best shot at the presidency in 1988 with the candidacy of Michael Dukakis, the former governor of Massachusetts. Hart made another unsuccessful bid for the nomination, but this time his candidacy imploded early in the process, thanks to a sex scandal.[107] Though, in the aftermath of that election, Dukakis was often grouped with Mondale and McGovern as the representative of a traditional (i.e., losing) Democratic Party, in the early 1980s he was one of the acknowledged members of the neoliberal movement. He was identified, for instance, as a member of the "neoliberal club" in the 1982 *Esquire* profile of the movement.[108] The rationale he gave for his candidacy was unimpeachably neoliberal. "This election is not about ideology; it's about competence," he declared as he accepted his party's nomination. "For all his rejection of labels," ran one report from the 1988 convention, "Mr. Dukakis represents a new kind of liberalism, one that arises naturally from the problem-solving demanded of the nation's governors. . . . Dukakis has tried to balance the traditional liberal view of government as the instrument of equity with a substantial dose of fiscal responsibility."[109] Tsongas was right in his assessment that his kind of politics was "just not exciting." Dukakis lost anyway. The defeat was not as lopsided as Mondale's, but Democrats could hardly claim that George H. W. Bush, Dukakis's victorious opponent, was a figure of comparable charisma to Reagan.

In December 1988, the *New Republic* ran what it billed as its "Quarterly Recriminations Issue."[110] Defeat, it seemed, was becoming the natural state of the Democratic Party. Although the Democrats kept control of the House of Representatives throughout the 1980s (indeed would hold it until the elections of 1994) and even regained the Senate in 1986, they had felt at a significant disadvantage for much of the decade. In a fundamental sense, conservatives won the battle of ideas. Policy debates after 1984 were conducted in a culture that was increasingly hostile to government activism, helped along by the Democrats' reliance on deficit reduction politics. The Democratic success in defending Social Security in the early 1980s had not translated into a broader appreciation for interventionist government. Neoliberalism, it seemed, had the effect only of reinforcing the Reagan agenda. During the 1988 campaign, Bush frequently cited Paul Tsongas in defense of his own proposed capital gains tax cut, much to the chagrin of Tsongas himself.[111] The narrowing of political options had the effect of draining debates on the Democratic side, rendering them particularist and technocratic. This was especially true in Congress, where cautious members had to keep a wary eye on a suspicious and tax-averse public. As Congressman George Miller, a Watergate Baby, complained in 1989, "You replaced visions and dreams with questions like 'How much does it cost?' There has been a decade here where, in some ways, you lost your voice. You really didn't quite want to speak out for universal health care or child care. . . . When the Reagan drumbeat came on the scene, it completely wiped out every other bit of noise. There was this ten-ton gorilla walking around town."[112]

Neoliberal versus New Democrat: Tsongas versus Clinton, 1992

Almost a decade before Paul Tsongas launched his own bid for the White House, his political career, and indeed even his life, had nearly been abruptly cut short. In 1983, Tsongas was diagnosed with non-Hodgkin's lymphoma, which induced him to retire from politics at the end of his first term in the Senate. His plan had been to seek reelection in 1984 and then to evaluate his ambitions for higher office as the next presidential cycle got underway. He had decided that he did not want to be "a career Washingtonian. It was going to be up or out." In common with many of the Watergate Babies, he saw little merit in a long career in congressional office. He wrote later of the shattering impact of the cancer not just on his personal life but also on his political identity: "It should have recognized that I was one of the up-and-coming New Democrats. I had something to say."[113] At the time, non-Hodgkin's lymphoma was regarded as incurable, and the forty-two-year-old Tsongas was forced into a sudden reckoning with his own mortality. The Tsongas family returned to Paul's childhood home in Lowell, Massachusetts. Tsongas later credited his struggle against cancer with tempering some of his callow ambition. He claimed in the 1990s that he found his earlier beliefs "unsettling."[114] When interviewed in 1992, Tsongas could immediately recall how many days it had been since he had first discovered a cancerous lump.[115]

By the end of the 1980s, however, Tsongas was apparently cancer-free thanks to a radical chemotherapy treatment and a bone marrow transplant. As the 1992 cycle approached, he began to contemplate a bid for the presidency and the possibility that he might put his interrupted career back on track.[116] His health was an issue that he planned to literally dive into. The day before he launched his campaign, in April 1991, Tsongas had invited a group of photojournalists to watch him swim lengths in Andover, Massachusetts, to demonstrate his robust good health. This unusual photo op may have made him the only presidential candidate to participate in a campaign event in Speedos.[117] He declared that if any rival candidate questioned his health, he would "challenge them to a 50-yard butterfly race in the pool of their choice." (In retirement, Tsongas had taken up swimming again, participating in senior league swim meets.)

For several months, he was the lone candidate in the race—a race largely defined by the candidates who declined to enter. Even as the lanes began to fill up, critics professed to be unimpressed with the qualities of the runners. Collectively, the field came to be known as the "Seven Dwarfs."[118] Despite the Republicans' long occupancy of the White House, incumbent George H. W. Bush was enjoying unusually high approval ratings, apparently juiced by a swift US victory in the first Gulf War, which dissuaded some of the more likely candidates (such as New York governor Mario Cuomo) from entering. That circumstance created space for an unlikely candidate—even an ex-senator who had nearly died from leukemia a few years earlier—to win the nomination.

Tsongas's principal in the 1992 primaries was, appropriately enough, a governor: Bill Clinton of Arkansas. Clinton's first role in national Democratic politics was a cameo in the Carter-Kennedy feud, when he acted as the chair of the health-care reform panel at the 1978 Democratic mini-convention in Memphis. Clinton was then midway through his first term as governor of Arkansas, a thirty-two-year-old wunderkind, a former Rhodes Scholar, law professor, and state attorney general, and now the second-youngest governor in the state's history. Two years before being elected as governor, Clinton had narrowly missed out on becoming a Watergate Baby in Congress, when he mounted an unsuccessful challenge to incumbent Republican John Paul Hammerschmidt in Arkansas's third district. Though defeated, Clinton lost to Hammerschmidt by only four points, no mean feat in a district that habitually returned the Republican by double-digit margins. Clinton's path to national prominence was rocky. He lost his first reelection bid in 1980, but returned to the office in the 1982 elections. In 1988, after some media speculation that he might be a candidate himself, Clinton delivered a meandering and overlong opening night address for the Democratic National Convention. Reportedly the biggest cheer of the evening came when Clinton uttered the words "In closing . . ."[119]

That mishap aside, Clinton's star continued to rise, largely thanks to his association with the DLC, which claimed vindication for its critique of orthodox Democratic liberalism in the aftermath of Dukakis's loss and was taking steps to increase its influence within the party's institutions. Much of the DLC's thinking was summarized in the seminal 1989 paper *The Politics of Evasion*, written by the academics William Galston and Elaine C. Kamarck for the DLC's house think tank, the Progressive Policy Institute. Both Galston and Kamarck had established careers in Democratic politics alongside their academic credentials. Galston had worked for Mondale's 1984 campaign and Al Gore's first bid for the presidency in 1988, having started as a campaign worker for Independent John Anderson in 1980; Kamarck had been a longtime DNC staffer as well as a campaign veteran. Democrats, they claimed, could no longer ignore the fact that "too many Americans have come to see the party as inattentive to their economic interests, indifferent if not hostile to their moral sentiments and ineffective in defense of their national security." The party had a choice, they concluded: "hunker down, change nothing," and wait for a political catastrophe to bring them back into office or address the party's weaknesses and articulate new policy solutions built around so-called middle-class values, "individual responsibility, hard work, [and] equal opportunity."[120] Somewhat counterintuitively, leading members of the DLC felt that the organization's purpose was to highlight ideological divisions within the party rather than create a facade of unity. "Pretending that divisions don't exist is hardly a constructive foundation for rebuilding our party," Al From remarked.[121]

Though a more instinctive conciliator than many of his DLC colleagues, Clinton shared their interpretation of the party's limitations and what it needed. Between 1990 and 1991, a crux for the organization as the next presidential election approached, Clinton served as chairman of the DLC. In that post, he oversaw the drive to transform the DLC into a national, mass membership organization and to shed its reputation as an elite, DC-centered outfit dominated by southerners. The goal was also to build, in the words of Al From, "an alternative infrastructure for the candidate or candidates delivering the message we hope the Democrats will emphasize in 1992."[122] In the 1988 cycle, the presidential candidates most strongly associated with the DLC—Tennessee senator Al Gore and Missouri congressman Dick Gephardt—had been able to count on no such organizational support. By the middle of 1991, thanks to their grassroots efforts, the organization could boast chapters in almost half of the states. At the DLC's convention in Cleveland in May 1991, Clinton gave a well-received keynote address that did much to obliterate memories of his interminable 1988 effort. "Dynamic," according to one delegate who claimed to have watched "in wonderment." "That's a guy who could do well in New Hampshire," remarked another.[123] Reflecting on the convention, David Broder concluded that the DLC had "done about all it can do" and that a presidential candidate would "have to take the next steps for the Democrats' revival."[124] Clinton, who announced his bid for the presidency in October, aspired to be that candidate.

The 1992 campaign would pit Clinton as a DLC-affiliated "New Democrat" against Tsongas as an independent "neoliberal" in a struggle for who would claim the role of modernizing party leader. There was significant overlap between these two movements, and there was a healthy dose of ego and personal antipathy in each candidate's hostility to the other.[125] There were, however, meaningful, if sometimes nuanced, differences between the two that influenced both the outcome of the race and the future of the party. Most notably, on social issues, Tsongas was more unabashedly liberal than Clinton. Though all candidates in the race made some effort to court LGBT voters, Tsongas could point to his early support of legislation to outlaw job discrimination on the grounds of sexual orientation, the first senator to champion such a civil rights law. He was the only candidate to regularly use the phrase "gay rights" in his stump speech, no matter the audience. Tsongas commanded considerable support among gay rights groups, which brought advantages to the campaign in terms of money and organization.[126]

Like Clinton, Tsongas's economic agenda was a direct challenge to the party's big-spending tradition. Tsongas dismissed conventional Democratic economics as "old nonsense," declaring that voters wanted "the truth": "We're grown-ups. We can handle it. . . . No more Santa Claus. No more giveaways." The Tsongas campaign condensed the senator's iconoclastic economic ideas into a handbook, "A Call to Economic Arms," which advocated investment tax credits and relaxed antitrust regulations.[127] Both were pro-business and skeptical of government overreach in the realm of economic management. However, in his effort to overwhelm Tsongas, Clinton (who offered a "New Covenant" in place of Tsongas's "Call") struck on many old-fashioned liberal themes and positioned himself as the more populist on economics. He asserted his commitment to redistributive justice, in contrast to Tsongas's supposedly laser-like focus on growth. There was, he said, "a fight in the Democratic Party with someone who says growth now, fairness later."[128] He accused Tsongas, who he called an "economic mechanic," of promoting a "coldblooded" plan that would favor the corporate world over ordinary Americans.[129] "You cannot redistribute wealth that is never created," Tsongas protested in response.[130]

On other issues, there was broad agreement. Though the Cold War had ended and the Soviet Union dissolved since the last time the Democrats had nominated a presidential candidate, foreign affairs played little role in the primaries. Indeed, both Tsongas and Clinton took the position that the collapse of the USSR "frees us up," as Tsongas put it, to focus on pressing domestic concerns. The candidates had nearly identical platforms on the defense budget and overseas troop reduction: Clinton wanted to reduce the defense budget by about a third, $100 billion, over five years; Tsongas wanted to reduce it by $105 billion over the same period. Both were in favor of the promotion of democracy, greater multilateralism, and the empowerment of the United Nations. Similarly, both emphasized the reinvigoration of the US economy as itself a security issue. Tsongas would frequently quote a line from the journalist David Halberstam, "The Cold War is over, Japan won."[131]

The nastiest exchanges turned not around issues, however, but around character. Tsongas called Clinton "cynical and unprincipled." He took to referring to the Arkansas governor as a "pander bear" because he would "say anything and do anything to get elected" (sometimes with a stuffed bear prop to illustrate the point).[132] He also accused Clinton—after the latter suggested that Tsongas's tax plan was "un-American"—of using "code words" to stoke anti-ethnic tensions. "Anyone who has an ethnic name is 'not American.' . . . Here you have a Democrat engaging in the kind of divisive politics the Republicans used in 1988." (The Clinton campaign brought out deputy campaign manager George Stephanopoulos, who was of Greek heritage, to answer those accusations.)[133] Whatever "vulnerabilities" he had, Tsongas asserted, "they're not vulnerabilities of character and judgment."[134] Clinton mostly tried to treat such attacks with airy indulgence. "I just think he's kind of frustrated," Clinton told one audience.

Where Clinton remained vulnerable on the "character" issue throughout the campaign and beyond, Tsongas fetishized his own righteousness. Joe Klein called him a "bran-muffin" candidate.[135] Tsongas was at a distinct disadvantage without Clinton's charisma. As a "Greek liberal from Massachusetts" he frequently drew comparisons with the colorless Dukakis. The humor columnist Dave Barry remarked that Tsongas was "so low-key that he might be capable of photosynthesis." His other major weakness was, of course, his health. He was frequently accompanied on the campaign trail by his oncologist to answer journalists' questions.[136]

The high point of the Tsongas campaign came with his early and convincing win in the New Hampshire primaries. "Hello, Washington, this is New Hampshire calling. Are you listening?" said the candidate in his victory speech. However, the real story—at least for much of the media—was Clinton's strong second place finish. The Arkansas governor had been embroiled in scandal, buffeted by revelations of his serial adultery and accusations that he had dodged the draft. That his candidacy could endure in the face of such controversies was remarkable to many observers. Clinton dubbed himself "the comeback kid" for his remarkable revival, a name soon taken up in the press.[137] Like Udall sixteen years earlier, it was Tsongas's support among affluent suburban voters that kept his campaign afloat. A similar core of voters would power him to victories in the Massachusetts and Maryland primaries.[138] As the campaign rolled on, however, Tsongas was routed by the resurgent Clinton. He was unable to expand his voter coalition to overcome his rival's advantage in the South (with the exception of Maryland and its obliging DC suburbs, Clinton won the primary in every state south of the

Mason-Dixon Line) and his support among African American voters, by then the most vital bloc for any aspiring Democratic presidential nominee. In an otherwise warm write-up of his campaign after he withdrew from the race in March, the New York Times editorial noted that Tsongas's "unusually principled" message "never reached much beyond well-educated, upper-income voters."[139]

Perhaps the most striking thing about the 1992 primaries was the fact that all of the top-tier candidates (Clinton, Tsongas, and the former California governor Jerry Brown, making another quixotic bid for the White House) were pushing some version of the "neoliberal" agenda. Unlike in previous cycles, the anti-neoliberal faction (represented in 1984 by Walter Mondale, and in 1984 and 1988 by Jesse Jackson, the DLC's most reliable sparring partner) was not significantly represented. In many respects, Tsongas was the candidate offering neoliberalism in its pure, undiluted form, while Clinton made strategic appeals to the traditional Democratic base. In April, Charles Peters urged Tsongas to reenter the presidential race to "elevat[e] the debate and giv[e] us time to figure out what we're getting into with Bill Clinton."[140] Even some members of the DLC worried about backsliding from Clinton, the eventual nominee and first Democratic president since Carter. In the days after the 1992 election, the DLC published a paper, coauthored by Galston and Kamarck, that appealed to Clinton to stick with the organization's moderate philosophy. The 1992 primaries, they concluded, had offered no "opportunity to encounter and overcome the most forceful advocates of the traditional Democratic party." In the absence of a mandate that a "clear-cut, ideological battle for the nomination" might have afforded, Clinton had to become a "Rooseveltian persuader" for DLC centrism.[141]

The 1992 primaries represented the last time that a candidate first elected to Congress in the 1974 Democratic wave election was a leading candidate for the party's presidential nomination.[142] They also revealed the extent to which the "neoliberal" ideas that had emerged from the class of '74 had come to dominate the party-wide conversation and define what was considered "mainstream" Democratic thinking. The congressional redoubt that had given the Democrats a platform throughout their long exile from the White House looked secure. As in 1974, the Democrats could also point to the fact that their party was driving significant demographic shifts within Congress, bringing the institution marginally closer to representing the nation. The numbers of African American and Hispanic members of Congress, overwhelmingly Democrats, increased sharply. The record four women elected to the Senate—including Carol Moseley Braun, the first black woman to serve as a senator and who took the total number of women in the upper chamber to six (all but one Democrats)—led to it being proclaimed the "Year of the Woman."[143] It was potentially ominous that Clinton had won the presidency with only a modest plurality of the popular vote (43 percent), only a shade higher than Dukakis had managed while losing in 1988. Moreover, Democrats had lost seats in both the House and the Senate, though they maintained their majorities in both chambers. Nonetheless, the elections seemed to have restored a pre-Reagan Democratic majority at the national level—a Democratic president with robust majorities in Congress.

1994

The End of the Permanent Democratic Congress

It was only four years earlier that the political scientist Norman Ornstein had written of the "permanent Democratic Congress" as one of the most solid realities of national political life. In 1994, that reality blew apart. The midterm elections that year inaugurated the most durable Republican congressional majorities in more than half a century. It was an unusual, and unpleasant, situation for the Democrats, who were accustomed to their tenuous grip on the White House but not on Congress. It was also what the "neoliberal" turn and the rise of "New Democrats" like Clinton were supposed to prevent. Two years earlier, *Times* correspondent Adam Clymer had credited "Clinton's coattails" with helping Democratic legislators to survive "tough Republican challenges."[1] Now, however, with the White House once more embroiled in scandals and Clinton's signature health-care reform having gone down in flames, it seemed clear that the unpopular Clinton had become a drag on Democrats running in congressional races.

It was an electoral bloodbath. Democrats lost 54 seats in the House of Representatives, leaving them with 204 seats to the GOP's 230. Fifteen House first-termers lost their bids for reelection. In the Senate, the Democrats lost eight seats. Within days, incumbent Democratic senator Richard Shelby of Alabama switched party affiliation and Colorado's Ben Nighthorse Campbell followed suit in March 1995 (both were reelected in 1998). This took the Republican Senate caucus to fifty-four. All together, they were the heaviest Democratic losses since 1946. The incumbent Democratic Speaker, Tom Foley, lost reelection in his Washington district—which he had first been elected to represent in 1964—and became the first Speaker to lose his seat since the 1860s. The party's Senate leader, George Mitchell, had declined to seek reelection (his seat had been won in a landslide by Republican Olympia Snowe). This left the party, for a brief moment, leaderless in both House and Senate. It was a fitting symbol of the confusion that had descended on the congressional Democratic Party.[2]

The election results threw up many similar symbolic encapsulations of the Democrats' plight. In Massachusetts, for instance, Ted Kennedy defeated a spirited challenge from businessman Mitt Romney, the son of George Romney, former governor of Michigan. Though Kennedy's margin over Romney was a shade over 17 percentage points, it was still the closest reelection of his political career. In Pennsylvania, first-term senator Harris Wofford, a veteran Democratic activist and former official in the Kennedy administration, was defeated by a young Republican congressman, Rick Santorum. Wofford's first victory, in a 1991 special election campaign, had been run by Clinton strategists Paul Begala and James Carville, and he had also made health-care reform, a centerpiece of Clinton's first-term agenda, a key plank of his campaign. In microcosm, Wofford's defeat seemed the clearest and most decisive rejection of Clinton.[3]

Democratic losses continued at the state level, where Republicans now occupied a majority of governorships for the first time since 1970.[4] New York's governor Mario Cuomo, seeking his fourth term in office, was toppled by a relatively obscure former lawyer and state politician, George Pataki. In Texas, George W. Bush, the son of the former president, unseated the Democratic governor of Texas, Ann Richards. (In Florida, the younger Bush brother, Jeb, was less fortunate, losing his bid to become governor to the incumbent, Lawton Chiles. Chiles was the only incumbent Democratic governor to be reelected that cycle.)

Republicans were understandably jubilant. On election night, to the cheering crowds at the Republican National Committee headquarters, the incoming Senate Majority Leader Bob Dole (who would become the party's presidential nominee two years later) declared that he had "never known a better night in electoral politics for the Republican Party, and the best is yet to come."[5] Georgia representative Newt Gingrich, who became the first Republican Speaker of the House since Joseph W. Martin Jr. in 1955, pledged to lead a transformation as sweeping as that of FDR and even predicted a "renew[al of] American civilization." In January, *Time* magazine put Gingrich on its cover alongside the strapline "King of the Hill."[6]

Since the New Deal, only Eisenhower had been fortunate enough to preside over Republican majorities in both House and Senate—and even those had been short-lived. Unlike in the 1950s, the Republican congressional majorities proved significantly more durable. Between 1995 and 2017, Republicans maintained unified control of Congress for twelve years. In an inversion of the previous status quo, the GOP had a majority in the House of Representatives for all but four of those twenty-two years. The permanent Republican House appeared to be one of Washington's new realities.

The 1994 elections—soon dubbed the "Republican Revolution"—were as consequential for the GOP as 1974 had been for the Democrats. In the 2012 cycle, for instance, a number of politicians who had played key roles in the elections—Gingrich, Romney, Santorum—would be vying for the Republican presidential nomination. But the Republicans in 1994 had achieved something that congressional Democrats had never quite managed in the preceding twenty years, despite their growing reliance on Congress as a national platform: they had run candidates across the country on a clear, formalized statement of their political beliefs and commitments, the "Contract with America." The contract was a brief statement, "a written commitment with no fine print," consisting of a series of guarantees for congressional reform (such as the reduction of House committees and committee staffs and the limiting of the terms of committee chairs) alongside a list of laws that the Republican majority would introduce within the first 100 days. These included bills to introduce a line-item veto, tax incentives for small businesses, and new work requirements for welfare recipients and to ensure that no US troops could be placed under UN command.[7]

The evidence that the contract was a key factor in the Republican wave is limited (in fact, Democratic consultant and Clinton adviser Paul Begala thought the contract was "the greatest gift to the Democratic Party since Medicare"), but it did enable the Republican Congress, and particularly the House under Gingrich (a key architect of the contract), to claim a mandate for a clear political agenda.[8] More than three hundred Republican congressional candidates had signed it, and it gave the incoming caucuses a policy platform around which they could unify and for which they could be held accountable.

Nonetheless, polling on the contract revealed contradictory public attitudes toward its components, which belies the idea that Americans had at
last swung firmly behind conservative ideas. A *New York Times*/CBS poll, for
instance, showed that 65 percent of Americans believed that government had
the "responsibility" to "take care of people who can't take care of themselves,"
that 47 percent wanted programs for impoverished children to be increased,
and that 71 percent wanted welfare recipients to continue receiving benefits
for as long as they worked. At the same time, a plurality of 44 percent blamed
"lack of effort" over circumstances for poverty, 48 percent wanted "welfare"
spending decreased, and an overwhelming majority of respondents (87 percent) wanted work requirements for welfare recipients.[9] Those contradictions played out in the subsequent political battles, as some key components
of the contract failed, others passed with the president's support, and Clinton
cruised to reelection in 1996.

A similar dynamic played out after the 2008 election, when Barack Obama
won the presidency—the first African American to do so and also the first
Democrat to win with more than 50 percent of the vote since Carter—and
commentators hailed the election as a new realignment, bringing the long
era of conservative domination to an end.[10] The journalist John Judis, for
example, wrote that Obama's election was "the culmination of a Democratic
realignment that began in the 1990s, was delayed by September 11, and re-
sumed with the 2006 election."[11] Shortly after President Obama embarked
on his second term in 2013, the *Huffington Post* ran the headline "The Reagan
Era Is Over, the Obama Era Has Begun."[12] However, the Obama era cannot
be understood as one of straightforward liberal triumph. Talk of a new Democratic realignment cannot explain the Republican victories in the 2010 or
2014 elections, or the outcome of the presidential election of 2016 for that
matter.

As Julian Zelizer has suggested, historians of American conservatism must
adjust their narratives to show "how conservatism unfolded in a dialectical
fashion with liberalism rather than as a replacement *to* liberalism."[13] American politics, at least from the 1970s onward, cannot be understood in terms
of neatly demarcated cycles of reform and reaction. The American public's
relationship with both Democratic liberalism and Republican conservatism
is too complex and contradictory to sustain such a conclusion. By 1984, an
American voter could cast his or her ballot for President Reagan (to provide
the optimistic, resolute leadership that America sorely needed after years of

crisis and drift) and for his or her district's Democratic representative (who would protect Social Security from the budget cutters) and see no contradiction. Despite decades of apparent conservative ascendancy, Americans continued to live comfortably with many of the legacies of New Deal and Great Society liberalism. Most notably, conservatives have not been able to retrench the activist state and have co-opted it to their own ends in some cases. It remains a significant presence in the lives of everyday Americans and largely because Americans want it there.

In a fundamental sense, conservatives won the battle of ideas as far as the abstract role of government was concerned. Policy debates since the 1970s have been conducted amid a culture that is increasingly hostile to government activism. As a result, the last quarter of the twentieth century was short on the kind of grand social welfare programs that had defined the Great Society. The sight of a Democratic president, Bill Clinton, declaring in the 1995 State of the Union address that "the era of big government is over" may be considered Reagan's most enduring success.[14] However, the Republican Party discovered that antipathy toward "government" sat uneasily alongside stubbornly durable public support for much of the government's practical activities. As the economist Paul Samuelson wrote in late 1994, the question of "Big Government's existence" had been "essentially settled." It "does too many people too much good and has created too many defenders." The anti-government climate was "less about undoing Big Government than reconciling our values to its permanence."[15]

Congress was a far from perfect arena for the development and testing of a coherent public philosophy to meet the challenges of this era. Nonetheless, it was the institutional bastion of Democratic strength, such as it was, from the 1970s onward, as the presidency remained largely out of reach and local and state party apparatuses decayed. It was the last place to fall to the Republican assault. Yet it proved ill-suited as the springboard for a Democratic revival. The high hopes of a more assertive legislative branch that accompanied the climax of the congressional reform movement evaporated with remarkable speed. A political culture centered on the president reasserted itself. Even with effective control of the legislature for most of this period (and uninterrupted control of the House throughout), there was little progress on a post–New Deal legislative agenda for the party, and little agreement on what such an agenda should look like. Unlike congressional Republicans in the early 1990s, the Democrats exhibited neither the inclination nor the ability to devise their own Contract with America to give definition to their congressional activities.

As Watergate Baby Tim Wirth of Colorado prepared to retire in 1992, he looked back on his arrival in Congress with considerable nostalgia. "It was a glory time," he said. "There was a tremendous sense of mutual mission. You really had a sense of why you were there and what you were doing."[16] Former president Gerald Ford was considerably less obliging about the Watergate Babies and their institutional legacy in a speech he gave the same year: "All they did was screw it up. . . . They took away the benefits of seniority, which created stability. . . . They undercut the capability of the leadership, both Democrat and Republican. . . . The net result is the House, in my judgement, has lost its capability to effectively handle the problems that are on its doorstep."[17] Neither assessment was wholly correct, however. That sense of "mutual mission" that Wirth so lionized dissipated quickly. But Ford too was ungenerous when he concluded that the reforms of the 1970s had left Congress unable to address itself to the problems that confronted the nation.

The case of one Watergate Baby, Henry Waxman of California, is instructive here. Waxman, a former member of the Young Democrats and the California assembly, had more experience than the average Watergate Baby when he arrived in Congress in 1975. He was also a protégé of Phillip Burton, who ensured that he was placed on several significant committees. On the same day that Burton was defeated for House majority leader in 1976, he successfully installed Waxman as the California delegation's representative on the Steering and Policy Committee, leapfrogging the more senior—and more conservative—Glenn Anderson.[18]

Unlike many other Watergate Babies, Waxman made a career of legislative politics. When he announced his retirement in January 2014, as the end of his twentieth consecutive term approached, the media response mixed elegy with panegyric. "Congressman's Exit Closes Book on 'Watergate Babies,'" ran the headline on one NPR blog. "When Waxman's departs, there will no longer be a House member who has been serving since that historic class of 75 Democrats was first elected in 1974."[19] By general consensus, Waxman left an enviable legislative legacy.[20] He had been a motive force in the Clean Air Act of 1990 (strengthening antipollution regulations, including for acid rain), the Ryan White Comprehensive AIDS Resources Emergency (CARE) Act of 1990 (the largest single medical program for Americans living with HIV/AIDS), the Food Quality Protection Act of 1996 (which established new regulations for pesticides), the Postal Accountability and Enhancement Act of 2006 (to improve transparency and accountability in the US Postal Service), the Family Smoking Prevention and Tobacco Control Act of 2009 (which gave the US Food and Drug Administration the right and ability to regulate tobacco), and more recently the Patient Protection and Affordable Care Act of 2010, popularly known as "Obamacare."[21] He was, wrote the *Washington Post*'s Harold Myerson, "liberalism's legislative genius."[22] He had been called the "Democrats' Eliot Ness" and the "Scariest Guy in Washington." His facial hair acquired its own nickname: the "mustache of justice."[23]

Waxman never held any office higher than that of committee chair. He never ran for a position in the House Democratic leadership, nor did he seek any statewide or national office. He never represented a constituency larger than a few hundred people. And yet he had an outsize impact on the lives of tens of millions of Americans. Waxman's career was unimaginable without the congressional reforms of the 1970s. His career also illustrates a remarkable irony of the Watergate Babies: that the class that burst into Congress with the intention of defenestrating the powerful conservative committee chairmen who had been gumming up liberal legislation for decades ended up being most successful at advancing liberalism through the very committees and subcommittees they had arrived to destroy. The "legislative dictatorship" that Ford had warned of back in 1974 may not have materialized, but a more diffuse and atomized "subcommittee government" certainly did.

The same Congress that obstructed Democratic efforts to hone a public philosophy for the post–New Deal order must also be acknowledged as the source of some of the most significant Democratic victories of the era. The institutional reforms of the 1970s both fragmented and stimulated liberal power throughout Congress. The cautious and reelection-conscious members were also "policy entrepreneurs," legislators keen to nurture substantial issue portfolios, for both self-interested and ideological motives. At this level, the postwar achievements of American liberalism were defended, and even expanded, albeit in less dramatic ways.

ABBREVIATIONS

CQA	*Congressional Quarterly Almanac*
CQWR	*Congressional Quarterly Weekly Report*
CSM	*Christian Science Monitor*
LAT	*Los Angeles Times*
NR	*New Republic*
NYT	*New York Times*
USNWR	*U.S. News & World Report*
WP	*Washington Post*
WP-TH	*Washington Post-Times Herald*
WSJ	*Wall Street Journal*

INTRODUCTION

1. Robert Shrum, *No Excuses: Concessions of a Serial Campaigner* (New York: Simon & Schuster, 2007), 46.

2. George McGovern, "Address Accepting the Presidential Nomination at the Democratic National Convention in Miami Beach, Florida," July 14, 1972, from *The American Presidency Project:* http://www.presidency.ucsb.edu/ws/?pid=25967#axzz2 ijdsgJda, accessed January 30, 2017.

3. It was assumed that if McGovern failed to clinch the nomination on the first ballot, he would likely be defeated on the second or third. A full account of the various challenges that the McGovern campaign had to confront can be found in Bruce Miroff, *The Liberals' Moment: The McGovern Insurgency and the Identity Crisis of the Democratic Party* (Lawrence: University Press of Kansas, 2009), 74–81.

4. Miroff, *The Liberals' Moment*, 81–82.

5. Indeed, during the convention, a group of senior Democratic and Republican Party officials, including Republican National Committee (RNC) chair Robert Dole and DNC chair Lawrence O'Brien, conducted fractious negotiations to determine what would happen in the event that the Democratic convention had not concluded by August 21. O'Brien was prepared to embrace a compromise, suggested by the mayor of Miami Beach, that Democratic and Republican delegates share the hall, but Dole refused, saying he "didn't want his clean-cut Republican delegates to be seen on television with people with long hair and blue jeans." Art Buchwald, "Democrats' Deadlock: Voting by Dawn's Early Light," *Washington Post-Times Herald* (hereafter *WP-TH*), July 13, 1972.

6. Joseph Alsop, "Nixon's Convention," *WP-TH*, July 12, 1972.

7. Dominic Sandbrook, *Eugene McCarthy: The Rise and Fall of Postwar American Liberalism* (New York: Alfred A. Knopf, 2004), 163–224; William Chafe, *Never Stop*

Running: Allard Lowenstein and the Struggle to Save American Liberalism (Princeton, NJ: Princeton University Press, 1998), 262–314.

8. South Dakota senator George McGovern was the commission's first chair, serving from 1969 to 1971. When he resigned to pursue a presidential bid, he was succeeded by Donald M. Fraser, a Minnesota congressman. A full analysis of the post-1968 reform of the party rules can be found in Byron E. Shafer, *Quiet Revolution: The Struggle for the Democratic Party and the Shaping of Post-Reform Politics* (New York: Russell Sage Foundation, 1983).

9. For a detailed account of McGovern's innovative and accomplished 1972 primary campaign, see Miroff, *The Liberals' Moment*, 41–71.

10. McGovern's request came in response to a letter from the House Caucus chairman Olin "Tiger" Teague, who had written to DNC chair Lawrence O'Brien suggesting that McGovern should make his pitch to the caucus members. Rowland Evans and Robert Novak, "McGovern Courts Congress," *WP-TH*, July 23, 1972.

11. Ben A. Franklin, "McGovern's Gain Embitters Labor," *NYT*, July 12, 1972.

12. Timothy N. Thurber, *The Politics of Equality: Hubert H. Humphrey and the African-American Freedom Struggle* (New York: Columbia University Press, 1999), 230.

13. Warren Weaver, Jr., "Democrats Gain 2 Seats and Have 57–43 Majority," *New York Times* (hereafter *NYT*), November 9, 1972; Steven V. Roberts, "The Elections: Praying For the 'Third Coming,'" *NYT*, November 12, 1975.

14. "Confidence Limited," *NYT*, November 8, 1972.

15. Miroff, *The Liberals' Moment*, 249.

16. Only the delegation from the Panama Canal Zone achieved the 50 percent target, though others came very close. Minnesota fielded a delegation that was 49 percent female, Massachusetts 48 percent, and Wisconsin 47 percent. Dorothy McCardle, "Democratic Convention: Giving Women a Piece of the Action," *Washington Post* (hereafter *WP*), June 18, 1972.

17. Westwood lasted only six months in the post. She was replaced by Robert Strauss in December 1972. R. W. Apple Jr., "Democrats Name Western Woman Party's Chairman," *NYT*, July 15, 1972.

18. The evening childcare center—complete with cribs, beds, and babysitters—was set up in a local elementary school and was intended to allow women delegates to attend sessions after 7 P.M. "Convention Child Care," *WP-TH*, January 26, 1972; McCardle, "Democratic Convention," *WP*, June 18, 1972.

19. The increase within state delegations between 1968 and 1972 was often even more dramatic. The proportion of African Americans in South Carolina's delegation had increased from 13 percent to 34.4 percent. In Louisiana from 18 to 43.2 percent, in Ohio from 3 to 20.6 percent, and in California from 5 to 18.8 percent. Robert McClory, "452 Blacks in Big Convention Role," *Chicago Daily Defender*, July 6, 1972.

20. Shirley Chisholm, *The Good Fight* (New York: Bantam, 1973).

21. E. J. Dionne, *They Only Look Dead: Why Progressives Will Dominate the Next Political Era* (New York: Simon & Schuster, 1996).

22. Miroff, *The Liberals' Moment*, 3–4, 6–7.

23. Jeffrey Bloodworth, *Losing the Center: The Decline of American Liberalism, 1968–1992* (Lexington: University Press of Kentucky, 2013), 3, 5.

24. Ronald Radosh, *Divided They Fell: The Demise of the Democratic Party, 1964–1996* (New York: Free Press, 1996), xi.

25. Michael Tomasky, *Left for Dead: The Life, Death, and Possible Resurrection of Progressive Politics in America* (New York: Free Press, 1996), 10–12.

26. Jefferson Cowie and Nick Salvatore, "The Long Exception: Rethinking the Place of the New Deal in American History," *International Labor and Working-Class History* 74 (Fall 2008): 5.

27. Sean Wilentz, *The Age of Reagan: A History, 1974–2008* (New York: Harper, 2008); Steven F. Hayward, *The Age of Reagan: The Fall of the Old Liberal Order, 1964–1980* (Roseville, CA: Forum, 2001), and *The Age of Reagan: The Conservative Counterrevolution, 1980–1989* (New York: Crown Forum, 2009).

28. Arthur M. Schlesinger Sr., "The Tides of National Politics," in *Paths to the Present* (New York: Macmillan, 1949); Arthur M. Schlesinger Jr., *The Cycles of American History* (London: Deutsch, 1987).

29. Walter Dean Burnham, *Critical Elections and the Mainsprings of American Politics* (New York: Norton, 1970), 181.

30. Alan Brinkley, "The Problem of American Conservatism," *American Historical Review* 99, no. 2 (April 1994): 409.

31. Mary C. Brennan, *Turning Right in the Sixties: The Conservative Capture of the GOP* (Chapel Hill: University of North Carolina Press, 1995). See also John A. Andrew III, *The Other Side of the Sixties: Young Americans for Freedom and the Rise of Conservative Politics* (New Brunswick, NJ: Rutgers University Press, 1997), and Nicol C. Rae, *The Decline and Fall of the Liberal Republicans: From 1952 to the Present* (New York: Oxford University Press, 1989).

32. Thomas Sugrue, *The Origins of the Urban Crisis: Race and Inequality in Postwar Detroit* (Princeton, NJ: Princeton University Press, 1996); Dan T. Carter, *From George Wallace to Newt Gingrich: Race in the Conservative Counterrevolution, 1963–1994* (Baton Rouge: Louisiana State University Press, 1996). See also Dan T. Carter, *The Politics of Rage: George Wallace, the Origins of the New Conservatism, and the Transformation of American Politics* (New York: Simon & Schuster, 1995).

33. Lisa McGirr, *Suburban Warriors: The Origins of the New American Right* (Princeton, NJ: Princeton University Press, 2001).

34. Kevin M. Kruse, *In God We Trust: How Corporate America Invented Christian America* (New York: Basic, 2015).

35. Nicole Hemmer, *Messengers of the Right: Conservative Media and the Transformation of American Politics* (Philadelphia: University of Pennsylvania Press, 2016).

36. Steven M. Teles, *The Rise of the Conservative Legal Movement: The Battle for Control of the Law* (Princeton, NJ: Princeton University Press, 2008).

37. Michael W. Flamm, *Law and Order: Street Crime, Civil Unrest, and the Crisis of Liberalism in the 1960s* (New York: Columbia University Press, 2005). See also, among others: Jonathan M. Schoenwald, *A Time for Choosing: The Rise of Modern American*

Conservatism (New York: Oxford University Press, 2001); John Micklethwait and Adrian Wooldridge, *The Right Nation: Why America Is Different* (London: Penguin, 2004); Geoffrey Kabaservice, *Rule and Ruin: The Downfall of Moderation and the Destruction of the Republican Party, From Eisenhower to the Tea Party* (New York: Oxford University Press, 2012); Laura Kalman, *Right Star Rising: A New Politics, 1974–1980* (New York: W. W. Norton, 2010); Dominic Sandbrook, *Mad As Hell: The Crisis of the 1970s and the Rise of the Populist Right* (New York: Alfred A. Knopf, 2011); Rick Perlstein, *Before the Storm: Barry Goldwater and the Unmaking of the American Consensus* (New York: Nation, 2001); Rick Perlstein, *Nixonland: The Rise of a President and the Fracturing of America* (New York: Scribner, 2008); Rick Perlstein, *The Invisible Bridge: The Fall of Nixon and the Rise of Reagan* (New York: Simon & Schuster, 2014); and Robert Mason, *Richard Nixon and the Quest for a New Majority* (Chapel Hill: University of North Carolina Press, 2004).

38. There are some exceptions. See, for instance, Jonathan Bell, *California Crucible: The Forging of Modern American Liberalism* (Philadelphia: University of Pennsylvania Press, 2012); Timothy Stanley, *Kennedy vs. Carter: The 1980 Battle for the Democratic Party's Soul* (Lawrence: University Press of Kansas, 2010); Bradford D. Martin, *The Other Eighties: A Secret History of America in the Age of Reagan* (New York: Hill and Wang, 2011); David Courtwright, *No Right Turn: Conservative Politics in a Liberal America* (Cambridge, MA: Harvard University Press, 2010); Bloodworth, *Losing the Center*.

39. Norman Ornstein, "The Permanent Democratic Congress," *Public Interest* (Summer 1990), 24.

40. Thomas C. Cochran, "'The "Presidential Synthesis' in American History," *American Historical Review* 53, no. 4 (July 1948): 748. See also Julian E. Zelizer, "Beyond the Presidential Synthesis: Reordering Political Time," in *A Companion to Post-1945 America*, ed. Jean-Christophe Agnew and Roy Rosenzweig (Malden, MA: Blackwell, 2006).

41. Kenneth Kato and Elizabeth Rybicki have argued that scholars' comparative neglect of Congress can partly be ascribed to "the inherent complex nature of a legislature. Focus and emphasis become constant problems in congressional history, forcing an endless series of choices. Should the emphasis be on events, organizations, or individuals? Should the focus be on the floor activities of Congress, the committee rooms, or the campaign trail?" Kenneth Kato and Elizabeth Rybicki, "Congressional History: A Literature Review," *OAH Magazine of History* 12, no. 4 (Summer 1998): 5.

42. A Gallup poll taken in 1981 showed that only 30 percent of Americans believed that less than 25 cents of every dollar collected in tax was wasted. Other polling firms show a similar collapse in public trust in the federal government. "Trust in Government," n.d., *Gallup.com*, accessed June 29, 2014, http://www.gallup.com/poll/5392/trust-government.aspx; "Public Trust in Government: 1958–2013," Pew Research Center for the People & the Press, October 18, 2013, accessed June 29, 2013, http://www.people-press.org/2013/10/18/trust-in-government-interactive/; "Government,"

Gallup.com, accessed June 29, 2013, http://www.gallup.com/poll/27286/government .aspx#3.

43. R. Shep Melnick, "Governing More but Enjoying It Less," in *Taking Stock: American Government in the Twentieth Century*, ed. Morton Keller and R. Shep Melnick (Cambridge: Cambridge University Press, 1999), 281, 301.

44. Robert A. Rutland, *The Democrats: From Jefferson to Carter* (Baton Rouge: Louisiana State University Press, 1979), 1.

45. Yanek Mieczkowski, *Gerald Ford and the Challenges of the 1970s* (Lexington: University Press of Kentucky, 2005), 65.

46. Lanny J. Davis, *The Emerging Democratic Majority: Lessons and Legacies from the New Politics* (New York: Stein and Day, 1974).

47. Burdett Loomis, *The New American Politician: Ambition, Entrepreneurship, and the Changing Face of Political Life* (New York: Basic, 1988).

48. Theodore J. Lowi, "What's New About Neoliberals," *WP*, June 16, 1985.

CHAPTER 1. "WE CAME HERE TO TAKE THE BASTILLE"

1. Philip Shabecoff, "A Blue-Collar Voter Discusses His Switch to Nixon," *NYT*, November 6, 1972.

2. Thomas J. Sugrue and John D. Skrentny, "The White Ethnic Strategy," in *Rightward Bound: Making America Conservative in the 1970s*, ed. Bruce J. Schulman and Julian E. Zelizer (Cambridge, MA: Harvard University Press, 2008). See also, Joe Merton, "Rethinking the Politics of White Ethnicity in 1970s America," *Historical Journal* 55, no. 3 (September 2012): 731–756.

3. Jefferson Cowie, "Nixon's Class Struggle: Romancing the New Right Worker, 1969–1973," *Labor History* 43, no. 3 (2002): 258–283; Ronald Radosh, *Divided They Fell: The Demise of the Democratic Party, 1964–1996* (New York: Free Press, 1996), xi.

4. Jefferson Cowie, *Stayin' Alive: The 1970s and the Last Days of the Working Class* (New York: New Press, 2010), 159.

5. The definitive history of this white backlash is Thomas Edsall and Mary Edsall, *Chain Reaction: The Impact of Race, Rights, and Taxes on American Politics* (New York: Norton, 1992).

6. Michael Kernan, "Out of the Inner Suburbs," *WP-TH*, September 2, 1973.

7. The Maryland fifth had seen a prolonged period of Democratic control since the New Deal, with the Republicans winning the seat for only one term after the Eisenhower landslide of 1952. In 1968, the seat was one of a handful to benefit from Nixon's coattails and elect a Republican, Lawrence Hogan. He was reelected twice with an increased majority on both occasions.

8. Bart Barnes, "Former Md. Representative Gladys N. Spellman, 70, Dies," *WP*, June 20, 1988.

9. Charles A. Krause, "Sen. Kennedy Makes Big Hit As Backer of Mrs. Spellman," *WP*, October 7, 1974.

10. Karen DeYoung, "They Say Gladys Spellman Is as Good as She Says," *WP*, October 25, 1976.

11. Hogan declined to run for reelection and instead made a bid for the Republican gubernatorial nomination. He lost in the primary. Harold J. Logan, "Spellman Seeks Hogan House Seat," *WP*, June 2, 1974.

12. B. D. Cohen, "Gladys Spellman Rings Up Reaction of Food Shoppers," *WP*, October 17, 1974.

13. Douglas Watson, "Spellman Wins Over Burcham; Gude, Holt Beat Democratic Foes," *WP*, November 6, 1974.

14. Alan Ehrenhalt, "Suburbia Gains Plurality in House But Not Influence," *WP*, April 28, 1974.

15. Lewis Chester, Godfrey Hodgson, and Bruce Page, *An American Melodrama: The Presidential Campaign of 1968* (New York: Viking, 1969), 376.

16. Richard L. Lyons, "Democrats Intensify Role in the House," *WP*, November 7, 1974.

17. Editorial, "Mr. Nixon's Game Plan," *NYT*, December 18, 1972.

18. "Impoundment" is the practice of a president simply refusing to spend money that Congress has appropriated for a particular executive function. As Gareth Davies has pointed out, the impoundment of appropriated funds was not a strategy that had begun with Nixon. Both Kennedy and Johnson had done it, for instance, and more frequently. Though partisanship explains some of the congressional opprobrium, what set Nixon's use of the power apart was the considerably larger sums he impounded and the fact that he used it to effectively defund entire programs, rather than simply shrinking them. Gareth Davies, *See Government Grow: Education Politics from Johnson to Reagan* (Lawrence: University Press of Kansas, 2007), 98.

19. "An Introspective and Angry Congress Begins Its Work," *Congressional Quarterly Weekly Report* (hereafter *CQWR*), January 6, 1973.

20. James M. Naughton, "Nixon-Congress Battle," *NYT*, March 14, 1973.

21. Despite coining that enduring critique of executive overreach, Schlesinger favored vigorous presidential leadership to overcome the potential for inaction encouraged by a constitution that "institutionalized conflict" and promoted inertia. Arthur M. Schlesinger Jr., *The Imperial Presidency* (Boston: Houghton Mifflin, 1989), viii, ix, viii.

22. James L. Sundquist, *The Decline and Resurgence of Congress* (Washington, DC: Brookings Institution, 1981), 155.

23. Despite this, from the outset the House and Senate Budget Committees were suspicious of encroachments by the Congressional Budget Office on their turf. When Dr. Alice Rivlin became the Congressional Budget Office's first director, Dr. William Capron, of Harvard's John F. Kennedy School of Government, advised her to move slowly in building the staff and observe a "flat rule" not to accept any staff member solely on House or Senate recommendation. Such internal conflicts undermined Congress's effectiveness against the executive. Letter, Dr. William Capron to Alice Rivlin, February 25, 1975, papers of Alice M. Rivlin, Manuscript Reading Room, Library of Congress, Box 2.

24. Gallup Poll (AIPO), August 1974. Retrieved August 19, 2013, from the iPOLL Databank, the Roper Center for Public Opinion Research, University of Connecticut,

http://ezproxy.ouls.ox.ac.uk:4032/data_access/ipoll/ipoll.html, last accessed January 30, 2017.

25. David S. Broder, "6 Senior House Republicans to Retire," *WP*, January 1, 1974.

26. Christopher Lydon, "Democrat Favored to Win House Seat in San Francisco Area in Special Election Tuesday," *NYT*, June 3, 1974.

27. Vander Veen was reelected to a full term in November 1974 but lost his seat to Republican Harold S. Sawyer in 1976. "Michigan Democrat Wins in Voting for Ford's Seat," *NYT*, February 19, 1974; Mary Russell, "VanderVeen [*sic*] Calls Victory a Signal for Nixon Ouster," *WP*, February 22, 1974; "Republicans Fear of Watergate," *Chicago Defender*, February 26, 1974.

28. Christopher Lydon, "Democrat Favored to Win House Seat in San Francisco Area in Special Election Tuesday," *NYT*, June 3, 1974.

29. "Text of President's Pardon of Nixon," *WP*, September 9, 1974.

30. Letter, Abraham Ribicoff to constituents, September 20, 1974, papers of Abraham Ribicoff, Library of Congress, Box 394.

31. Richard Dudman, "Is Ford Protecting Nixon," *St. Louis Post-Dispatch*, September 17, 1974, offprint in the papers of John F. Osborne, Library of Congress, Box 42; Editorial, "Mr. Ford's Folly," *NYT*, September 15, 1974.

32. "In the People's House," *NYT*, October 6, 1974.

33. Naughton, "Nixon-Congress Battle."

34. Haynes Johnson, "Ford's Historic Visit: Questions Remain," *WP*, October 18, 1974; James M. Naughton, "History Played Out on Familiar Stage," *NYT*, October 18, 1974.

35. Holtzman joked later that it may have been sexism that led her to be her brother's running mate, or perhaps that he was "a half-hour older." "Elizabeth Holtzman," *NYT*, June 22, 1972.

36. "Elizabeth Holtzman," *NYT*, June 22, 1972.

37. Thomas P. Ronan, "A Woman Leader in Brooklyn to Challenge Celler in Primary," *NYT*, March 29, 1972.

38. "Court Dismisses Celler's Suit to Nullify Democratic Primary," *NYT*, August 30, 1972; Elizabeth Holtzman, "How to Be Young and Female in Congress," *Politico Magazine*, February 15, 2015, accessed July 25, 2018, https://www.politico.com/magazine/story/2015/02/elise-stefanik-elizabeth-holtzman-advice-115071.

39. Maurice Carroll, "Miss Holtzman, Vowing Reform, Prepares to Sit in Rep. Celler's Congressional Seat," *NYT*, October 2, 1972.

40. The *Times* published an op-ed composed of excerpts from a speech Holtzman had made to New York Women in Communications. Elizabeth Holtzman, "Exercising Freshperson Power," *NYT*, April 14, 1974.

41. Holtzman had sought a seat on the Commerce Committee but "was told by House leadership that there was no opening for a New York Democrat" there. Richard L. Madden, "Miss Holtzman Given Judiciary Post."

42. Holtzman cited Article 1, Section 6, which forbids a sitting member of Congress from appointment to any federal office if the emoluments for that office have

been increased during their term. Ford had voted for a bill in October 1973 that made the eligibility criteria for cost of living increases in congressional and civil service retirement annuities more generous. The committee rejected Holtzman's motion to table the nomination. Marjorie Hunter, "House Unit Backs Ford Nomination," *NYT*, November 30, 1973.

43. Grace Lichtenstein, "Rep. Holtzman, One of Six Likely Winners in Brooklyn, Is a TV Personality in her Second Race," *NYT*, October 31, 1973.

44. Julian E. Zelizer, *On Capitol Hill: The Struggle to Reform and Its Consequences, 1948–2000* (Cambridge, MA: Cambridge University Press, 2004), 158.

45. Marquis Childs, "Euphoria among the Democrats," *WP*, October 8, 1974.

46. David S. Broder, "Election '74: The Year of the Democrats," *WP*, October 6, 1974.

47. Christopher Lydon, "The Awful Arithmetic," *NYT*, April 21, 1974, 213.

48. "1974 Elections: A Major Sweep for the Democrats," *Congressional Quarterly Almanac* (hereafter *CQA*) 30 (1974): 839–840.

49. Zelizer, *On Capitol Hill*, 163.

50. Diane Granat, "Whatever Happened to the Watergate Babies?" *CQWR*, March 3, 1984.

51. "New Congress Is Youngest Since World War II," *CQA* 30 (1974): 852–853.

52. Edgar would be reelected five times, retiring in 1987 to mount an unsuccessful Senate run as the longest-serving Democrat from the district. Granat, "Whatever Happened to the Watergate Babies?"

53. Fithian had been Landgrebe's opponent in 1972, losing in the general election by almost 10 points. In 1974, he won 61 percent to Landgrebe's 38 percent. Fithian was the first Democrat to represent the district since 1935. James M. Naughton, "Senate and House Margins Are Substantially Enlarged," *NYT*, November 6, 1974.

54. The Senate continued to boast only one African American member, liberal Republican Edward Brooke of Massachusetts, who would lose his seat to Democrat Paul Tsongas in 1978. No other black American would serve in the upper chamber until 1993.

55. While the Senate remained an all-male body, the Ninety-Fourth Congress saw a record 18 women serving in the House. "New Congress Is Youngest Since World War II," *CQA*.

56. Broder, "Election '74: The Year of the Democrats."

57. Lily Geismer, in her recent study of politically conscious residents of Boston's Route 128 suburbs, has shown how crucial highly educated white-collar suburbanites in high-tech jobs have become to the Democratic Party since the 1970s, with their priorities and their prejudices reflected in the national party's agenda. Lily Geismer, *Don't Blame Us: Suburban Liberals and the Transformation of the Democratic Party* (Princeton, NJ: Princeton University Press, 2014).

58. "Suburbs and the South: Democratic Gold Mines," *CQA* 30 (1974): 854.

59. This meant that nine of the region's eleven governorships were in Democratic hands. Maine's gubernatorial race was won in an upset by the independent candidate,

James B. Longley. Only New Hampshire still had a Republican governor, Meldrim Thomson Jr. Stephen Isaacs, "Democrats Sweep Most of Northeast's Governorships," *WP*, November 6, 1974.

60. Isaacs, "Democrats Sweep Most of Northeast's Governorships."

61. Tsongas for Senate Leaflet, 1978, Paul E. Tsongas, Congressional Collection, Center for Lowell History, University of Massachusetts, Lowell, Box 51B.

62. Paul E. Tsongas, *Journey of Purpose: Reflections on the Presidency, Multiculturalism, and Third Parties* (New Haven, CT: Yale University Press, 1995), 12.

63. "Tsongas Runs for Congress in the 5th District," *Boston Globe*, May 23, 1974.

64. "A Tight Tsongas-Cronin Race," *Boston Globe*, November 4, 1974.

65. Richard F. Fenno Jr., *Senators on the Campaign Trail: The Politics of Representation* (Norman: University of Oklahoma Press, 1996), 22–31.

66. Rowland Evans and Robert Novak, "John Glenn's Political Orbit," *WP*, September 14, 1974.

67. William E. Farrell, "Victory by Glenn Linked to Image," *NYT*, May 9, 1974; Jules Witcover, "Metzenbaum-Glenn Race Under Nixon Shadow," *WP*, May 5, 1974.

68. Marquis Childs, "Euphoria among the Democrats," *WP*, October 8, 1974.

69. Mary Russell, "Democrats Put Halt to Republican Momentum in South," *WP*, November 6, 1974.

70. Dale Bumpers, *The Best Lawyer in a One-Lawyer Town: A Memoir* (New York: Random House, 2003), 235, 238. See also, Randall Bennett Woods, *Fulbright: A Biography* (Cambridge: Cambridge University Press, 1995), 654–671.

71. Russell, "Democrats Put Halt to Republican Momentum in South."

72. Paul R. Wieck, "How They Won in Colorado," *New Republic* (hereafter *NR*), November 23, 1974, 8.

73. Letter, Gary Hart to Mr. J. J. Hofmeister, July 9, 1974, papers of Gary W. Hart, University of Colorado, Boulder, Box 53.

74. Miroff, *The Liberals' Moment*, 44, 154; David S. Broder, "Hart Sheds '72 Image," *WP*, September 8, 1974.

75. Miroff, *The Liberals' Moment*, 286; *Right from the Start* (1973) quoted in Gary Hart, *The Thunder and the Sunshine: Four Seasons in a Burnished Life* (Golden, CO: Fulcrum, 2010), 22.

76. Letter, "Dear Friend," Hart for Senate 1974, November 12, 1973, papers of Gary W. Hart, University of Colorado, Boulder, Box 53.

77. Campaign flier, Hart for Senate 1974, undated, papers of Gary W. Hart, University of Colorado, Boulder, Box 53.

78. Speech, Gary Hart, "Now It's Our Turn," delivered at Costigan-Cervi Democratic Club, April 9, 1974, papers of Gary W. Hart, University of Colorado, Boulder, Box 53.

79. Norman C. Miller, "The Transformation of Gary Hart," *Wall Street Journal* (hereafter *WSJ*), October 28, 1974. See also, Broder, "Hart Sheds '72 Image."

80. Gary Hart, "The End of the New Deal," Remarks at the University of Denver, September 25, 1974, papers of Gary W. Hart, University of Colorado, Boulder, Box 54.

81. Ethan Rarick, *California Rising: The Life and Times of Pat Brown* (Berkeley: University of California Press, 2005), 1, 3.

82. See Matthew Dallek, *The Right Moment: Ronald Reagan's First Victory and the Decisive Turning Point in American Politics* (New York, NY: Oxford University Press, 2000).

83. Jerry Brown, untitled speech, 1974, papers of Edmund G. (Jerry) Brown, Jr., University of Southern California, Box B-32-9; Bell, *California Crucible*, 270.

84. Bill Boyarsky, "Brown's Campaign—Old-Fashioned but Mod," *Los Angeles Times*, May 29, 1974.

85. Brown for Governor, 1974, election leaflet, papers of Jerry Brown, University of Southern California, Box B-32-9.

86. "1974 Elections: A Major Sweep for the Democrats," *CQA* 30, 1974, 839.

87. David S. Broder, "Big Majority of Big Spenders," *WP*, November 3, 1974.

88. Letter, Hart to Hubert Humphrey, December 5, 1974, papers of Gary W. Hart, University of Colorado Boulder, Box 53.

89. Letter, Hart to William McCormick Blair, January 3, 1974, papers of Gary W. Hart, University of Colorado Boulder, Box 53.

90. Eric Alterman and Kevin Mattson, *The Cause: The Fight for American Liberalism from Franklin Roosevelt to Barack Obama* (New York: Viking, 2012), 186.

91. Perlstein, *Nixonland*, 6.

92. William Schneider, "JFK's Children: The Class of '74," *Atlantic Monthly*, March 1989.

93. Wirth shared the faith of his colleague Gary Hart in increasing citizen participation. "I hope that some of the current lack of faith in government," he wrote, "can be dispelled by fostering more citizen participation in public affairs." "The Wirth Washington Letter," No. 2, December 1975, papers of Timothy E. Wirth, University of Colorado Boulder, Box 2.

94. Daniel Patrick Moynihan, *Coping: Essays on the Practice of Government* (New York: Random House, 1973), 27.

95. Robert G. Kaufman, *Henry M. Jackson: A Life in Politics* (Seattle: University of Washington Press, 2000), 313, 329.

96. Randall Rothenberg, *The Neoliberals: Creating the New American Politics* (New York: Simon & Schuster, 1984), 22.

97. Schneider, "JFK's Children."

98. Sanford J. Ungar, "Bleak House: Frustration on Capitol Hill," *Atlantic Monthly*, July 1977.

99. Steven M. Gillon, *The Pact: Bill Clinton, Newt Gingrich, and the Rivalry That Defined a Generation* (New York: Oxford University Press, 2008), 9. See also, Maurice Isserman and Michael Kazin, *America Divided: The Civil War of the 1960s* (3rd ed., New York: Oxford University Press, 2008) and Mark H. Lytle, *America's Uncivil Wars: The Sixties Era from Elvis to the Fall of Richard Nixon* (New York: Oxford University Press, 2006).

100. Stephen Green, "New Members in House Planning for Bloc Voting," *WP*, November 30, 1974.

101. Granat, "Whatever Happened to the Watergate Babies?"

102. G. Calvin Mackenzie and Robert Weisbrot, *The Liberal Hour: Washington and the Politics of Change in the 1960s* (New York: Penguin, 2008), 38.

103. Schneider, "JFK's Children."

104. M. Robert Carr, interview with the author, via Skype, March 14, 2013.

105. Richard Bolling, *House Out of Order* (New York: Dutton, 1965), 221.

106. Granat, "Whatever Happened to the Watergate Babies?"

107. Bruce Wolpe, interview with the author, Washington, DC, January 20, 2012.

108. Jack Anderson, "When Will the Old Men of Congress Be Forced to Quit?" *Parade*, April 26, 1970, offprint in the papers of Patsy T. Mink, Library of Congress, Box 679.

109. Common Cause, Report from Washington, vol. 5, no. 2, December 1974– January 1975, in the papers of Patsy T. Mink, Library of Congress, Box 680.

110. Peter C. Stuart, "Mills's Authority Wanes in Congress," *Christian Science Monitor* (hereafter *CSM*), December 4, 1974.

111. Zelizer, *On Capitol Hill*, 159.

112. John Jacobs, *A Rage for Justice: The Passion and Politics of Phillip Burton* (Berkeley: University of California Press, 1995), 262.

113. Caucus Minutes, December 2, 1974, papers of the House Democratic Caucus, Library of Congress, Box 4.

114. Mary Russell, "Mills Will Lose Chairmanship, Albert Confirms," *WP*, December 5, 1974.

115. Herblock cartoon, 1974, papers of Phillip Burton, Bancroft Library, University of California, Berkeley, Carton 12.

116. Jacobs, *A Rage for Justice*, 268.

117. Hearings before the Caucus on the Organization of the Ninety-Fourth Congress, January 16, 1975, papers of the House Democratic Caucus, Library of Congress, Box 5.

118. Zelizer, *On Capitol Hill*, 171.

119. Zelizer, *On Capitol Hill*, 170.

120. Hearings before the Caucus on the Organisation of the Ninety-Fourth Congress, January 13, 1975, papers of the House Democratic Caucus, Library of Congress, Box 5.

121. Granat, "Whatever Happened to the Watergate Babies?"

122. Thomas P. O'Neill Jr. and William Novak, *Man of the House: The Life and Political Memoirs of Speaker Tip O'Neill* (New York: Random House, 1987), 283–284.

123. Burdett Loomis, *The New American Politician: Ambition, Entrepreneurship, and the Changing Face of Political Life* (New York: Basic, 1988), 4.

124. Ungar, "Bleak House."

125. Richard D. Lyons, "House Democrats Vote to Weaken Seniority System," *NYT*, December 5, 1974.

126. Barbara Sinclair, "Congressional Reform," in *The American Congress: The Building of* Democracy, ed. Julian E. Zelizer (Boston: Houghton Mifflin, 2004), 630.

127. Hubert H. Humphrey, "Notes and Memoranda: The Senate on Trial," *American Political Science Review* 44, no. 3 (September 1950): 651.

128. Zelizer, *On Capitol Hill*, 173–175. See also, Walter F. Mondale and Dave Hage, *The Good Fight: A Life in Liberal Politics* (New York: Scribner, 2010), 111–134.

129. Granat, "Whatever Happened to the Watergate Babies?"

130. Schneider, "JFK's Children."

131. Zelizer, *On Capitol Hill*, 34.

132. Harry McPherson, *A Political Education* (Boston: Little, Brown, 1972), 30.

133. Zelizer, *On Capitol Hill*, 34.

134. Arthur M. Schlesinger, "The Future of Liberalism: I. The Challenge of Abundance," *The Reporter* (May 3, 1956).

135. Joseph Kraft, "Divergence Among the Democrats," *WP*, November 7, 1974.

136. Bruce Wolpe, author interview.

137. "Congressional Government: Can It Happen?" *CQWR*, June 28, 1975.

CHAPTER 2. "THE LAST ELECTION MEANS
THE BUCK STOPS HERE"

1. David S. Broder, "The Democrats Dilemma," *Atlantic*, March 1974.

2. Midterm conventions had been mooted before. In 1937, for instance, former president Herbert Hoover had endorsed the idea as a means of reenergizing the Republican Party against FDR's surging Democrats. As a mechanism of policy formulation, the midterm convention enjoyed the support of many political scientists, and the question had been intermittently taken up by both parties' national committees. The Democrats were the first to experiment with the format. William Chapman, "Off-Year Democratic Convention Eyed," *WP*, May 20, 1972; "Hoover Favors Mid-Term Rally of Republicans," *WP*, August 9, 1937; Editorial, "Midterm Conventions," *WP*, April 3, 1953.

3. Kathryn J. McGarr, *The Whole Damn Deal: Robert Strauss and the Art of Politics* (New York: PublicAffairs, 2011), 154.

4. Edward T. Folliard, "The Appeal of Harry Truman," *WP*, April 28, 1974.

5. "Truman-Mania," *NBC Evening News*, April 13, 1975, Vanderbilt; William Chapman, "Truman Tells It His Way—Scorchingly," *WP*, November 22, 1973; "Senate Votes to Create Truman Scholarships," *WP*, August 8, 1974; "Truman Portrait Hung in White House by Ford," *NYT*, August 21, 1974, 25.

6. William V. Shannon, "Another Truman?" *NYT*, July 2, 1975.

7. DNC sample fund-raising letter, 1974 Campaign Sourcebook, Published by the Democratic National Committee, Office of the Congressional Liaison, "Campaign '74 Source Book—DNC," Jimmy Carter Library, Box 1.

8. "Hoover Favors MidTerm Rally of Republicans," *WP*, August 9, 1937.

9. Editorial, "Midterm Conventions," *WP*, April 3, 1953.

10. Myra MacPherson, "Mr. Chairman: The Texas Touch of Bob Strauss," *WP*, January 5, 1975; Paul R. Wieck, "Chairman Strauss' Hot Seat," *NR*, April 20, 1974.

11. McGarr, *The Whole Damn Deal*, 136, 141.

12. MacPherson, "Mr. Chairman."

13. Paul R. Wieck, "Everything Hunky-dory in Kansas City," *NR*, December 21, 1974.

14. Rowland Evans and Robert Novak, "Toward a Democratic Collision," *WP*, December 9, 1974; MacPherson, "Mr. Chairman."

15. David S. Broder, "Democrats Adopt Their First Charter," *WP*, December 8, 1974.

16. R. W. Apple Jr., "Conservative Parley Taken up with Talk of 3d Party," *NYT*, February 15, 1975.

17. William A. Rusher, "A New Party: Eventually, Why Not Now?" *National Review*, May 23, 1975.

18. Yanek Mieczkowski, *Gerald Ford and the Challenges of the 1970s* (Lexington: University Press of Kentucky, 2005), 65.

19. "Congressional Government: Can It Happen?" *CQWR*, June 28, 1975.

20. "Transcript of President Ford's Address to Joint Session of Congress and the Nation," *NYT*, August 13, 1974.

21. Minutes of the Democratic Caucus for the Organization of the Ninety-Fourth Congress, December 2, 1974, papers of the House Democratic Caucus, Library of Congress, Box 4.

22. *Time*, November 18, 1974.

23. See Robert V. Remini, *The House: The History of the House of Representatives* (New York: Smithsonian Books, 2006), chapters 11 and 12.

24. Philip Shabecoff, "Ford Warns G.O.P. On Rivals' Sweep," *NYT*, October 17, 1974; Philip Shabecoff, "Ford Says a 'Runaway Congress' Would Harm Peace," *NYT*, October 30, 1974.

25. Mary Russell, "GOP Fears Return of 'King Caucus' in House Next Year," *WP*, July 29, 1974.

26. Burton had won a special election in California's sixth district in early 1964—only a few months before LBJ would reveal his "Great Society"—as a supporter of expanding health care and civil rights. He had also expressed some sympathy toward the idea of improving relations with China and Cuba. In an uncharacteristic show of humility, he promised that he would be "going to do a lot of listening and learning. They've been running that shop a long time without me." A year later, he was a vice chair of the pro-reform Democratic Study Group. "New Man in House Promises Silence," *NYT*, February 23, 1964; "Democratic Liberals Elect Representative Thompson," *NYT*, March 4, 1965.

27. Jacobs, *A Rage for Justice*, xx.

28. John A. Farrell, *Tip O'Neill and the Democratic Century* (Boston: Little, Brown, 2001), 388.

29. David E. Rosenbaum, "Congress Has Its Reform; Now What?" *NYT*, December 8, 1974.

30. Dominic Sandbrook, *Eugene McCarthy: The Rise and Fall of Postwar American Liberalism* (New York: Alfred A. Knopf, 2004), 76–79.

31. Political Report, "Democratic Study Group Shifts Role in 91st Congress," October 10, 1969, papers of the Democratic Study Group, Library of Congress, Part II, Box 1.

32. Interview with Conlon, July 5, 1974, papers of the Democratic Study Group, Library of Congress, Part II, Box 2.

33. Interview with Conlon, July 5, 1974, papers of the Democratic Study Group, Library of Congress, Part II, Box 2.

34. Interview with Conlon, July 5, 1974, papers of the Democratic Study Group, Library of Congress, Part II, Box 2; Jacobs, *A Rage for Justice*, 222.

35. "Uprising on Capitol Hill," *NYT*, February 18, 1970; "Rebellion in the House," *NYT*, March 22, 1970; Marjorie Hunter, "House Democrats Uphold Seniority by 30-Vote Margin," *NYT*, February 4, 1971; editorial, "The Stifling Hand of Seniority," *WP-TH*, January 11, 1971; Mary Russell, "Revolt on Capitol Hill," *WP*, February 4, 1976.

36. Jacobs, *A Rage for Justice*, 229.

37. "Battle Looms in Democratic Study Group," *WP-TH*, February 23, 1971.

38. Jacobs, *A Rage for Justice*, 220.

39. "Study Unit Split on Chief," *WP-TH*, February 25, 1971.

40. Myrna Oliver, "James C. Corman; 10-Term Valley Congressman Championed Civil Rights, Welfare Legislation," *Los Angeles Times* (hereafter *LAT*), January 3, 2001.

41. Jacobs, *A Rage for Justice*, 229; "Democratic Study Group Elects Burton," *WP-TH*, March 10, 1971.

42. Lou Cannon, "Burton Will Spark Liberals," *St. Paul Pioneer Press*, March 15, 1971, clipping in the Phillip Burton papers, Bancroft Library, Carton 10.

43. Jacobs, *A Rage for Justice*, 230–231, 241–247; Farrell, *Tip O'Neill and the Democratic Century*, 394.

44. Jacobs, *A Rage for Justice*, 233.

45. M. Robert Carr, author interview.

46. Democratic Study Group ad, *NYT*, September 15, 1974, emphasis in original.

47. Letter, Tim Wirth to Phillip Burton, July 15, 1974, Phillip Burton papers, Bancroft Library, Carton 4.

48. Jacobs, *A Rage for Justice*, 252–254; Gerald R. Rosen, "The Most Powerful Man in Congress?" *Dun's Review*, Offprint in the papers of the Democratic Study Group, Library of Congress, Part II, Box 2.

49. Letter, Terry M. Moshenko to Phillip Burton, July 18, 1974; Letter, Jim Lloyd to Phillip Burton, July 17, 1974, Phillip Burton papers, Bancroft Library, Carton 4.

50. "Demo Study Group Now Dominant House Power," *Evansville Courier*, clipping in the papers of the Democratic Study Group, Library of Congress, Part II, Box 26.

51. "Visit from 'Fishbait' Sets Liberals Buzzing," *Greensboro Daily News*, November 24, 1972, offprint in the papers of the Democratic Study Group, Library of Congress, Part II, Box 26; Richard L. Lyons, "House Dixie Bloc Losing Clout," *WP*, February 15, 1973.

52. Mary Russell, "Liberal House Democrat Contest: Loyalist vs. Independent," *WP*, February 26, 1979.

53. Richard E. Cohen, "The DSG's Identity Crisis," *CQWR*, January 27, 1979.

54. Saul B. Shapiro, "Picking Up the Pieces: Whatever Became of the DSG?" *Nation*, August 8–15, 1981.

55. Statement of Richard P. Conlon, Task Force on Work Management House Commission on Administrative Review, June 1, 1977, papers of the Democratic Study Group, Library of Congress, Part II, Box 3.

56. Letter, Richard Conlon to Bill Hansel, July 18, 1977, papers of the Democratic Study Group, Library of Congress, Part II, Box 50.

57. Editorial, "The Democratic Caucus in Command," *WP*, January 20, 1975.

58. Jacobs, *A Rage for Justice*, 257.

59. By 1966, the conservative broadcaster Fulton Lewis Jr. was denouncing Burton as one of a group of California-based "radical leftists" and "peaceniks." Fulton Lewis Jr., "Calif. Democrats Nominate Peaceniks for Congress," *Human Events*, July 2, 1966, offprint in the Phillip Burton papers, Bancroft Library, Carton 10.

60. Common Cause press release, March 1, 1973; Letter, John W. Gardner to Phillip Burton, March 2, 1973, Phillip Burton papers, Bancroft Library, Carton 11.

61. Telegram, Cesar Chavez to Phillip Burton, April 25, 1972, Phillip Burton papers, Bancroft Library, Carton 3.

62. Jacobs, *A Rage for Justice*, 259.

63. John Pierson, "A New Boss for House Democrats?" *WSJ*, November 29, 1974.

64. Pierson, "A New Boss for House Democrats?"

65. Caucus minutes, December 2, 1974, papers of the House Democratic Caucus, Library of Congress, Box 4.

66. Mary Russell, "Burton Wins; Mills Set Back," *WP*, December 3, 1974.

67. William Safire, "Too Big a Majority," *NYT*, January 23, 1975; William Safire, "Reagan vs. 'McGovernment,'" *NYT*, March 31, 1975.

68. Jim Orton cartoon, April 1, 1975, Phillip Burton papers, Bancroft Library, Carton 12.

69. Lacey Fosburgh, "Antiwar Rally Draws 300 Here; Mrs. Abzug Urges No Letdown in Effort," *NYT*, October 16, 1970; "Capitol Peace Group Is Met by Mrs. Abzug," *NYT*, May 13, 1971; "Bella Abzug," *NYT*, April 1, 1998.

70. M. Robert Carr, author interview. At one meeting of the House Democrats in 1975, confronted with the new members, Abzug reportedly exclaimed, "My God, the reinforcements have arrived!" John E. Yang, "In the Wake of Watergate, Reformers Charged Hill," *WP*, June 15, 1992.

71. M. Robert Carr, author interview.

72. Hearings, Special Democratic Caucus for Consideration of Resolution Opposing Further Military Assistance to Cambodia and Vietnam, and Resolution Supporting the Emergency Employment Appropriations Act of 1975, March 12, 1975, papers of the House Democratic Caucus, Library of Congress, Box 6.

73. John W. Finney, "House Democrats Opposed, 189–49, to Cambodian Aid," *NYT*, March 13, 1975.

74. Between 1974 and 1978, the House Committee on Foreign Affairs was renamed the Committee on International Relations. Jacobs, *A Rage for Justice*, 274.

75. Hearings, Special Democratic Caucus, Cambodia/Vietnam resolution, March 12, 1975, papers of the House Democratic Caucus, Library of Congress, Box 6.

76. David S. Broder, "The Rule of 'King Caucus,'" *WP*, March 19, 1975.

77. "House Democrats: Dispute over Caucus Role," *CQWR*, May 3, 1975.

78. Ibid.

79. Burton was one of four Democrats who attended. He chose the other three: Abner Mikva, Don Fraser, and Thomas Foley. Rowland Evans and Robert Novak, "A Warning About Vetoes," *WP*, March 30, 1975.

80. Marjorie Hunter, "A California Democrat Delivers the Votes in the House," May 23, 1975.

81. Phillip Burton newsletter, n.d., Phillip Burton papers, Bancroft Library, Carton 11.

82. Veto of the Emergency Employment Appropriation Act, 1975, June 2, 1975, Congressional Serial Set, Vol. No. 13109–3, Session Vol. No. 1–3, Ninety-Fourth Congress, 1st Session, H.Doc. 169.

83. Minutes, Special Democratic Caucus, papers of the House Democratic Caucus, Library of Congress, Box 6; Nancy Hicks, "House Fails to Override Veto of Bills to Add Jobs," *NYT*, June 5, 1975.

84. *Congressional Record—House*, 121:13, June 4, 1975, 16863, 16869.

85. Richard L. Lyons, "Veto of Housing Subsidy Bill Upheld," *WP*, June 26, 1975; Richard L. Madden, "Housing Bill Veto Upheld in House on 268–157 Tally," *NYT*, June 26, 1975.

86. A. James Reichley, *Conservatives in an Age of Change: The Nixon and Ford Administrations* (Washington, DC: Brookings Institution, 1981), 323.

87. Larry L. King, "Congress Gums It Up," *NYT*, June 15, 1975; Editorial, "Governing by Posture," *NYT*, June 30, 1975.

88. Marjorie Hunter and David E. Rosenbaum, "Defeats Split Bitter House Democrats," *NYT*, July 2, 1975.

89. Richard L. Lyons, "Vetoes Frustrate Democrats," *WP*, June 17, 1975.

90. David S. Broder, "Why Congress Is Floundering," *WP*, August 13, 1975.

91. Rhodes Cook, "1976 Election Showed Erosion of GOP Base," *CQWR*, March 19, 1977.

92. According to Nigel Bowles, whereas Carter won 50.1 percent of the popular vote, victorious Democrats averaged 56.2 percent in House races and 54.4 percent in Senate races. House Democrats ran ahead of Carter by between 4 and 9 percentage points in every region of the country. Nigel Bowles, *The White House and Capitol Hill: The Politics of Presidential Persuasion* (Oxford: Clarendon, 1987), 190–191.

93. Myron Struck, "As It Strikes Struck," *Roll Call*, November 18, 1976, clipping in the papers of Phillip Burton, Bancroft Library, Carton 13.

94. "Albert May Face a Revolt in the House," *NYT*, June 14, 1976; "Albert to Get Bid for 'Party Unity,'" *NYT*, June 18, 1975.

95. As he claimed in the interview that Burton was "a lot more moderate than he appears to be," the remark is a lot less of a rebuke than it might at first appear. "Albert Is Hailed in House; Drive for Key Posts Is On," *NYT*, June 8, 1976; Lois Romano, "Interview with Albert," *Roll Call*, June 17, 1976, offprint in the papers of Phillip Burton, Bancroft Library, Carton 13.

96. Letter, Phillip Burton to Morris K. Udall, June 7, 1976, papers of Morris K. Udall, University of Arizona, Box 662.

97. Richard D. Lyons, "Leadership of House: Struggle Involves Ideology and Legislation," *NYT*, March 31, 1976; David S. Broder, "The House Contest: Four Personalities," *WP*, December 1, 1976; Richard Bolling, *House Out of Order* (New York: Dutton, 1965).

98. "Phillip Burton Says He'll Be Demo Leader," *S.F. Examiner*, May 27, 1976, offprint in the papers of Phillip Burton, Bancroft Library, Carton 13; Mary Russell, "The Struggle," *WP*, June 6, 1976.

99. "Humphrey Will Seek Leadership," *WP*, June 18, 1976.

100. Albert R. Hunt, "Two Close Democratic Leadership Fights Could Decide New Congress's Disposition," *WSJ*, November 19, 1976, offprint in the papers of Phillip Burton, Bancroft Library, Carton 13.

101. Letter, Tip O'Neill to Phillip Burton, n.d., papers of Phillip Burton, Bancroft Library, Carton 10; Farrell, *Tip O'Neill and the Democratic Century*, 390.

102. Mary Russell, "House Leader Race Narrowed to Two," *WP-TH*, November 17, 1972.

103. Jacobs, *A Rage for Justice*, 237–238.

104. Marjorie Hunter, "Democratic Bloc Seek to End Appointment of House Whip," *NYT*, December 30, 1972; Minutes, Caucus Meeting, January 2, 1973, in papers of the House Democratic Caucus, Library of Congress, Box 3.

105. Farrell, *Tip O'Neill*, 435.

106. Bruce F. Freed, "Albert Retirement Promises Leadership Fight," *CQ*, June 12, 1976.

107. Daniel Rapoport, "Wright: No Unkind Words," *WP*, January 3, 1977.

108. John M. Barry, *The Ambition and the Power* (New York: Viking, 1989), 11–12.

109. Seventeen members of the Texas Democratic delegation signed a letter in support of Wright's candidacy, including Barbara Jordan, Charles Wilson, George Mahon, and Burton's old adversary Olin Teague. "Dear Colleague" letter from George Mahon et al., September 22, 1976, papers of Morris K. Udall, University of Arizona, Box 662.

110. Bruce I. Oppenheimer and Robert L. Peabody, "The House Majority Leadership Contest, 1976," prepared for the American Political Science Association, September 1–4, 1977, 34, papers of Phillip Burton, Bancroft Library, Carton 13.

111. Marion Clark and Rudy Maxa, "Closed-Session Romance on the Hill," *WP*, May 23, 1976.

112. "Rep. Hays Defers Trip, Denies Aide's Accusation," *NYT*, May 24, 1976; Lucinda Franks, "Hays, in Reversal, Admits Affair with Staff Member," *NYT*, May 26, 1976.

113. Laurence Stern and Walter Pineus, "Wayne Hays' Power Base: Political IOUs," *WP*, June 8, 1976.

114. Mary Russell, "Hays Rebuffs Albert, Keeps Campaign Post," *WP*, January 30, 1975; T. R. Reid, "Changing the Guard at Common Cause," *WP*, May 15, 1977.

115. Common Cause Press Release, "Common Cause Lauds Burton's Leadership on Congressional Reform," March 1, 1973, papers of Phillip Burton, Bancroft Library,

Carton 11. Letter, John W. Gardner to Burton, March 6, 1975, papers of Phillip Burton, Bancroft Library, Carton 10.

116. Richard D. Lyons, "O'Neill Bids Hays Give Up His House Chairmanships," *NYT*, June 3, 1976; Richard D. Lyons, "Democrats Remove Hays as Head of Campaign Unit," *NYT*, June 10, 1976.

117. Lucinda Franks, "Hays's Pill Dose Called 10 Times Usual," *NYT*, June 12, 1976; "Hays Terms Overdose of Pills a Mishap, Not Suicide Attempt," *NYT*, July 4, 1976.

118. "Hays Resignation of Chairmanship Accepted by House," *NYT*, June 22, 1976; Minutes, Democratic Caucus, Regular Meeting, June 23, 1976, papers of the House Democratic Caucus, Library of Congress, Box 7.

119. Mary Russell, "Hays to Retire; He Cites Health, 'Harassment,'" *WP*, August 14, 1976.

120. Russell, "Hays Rebuffs Albert, Keeps Campaign Post."

121. Editorial, "The Trouble with Mr. Hays," *WP*, January 22, 1975.

122. Myron Struck, "House GOP Making Issue of Hays-Ray Fray," *Roll Call*, June 17, 1976; "Ford Says Hays Case Disturbs Him and Nation," *NYT*, June 5, 1976.

123. Bruce F. Freed, "Democrats Fear Fallout from Hays Affair," *CQWR*, May 29, 1976.

124. Phillip Burton, Memorandum, November 16, 1976, papers of Phillip Burton, Bancroft Library, Carton 10.

125. Herblock cartoon, *WP*, December 2, 1976, offprint in the papers of Phillip Burton, Bancroft Library, Carton 13.

126. Tom Eastham, "Phil Burton–," *San Francisco Examiner*, November 14, 1976, offprint in the papers of Phillip Burton, Bancroft Library, Carton 13.

127. Richard L. Madden, "Carter's Relationship with Congress May Depend on a Series of Leadership Battles before He Takes Office," *NYT*, November 13, 1976.

128. Walter Taylor, "Democrats' Jockeying Includes Factional Recruiting of Freshman," *Washington Star*, November 23, 1976, offprint in the papers of Phillip Burton, Bancroft Library, Carton 13.

129. They were Michael T. Blouin (Iowa), William T. Brodhead (Michigan), Joseph L. Fisher (Virginia), James J. Florio (New Jersey), George Miller and Norman Y. Mineta (California), and Toby Moffett (Connecticut). "Dear Colleague" letter from Michael T. Blouin et al., December 2, 1976, papers of Phillip Burton, Bancroft Library, Carton 13.

130. Tom Eastham and John Hall, "Why Burton Lost House Battle," *San Francisco Examiner*, December 7, 1976, offprint in the papers of Phillip Burton, Bancroft Library, Carton 13.

131. Myron Struck, "Survey Shows Burton Ahead in House Majority Leader Race," *Roll Call*, December 9, 1976; Leo Rennerts, "Burton Is Favorite in Majority Leader Race in House," *Sacramento Bee*, December 5, 1976, offprints in the papers of Phillip Burton, Bancroft Library, Carton 13.

132. M. Robert Carr, author interview.

133. Eastham and Hall, "Why Burton Lost House Battle."

134. Richard L. Lyons, "Soothing Bridge-Builder," *WP*, December 7, 1976.

135. J. F. terHorst, "The House Is a Bit Shaky," *LAT*, December 14, 1976, offprint in the papers of Phillip Burton, Bancroft Library, Carton 13.

136. John Fogarty, "Burton: No Relaxing, No Regrets," *WP*, January 3, 1977.

137. Eastham and Hall, "Why Burton Lost in House Battle."

138. Reg Murphy, "Carter's Role in Burton's Loss," *S.F. Examiner*, December 12, 1978, offprint in the papers of Phillip Burton, Bancroft Library, Carton 13.

139. Spencer Rich, "Ideologies Will Clash in Senate Leader Race," *WP*, June 11, 1976.

140. Philip Shabecoff, "Rep. Burton Held Likely to Seek House Leader's Fort," *NYT*, February 23, 1978.

141. Granat, "Whatever Happened to the Watergate Babies?"

CHAPTER 3. PEANUTS

1. Garry Wills, *Lead Time: A Journalist's Education* (Boston: Mariner, 2004), 193.

2. Jules Witcover, *Marathon: The Pursuit of the Presidency, 1972–1976* (New York: Viking, 1977), 117–118.

3. Randy Sanders profiles four southern gubernatorial candidates who won statewide elections through that brand of politics. The four he profiles are Carter, Dale Bumpers of Arkansas, Reubin Askew of Florida, and John West of South Carolina. These four were motivated by a mix of principle and political calculation. The Voting Rights Act meant that African Americans were now an electoral bloc that southern whites could no longer exclude or ignore. But they also embraced the moral case for civil rights and the need for the South to transcend its racial history. Randy Sanders, *Mighty Peculiar Elections: The New South Gubernatorial Campaigns of 1970 and the Changing Politics of Race* (Baton Rouge: Louisiana State University Press, 2007).

4. Cover headline, "Dixie Whistles a Different Tune," "The Nation: A New Day A'Coming in the South," *Time*, May 31, 1971.

5. Max Frankel, "A Stunning Sweep," *NYT*, July 13, 1972.

6. Wayne King, "Georgia's Gov. Carter Enters Democratic Race for President," *NYT*, December 13, 1974.

7. Sanford J. Ungar, "How Jimmy Carter Does It," *Atlantic Monthly*, July 1976.

8. David E. Rosenbaum, "Carter's Position on Issues Designed for Wide Appeal," *NYT*, June 11, 1976.

9. J. Brooks Flippen, *Jimmy Carter, the Politics of Family, and the Rise of the Religious Right* (Athens: University of Georgia Press, 2011), 99–100; Edward D. Berkowitz, *Something Happened: A Political and Cultural Overview of the Seventies* (New York: Columbia University Press, 2006), 108. At the end of Carter's first year in office, *Time* magazine devoted a cover story to the rising evangelical movement. "The Evangelicals: New Empire of Faith," *Time*, December 26, 1977.

10. Zachary J. Lechner, "'Fuzzy as a Georgia Peach': The Ford Campaign and the Challenge of Jimmy Carter's Southernness," *Southern Cultures* 23, no. 4 (Winter 2017): 63.

11. Burton I. Kaufman and Scott Kaufman, *The Presidency of James Earl Carter, Jr.* (2nd ed., rev., Lawrence: University Press of Kansas, 2006), 14.

12. Witcover, *Marathon*, 107–109.

13. Although Ford came surprisingly close to beating Carter in that November's elections, there was never any serious danger of the Democrats losing their majorities in the House or the Senate. Democratic control of Congress was assured regardless of who occupied the White House.

14. Carson and Johnson, *Mo*, 3–4; Jeffrey Bloodworth, *Losing the Center: The Decline of American Liberalism, 1968–1992* (Lexington: University Press of Kentucky, 2013), 179–180.

15. Carson and Johnson, *Mo*, 49, 135; Mark Shields, "Mo Udall's Monuments," *NYT*, April 23, 1991.

16. It was an asset he deliberately cultivated. One article from 1975 noted that Udall kept two loose-leaf scrapbooks of anecdotes, one-liners, jokes, clippings on hand. By that point, they numbered 377 pages, indexed by topic. R. R., "What Makes Mo Udall Laugh?" *WP*, February 16, 1975.

17. Udall's 1988 memoir was titled *Too Funny to Be President.* Morris K. Udall, Bob Neuman, and Randy Udall, *Too Funny to Be President* (New York: Henry Holt, 1988); Molly Ivins, "Liberal from Goldwater Country," *NYT*, February 1, 1976.

18. Carson and Johnson, *Mo*, 58–59; Richard Severo, "Morris K. Udall, Fiercely Liberal Congressman, Dies at 76," *NYT*, December 14, 1998.

19. Carson and Johnson, *Mo*, 64.

20. Udall's involvement stemmed from a letter sent by ex-GI Ron Ridenhour, which induced him to lobby the House Armed Services Committee to undertake the investigation. Of thirty recipients, Udall was the only congressman to act on Ridenhour's missive. Myra MacPherson, "Mo Udall, Triumph of the Good Guy," *WP*, December 29, 1985.

21. Puckish even in defeat, after Udall lost his bid to supplant Hale Boggs as House majority leader, he turned his "MO" button upside down so that it read "OW." Severo, "Morris K. Udall, Fiercely Liberal Congressman, Dies at 76."

22. Carson and Johnson, *Mo*, 104–116.

23. Stewart Dill McBride, "Udall: Wit, Pragmatism in Early Campaigning," *CSM*, February 4, 1975; MacPherson, "Mo Udall, Triumph of the Good Guy."

24. Andrew Schneider, "For the Easygoing Arizona Rebel, Mo Udall, It's Do or Die Time in His Campaign," *People*, March 1, 1976.

25. Jules Witcover, *The Making of an Ink-Stained Wretch: Half a Century Pounding the Political Beat* (Baltimore, MD: Johns Hopkins University Press, 2005), 203.

26. Carson and Johnson, *Mo*, 164.

27. Larry L. King, "Unbowed Udall," *NYT*, July 14, 1976.

28. "Morris Udall: The Candidate on the Issues: An Interview," *WP*, April 25, 1976.

29. Charles Mohr, "'The Hour Is Very Late,' Udall Says, And He's the 'Only Viable' Liberal Left," *NYT*, March 18, 1976.

30. Bloodworth, *Losing the Center*, 185–188.

31. William Chapman, "The Good-Times Democrats: 'The War Is Over,'" *WP*, March 28, 1976.

32. For more on ROAR and the Boston antibusing protests, see Kathleen Banks Nutter, "'Militant Mothers': Boston, Busing, and the Bicentennial of 1976," *Historical Journal of Massachusetts* 38, no. 2 (Fall 2010): 52–75.

33. William Chapman, "He Defends His Position," *WP*, March 1, 1976.

34. "Morris Udall: The Candidate on the Issues; An Interview," *WP*, April 25, 1976.

35. William Chapman, "The Good-Times Democrats: 'The War Is Over,'" *WP*, March 28, 1976.

36. William Chapman, "Mass. Shirks Liberalism of '72," *WP*, March 4, 1976.

37. MacPherson, "Mo Udall, Triumph of the Good Guy."

38. George F. Will, "The Loneliness of the Long-Distance Liberal," *Newsweek*, May 3, 1976.

39. Chapman, "The Good-Times Democrats."

40. Jules Witcover, "Carter Race Will Follow Early Plans," *WP*, September 7, 1976.

41. Leuchtenburg, *In the Shadow of FDR*, 185; Tom Wicker, "Franklin D. Roosevelt Carter," *NYT*, September 21, 1976.

42. Nigel Bowles, *The White House and Capitol Hill: The Politics of Presidential Persuasion* (Oxford: Clarendon, 1987), 3.

43. John Dumbrell, *The Carter Presidency: A Re-evaluation* (2nd ed., Manchester: Manchester University Press, 1995), 40; Dom Bonafede, "Carter's Relationship with Congress—Making a Mountain Out of a 'Moorehill,'" *National Journal*, March 26, 1977.

44. Martin Tolchin, "Carter's Congress Lobbyist Battles Problems of Office," *NYT*, February 25, 1977.

45. Mary McGrory, "How Jimmy Carter Lost the Best Friend He Had on the Hill," *Washington Star*, August 1, 1978, offprint in the papers of Mary McGrory, Library of Congress, Box 105.

46. Jeffrey K. Stine, "Environmental Policy during the Carter Administration," in *The Carter Presidency: Policy Choices in the Post-New Deal Era*, ed. Gary M. Fink and Hugh Davis Graham (Lawrence: University Press of Kansas, 1998), 182.

47. As the environmental historian Donald Worster argues, "The American West can best be described as a modern *hydraulic society* . . . a social order based on the intensive, large-scale manipulation of water and its products for an arid setting." Donald Worster, *Rivers of Empire: Water, Aridity, and the Growth of the American West* (New York: Oxford University Press, 1985), 6.

48. US Office of the Federal Register, *Public Papers of the Presidents of the United States: Jimmy Carter, 1977: Book I—January 20 to June 24, 1977* (Washington, DC: National Archives and Record Service, 1977), 207–208.

49. Carter, *White House Diary*, 23.

50. Mercer Cross, "Carter vs. Congress: At War over Water," *CQWR*, March 19, 1977, 481.

51. An invaluable conduit between the Carter administration and the Senate, Mondale "spent much of his time attending to crises and mollifying senators offended by

White House misjudgements and errors" in the first months of Carter's presidency. Memo, Bill Smith to Walter F. Mondale, March 21, 1977, papers of Walter F. Mondale, Minnesota Historical Society, Box 153.L.20.2F; Bowles, *The White House and Capitol Hill*, 198.

52. Cross, "Carter vs. Congress," 484.

53. Martin Tolchin, "Byrd Tells Carter Senate Is Angered by Unilateral Acts," *NYT*, March 12, 1977.

54. Cross, "Carter vs. Congress," 482.

55. Position paper, Gary Hart, "Labor: Where Gary Hart Stands," n.d. [1980], papers of Gary W. Hart, University of Colorado Boulder, Box 53.

56. Jimmy Carter, *Keeping Faith: Memoirs of a President* (Fayetteville: University of Arkansas Press, 1995), 78.

57. Letter, Carter to Members of Congress, March 16, 1977, "Water Projects, 2/18/77–10/6/78 [CF, O/A 625]" folder, Office of the Congressional Liaison, Frank Moore Subject Files, Jimmy Carter Presidential Library, Box 50.

58. "Please excuse the silly analogy, but I wanted to report the Senator's conversation accurately," added Moore. Memo, Frank Moore to Carter, April 5, 1977, "Water Projects Briefing, 3/10/77 [O/A 6748]" folder, Office of the Congressional Liaison, Frank Moore Subject Files, Jimmy Carter Presidential Library, Box 50.

59. Stine, "Environmental Policy," in *Carter Presidency*, ed. Fink and Graham, 187; Edward Walsh, "$10 Billion Public Works Bill Is Signed," *WP*, August 9, 1977.

60. Dumbrell, *The Carter Presidency*, 40.

61. Stine, "Environmental Policy," in *Carter Presidency*, ed. Fink and Graham, 185.

62. Carter, *Keeping Faith*, 78.

63. Dumbrell, *The Carter Presidency*, 40–41.

64. W. Carl Biven, for instance, described it as "the last hurrah of those whose mindsets took shape in the New Deal-Great Society policy era." The economist Brian Dimitrovic was blunter, dismissing Humphrey-Hawkins as a retreat into the comfort zone of "bald Keynesianism." Dominic Sandbrook, meanwhile, said Humphrey-Hawkins was "a welcome rallying point" in "an era when liberalism seemed to have run out of gas" but also "an exercise in public relations rather than sensible economic management." W. Carl Biven, *Jimmy Carter's Economy: Policy in an Age of Limits* (Chapel Hill: University of North Carolina Press, 2002), 33; Brian Domitrovic, "Gross as a Mountain," *Journal of Policy History* 23, no. 3 (2011): 439; Dominic Sandbrook, *Mad as Hell: The Crisis of the 1970s and the Rise of the Populist Right* (New York: Alfred A. Knopf, 2011), 45.

65. Susan M. Hartmann, "Liberal Feminism and the Shaping of the New Deal Order," in *Making Sense of American Liberalism*, ed. Jonathan Bell and Timothy Stanley (Urbana: University of Illinois Press, 2012), 203.

66, Timothy N. Thurber, *The Politics of Equality: Hubert H. Humphrey and the African-American Freedom Struggle* (New York: Columbia University Press, 1999), 233–255.

67. Jefferson Cowie, *Stayin' Alive: The 1970s and the Last Days of the Working Class* (New York: New Press, 2010), 261.

68. FDR had arrived in the White House in 1933 with an interest in planning ideas. Beginning with the National Recovery Administration (NRA)—a body that promoted government-regulated cartelization through industry codes, wage and price scales, and the prohibition of unfair practices—the planning impulse ran through much of the New Deal. Otis Graham notes that while the NRA was "a sloppy, poorly coordinated effort" at planning, the Roosevelt administration's methods became more sophisticated with time. Otis L. Graham Jr., *Toward a Planned Society: From Roosevelt to Nixon* (New York: Oxford University Press, 1976), 16–20, 28–31. See also, Patrick Reagan, *Designing A New America: The Origins of New Deal Planning, 1890–1943* (Amherst: University of Massachusetts Press, 1999).

69. Wassily Leontief, "For a National Economic Planning Board," *NYT*, March 14, 1974.

70. Leontief pitched this new board as a revival of Roosevelt's National Resourecs Planning Board. Leontief, "For a National Economic Planning Board." These ideas had currency even among those who were wary of planning. Sociologist Daniel Bell wrote of his conviction that "we in America are moving away from a society based on a private-enterprise market system toward one in which the most important economic decisions will be made at the political level, in terms of consciously defined 'goals' and 'priorities.'" Daniel Bell, *The Coming of Post-Industrial Society: A Venture in Social Forecasting* (special anniversary ed.; New York: Basic, 1999 [orig. 1973]), 297–298.

71. "Diverse Group Advocates Economic Planning for U.S.," *NYT*, February 28, 1975.

72. The act would not only have created the infrastructure for economic planning but also have required the president to submit a biennial "balanced economic growth plan" to Congress and have established a process for federal agencies, state and local governments, and citizens to be involved in scrutinizing and amending the plan. Eileen Shanahan, "Planned Economy Urged in Senate," *NYT*, May 13, 1975

73. James P. Gannon, "Humphrey's Passing Marks the Passing of a Political Era," *WSJ*, January 16, 1978.

74. When the thesis was published in 1970, Humphrey wrote in a new preface that he retained "much affection" for the work and that there were "some sound lessons for today in President Roosevelt's activist political judgements." Hubert Humphrey, *The Political Philosophy of the New Deal* (Baton Rouge: Louisiana State University Press, 1970), ix–x, 6, 99, 108.

75. Humphrey was a longtime champion of civil rights. He had started his career in national politics with a barnstorming speech to the 1948 party convention urging his fellow Democrats to "get out of the shadow of state's rights and walk forthrightly into the bright sunshine of human rights." One of his proudest achievements in the Senate was acting as floor manager for the 1964 Civil Rights Act. Carl Solberg, *Hubert Humphrey: A Biography* (New York: Norton, 1984), 174. Humphrey's early career is more fully detailed in Jennifer Delton, *Making Minnesota Liberal: Civil Rights and the Transformation of the Democratic Party* (Minneapolis: University of Minnesota Press,

2002). For a full account of the floor fight over the 1964 Civil Rights Act, see Robert Mann, *The Walls of Jericho: Lyndon Johnson, Hubert Humphrey, Richard Russell and the Struggle for Civil Rights* (San Diego: Harcourt Brace, 1996).

76. Erik van den Berg, "Supersalesman for the Great Society: Vice President Hubert H. Humphrey, 1965–1969," *American Studies International* 36, no. 3 (October 1998): 59–72.

77. For a detailed account of Humphrey's benighted 1968 campaign, see Lewis Chester, Godfrey Hodgson, and Bruce Page, *An American Melodrama: The Presidential Campaign of 1968* (New York: Viking, 1969), and Michael A. Cohen, *American Maelstrom: The 1968 Election and the Politics of Division* (New York: Oxford University Press, 2016).

78. Chester, Hodgson, and Page, *An American Melodrama*, 634.

79. Hubert H. Humphrey, Announcement Statement, June 14, 1970, papers of Hubert H. Humphrey, Minnesota Historical Society, St. Paul, MN, Box 150.J.19.3B.

80. In 1968, Humphrey had tried to defuse Wallace's potent "law and order" platform by reconceptualizing the problem as one of "order and justice." His solution to urban unrest was to promise not only more effective policing tactics but also that the inequalities that triggered the unrest would be addressed. Hubert Humphrey, Remarks at National Press Club Luncheon, Washington, DC, June 20, 1968, papers of Hubert H. Humphrey, Minnesota Historical Society, St. Paul, MN, Box 150.F.13.8(F).

81. Richard M. Scammon and Ben J. Wattenberg, *The Real Majority* (New York: Coward-McCann, 1970), 21, 45–46, 70–71. One reviewer dismissed *The Real Majority* as "third-rate Machiavelli" and compared reviewing it to "trying to use a smog-ball as a punching bag." John Leonard, "Books of the Times: Third-Rate Machiavelli," *NYT*, September 25, 1970.

82. The speech's theme and title, and the choice of venue, seem to have been Wattenberg's idea. Senator Kennedy had been invited to speak at the American Bar Association as well, Wattenberg told Humphrey, "so between the two of you there is bound to be good *national* press coverage." Memo, Wattenberg to Hubert H. Humphrey, July 24, 1970, papers of Hubert H. Humphrey, Minnesota Historical Society, Box 148.A.12.6F.

83. Hubert H. Humphrey, "'Liberalism' and 'Law and Order': Must There Be a Conflict?" Remarks at the American Bar Association, St. Louis, August 11, 1970, papers of Hubert H. Humphrey, Minnesota Historical Society, Box 150.J.18.6F.

84. Letter, Hubert H. Humphrey to O'Brien, August 18, 1970, papers of Hubert H. Humphrey, Minnesota Historical Society, Box 150.J.19.1B.

85. Memo, Hubert H. Humphrey to Jack Chestnut, Norman Sherman, D. J. Leary, June 19, 1970, papers of Hubert H. Humphrey, Minnesota Historical Society, Box 150.J.19.1B.

86. Iwan W. Morgan, "Hubert Humphrey's Last Hurrah: The 1977 Senate Leadership Election and the Decline of the New Deal Tradition," *Mid-America: An Historical Review* 79, no. 3 (Fall 1997): 295.

87. Solberg, *Hubert Humphrey*, 424.

88. James R. Gaines and Bernice Buresh, "Hubert Gets a Leg Up," *Newsweek*, August 18, 1975.

89. Clayton Fritchey, "Humphrey's New Hurrah," *Washington Post-Times Herald* (hereafter *WP-TH*), March 10, 1973.

90. Hubert H. Humphrey, "National Economic Planning: Pro and Con," *NYT*, December 21, 1975.

91. As early as 1965, the musical satirist Tom Lehrer had joked of Vice President Humphrey's loss of status and influence in song: "Once a fiery liberal spirit / Ah, but now when he speaks he must clear it / Second fiddle's a hard part, I know / When they don't even give you a bow." Tom Lehrer, "Whatever Became of Hubert," *That Was the Year That Was*, [CD] (Warner Bros. Records Inc. & Rhino Entertainment Company, 2000 [1965]).

92. Hunter S. Thompson, *Fear and Loathing on the Campaign Trail '72* (London: Harper Perennial, [1973] 2005), 129, 199.

93. Humphrey quoted in "The Hubert Humphrey Record," *U.S. News & World Report*, July 1, 1968.

94. Leontief, "For a National Economic Planning Board."

95. Douglas Flamming, *Bound for Freedom: Black Los Angeles in Jim Crow America* (Oakland: University of California Press, 2004), 48–49.

96. Flamming, *Bound for Freedom*, 168–187.

97. In 1974, when he first introduced his full employment bill with Humphrey, Hawkins's district was 54 percent African American (76 percent nonwhite including Hispanic and Japanese American residents) with a median income of $7,060. Eighteen percent of families lived on incomes below $3,000. Michael Barone, Grant Ujifusa, Douglas Matthews, *The Almanac of American Politics, 1974* (London: Macmillan, 1974), 102; Alan Ehrenhalt, ed., *Politics in America: Members of Congress in Washington and at Home 1984* (Washington, DC: CQ, 1983), 175–177.

98. Ehrenhalt, ed., *Politics in America*, 175–177; Michael Barone and Grant Ujifusa, *The Almanac of American Politics, 1982* (Washington, DC: Barone, 1981), 133–134.

99. George Lardner Jr., "CORE Leaders Assails Black Caucus," *WP-TH*, February 11, 1972; "Fifty CORE Members Seek Antibusing Voice," *WP-TH*, February 12, 1972.

100. Cowie, *Stayin' Alive*, 269; Josh Sides, *L.A. City Limits: African American Los Angeles from the Great Depression to the Present* (Berkeley: University of California Press, 2003), 154, 157, 177; Ward Sinclair, "Augustus F.: The Other, Unknown Half of Humphrey Hawkins," *WP*, February 1, 1978.

101. Thurber, *The Politics of Equality*, 4–5.

102. Hawkins added that the situation may be even worse, given the notorious difficulties the Department of Labor faced in amassing statistics from black communities. Augustus Hawkins, "The Economic Status of Blacks," *New York Amsterdam News*, December 28, 1974.

103. Thurber, *The Politics of Equality*, 236.

104. "Ford Sees Congressional Black Caucus," *Sun Reporter*, August 31, 1974.

105. Alan Brinkley, "World War II and American Liberalism," in *The War in American Culture: Society and Consciousness During World War II*, ed. Lewis A. Erenberg and Susan E. Hirsch (Chicago: University of Chicago Press, 1996), 319–320.

106. "Whether there is to be unemployment or full employment even after the armistice," wrote the *Pittsburgh Courier* in early 1944, "depends upon the intelligence and over-all scope of planning now." "Job Fear Hurled at Negroes," *Pittsburgh Courier*, April 15, 1944.

107. Alan Brinkley, *The End of Reform: New Deal Liberalism in Recession and War* (New York: Alfred A. Knopf, 1995), 260–263; Alonzo L. Hamby, *Beyond the New Deal: Harry S. Truman and American Liberalism* (New York: Columbia University Press, 1973), 63–64.

108. As Helen Lachs Ginsburg has noted, this included *"persons not in the labor force as it is traditionally measured. So all* meant just that: women, older and younger people, physically and mentally handicapped people, members of racial, ethnic, national or religious minorities, veterans, ex-drug addicts, and former prisoners." Helen Lachs Ginsburg, "Historical Amnesia: The Humphrey-Hawkins Act, Full Employment and Employment as a Right," *Revolutionary Black Political Economy* 39 (2012): 130.

109. Editorial, "A Job for Everyone," *NR*, March 27, 1976.

110. As Judith Stein notes, when, for example, a plant had to lay off workers, management had to decide whether to observe the union-backed seniority principle (last hired, first fired) and thus obliterate gains in diversifying the workforce since the 1960s. Such cases brought the NAACP's Legal Defense Fund into public conflict with otherwise progressive unions, such as the United Steelworkers. Judith Stein, *Pivotal Decade: How the United States Traded Factories for Finance in the Seventies* (New Haven, CT: Yale University Press, 2010), 140–141.

111. Jefferson Cowie suggests Humphrey and Hawkins were pursuing the "seventies alchemy" of "turning the leaden and divisive policies of race into the golden unity of class." Cowie, *Stayin' Alive*, 269; Stein, *Pivotal Decade*, 141–142.

112. Augustus F. Hawkins, speech before the Full Employment Conference, Hunter College, N.Y., February 15, 1975, papers of Augustus F. Hawkins, University of California, Los Angeles, Department of Special Collections, Box 84.

113. Augustus F. Hawkins, highlights of address at Full Employment Conference, Urban Center, Columbia University, March 2, 1974, papers of Augustus F. Hawkins, University of California, Los Angeles, CA, Box 84.

114. David S. Broder, "Jobs and the Government," *WP*, September 1, 1975.

115. Hubert H. Humphrey, testimony before the Senate Committee on Banking, Housing and Urban Affairs, August 15, 1974, papers of Hubert H. Humphrey, Minnesota Historical Society, Box 150.G.1.3B.

116. Humphrey asked Dr. Norman Beckman, acting director of the Congressional Research Service, to prepare a draft review that the senator could put into "final 'Humphrey' form" before sending it to the editors. Letter, Hubert H. Humphrey to Norman Beckman, December 29, 1975, papers of Hubert H. Humphrey, Minnesota Historical Society, Box 150.G.1.3B.

117. Hubert H. Humphrey, "National Policy Planning: Roosevelt to Nixon," *Congressional Record* 122, no. 27, March 1, 1976, offprint in the papers of Hubert H. Humphrey, Minnesota Historical Society, Box 150.G.1.3B.

118. James W. Compton, executive director of the Chicago Urban League, cited these statistics in his testimony to the JEC. "Jobs and Prices in Chicago," Hearing before the Joint Economic Committee, Ninety-Fourth Congress, First session, *Congressional Serial Set*, October 20, 1975, 25.

119. "Jobs and Prices in Chicago," Hearing before the Joint Economic Committee, Ninety-Fourth Congress, First session, *Congressional Serial Set*, October 20, 1975, 30–32, 24–30, 76–80, 85–88, 103–114.

120. Editorial, "A Job for Everyone."

121. Report of the Joint Economic Committee on the January 1976 Economic Report of the President, Ninety-Fourth Congress, 2nd Session, S.Rpt. 690, *Congressional Serial Set*, March 10, 1976, 5–9.

122. Although he was careful not to endorse the Humphrey-Hawkins bill, sitting vice president Nelson Rockefeller, who had a long-established interest in national economic planning, delivered some opening remarks for the conference, saying that there was "no better time than this bicentennial year to review the objectives of the Employment Act of 1946." Hobart Rowen, "With a Helping Hand from Rockefeller: 2-Day Conference on Full-Employment Legislation Launched," *WP*, March 19, 1976.

123. The *U.S. News & World Report* figures were based on those respondents who opted to make such a prediction. Approximately one quarter declined to. "Poll of Democratic Leaders—'It Looks Like Humphrey,'" *U.S. News & World Report* (hereafter *USNWR*), November 17, 1975.

124. In February 1976, Ford told reporters, "I have said repeatedly, and I see no reason to change, that my good friend Hubert Humphrey will probably be the nominee." US Office of the Federal Register, *Public Papers of the Presidents of the United States: Gerald R. Ford, 1976–77; Book I—January 1 to April 9, 1976* (Washington, DC: National Archives and Records Administration, 1979), 478.

125. Humphrey was, argues Judith Stein, "the lone candidate who stood for a clear alternative to Ford economics" by 1976. Stein, *Pivotal Decade*, 130, 137.

126. Conservative economist Murray Weidenbaum complained that opposing Humphrey-Hawkins "has become the economic equivalent of attacking the flag and apple pie." Melville J. Ulmer, "Taking a Dim View of Humphrey-Hawkins," *NR*, June 12, 1976; Murray L. Weidenbaum, "The Case Against the Humphrey-Hawkins Bill," *Challenge* 19, no. 4 (September/October 1976): 21.

127. Leonard Silk, "Carter's Economics," *NYT*, July 14, 1976; Biven, *Jimmy Carter's Economy*, 33–34.

128. Thurber, *The Politics of Equality*, 241.

129. Edward J. Walsh, "Ford Assails Hill's Plans on Economy," *WP*, April 27, 1976.

130. "Jobs and Prices in Chicago," 47; "Fed Cuts Money-Growth Target Slightly," *NYT*, May 4, 1976.

131. Godfrey Sperling Jr., "With Humphrey out of Race, Carter Campaign Surges," *CSM*, April 30, 1976; Morgan, "Hubert Humphrey's Last Hurrah," 287.

132. Christopher Lyon, "Humphrey to Undergo Surgery; Still Seeks Majority Leadership," *NYT*, October 2, 1976.

133. Joseph Lelyveld, "Liberals, Despite Humphrey Ties, Are Expected to Elect Byrd Today," *NYT*, January 4, 1977.

134. Time/Yankelovich, Skelly, August 1976; Time/Yankelovich, Skelly, March 1977; ORC Public Opinion Index, November 1980. Polls retrieved February 12, 2011, from the iPOLL Databank: http://ezproxy.ouls.ox.ac.uk:4032/data_access/ipoll/ipoll.html.

135. Memo, Valerie Pinson to Frank Moore, March 28, 1977, "House Memoranda, 2/24/77–11/10/80" folder, Office of the Congressional Liaison, Frank Moore Subject Files, Jimmy Carter Presidential Library, Atlanta, GA, Box 32.

136. Memo, Stuart Eizenstat to Bert Carp, April 11, 1977, "Humphrey-Hawkins [Bill][O/A 6345][2]" folder, Domestic Policy Staff, Stuart E. Eizenstat Subject Files, Jimmy Carter Presidential Library, Box 221.

137. Letter, Humphrey and Hawkins to Carter, June 10, 1977, "Humphrey-Hawkins [Bill][O/A 6345][2]" folder, Domestic Policy Staff, Eizenstat Subject Files, Jimmy Carter Presidential Library, Box 221.

138. Warren Brown, "President Is Taken to Task," *WP*, July 25, 1977.

139. J. Zamga Browne, "Jordan Endorses Humphrey-Hawkins Bill," *New York Amsterdam News*, November 26, 1977.

140. "We Need Jobs!—NAACP to Carter," *New York Amsterdam News*, October 8, 1977.

141. Donald P. Baker, "On the Road," *WP*, May 8, 1978.

142. Memo, Bert Lance to Carter, May 31, 1977, "Humphrey-Hawkins Jobs Bill, 6/6/77–10/27/78 [O/A 6748])" folder, Office of the Congressional Liaison, Moore Subject Files, Jimmy Carter Presidential Library, Box 32.

143. Memo, Schultze to Eizenstat, September 7, 1977, "Humphrey-Hawkins [Bill] [O/A 6342][1]" folder, Domestic Policy Staff, Eizenstat Subject Files, Jimmy Carter Presidential Library, Box 221.

144. Memo, Eizenstat to Carter, Bert Lance, June 4, 1977, "Humphrey-Hawkins Jobs Bill, 6/6/77–10/27/78 [O/A 6748])" folder, Office of the Congressional Liaison, Moore Subject Files, Jimmy Carter Presidential Library, Box 32.

145. Memo, Eizenstat and Schultze to Carter, October 19, 1977, "Humphrey-Hawkins Jobs Bill, 6/6/77–10/27/78 [O/A 6748]" folder, Office of the Congressional Liaison, Moore Subject Files, Jimmy Carter Presidential Library, Box 32.

146. Memo, Hubert H. Humphrey to Jerry Jasinowski, June 16, 1975, papers of Hubert H. Humphrey, Minnesota Historical Society, Box 148.A.12.4F.

147. Benjamin Waterhouse, "The Conservative Mobilization Against Liberal Reform: Big Business Day, 1980," in *What's Good for Business: Business and American Politics since World War II*, ed. Kim Phillips-Fein and Julian Zelizer (New York: Oxford University Press, 2012), 237. See also, Kim Phillips-Fein, "'If Business and the Country Will Be Run Right': The Business Challenge to the Liberal Consensus, 1945–1964," *International Labor and Working-Class History* 72 (Fall, 2007): 192–215.

148. James H. Evans, ". . . And What Congress Proposes," *NYT*, January 23, 1977.

149. Benjamin C. Waterhouse, *Lobbying America: The Politics of Business from Nixon to NAFTA* (Princeton, NJ: Princeton University Press, 2014), 130–132.

150. Memo, Eizenstat to Carter, October 6, 1977, "Humphrey-Hawkins [Bill] [O/A 6345] [2]" folder, Box 221, Domestic Policy Staff, Eizenstat Subject Files, Jimmy Carter Presidential Library.

151. Thurber, *The Politics of Equality*, 246; Cowie, *Stayin' Alive*, 275.

152. Art Pine, "Advice Not Taken: Charles Schultze Finds Role Tough," *WP*, November 27, 1977; Art Pine, "Pass Jobs Bill, Administration Asks Congress," *WP*, February 8, 1978.

153. Before the Vietnam War blasted a hole in the side of Cold War liberalism, Keyserling had advocated a "guns as butter" strategy, in which increased defense spending would be the engine of a full employment economy. Edmund F. Wehrle, "Guns, Butter, Leon Keyserling, the AFL-CIO, and the Fate of Full Employment Economics," *The Historian* 66, no. 4 (2004): 730–748.

154. Donald K. Pickens, *Leon H. Keyserling: A Progressive Economist* (Lanham, MD: Lexington, 2009), 198.

155. A. H. Raskin, "Jobless Benefits: Demand Strains Supply," *NYT*, January 26, 1975.

156. Susan Hartmann has shown that many liberal feminists placed material security at the heart of their campaigning: "Rather than deviating from the New Deal policy order, liberal feminists sought to include women within its benefits and to expand its regulatory and social provision powers to accommodate women's dual roles as workers and mothers." Hartmann, "Liberal Feminism and the Shaping of the New Deal Order," 203.

157. Deirdre Carmody, "Feminists Shifting Emphasis from Persons to Politics," *NYT*, August 21, 1972.

158. Soma Golden, "Betty Friedan Suggests Women Must Develop Economic Allies," *NYT*, November 3, 1975.

159. Thomas P. Ronan, "Women Stress Feminist Issues in Rally Opposite the Garden," *NYT*, July 11, 1976.

160. NOW was unsuccessful in persuading the bill's drafters to specify that the full-employment target rate should be applied to "*each* worker group" rather than just to the labor force in general. Robert O. Self, *All in the Family: The Realignment of American Democracy Since the 1960s* (New York: Hill and Wang, 2012), 325–327.

161. Cowie, *Stayin' Alive*, 272.

162. The AFL-CIO dismissed the right to sue as unworkable and unnecessary, though the more liberal UAW argued that the right to a job would be meaningless. Helen Lachs Ginsburg, an academic economist and "participant observer" in the Humphrey-Hawkins negotiations, was at a loss to explain the AFL-CIO's opposition: "Speculation about other possible reasons heard by the author at the time, included a fear of flooding the labor market with job seekers; not having a high priority because unemployment didn't affect union members directly; and the racism of some unions, particularly in the building trades, where minorities were pushing for affirmative action." Ginsburg, "Historical Amnesia," 131.

163. Press release, "Humphrey, Hawkins Pleased with Agreement on Full Employ-ment Bill; Predict Favorable Action Early Next Year," November 14, 1977, papers of Augustus F. Hawkins, University of California, Los Angeles, Box 84.

164. Memo, John Carr to FEAC board, local coalitions, other interested persons, November 29, 1977, papers of Augustus F. Hawkins, University of California, Los An-geles, Box 84.

165. Ray Marshall, Statement before the Employment Opportunities Subcommit-tee, House of Representatives, February 7, 1978, papers of Augustus F. Hawkins, Uni-versity of California, Los Angeles, Box 84.

166. Hatch voted against the bill anyway. Tracy Roof, *American Labor, Congress, and the Welfare State, 1935–2010* (Baltimore, MD: Johns Hopkins University Press, 2011), 164.

167. Jimmy Carter, "Full Employment and Comprehensive Employment and Training Act Bills Remarks on Signing H.R. 50 and S. 2570 into Law," October 27, 1978. Online by Gerhard Peters and John T. Woolley, *The American Presidency Proj-ect*, accessed June 22, 2017, http://www.presidency.ucsb.edu/ws/?pid=30057; Ed-ward Walsh, "Humphrey-Hawkins Measure Is Signed by the President," *WP*, Oc-tober 28, 1978.

168. Roof, *American Labor, Congress, and the Welfare State*, 165.

169. M. Robert Carr, interview with the author, via Skype, March 14, 2013.

170. "Carter Blows the Horn of the Wrong Horatio," *NYT*, August 15, 1980.

CHAPTER 4. PERSONA NON CARTER

1. David S. Broder and Bill Peterson, "Key Democrats to Shun Midterm Parley," *WP*, December 4, 1978.

2. Adam Clymer, "Democrats Dominate," *NYT*, November 8, 1978.

3. Warren J. Weaver Jr., "Democrats in Memphis: Of Birds, Sorghum, and Sincer-ity," *NYT*, December 9, 1978.

4. "Reflections on Memphis," *WP*, December 12, 1978.

5. Memo, Rafshoon, Greg Schneiders, and Bernie Aronson to Carter, November 2, 1978, "Midterm Conference [CF 187]" folder, Office of the Assistant to the Presi-dent for Communications (OAPC), Retired Office Files, Jimmy Carter Presidential Library, Box 55.

6. Terence Smith, "Carter's Dual Role in Memphis: A Politician as Well as a Presi-dent," *NYT*, December 10, 1978.

7. Alan Ehrenhalt, "The Democratic Left Faces a Dilemma," *CQWR*, December 16, 1978, 3431.

8. Edward M. Kennedy, Remarks at the Workshop on Health Care, Democratic National Committee, Midterm Convention, Memphis, TN, December 9, 1978, papers of Adam Clymer, John F. Kennedy Presidential Library, Box 12.

9. Myra McPherson, "Heeeeere's Teddy!" *WP*, December 11, 1978; Interview with Jimmy Carter, May 15, 1998, papers of Adam Clymer, John F. Kennedy Presidential Library, Box 3.

10. Adam Clymer, "Carter's Clash with Kennedy," *NYT*, December 13, 1978.

11. Bill Peterson, "Draft-Kennedy Advocates Kick Off Campaign in Minnesota," *WP*, June 11, 1979.

12. Broder and Peterson, "Key Democrats to Shun Midterm Parley."

13. Remnick noted that such affectations gave Moynihan the appearance of a statesman out of time, "an American Edmund Burke taking dominion on the Hill." David Remnick, "The Family Crusader, Belying Labels, Drawing Crowds & Loving It All," *WP*, July 16, 1986.

14. Along with the names of the organizing committee, this statement of political principles featured a "partial list" of some 72 high-profile sponsors. These included Ben Wattenberg, civil rights activist Bayard Rustin, lawyer Max M. Kampelman, Harvard professors Daniel Bell and Nathan Glazer, congressmen Thomas Foley and Richard Bolling, economist Leon Keyserling, *Commentary* editor Norman Podhoretz, business executive Richard Ravitch, journalist and white ethnic activist Michael Novak, and labor leaders Albert Shanker and Louis Stulberg. Coalition for a Democratic Majority ad, *NYT* and *WP-TH*, December 7, 1972.

15. Michael Harrington, "The Welfare State and Its Neoconservative Critics," *Dissent*, Autumn 1973.

16. Gary J. Dorrien, *The Neoconservative Mind: Politics, Culture, and the War of Ideology* (Philadelphia: Temple University Press, 1993), 2.

17. Maurice Isserman, *The Other American: The Life of Michael Harrington* (New York: PublicAffairs, 2000), 303–308.

18. John Ehrman, *The Rise of Neoconservatism: Intellectuals and Foreign Affairs, 1945–1994* (New Haven, CT: Yale University Press, 1995), 34.

19. Moynihan was an accomplished social scientist, who had devoted much of his career to questions of public policy, sociology and politics. Michael Barone famously described him as "the nation's best thinker among politicians since Lincoln and its best politician among thinkers since Jefferson." Michael Barone and Grant Ujifusa, *The Almanac of American Politics, 2000* (Washington, DC, 1999), 1090.

20. The report argued that disproportionately high rates of black unemployment, poverty and welfare enrolment, as well as the pervasive legacy of slavery and discrimination, had led to the "profound weakening of Negro family structure." In the report's most resonant phrase, Moynihan suggested that a "tangle of pathology" perpetuated a black underclass. The response to the report's publication was explosive and Moynihan was accused of racism, cultural bias, and victim blaming. US Department of Labor, *The Negro Family: The Case for National Action* (Washington, DC, 1965); See also James T. Patterson, *Freedom Is Not Enough: The Moynihan Report and America's Struggle Over Black Family Life from LBJ to Obama* (New York: Basic, 2010), and Daniel Geary, *Beyond Civil Rights: The Moynihan Report and Its Legacy* (Philadelphia: University of Pennsylvania Press, 2015).

21. For a detailed account of Moynihan's time as a member of the Nixon administration, see Stephen Hess, *The Professor and the President: Daniel Patrick Moynihan in the Nixon White House* (Washington, DC: Brookings Institution, 2015).

22. The white working class, he wrote to Nixon in May 1969, must "see what it *is* getting out of government, and even, perhaps, to provide it more." Achieving this required that social problems should no longer be defined as to "separate blacks (and to a degree Hispanics) from the rest of society." Memo, Daniel Patrick Moynihan to Nixon, May 17, 1969, papers of Daniel Patrick Moynihan, Library of Congress, Part I, Box 247.

23. Memo, Daniel Patrick Moynihan to Nixon, March 26, 1969, and memo, Daniel Patrick Moynihan to Nixon, April 1, 1969, papers of Daniel Patrick Moynihan, Library of Congress, Part I, Box 247.

24. For more on FAP, see Daniel Patrick Moynihan, *The Politics of a Guaranteed Income: The Nixon Administration and the Family Assistance Plan* (New York: Vintage, 1973), and Gareth Davies, *From Opportunity to Entitlement: The Transformation and Decline of Great Society Liberalism* (Lawrence: University Press of Kansas, 1996), 211–233.

25. Memo, Daniel Patrick Moynihan to Nixon, January 16, 1970, papers of Daniel Patrick Moynihan, Library of Congress, Part I, Box 255.

26. "The memo, if couched in the language of a Southern saloon," editorialized the *New York Post*, "might be summarized in the sentence 'those people never had it so good' and it is time to mute national debate about their alleged troubles." Editorial, "With All 'Benign Neglect,'" *New York Post*, March 2, 1970. Other interpretations were similarly hostile: "Moynihan Idea Draws Anger . . . As Usual," *Newsday*, March 2, 1970; Editorial, "Let Us Lower Our Voices, But Not to 'Benign Neglect,'" *Detroit Free Press*, March 3, 1970; Mary McGrory, "Tone of Moynihan Memo Will Infuriate Blacks," *Boston Globe*, March 3, 1970; offprints in the papers of Daniel Patrick Moynihan, Library of Congress, Part I, Box 255.

27. Daniel Patrick Moynihan, "The United States in Opposition," *Commentary*, March 1975.

28. "Moynihan Says U.N. Must Bar Resolution Condemning Zionism," *NYT*, October 22, 1975.

29. Moynihan discusses his tenure at the UN in *A Dangerous Place* (with Suzanne Weaver; Boston: Little, Brown, 1978). For a detailed and sympathetic account of the battle over Resolution 3379, see Gil Troy, *Moynihan's Moment: America's Fight Against Zionism as Racism* (New York: Oxford University Press, 2013).

30. Clayton Fritchey, "Moynihan-Kissinger Split: A Matter of Style," *WP*, December 6, 1975; Troy, *Moynihan's Moment*, 9.

31. "A Fighting Irishman at the U.N.," *Time*, January 26, 1976.

32. "Moynihan Sees U.N. Assembly Voting Anti-Zionism Resolution," *NYT*, October 27, 1975; Hodgson, *Gentleman from New York*, 259.

33. Editorial, "Final(?) Questions on Moynihan," *Nation*, February 14, 1976.

34. From the 1960s, with mounting outlays and declining revenues, New York City became dangerously reliant on the sale of notes and bonds to service a growing budget deficit and meet its annual operating costs. By early 1975, Manhattan banks were refusing to underwrite any further loans, and the city was forced to turn to the federal

government for relief. Roger Biles, *The Fate of Cities: Urban America and the Federal Government, 1945–2000* (Lawrence: University Press of Kansas, 2011), 201; Vincent J. Cannato, *The Ungovernable City: John Lindsay and His Struggle to Save New York* (New York: Basic, 2002), 548–553.

35. Ford eventually relented and signed the New York City Seasonal Financial Act, which authorized loans of $2.3 billion in each of the three subsequent financial years. Biles, *Fate of Cities*, 210–212. For more on the crisis and its resolution, see Seymour P. Lachlan and Robert Polner, *The Man Who Saved New York: Hugh Carey and the Great Fiscal Crisis of 1975* (Albany: State University of New York Press, 1975).

36. A more detailed analysis of this campaign forms the basis of my article, Patrick Andelic, "Daniel Patrick Moynihan, the 1976 New York Senate Race, and the Struggle to Define American Liberalism," *Historical Journal* 57, no. 4 (December 2014): 1,111–1,133.

37. Jonathan Soffer, *Ed Koch and the Rebuilding of New York City* (New York: Columbia University Press, 2010), 98.

38. Godfrey Hodgson, *Gentleman from New York: Daniel Patrick Moynihan, A Biography* (Boston: Houghton Mifflin, 2000), 265.

39. Ken Bode and William Straus, "The New York Senate Race: Five Is a Crowd," *NR*, August 21–28, 1976; "A.F.L.-C.I.O. Aide Backs Moynihan," *NYT*, March 25, 1976.

40. One *Daily News* poll taken before he announced his candidacy showed that support for Moynihan's actions in the UN stood at 78 percent among Jewish respondents, 60 percent of whom favored his entry into the race; "Moynihan for Senate Run Favored," *Daily News*, March 1, 1976, clipping in the papers of Norman Podhoretz, Library of Congress, Box 2.

41. Douglas Schoen, *Pat: A Biography of Daniel Patrick Moynihan* (New York: Harper & Row, 1979), 250, 253–254; Bode and Straus, "The New York Senate Race: Five Is a Crowd."

42. The note to editors and correspondents attached to the first speech, from communications director Richard T. Stout, announced that the four upcoming statements would "form the centerpiece of [Moynihan's] campaign." Richard T. Stout, "Note to Editors and Correspondents," August 25, 1976, papers of Daniel Patrick Moynihan, Library of Congress, Part I, Box 493.

43. Daniel Patrick Moynihan, "A Nation Worth Defending," August 25, 1976; Daniel Patrick Moynihan, "New York State and the Liberal Tradition," August 28, 1976; Daniel Patrick Moynihan, "Saving New York City," August 30, 1976; Daniel Patrick Moynihan, "In Defense of the Family," September 1, 1976, papers of Daniel Patrick Moynihan, Library of Congress, Part I, Box 493.

44. Maurice Carroll, "Mrs. Abzug Offers to Aid Winner; Buckley Calls Moynihan 'to the Left,'" *NYT*, September 16, 1976.

45. Albert R. Hunt, "In the Senate Race, One Campaign Issue Is FDR's 'New Deal,'" *WSJ*, October 15, 1976; "Buckley TV Ads Spur New, Tougher Stance," *NYT*, October 27, 1976.

46. Hodgson, *Gentleman from New York*, 272.

47. CQ Press, *Guide to U.S. Elections*, Vols. I–II, 793, 1457.

48. Timothy Stanley, *Kennedy vs. Carter: The 1980 Battle for the Democratic Party's Soul* (Lawrence: University Press of Kansas, 2010), 29–30.

49. Michael Novak, "Isn't It Time We Had a Senator?" [Periodical unknown], August 23, 1976, offprint in the papers of Norman Podhoretz, Box 2.

50. Albert R. Hunt, "In This Senate Race, One Campaign Issue Is FDR's 'New Deal,'" *WSJ*, October 15, 1976.

51. Ira Shapiro, *The Last Great Senate: Courage and Statesmanship in Times of Crisis* (New York: PublicAffairs, 2012), x.

52. Eventually his staff persuaded him to abandon this latter habit. Letter, Daniel Patrick Moynihan to Safire, June 23, 1984, papers of Daniel Patrick Moynihan, Library of Congress, Part II, Box 9; Daniel Patrick Moynihan and Steven R. Weisman, eds., *Daniel Patrick Moynihan: A Portrait in Letters of an American Visionary* (New York: PublicAffairs, 2010), 440.

53. Edward C. Burks, "Moynihan's Flamboyance and Quick Wit Draw Attention to Washington Freshman," *NYT*, November 7, 1977.

54. Hodgson, *Gentleman from New York*, 270.

55. Edward C. Burks, "Moynihan Gets a Major Post in the Senate," *NYT*, February 10, 1977.

56. Biles, *The Fate of Cities*, 222; "Excerpt from an Interview with Jimmy Carter on Urban Affairs," *NYT*, March 31, 1976; Jack Egan, "Carter Might Back Form of N.Y. Loan Guarantee," *WP*, October 19, 1976.

57. Thomas P. Ronan, "Carter Campaigns with Moynihan," *NYT*, October 1, 1976; Moynihan flyer, papers of Daniel Patrick Moynihan, Part I, Box 490.

58. According to Moynihan, who quoted Powell, these remarks were reported by the *Albany Times-Union* on November 11, 1976. Daniel Patrick Moynihan, "How to Politicize the Economics of Growth—And Why Not To," Address before the White House Conference on Balanced Growth and Economic Development, January 31, 1978, "Senate—General Correspondence, 4/14/77–2/9/78 [CF, O/A 536]," OCL, Frank Moore Subject Files, Jimmy Carter Presidential Library, Box 47.

59. Maurice Carroll, "Moynihan Planning to Talk with Beame," *NYT*, November 5, 1976.

60. Daniel Patrick Moynihan, "What a Senator Can Do for New York," Speech to the City Club of NY, October 29, 1976, papers of Daniel Patrick Moynihan, Library of Congress, Part I, Box 493.

61. Mondale phoned Moynihan the same day to assure him that the remarks of the unnamed aide did not reflect the president's views and that if Carter could "find the son of a bitch," he would fire him. The aide was not found. Rowland Evans and Robert Novak, "A Sharp Edge in Carter-Moynihan Relations," *WP*, July 29, 1977; Memo, Daniel Patrick Moynihan to Elliot Abrams, Charles Horner, Tim Russert, Checker Finn, July 29, 1977, papers of Daniel Patrick Moynihan, Library of Congress, Part II, Box 1.

62. Kahlenberg, *Tough Liberal*, 224–225.

63. Paul C. Warnke, "Apes on a Treadmill," *Foreign Policy* 18 (Spring 1975): 12–29.

64. "Coalition for Democratic Majority Is Identified as Anti-Warnke Group," *NYT*, February 4, 1977.

65. *Congressional Record*, 95–1, March 4, 1977, 6,395–6,396.

66. Edward C. Burks, "Moynihan: How He Won His Senate Spurs," *NYT*, April 5, 1977.

67. Rowland Evans and Robert Novak, "Moynihan's Rubicon," *WP*, April 1, 1977.

68. Rowland Evans and Robert Novak, "A Coalition Comes to Life," *WP*, July 9, 1977.

69. Letter, Daniel Patrick Moynihan to Carter, June 24, 1977, papers of Daniel Patrick Moynihan, Library of Congress, Part II, Box 1.

70. The figures were taken from Professor Erik Johnsen of SUNY Plattsburgh, New York; Hodgson, *Gentleman from New York*, 287.

71. Hodgson, *Gentleman from New York*, 289; Daniel Patrick Moynihan, "What Will They Do for New York," *NYT*, January 27, 1980.

72. "Moynihan Criticizes Federal 'Bias,'" *NYT*, June 27, 1977.

73. Letter, Carter to Daniel Patrick Moynihan, September 14, 1977, papers of Daniel Patrick Moynihan, Library of Congress, Part II, Box 1.

74. Letter, Daniel Patrick Moynihan to Carter, September 28, 1977, papers of Daniel Patrick Moynihan, Library of Congress, Part II, Box 1; Edward C. Burks, "2 Carter Advisers Back Moynihan 'In Certain Respects' on Aid Bias," *NYT*, September 28, 1977.

75. Edward C. Burks, "Northeast and Middle West Join in Congress in Bid for More Aid," *NYT*, June 13, 1977.

76. Carter, *White House Diary*, 165, 199.

77. Hodgson, *Gentleman from New York*, 286–288; For a detailed account of the passage of the New York City Loan Guarantee Act of 1978, see Shapiro, *The Last Great Senate*, 185–200.

78. Lou Cannon, "In California, a Ceiling Is Proposed," *WP*, April 17, 1978; Andrew Rolle, "Howard Jarvis: Taxpayers' Santa Tells His Story," *LAT*, December 9, 1979; Editorial, "Mutiny in California," *NR*, June 3, 1976.

79. Morton Kondracke, "The Moynihan Movement," *NR*, July 22, 1978.

80. Clayton Fritchey, "The New Moynihan," *WP*, August 3, 1981.

81. William F. Buckley, "Why Not Moynihan?" *National Review*, June 22, 1980.

82. *Nation*, September 22, 1979.

83. Shapiro, *The Last Great Senate*, 248, 308; Irvin Molotsky, "Moynihan Prefers the Role of a Neutral," *NYT*, March 17, 1980.

84. Norman Podhoretz, *Ex-Friends: Falling Out with Allen Ginsberg, Lionel & Diana Trilling, Lillian Hellman, Hannah Arendt, and Norman Mailer* (New York: Free Press, 1999), 101.

85. Letter, Daniel Patrick Moynihan to Peter Steinfels, papers of Daniel Patrick Moynihan, Library of Congress, Part II, Box 1.

86. John H. Fenton, "Kennedy Assailed in Debate," *NYT*, August 28, 1962; Stanley, *Kennedy vs. Carter*, 32–40.

87. Burton Hersh, *The Shadow President: Ted Kennedy in Opposition* (South Royalton, VT: Steerforth, 1997), 11.

88. A brief, lucid account of the Chappaquiddick accident can be found in Adam Clymer, *Edward M. Kennedy: A Biography* (New York: Harper Perennial, 2009), 139–149.

89. William E. Leuchtenburg, *In the Shadow of FDR: From Harry Truman to Barack Obama* (4th ed., rev. and updated, Ithaca, NY, and London, 2009), 63–120; Hersh, *The Shadow President*, 38.

90. "The Non-Candidacy of Edward Moore Kennedy," *Time*, November 29, 1971.

91. William Chapman, "Busing Foes Boo Kennedy in Boston," *WP*, September 10, 1974; Stanley, *Kennedy vs. Carter*, 41, 50.

92. Editorial, "The Kennedy-Wallace Summit," *CSM*, July 7, 1987.

93. Hersh, *The Shadow President*, 14–15; Anne Taylor Fleming, "Kennedy: Time of Decision," *NYT*, June 24, 1979.

94. "Uproar Over Medical Bills," *USNWR*, March 28, 1977.

95. Eliot Marshall, "HEW's Half-Measure," *NR*, May 7, 1977.

96. Stanley, *Kennedy vs. Carter*, 51.

97. Edward M. Kennedy, *True Compass: A Memoir* (New York: Twelve, 2009), 359.

98. Fleming, "Kennedy"; Hersh, *The Shadow President*, xv.

99. In another parallel with Hubert Humphrey, Kennedy had lost his post as Senate majority whip, the only leadership position he ever held, to Robert Byrd. Spencer Rich, "Byrd Ousts Kennedy As Senate Whip," *WP*, January 22, 1971.

100. Stanley, *Kennedy vs. Carter*, 52–53.

101. David Blumenthal and James A. Morone, *The Heart of Power: Health and Politics in the Oval Office* (Berkeley: University of California Press, 2009), 252–253; Peter G. Bourne, *Jimmy Carter: A Comprehensive Biography from Plains to Post-Presidency* (New York: Scribner, 1997), 433.

102. National Democratic Party Platform, 1976, papers of Thomas P. (Tip) O'Neill Jr., John J. Burns Library, Boston College, Legislative Files, Democratic Steering & Policy Committee, Sub-subseries 7, Box 57.

103. During the campaign, Carter had courted the UAW, consulting extensively with the union before delivering a major speech on health insurance. The support of the UAW was vital to Carter's victories in Iowa and Florida, among other states. Taylor E. Dark, *The Unions and the Democrats: An Enduring Alliance* (Ithaca, NY: ILR, 1999), 101–102; Bourne, *Jimmy Carter*, 432.

104. Memo, Bourne to Jordan, June 20, 1977, "National Health Insurance [CF, O/A 40]" folder, DPS, Eizenstat Subject Files, Jimmy Carter Presidential Library, Box 240.

105. Memo, Bourne to Carter, December 12, 1977; Memo, Jordan to Bourne, July 8, 1977; Memo, Eizenstat to Jordan, July 5, 1977, "National Health Insurance [CF, O/A 40]" folder, DPS, Eizenstat Subject Files, Jimmy Carter Presidential Library, Box 240; Author interview with Peter Bourne, November 19, 2013.

106. Joseph A. Califano Jr., *Inside: A Public and Private Life* (New York: PublicAffairs, 2004), 329.

107. Bourne to Jordan and Eizenstat, August 1, 1977, "National Health Insurance [CF, O/A 40]" folder, DPS, Eizenstat Subject Files, Jimmy Carter Presidential Library, Box 240.

108. Memo, Joe Onek and Bob Havely to Eizenstat, September 27, 1977, "National Health Insurance [CF, O/A 40]" folder, Domestic Policy Staff, Eizenstat Subject Files, Jimmy Carter Presidential Library, Box 240.

109. Edward M. Kennedy, Tribute to Leonard Woodcock at the United Auto Workers Convention, Los Angeles, CA, May 16, 1977, papers of Adam Clymer, John F. Kennedy Presidential Library, Box 12.

110. Memo, Eizenstat to Jordan, Bourne, August 2, 1977, "National Health Insurance [CF, O/A 40]" folder, Domestic Policy Staff, Eizenstat Subject Files, Jimmy Carter Presidential Library, Box 240.

111. Lawrence Meyer, "Carter Raps 'Spend More' Attitude in Health Care," *WP*, June 17, 1977; Richard D. Lyons, "Carter and Health Care Costs," *NYT*, April 30, 1977.

112. Memo, Stuart E. Eizenstat to Jimmy Carter, July 27, 1978, papers of Adam Clymer, John F. Kennedy Presidential Library, Box 12.

113. Blumenthal and Morone, *Heart of Power*, 267–268.

114. Bell quoted in Hersh, *The Shadow President*, 29.

115. Alan Ehrenhalt, "The New Congress: A Small Step to the Right," *CQA* 34, 1978, 3-B, 4-B; Jimmy Carter, *Keeping Faith: Memoirs of a President* (Fayetteville: University of Arkansas Press, 1995), 77.

116. Memo, Greg Schneiders to Gerald Rafshoon, n.d., "National Health Insurance [3]" folder, Office of the Assistant to the President for Communications (OAPC), Rafshoon Subject Files, Jimmy Carter Presidential Library, Box 4.

117. Blumenthal and Morone, *The Heart of Power*, 275.

118. Transcript, *Today Show*, Tom Brokaw interview with Edward M. Kennedy, papers of Adam Clymer, John F. Kennedy Presidential Library, Box 7.

119. Memo, Powell to Carter, May 18, 1979, "National Health Insurance [CF, O/A 729][3]" folder, Eizenstat Subject Files, Domestic Policy Staff, Jimmy Carter Presidential Library, Box 241.

120. Philip J. Funigiello, *Chronic Politics: Health Care Security from FDR to George W. Bush* (Lawrence: University Press of Kansas, 2005), 191.

121. Jimmy Carter, *White House Diary* (New York: Farrar, Straus and Giroux, 2010), 527.

122. For a detailed treatment of the speech, the events surrounding it, and its legacy, see Kevin Mattson, *"What the Heck Are You Up to Mr. President?": Jimmy Carter, America's "Malaise," and the Speech That Should Have Changed the Country* (New York: Bloomsbury, 2009).

123. Kennedy, *True Compass*, 367.

124. Blumenthal and Morone, *The Heart of Power*, 278.

125. Memo, Mo Udall to Bob and Ron, June 6, 1977, papers of Morris K. Udall, University of Arizona, Box 662.

126. Before setting off in pursuit of the White House, Udall had seriously considered bidding for one of Arizona's Senate seats, either by challenging his friend Barry

Goldwater in 1974 or by running for the seat that became vacant after Paul Fanin announced his retirement in 1976. Letter, Mo Udall to George McGovern, February 22, 1973, papers of Morris K. Udall, University of Arizona, Box 21; Letter, Dennis DeConcini to Mo Udall, February 18, 1976, papers of Morris K. Udall, University of Arizona, Box 23.

127. The other four, according to Bracy, were Hubert Humphrey, Walter Mondale, Jerry Brown, and Ted Kennedy. It is striking that Bracy did not consider Jimmy Carter, then on the verge of winning the presidency, one of the country's "top" Democrats. Memo, Terry Bracy to Mo Udall, November 2, 1976, papers of Morris K. Udall, University of Arizona, Box 23.

128. Carson and Johnson, *Mo: The Life & Times of Morris K. Udall* (Tucson: University of Arizona Press, 2001), 182–183.

129. The only US territory where that was higher was the District of Columbia, where, for obvious reasons, the federal government held 26 percent of the land. Kirschten, "There's More Rhetoric than Reality in the West's 'Sagebrush Rebellion.'" Lou Cannon, "Sagebrush Rebellion Challenges U.S. Grip on Western Land," *WP*, April 9, 1979.

130. Quoted in Carroll B. Foster, "The 'Sagebrush Rebellion' and the Alaska Lands Bill in the U.S. Congress," *Legislative Studies Quarterly* 8, no. 4 (November 1983): 658.

131. Kirschten, "There's More Rhetoric than Reality in the West's 'Sagebrush Rebellion'"; James Morton Turner, *The Promise of Wilderness: American Environmental Politics since 1964* (Seattle: University of Washington Press, 2012), 228.

132. Foster, "The 'Sagebrush Rebellion' and the Alaska Lands Bill," 658; Jeffrey Bloodworth, *Losing the Center: The Decline of American Liberalism, 1968–1992* (Lexington: University Press of Kentucky, 2013), 177–179.

133. Turner, *The Promise of Wilderness*, 228.

134. Memo, Tom Donilon to "Bob," October 13, 1977, "[President's] Western Trip, 10/21–23/77 [CF, O/A 536]" folder, Office of the Congressional Liaison (OCL), Frank Moore Subject Files, Jimmy Carter Presidential Library, Box 45.

135. Lou Cannon, "Mondale, Touring West, Told of Coal Boom Towns' Social and Economic Problems," *WP*, January 12, 1978; Lou Cannon, "Carter in Full Retreat in 'War on West,'" *WP*, January 15, 1979.

136. "The Big Federal Land Grab," *Conservative Digest* 4 (December 1978): 7–11, cited in James Morton Turner, "'The Specter of Environmentalism': Wilderness, Environmental Politics, and the Evolution of the New Right," *Journal of American History* 96, no. 1 (June 2009): 130.

137. This claim was supported largely by anecdotal evidence. The article cited no polling data or large-scale quantitative analyses, alluding only to "a range of evidence and persons interviewed across the country." John Herbers, "West Taking South's Place as Most Alienated Area," *NYT*, March 18, 1979.

138. Foster, "The 'Sagebrush Rebellion' and the Alaska Lands Bill in the U.S. Congress," 658.

139. Cannon, "Sagebrush Rebellion Challenges U.S. Grip on Western Land."

140. Kirschten, "There's More Rhetoric than Reality in the West's 'Sagebrush Rebellion.'"

141. US Office of the Federal Register, *Public Papers of the Presidents of the United States: Jimmy Carter, 1979: Book 2—June 23 to December 31, 1979* (Washington, DC: National Archives and Record Service, 1980), 1,363.

142. Mark Stevens, "Utah's Governor—Determined Crusader for States' Rights," *CSM*, March 3, 1980.

143. Richard D. Lamm, "Whither the Democratic Party?" *NYT*, February 1, 1976; Richard D. Lamm, "Out West, Worries," *NYT*, August 12, 1980.

144. Kirschten, "There's More Rhetoric than Reality in the West's 'Sagebrush Rebellion.'"

145. Myra McPherson, "Mo Udall, Triumph of the Good Guy," *WP*, December 29, 1985.

146. Carson and Johnson, *Mo*, 195.

147. Carson and Johnson, *Mo*, 196.

148. Turner, "The Specter of Environmentalism," 130.

149. Carson and Johnson, *Mo*, 195, 201.

150. Memo, Mo Udall to Private Files, April 28, 1977, papers of Morris K. Udall, University of Arizona, Box 662.

151. Memo, Mo Udall to Files, May 3, 1977, papers of Morris K. Udall, University of Arizona, Box 662.

152. Memo, Mo Udall to Mo Udall Files, January 18, 1978, papers of Morris K. Udall, University of Arizona, Box 662.

153. A full account of the struggle, and Udall's role in it, can be found in Carson and Johnson, *Mo*, 193–202.

154. US Office of the Federal Register, *Public Papers of the Presidents of the United States: Jimmy Carter, 1980–81: Book III—September 29, 1980 to January 20, 1981* (Washington, DC: National Archives and Record Service, 1982), 2,756.

155. Carson and Johnson, *Mo*, 194.

156. McPherson, "Mo Udall, Triumph of the Good Guy."

157. "Udall Outdoes Sherman," *Boston Globe*, July 31, 1980.

158. Statement by Mo Udall, December 18, 1979, Morris K. Udall, University of Arizona, Box 664.

159. Statement, n.d., papers of Morris K. Udall, University of Arizona, Box 664.

160. Timothy Stanley attributes Kennedy's failure to foreign policy crises that boosted Carter's domestic popularity, to the incompetence of Kennedy's campaign, and to the senator's personal baggage. Stanley, *Kennedy vs. Carter*.

161. Curtis Wilkie and Thomas Oliphant, "Kennedy Has His Say," *Boston Globe*, August 13, 1980.

162. Ward Sinclair, "Keynoter Udall: Reformer and Mediator," *WP*, August 11, 1980.

163. Steven V. Roberts, "Some Key Democratic Leaders at the Convention," *NYT*, August 11, 1980.

164. Mo Udall, Text of Keynote Address, Democratic National Convention, NYC, August 11, 1980, papers of Morris K. Udall, University of Arizona, Box 25.

CHAPTER 5. MARAUDERS AT THE GATES

1. Julian E. Zelizer, *Jimmy Carter* (New York: Times, 2010), 125.

2. Carter's relationship with evangelical voters, and the circumstances that led to his ultimate loss of that bloc to Reagan, are detailed in J. Brooks Flippen, *Jimmy Carter, the Politics of Family, and the Rise of the Religious Right* (Athens: University of Georgia Press, 2011).

3. The demographic figures came from a *NYT*/CBS poll conducted in October 1980. CQ Press, *Guide to U.S. Elections, Volume I*, 792, 794; editorial, "Woe Is the Democrats," *WP*, November 11, 1980; Adam Clymer, "The Collapse of a Coalition," *NYT*, November 5, 1980.

4. "Woe Is the Democrats."

5. David S. Broder, "Is It a New Era?" *WP*, November 19, 1981.

6. Lynn Rossellini, "In Capital, Stunned Democrats Lament Amid Republicans' Glee," *NYT*, November 6, 1980.

7. Martin Tolchin, "Democrats Expected to Keep Majorities in Congress," *NYT*, September 2, 1980.

8. Richard L. Lyons, "House Democrats Retain Power, But with Limits," *WP*, November 6, 1980.

9. "Political Shift to Right—Will It Last in '80s?" *USNWR*, February 23, 1981.

10. David S. Broder, "A Sharp Right Turn," *WP*, November 6, 1980.

11. Moynihan was trying to impress on the incoming DNC chairman the importance of the East, and of New York in particular, to the Democratic Party, but his data were persuasive. For instance, of the ten states the Democratic candidate had won in four of the previous six presidential elections, seven were Eastern (Maryland, Massachusetts, New York, Pennsylvania, Rhode Island, West Virginia, and, included though not a state, the District of Columbia). Daniel Patrick Moynihan, "The East Is Now the Electoral Base of the Democratic Party," Memorandum for the Candidates for Chair of the Democratic National Committee, January 22, 1981, papers of Daniel Patrick Moynihan, Library of Congress, Part II, Box 3.

12. To combat this deficiency, Losser proposed a DNC Grassroots Task Force, modeled on Republican efforts in the 1970s. Memo, Sheryl Losser to Charles Manatt, January 27, 1981, papers of Tip O'Neill, John J. Burns Library, Staff Files, Kirk O'Donnell Files, Sub-Subseries 4, Box 3.

13. Edward Walsh, "Bill Brock: Architect of Republican Revival," *WP*, November 20, 1980.

14. Pamela C. Harriman, "Rebuilding the Party from the Grass Roots Up," *WP*, November 26, 1980.

15. Hedrick Smith, "A Turning Point Seen," *NYT*, November 6, 1980.

16. Hedrick Smith, "Reformer Who Would Reverse the New Deal's Legacy," *NYT*, January 21, 1981.

17. Broder, "Is It a New Era?"

18. Bill Peterson, "Democrats Hope, But Mostly Hurt After Worst Beating in 28 Years," *WP*, November 6, 1980.

19. Godfrey Hodgson, *The World Turned Right Side Up: A History of the Conservative Ascendancy in America* (Boston: Houghton Mifflin, 1996), 3.

20. USOFR, *Public Papers of the Presidents: Ronald Reagan, 1981, January 20 to December 31, 1981*, 1. As Gareth Davies writes, "Whether or not there was a Reagan Revolution, there was at least a revolutionary movement during the first six months or so, when defenders of the welfare state were on the run, overwhelmed by the president's popularity and by the widespread sense that excessive government spending lay at the heart of the nation's inflationary crisis." Gareth Davies, "The Welfare State," in *The Reagan Presidency: Pragmatic Conservatism and Its Legacies*, ed. W. Elliot Brownlee and Hugh Davis Graham (Lawrence: University Press of Kansas, 2003), 211.

21. Despite the headline, *NR*'s editorial barely mentioned Anderson and instead focused on Jimmy Carter's shortcomings as president. In four years, wrote the editors, Carter had "failed by both the general standards of competent administration and the special standards of the liberal agenda. . . . Now Carter asks liberals to support him for reelection. We say no." Editorial, "John Anderson for President," *NR*, October 4, 1980. Anderson also received the support of civil rights lawyer Joseph Rauh and Arthur Schlesinger. The latter was a Carter skeptic of long vintage, having not cast a vote for president in 1976. Arthur M. Schlesinger Jr., *Journals, 1952–2000*, ed. Andrew Schlesinger and Stephen Schlesinger (London: Atlantic, 2007), 503–506; Letter, Rauh to John Anderson, June 22, 1981, papers of Joseph A. Rauh, Library of Congress, Box 1. For a detailed account of Anderson's 1980 campaign, see Jim Mason, *No Holding Back: The 1980 John B. Anderson Presidential Campaign* (Lanham, MD: University Press of America, 2011).

22. Peter D. Hart, "The Regeneration of the Democrats," n.d., papers of Tip O'Neill, John J. Burns Library, Staff Files, O'Donnell Files, Sub-subseries 4–5, Box 5.

23. Morton Kondracke, "A Doubtful New Order," *NR*, November 15, 1980.

24. Editorial, "Democrats for Congress," *NR*, October 25, 1980.

25. Lyons, "House Democrats Retain Power, But with Limits."

26. Schlesinger, *Journals*, 491.

27. Gregg Easterbrook, "What's Wrong with Congress?" *Atlantic Monthly*, December 1984.

28. Rossellini, "In Capital, Stunned Democrats Lament Amid Republicans' Glee."

29. Granat, "Whatever Happened to the Watergate Babies?"

30. Easterbrook, "What's Wrong with Congress?"

31. Marjorie Hunter, "Televised Coverage of the House Begins Today on a Limited Basis," *NYT*, February 19, 1979; Barbara Matusoio, "Congress on TV; Look Out, Mork and Mindy," *WP*, July 29, 1979; Donald A. Ritchie, *Reporting from Washington: The History of the Washington Press Corps* (New York: Oxford University Press, 2005), 212–213.

32. Memo, Burt Hoffman to O'Neill, November 10, 1980, papers of Tip O'Neill, John J. Burns Library, Staff Files, O'Donnell Files, Sub-Subseries 4, Box 4.

33. William A. Henry III, "The Unlikely Cult Figure," *NR*, February 11, 1987.

34. Sanford J. Ungar, "Bleak House: Frustration on Capitol Hill," *Atlantic Monthly*, July 1977.

35. In case the metaphor was too subtle, the passenger addressed the O'Neill character as "Congressman" throughout. John A. Farrell, *Tip O'Neill and the Democratic Century* (Boston: Little, Brown, 2001), 534; Robert McLean, "GOP Aiming at Tip O'Neill," *Boston Globe*, January 16, 1980; Alan Ehrenhalt, "O'Neill's Look-Alike Stars in GOP Film for Hill Races," *Washington Star*, January 30, 1980, offprints in the papers of Tip O'Neill, John J. Burns Library, Press Relations, Clippings, Box 24.

36. "Youngest House Member Lodges Attack on O'Neill," *WP*, July 12, 1981.

37. Edward Walsh, "Conservative Democrats in House Signal Change," *WP*, November 28, 1980.

38. Lou Cannon and Richard L. Lyons, "40 Conservative House Democrats Ask Reagan for More Budget Cuts," *WP*, March 6, 1981.

39. John W. Mashek, "Democrats' First Step on Road Back," *USNWR*, March 9, 1981.

40. Farrell, *Tip O'Neill*, 544–545.

41. Steven V. Roberts, "Democratic Legislators, Shaken by Losses, Hoping to Rebuild Ties with the Middle Class," *NYT*, November 15, 1980.

42. Godfrey Hodgson, *All Things to All Men: The False Promise of the Modern American Presidency* (London: Weidenfeld and Nicolson, 1980), 15–16; Fred I. Greenstein, *The Hidden-Hand Presidency: Eisenhower as Leader* (New York: Basic, 1982).

43. Iwan Morgan, *The Age of Deficits: Presidents and Unbalanced Budgets from Jimmy Carter to George W. Bush* (Lawrence: University Press of Kansas, 2009), 79–80.

44. White and Wildavsky quoted in Morgan, *The Age of Deficits*, 1.

45. An NBC/News/Associated Press poll from May 1981 found that 69 percent of respondents believed that federal income taxes were "too high" or "much too high." A Cambridge Reports National Omnibus Survey poll from April had found that 58 percent of respondents believed that federal income taxes "discouraged [people] from working harder." NBC News/Associated Press Poll, May 1981. Cambridge Reports National Omnibus Survey, April 1981. Retrieved October 2, 2014 from the *iPOLL Databank*, http://ezproxy-prd.bodleian.ox.ac.uk:3170/data_access/ipoll/ipoll.html.

46. John Ehrman, *The Eighties: America in the Age of Reagan* (New Haven, CT: Yale University Press, 2005), 54–55.

47. Morgan, *The Age of Deficits*, 84–85.

48. Mashek, "Democrats' First Step on Road Back."

49. Adam Clymer, "Democrats Lie Low—for Good Reason," *NYT*, July 5, 1981.

50. Robert Ajemian, "Tip O'Neill on the Ropes," *Time*, May 18, 1981, offprint in the papers of Tip O'Neill, John J. Burns Library, Press Relations, Clippings, Box 24.

51. John Ohman cartoon, May 9, 1981, papers of Tip O'Neill, John J. Burns Library, Press Relations, Clippings, Box 24.

52. David Farrell, "Speaker O'Neill to Retire Next Year?" *Boston Globe*, March 30, 1981, offprint in the papers of Tip O'Neill, John J. Burns Library, Press Relations, Clippings, Box 24.

53. Ajemian, "Tip O'Neill on the Ropes."

54. Iwan W. Morgan, "Reaganomics and Its Legacy," in *Ronald Reagan and the 1980s*, ed. Hudson and Davies, 103–104.

55. Louis Fisher, "Reagan's Relations with Congress," in *The Reagan Presidency: An Incomplete Revolution?*, ed. Dilys M. Hill, Raymond A. Moore, and Phil Williams (Basingstoke: Macmillan, 1990), 97.

56. Memo, Patrick H. Caddell to the Democratic Leadership, February 20, 1982, papers of Tip O'Neill, John J. Burns Library, Staff Files, O'Donnell Files, Sub-subseries 13–14, Box 12; Farrell, *Tip O'Neill*, 585.

57. Farrell, *Tip O'Neill*, 24.

58. Memo, Jerry Colbert to Tip O'Neill, n.d., papers of Tip O'Neill, John J. Burns Library, Staff Files, O'Donnell Files, Sub-Subseries 4, Box 3.

59. Steven V. Roberts, "O'Neill TV Appearances a Major Shift in Strategy," *NYT*, June 9, 1981; Transcript (rush), ABC, Issues and Answers, June 7, 1981, papers of Tip O'Neill, John J. Burns Library, Press Relations, Speeches, Box 6.

60. Memo from O'Donnell to Tip O'Neill, August 4, 1981, papers of Tip O'Neill, John J. Burns Library, Staff Files, O'Donnell Files, Sub-subseries 14–1, Box 13.

61. Richard Locher cartoon, *Chicago Tribune*, June 23, 1981, offprint in the papers of Tip O'Neill, John J. Burns Library, Press Relations, Clippings, Box 24.

62. Mary Battiata, "Gridiron Dinner: Labor of Lampoonery," *WP*, March 30, 1981.

63. Daniel P. Moynihan, *Came the Revolution: Argument in the Reagan Era* (San Diego: Harcourt Brace Jovanovich, 1988), 5–7.

64. Letter, Daniel Patrick Moynihan to Theodore White, April 29, 1980, papers of Daniel Patrick Moynihan, Library of Congress, Part II, Box 3.

65. That same month, Norman Podhoretz declared in a public lecture that after years of resisting the label "neoconservative," he was "willing now, however reluctantly, to accept the designation." This suggested a solidifying of political factions in the Reagan era. Norman Podhoretz, Lecture, "Liberalism and Neoconservatism," March 11, 1981, papers of Norman Podhoretz, Library of Congress, Box 2.

66. Ehrman, *The Eighties*, 52–53; David Stockman, *The Triumph of Politics: How the Reagan Revolution Failed* (New York: Harper & Row, 1986), 21.

67. Stockman, *The Triumph of Politics*, 2.

68. Ehrman, *The Eighties*, 53; Hedrick Smith, "Stockman Is Ruffling Feathers in Seeking Budget Cuts," *NYT*, February 4, 1981; Walter Shapiro, "The Stockman Express," *WP*, February 8, 1981.

69. Eric Laursen, *The People's Pension: The Struggle to Defend Social Security Since Reagan* (Oakland, CA: AK, 2012), 36; Gar Alperovitz and Jeff Faux, "An Alternative Policy to Prevent 'Dunkirk,'" *NYT*, January 7, 1981.

70. Art Pine, "Democrats Vow to Fight on Social Security Cuts," *WP*, May 14, 1981.

71. Godfrey Hodgson, *Gentleman from New York: Daniel Patrick Moynihan, A Biography* (Boston: Houghton Mifflin, 2000), 298; Martin Tolchin, "Byrd Assails Cuts in Social Security as 'Harsh' and Breach of Promise," *NYT*, May 16, 1981; Alison Muscatine and Mary Thornton, "House Democrats Attack Reagan Social Security

Plan," *Washington Star*, May 14, 1981, offprint in the papers of Tip O'Neill, John J. Burns Library, Box 25; Daniel Patrick Moynihan, "Beyond 96–0," *NYT*, May 22, 1981.

72. Martha Derthick, *Policymaking for Social Security* (Washington, DC: Brookings Institution, 1979), 381–411; Laursen, *The People's Pension*, 34.

73. Martha Derthick and Steven M. Teles, "Riding the Third Rail: Social Security Reform," in *The Reagan Presidency*, ed. Brownlee and Davis, 183.

74. Laursen, *The People's Pension*, 5.

75. Douglas E. Kneeland, "Reagan Vows to Support Social Security Program," *NYT*, September 8, 1980.

76. Ronald Reagan, *Speaking My Mind: Selected Speeches* (London: Hutchinson, 1990), 31.

77. Derthick and Teles, "Riding the Third Rail," 182.

78. William Greider, "The Education of David Stockman," *Atlantic Monthly*, December 1, 1981; Jack Germond and Jules Witcover, "Social Security Plans Caught GOP Off Guard," *Washington Star*, May 18, 1981, offprint in the papers of Tip O'Neill, John J. Burns Library, Box 25.

79. Edward D. Berkowitz, *America's Welfare State: From Roosevelt to Reagan* (Baltimore: Johns Hopkins University Press, 1996), 74.

80. Edward D. Berkowitz, *Mr. Social Security: The Life of Wilbur J. Cohen* (Lawrence: University Press of Kansas, 1995), 297–307; Mike Causey, "Gray Power Lobby Set to Fight Cut in COLA," *WP*, June 17, 1981.

81. Warren J. Weaver Jr., "Coalition Plans Drive Against Move to Trim Social Security Benefits," *NYT*, May 14, 1981.

82. Spencer Rich, "Plight of Social Security Is Being Exaggerated, Democrats Charge," *WP*, July 8, 1981.

83. David S. Broder, "Reagan Backs Off Televised Speech on Social Security," *WP*, July 26, 1981.

84. In a letter to O'Neill proposing this body, Reagan referred to it as a "bipartisan Blue Ribbon Task Force." Letter, Reagan to O'Neill, September 24, 1981, papers of Tip O'Neill, John J. Burns Library, Box 26.

85. Berkowitz, *America's Welfare State*, 74.

86. For an account of Volcker's Fed policies, see Iwan Morgan, "Monetary Metamorphosis: The Volcker Fed and Inflation," *Journal of Policy History*, 24, no. 4 (2012): 545–571.

87. Moynihan and Weisman, eds., *Moynihan: Portrait in Letters*, 438.

88. Richard L. Strout, "Senator Moynihan, A Liberal-Conservative Hybrid," *CSM*, March 26, 1982.

89. Daniel Patrick Moynihan, "Reagan's Bankrupt Budget," *NR*, December 31, 1983.

90. Geider, "Education of David Stockman."

91. Letter, Daniel Patrick Moynihan to Arthur O. Sulzberger, July 28, 1981, enclosed clipping: "Democratic Unity Faces Test on Tax," *NYT*, July 28, 1981, papers of Daniel Patrick Moynihan, Library of Congress, Part II, Box 3. Moynihan had ringed the

paragraph in the enclosed article that identified him as one of the "liberals from the Northeast."

92. Fred Barnes, "Pat Moynihan, Neoliberal," *NR*, October 21, 1981.

93. "Et Tu, Moynihan," *National Review*, August 5, 1983.

94. Chester E. Finn Jr. *Troublemaker: A Personal History of School Reform Since Sputnik* (Princeton, NJ: Princeton University Press, 2008), 92.

95. Stockman, *The Triumph of Politics*, 244.

96. Maurice Carroll, "Conservatives Open an Anti-Moynihan Drive," *NYT*, November 22, 1981.

97. Headline, "Democratic Party," *NBC News*, November 15, 1980, Vanderbilt Television News Archive.

98. Frank Lynn, "In New York, an Invisible G.O.P. Race," *NYT*, July 20, 1982.

99. Maurice Carroll, "Mrs. Sullivan and Moynihan Trade Charges," *NYT*, October 12, 1982; Josh Barbanel, "Mrs. Sullivan Attacking Moynihan as Too Liberal," *NYT*, September 25, 1982.

100. Carroll, "Mrs. Sullivan and Moynihan Trade Charges."

101. Maurice Carroll, "Moynihan Assails G.O.P Fund Ballot," *NYT*, October 30, 1982.

102. CQ Press, *Guide to U.S. Elections, Vol. II*, 1,439, 1,448–1,449, 1,452, 1,457, 1,469; Maurice Carroll, "Moynihan Wins Overwhelming Victory," *NYT*, November 3, 1982.

103. Derthick and Teles, "Riding the Third Rail," 198.

104. Judith Miller, "Breakfast Stir: Glenn on Social Security," *NYT*, August 13, 1982.

105. Letter, Daniel Patrick Moynihan to Lane Kirkland, August 13, 1982, papers of Daniel Patrick Moynihan, Library of Congress, Part II, Box 5.

106. Ronald Reagan and Douglas Brinkley, eds., *The Reagan Diaries* (New York: HarperCollins, 2007), 119.

107. Edward Cowan, "Dole Holds Meeting to Seek a Social Security Concession," *NYT*, January 5, 1983.

108. Editorial, "A Reasonable Compromise," *WP*, January 17, 1983.

109. Daniel Patrick Moynihan, "More Than Social Security Was at Stake," *WP*, January 18, 1983.

110. Letter, Daniel Patrick Moynihan to James Reston, December 16, 1982, papers of Daniel Patrick Moynihan, Library of Congress, Part II, Box 5.

111. Stockman, *The Triumph of Politics*, 193.

112. Stockman, *The Triumph of Politics*, 7, 11.

113. Letter, Daniel Patrick Moynihan to Jim Wright, January 27, 1984, papers of Daniel Patrick Moynihan, Library of Congress, Part II, Box 7.

114. Derthick and Teles, "Riding the Third Rail," 184, 203–204.

115. See Nelson Lichtenstein, "Ideology and Interest on the Social Policy Home Front," in *Presidency of George W. Bush*, ed. Zelizer, 169–198.

116. The new resolution mandated that there would be 900 delegates. Of those, 369 would be DNC members, 369 would be chosen by state party committees, and a further 100 were to be named by Manatt, subject to the approval of the party's executive

committee. All Democratic governors were invited, as were twenty-four House members, and eight senators. David S. Broder, "Democrats, in Turnabout, Shrink Size of '82 Mid-Term Convention," *WP*, June 6, 1981.

117. David S. Broder, "Democrats Unite in Picking Chairman," *WP*, February 28, 1981; Jacqueline Trescott, "The Politics of Pragmatism," *WP*, February 28, 1981.

118. T. Rees Shapiro, "Charles T. Manatt, Former Chairman of Democratic National Committee, Dies at 75," WP, July 23, 2011.

119. Francis X. Clines, "Workshops at Democratic Mini-Convention Mix Party Hoopla and Cynicism," *NYT*, June 26, 1982.

120. William Greider, "A Dull Democratic Party," *Rolling Stone*, August 5, 1982.

121. Elizabeth Bumiller, "The DNC Does Philly," *WP*, June 25, 1982.

122. Greider, "A Dull Democratic Party."

123. Peter McGrath, Gloria Borger, Howard Fineman, John J. Lindsay, and Rich Thomas, "The Next Two Years in the New Congress," *Newsweek*, November 15, 1982, offprint in the papers of Tip O'Neill, Staff Files, O'Donnell Files, Sub-subseries 4–5, Box 5.

124. Farrell, *Tip O'Neill*, 595–596; Letter from John LeBoutillier, papers of Tip O'Neill, John J. Burns Library, Staff Files, O'Donnell Files, Sub-subseries 14–1, Box 13.

125. Merit Report, October 1982. Retrieved September 28, 2014 from the iPOLL Databank, http://ezproxy-prd.bodleian.ox.ac.uk:3170/data_access/ipoll/ipoll.html.

126. Kevin P. Phillips, "'82 Democratic Gains, '84 Democratic Pains," *NYT*, October 17, 1982.

127. David S. Broder, "Kirk to Seek Cancellation of Midterm Convention," *WP*, May 10, 1985; Paul Taylor, "Party Rejects '86 Midterm Convention," *WP*, June 26, 1985.

CHAPTER 6. "REAGANISM WITH A HUMAN FACE"?

1. The definitive history of ADA, covering its peak years as a liberal vanguard, is Steven M. Gillon, *Politics and Vision: The ADA and American Liberalism, 1947–1985* (New York: Oxford University Press, 1987). Scott Kamen has offered a revisionist take on ADA, arguing that it had not been constrained by anticommunist dogma but rather remained committed to ambitious social democratic ideas well into the 1960s. Scott Kamen, "Rethinking Postwar Liberalism: The Americans for Democratic Action, Social Democracy, and the Struggle for Racial Equality," *The Sixties: A Journal of History, Politics, and Culture* 11, no. 1 (2018): 69–92. See also, Kevin Mattson, *When America Was Great: The Fighting Faith of Postwar Liberalism* (New York: Routledge, 2004).

2. Tsongas added that his former colleagues in the House were inclined to "feel their re-election is in the national interest," a sentiment that was "multipl[ied] . . . when you get to the Senate." "Tsongas Says Senators Need Dose of Humility," *NYT*, November 11, 1978.

3. Richard F. Fenno Jr., *Senators on the Campaign Trail: The Politics of Representation* (Norman: University of Oklahoma Press, 1996), 47.

4. B. Drummond Ayres Jr., "Tsongas Played Underdog Role to Oust Brooke in Senate Race," *NYT*, November 9, 1978.

5. Sue Warner, "Liberal Laments," *WP*, June 16, 1980.

6. Warner, "Liberal Laments."

7. David S. Broder, "Politically Passé?" *WP*, June 25, 1980; "Bunker Liberalism: Find Realistic Solutions for Tomorrow's Problems," *WP*, November 9, 1980.

8. Broder, "Politically Passé?"; "Bunker Liberalism."

9. Curt Suplee, "The Tsongas Liberalism," *WP*, September 23, 1981.

10. Steven V. Roberts, "A.D.A. Debates Role of Liberalism in a Year of Losses and Budget Cuts," *NYT*, June 15, 1980.

11. Warner, "Liberal Laments," *WP.*

12. Roberts, "A.D.A. Debates Role of Liberalism in a Year of Losses and Budget Cuts."

13. Fenno, *Senators on the Campaign Trail*, 51.

14. Rothenberg would go on to write a book chronicling the emergence of the neoliberals and taxonomizing their ideology. Randall Rothenberg, "The Neoliberal Club," *Esquire*, February 1982.

15. Kenneth Baer identifies the neoliberals as one of the forerunners of the DLC in his history of the organization. Baer, *Reinventing Democrats*, 32–33.

16. Headline: "Democratic Party," *NBC News*, November 15, 1980, Vanderbilt Television News Archive, Vanderbilt University.

17. Letter, Daniel Patrick Moynihan to Tom Wicker, May 19, 1980, papers of Daniel Patrick Moynihan, Part II, Box 2.

18. Tom Wicker, "Democrats in Search of Ideas," *NYT*, January 25, 1981.

19. "97th Congress—Young, Energetic, Pragmatic," *USNWR*, January 12, 1981; Mashek, "Democrats' First Step on Road Back."

20. "Democrats Set Up Study Group Aimed at Developing New Ideas," *NYT*, March 1, 1981.

21. Adam Clymer, "Democrats: New Views," *NYT*, September 24, 1981.

22. Adam Clymer, "Democrats Propelling 3 Strategies on Economics into Battle of Ideas," *NYT*, October 15, 1981.

23. Gary Hart, "The End of the New Deal," papers of Gary W. Hart, University of Colorado Boulder, Box 54.

24. Memo, Rick Brown to Gary Hart, May 25, 1979, papers of Gary W. Hart, University of Colorado Boulder, Box 55.

25. Kenneth T. Walsh, "Colorado: Hart Trouble," *NR*, October 25, 1980; Gary Hart, nomination acceptance speech, n.d., papers of Gary W. Hart, University of Colorado Boulder, Box 55.

26. Hedrick Smith, "Senator Hart Tackles Party Renewal," *NYT*, December 28, 1981.

27. Kondracke also mentioned Tsongas as an example of a "neoliberal" trailblazer. Rothenberg, *The Neoliberals*, 17.

28. Rothenberg, *The Neoliberals*, 45; "Bunker Liberalism".

29. Tsongas, Statement of US Senate Candidacy, May 18, 1978, Paul Efthemios Tsongas collection, Center for Lowell History, Box 51B; Steven V. Roberts, "Democrats: An Aye for Business," *NYT*, March 1, 1981.

30. Gary Hart, *The Thunder and the Sunshine: Four Seasons in a Burnished Life* (Golden, CO: Fulcrum, 2010), 40.

31. Tsongas, speech at the Centennial Celebration of the Department of Electrical Engineering at M.I.T., Cambridge, MA, October 2, 1982, Paul E. Tsongas collection, Center for Lowell History, Box 60C.

32. Thomas B. Edsall, "'Atari Democrats' Join Party Conflicts Revived by Gains," *WP*, November 7, 1982.

33. R. James Woolsey, "The Kind of Critic the Military Needs," *WP*, June 18, 1980; Michael Kramer, "Where Does Hart Stand?" *New York*, April 9, 1984.

34. "A basic strategic fact," said Hart, "is that the United States is a sea power, not a land power." Rothenberg, *The Neoliberals*, 115.

35. Adam Clymer, "Reagan Evoking Rising Concern, New Poll Shows," *NYT*, March 19, 1982; Barry Sussman, "Criticism of Foreign Policy Growing," *WP*, January 20, 1984.

36. Steven V. Roberts, "Senate Bill Seeks a Rein on the U.S. in Latin America," *NYT*, March 1982.

37. Patrick E. Taylor and Don Oberdorfer, "Nicaragua Activities Questioned," *WP*, April 14, 1983.

38. "Hart on El Salvador: It's Their War," *WP*, February 28, 1982.

39. TRB, "Neoliberals, Paleoliberals," *NR*, April 9, 1984.

40. Barbara Gamerekian, "To Magazine Founder, Capital Doesn't Function Well," *NYT*, April 22, 1982.

41. Eric Redman, "Empire-Building on the Potomac," *WP*, June 1, 1980.

42. In the same column, Peters suggested that perhaps the reason Carter lost the election was that he had "begun to bore his fellow Americans. . . . Switch the channel, change the show." Charles Peters, "Why the Democrats Lost, and Why Criminals Go Free," *WP*, December 21, 1980.

43. Charles Peters, "A Neo-liberal's Manifesto," *WP*, September 5, 1982.

44. Charles Peters, "Neoliberals," *WP*, July 21, 1985; Walter Goodman, "Neo-Liberals and the Fight for the Political Center," *NYT*, October 26, 1983.

45. Theodore J. Lowi, "What's New About Neoliberals?" *WP*, June 16, 1985; Charles Peters, "Neoliberals," *WP*, July 21, 1985.

46. Statement of Senator Paul Tsongas, September 24, 1979, Paul E. Tsongas collection, Center for Lowell History, Box 62C.

47. Scully quoted in Rothenberg, *The Neoliberals*, 19; Robert M. Kaus, "Reaganism with a Human Face," *NR*, November 25, 1981.

48. Arthur Schlesinger Jr., "American Politics on a Darkling Plain," *WSJ*, March 16, 1982, offprint in the Paul E. Tsongas collection, Center for Lowell History, Box 57A.

49. "On Capitol Hill," *WP*, April 7, 1979.

50. Karl Gerard Brandt, "The Ideological Origins of the New Democrat Movement," *Louisiana History* 48, no. 3 (Summer 2007): 281.

51. From, *The New Democrats and the Return to Power* (New York: Palgrave Macmillan, 2013), 32.

52. Brandt, "The Ideological Origins of the New Democrat Movement," 278, 283.

53. Adam Clymer, "Democrats: New Views," *NYT*, September 24, 1981.

54. Baer, *Reinventing Democrats*, 40.

55. Brandt, "Ideological Origins," 284.

56. House Democratic Caucus press release, April 8, 1981; Statement of Democratic Economic Principles, April 8, 1981, papers of Tip O'Neill, John J. Burns Library, Staff Files, O'Donnell Files, Sub-Subseries 4, Box 4.

57. Caucus Committee on Party Effectiveness, *Rebuilding the Road to Opportunity: A Democratic Direction for the 1980s*, September 1982, papers of the House Democratic Caucus, Library of Congress, Box 63.

58. Joseph Kraft, "Economic Realism Is Back," *WP*, September 28, 1980.

59. Letter, Gillis Long to O'Neill, December 16, 1981, papers of Tip O'Neill, John J. Burns Library, Box 22.

60. From, *The New Democrats and the Return to Power*, 31.

61. Steven M. Gillon, *The Democrats' Dilemma: Walter F. Mondale and the Liberal Legacy* (New York: Columbia University Press, 1992), 310.

62. Edward Cowan, "Reagan Aides Defend Deficits," *NYT*, December 9, 1981.

63. Peter T. Kilborn, "Democrats Search for a Winning Issue," *NYT*, February 26, 1984; Paul Tsongas, "Only a Summit Will Do," *Boston Globe*, December 13, 1983, offprint in the Paul E. Tsongas collection, Center for Lowell History, Box 1B.

64. Jonathan Fuerbringer, "Democrats Insist on Military Cuts in Deficit Talks," *NYT*, February 10, 1984.

65. Francis X. Clines, "President Denies Blame for Deficit," *NYT*, October 8, 1983; Herbert H. Denton and William Chapman, "Reagan Backs Balanced-Budget Amendment," *WP*, July 13, 1982.

66. Jude Wanniski, "The Balanced Budget Amendment: The Idea Is Ludicrous," *WP*, August 1, 1982; Alice M. Rivlin, interview with the author, January 9, 2012; "Constitutional Con," *NYT*, August 1, 1982.

67. Helen Dewar, "Democrats Vow Own Cuts," *WP*, February 2, 1984.

68. See Iwan W. Morgan, "Monetary Metamorphosis: The Volcker Fed and Inflation," *Journal of Policy History* 24, no. 4 (2012): 545–571.

69. Steven V. Roberts, "On the Deficit, 'A World Turned Upside Down,'" *NYT*, December 28, 1984.

70. James D. Savage, *Balanced Budgets and American Politics* (Ithaca, NY: Cornell University Press, 1988), 222–232.

71. Paul E. Tsongas, speech before the National Press Club, October 5, 1982, Paul E. Tsongas collection, Center for Lowell History, Box 1B.

72. The Commission recommended, and received some backing for, 30 percent of the convention to be made up of unpledged delegates. In the event, the DNC opted for 14 percent super delegates. "Excerpts from the Democratic Commission's Report on New Convention Rules," *NYT*, March 27, 1982; Adam Clymer, "Democrats Alter Delegate Rules, Giving Top Officials More Power," *NYT*, March 27, 1982.

73. Minutes, Democratic Caucus, Regular Meeting, July 20, 1983; Minutes, Democratic Caucus, Regular Meeting, July 13, 1983; Minutes, Democratic Caucus, Regular

Meeting, November 15, 1983; Democratic Caucus, Regular Meeting, June 12, 1984, papers of the House Democratic Caucus, Library of Congress, Boxes 18, 19.

74. Farrell, *Tip O'Neill*, 678–679.

75. Lois Romano, "Jesse Jackson: His Charismatic Crusade for the Voters at the End of the Rainbow Coalition," *WP*, July 31, 1983. For more on the "Rainbow Coalition" and the political legacy of the Jackson campaign, see Lorenzo Morris and Linda F. Williams, "The Coalition at the End of the Rainbow," in *Jesse Jackson's 1984 Presidential Campaign: Challenge and Change in American Politics,* ed. Lucius J. Barker and Ronald W. Waters (Urbana: University of Illinois Press, 1989).

76. In 1982, 237 of the 376 House candidates endorsed by the AFL-CIO's Committee on Political Education (COPE) won their elections. So too did twenty of the thirty-one senatorial and twenty-four of the thirty-three gubernatorial candidates endorsed. Kathy Sawyer, "List Labor as One of the Midterm Winners," *WP*, November 9, 1982.

77. Roberts, "Democrats."

78. Underlined text as in original. Memo, Bill Hamilton to Tip O'Neill, Coelho, March 23, 1984, papers of Tip O'Neill, John J. Burns Library, Party Leadership/Administrative Files, Democratic Party, Box 30.

79. David S. Broder, "Hart Defeats Mondale in New Hampshire Upset," *WP*, February 29, 1984.

80. George Lardner and Dan Balz Jr., "Mondale Turns Combative, Clashes with Hart in Debate," *WP*, March 12, 1984.

81. Fay S. Joyce, "Hart Sees Triumph for His Ideas, if Not for Himself," *NYT*, July 22, 1984.

82. Dan Balz and Milton Coleman, "Accepting Nomination, Mondale Offers Voters Era of 'New Realism,'" *WP*, July 20, 1984; Rich Jaroslovsky and Jeanne Saddler, "Mondale Accepts the Nomination, Vows to Raise Taxes, Shrink Deficit," *WSJ*, July 20, 1984.

83. David Hoffman and John M. Berry, "Reagan, Mondale Tax Brawl Defies Political Convention," *WP*, July 29, 1984.

84. Eric Alterman and Kevin Mattson, *The Cause: The Fight for American Liberalism from Franklin Roosevelt to Barack Obama* (New York: Viking, 2012), 317.

85. Gil Troy, *Morning in America: How Ronald Reagan Invented the 1980s* (Princeton, NJ: Princeton University Press, 2005), 148–149.

86. "Prouder, Stronger, Better," 1984, *The Living Room Candidate: Presidential Campaign Commercials, 1952–2012*, Museum of the Moving Image, http://www.living roomcandidate.org/commercials/1984.

87. Farrell, *Tip O'Neill*, 646.

88. Richard A. Viguerie, "Reagan's Campaign Double-Crossed the G.O.P.," *NYT*, November 12, 1984.

89. Troy, *Morning in America*, 172.

90. Editorial, "The Reagan Triumph," *WP*, November 7, 1984.

91. William Schneider, "An Uncertain Consensus," *National Journal*, November 10, 1984.

92. Admittedly, this had shrunk from 48–26 percent in 1980 and the high of 49–20 percent in 1977, the first year of Carter's presidency. George H. Gallup, *The Gallup Poll: Public Opinion 1972–1977: Volume Two, 1976–1977* (Wilmington, DE: Scholarly Resources, 1978), 1,172; George H. Gallup, *The Gallup Poll: Public Opinion 1980* (Wilmington, DE: Scholarly Resources, 1981), 249; George Gallup Jr., *The Gallup Poll: Public Opinion 1985* (Wilmington, DE: Scholarly Resources, 1986), 24.

93. Harris Survey, November 1984. Retrieved September 23, 2014, from the iPOLL Databank, http://ezproxy-prd.bodleian.ox.ac.uk:3170/data_access/ipoll/ipoll.html.

94. James Q. Wilson, "Realignment at the Top, Dealignment at the Bottom," in *The American Elections of 1984*, ed. Austin Ranney (Durham, NC: Duke University Press, 1985), 297.

95. Albert R. Hunt, "The Campaign and the Issues," in *The American Elections of 1984*, ed. Austin Ranney, 130.

96. Troy, *Morning in America*, 147.

97. Robert S. Strauss, "Enough Hand-Wringing by the Democrats," *NYT*, May 24, 1985.

98. Fred Barnes, "The Majority Complex," *NR*, August 5, 1985.

99. "What Now?" *NR*, November 26, 1984.

100. MacPherson, "Mo Udall, Triumph of the Good Guy."

101. Milton Coleman and Dan Balz, "34 Governors Strut as Democrats' New Hope," *WP*, February 24, 1985; Maurice Carroll, "Cuomo Sees Larger Role for Democratic Governors," *NYT*, February 17, 1985.

102. Ronald Brownstein, "Babbitt's New Politics," *National Journal*, March 9, 1985.

103. Dan Balz, "Southern and Western Democrats Launch New Leadership Council," *WP*, March 1, 1985; Phil Gailey, "Dissidents Defy Top Democrats; Council Formed," *NYT*, March 1, 1985.

104. Michael Kinsley, "See Dick Run," *WP*, January 28, 1988.

105. Balz, "Southern and Western Democrats Launch New Leadership Council"; Gailey, "Dissidents Defy Top Democrats." *NYT*; Kinsley, "See Dick Run."

106. For more on the DLC's campaign to refashion the Democratic Party in their own image, see Baer, *Reinventing Democrats*.

107. Matt Bai, "How Gary Hart's Downfall Forever Changed American Politics," *NYT*, September 18, 2014.

108. Randall Rothenberg, "The Neoliberal Club," *Esquire*, February 1982.

109. Robin Toner, "The Orderly Rise of a New Kind of Democrat," *NYT*, July 24, 1988.

110. *New Republic*, December 5, 1988.

111. By this point, Tsongas was retired from the Senate. He had announced his intention to step down after being diagnosed with cancer in 1983. He maintained some informal links with the Dukakis campaign. "Transcript of the First TV Debate

between Bush and Dukakis," *NYT*, September 26, 1988; "Tsongas Cites Views on Capital Gains Tax," *NYT*, October 7, 1988.

112. Schneider, "JFK's Children."

113. Paul E. Tsongas, *Journey of Purpose: Reflections on the Presidency, Multiculturalism, and Third Parties* (New Haven, CT: Yale University Press, 1995), 3–4, 17.

114. Tsongas, *Journey of Purpose*, 18.

115. Christopher B. Daly, "After Beating a Rare Cancer, Paul Tsongas Sets His Sights on the Presidency," *WP*, January 28, 1992.

116. Daly, "After Beating a Rare Cancer, Paul Tsongas Sets His Sights on the Presidency."

117. "Tsongas Goes Swimming," April 29, 1992, *C-SPAN*, uploaded May 30, 2016, accessed July 17, 2018, https://www.c-span.org/video/?c4600321/tsongas-swimming.

118. Robin Toner, "Democrats Pass Torch as Bearers Seek Light," *NYT*, September 21, 1991.

119. Thomas B. Edsall, "Gov. Clinton Wears Out Welcome with Nominating Speech," *WP*, July 21, 1988.

120. Galston had worked in the presidential campaigns of Walter Mondale and Al Gore (1988). Kamarck had been a senior staffer in the DNC, had worked for the Carter and Mondale presidential campaigns, as well as that of Bruce Babbitt in 1987–1988. Both would go on to senior policy roles in the Clinton administration. William Galston and Elaine C. Kamarck, *The Politics of Evasion: Democrats and the Presidency*, Progressive Policy Institute, September 1989, 2, 18–20, accessed August 15, 2018, https://www.progressivepolicy.org/publications/policy-memo/the-politics-of -evasion-democrats-and-the-presidency/.

121. Jon F. Hale, "The Making of the New Democrats," *Political Science Quarterly* 110, no. 2 (Summer 1995): 221.

122. David S. Broder, "Moderate Democrats Trying to Grow Grass Roots," *WP*, December 12, 1990.

123. David S. Broder and Dan Balz, "Democratic Group Finds No Champion," *WP*, May 9, 1991.

124. David S. Broder, "The DLC At Six," *WP*, May 12, 1991.

125. Kenneth Baer identifies neoliberalism as one of the forerunners of the DLC's critique. Baer, *Reinventing Democrats*.

126. Lloyd Grove, "Paul Tsongas's Precarious Stand," *WP*, March 6, 1992.

127. Lloyd Grove, "Paul Tsongas, Feeling His Oats," *WP*, February 15, 1992.

128. Gwen Ifill, "Clinton Finds a Theme: He Is Not Paul Tsongas," *NYT*, March 5, 1992.

129. Dan Balz, "Clinton Denounces Tsongas," *WP*, February 28, 1992.

130. Steven Mufson, "Divergent Views on Economic Policy," *WP*, March 9, 1992.

131. Don Oberdorfer, "Democrats Offer Broad Themes for U.S. Role in Post-Cold War Era," *WP*, March 15, 1992.

132. Gillon, *The Pact*, 16; David S. Broder, "Tsongas Calls Clinton 'Cynical,' 'Unprincipled,' Divisive Confirmed," *WP*, March 7, 1992.

133. Joe Klein, "The Last Harrumph," *New York Magazine*, March 23, 1992.

134. R. W. Apple Jr., "Tsongas Steps Up Attack on Clinton," *NYT*, March 12, 1992.

135. Joe Klein, "The Last Harrumph," *New York Magazine*, March 23, 1992.

136. Lloyd Grove, "Paul Tsongas, Feeling His Oats," *WP*, February 15, 1992.

137. Robin Toner, "Buchanan at 40%," *NYT*, February 19, 1992. Clinton's 1992 campaign, with particular focus on the New Hampshire primary, is detailed in Mark White, "Vicissitudes: 1992 and the Road to the White House," in *The Presidency of Bill Clinton: The Legacy of a New Domestic and Foreign Policy*, ed. Mark White (London: I. B. Tauris, 2012).

138. R. W. Apple Jr., "Washington's Suburbs Offer Tsongas a Chance to Win Again," *NYT*, February 27, 1992.

139. Editorial, "Mr. Tsongas Departs, Gracefully," *NYT*, March 20, 1992.

140. Charles Peters, "Tsongas, Role Model for '92," *NYT*, April 9, 1992.

141. Dan Balz, "A Message from the Moderates," *WP*, November 12, 1992.

142. In addition to Tsongas, Iowa senator Tom Harkin, first elected to the House of Representatives in 1974, was also a candidate in 1992. The last Watergate Baby to seek the presidency was Christopher Dodd in 2008.

143. Adam Clymer, "On Clinton's Coattails, Many Democrats Blunt Anti-Incumbent Anger," *NYT*, November 4, 1992; "'Year of the Woman,' as Predicted," *NYT*, November 4, 1992.

EPILOGUE. 1994: THE END OF THE
PERMANENT DEMOCRATIC CONGRESS

1. Adam Clymer, "On Clinton's Coattails, Many Democrats Blunt Anti-Incumbent Anger," *NYT*, November 4, 1992.

2. Kevin Merida, "Many Democratic House Freshmen Won't Be Returning," *WP*, November 10, 1994.

3. "Northeast: Two Kennedy Victories Are Among the Bright Spots for Democrats; Washington Goes Back to Barry," *NYT*, November 10, 1994; "Vote '94: The Nation, State by State: The Mid-Atlantic: Pennsylvania," *WP*, November 10, 1994.

4. David S. Broder, "Vote May Signal GOP Return as Dominant Party," *WP*, November 10, 1994.

5. Richard L. Berke, "G.O.P. Wins Control of Senate and Makes Big Gains in House; Pataki Denies Cuomo 4th Term," *NYT*, November 9, 1994.

6. Maureen Dowd, "Vengeful Glee (and Sweetness) and Gingrich's Victory Party," *NYT*, November 9, 1994; *Time*, January 9, 1995.

7. The full text of the Contract is available in Lori Cox Han and Diane J. Heith, *Presidents and the American Presidency* (New York: Oxford University Press, 2012), 209. Also available on Oxford University Press's accompanying resources website, accessed August 27, 2018, https://global.oup.com/us/companion.websites/9780195385168/resources/chapter6/contract/america.pdf.

8. Katherine Q. Seelye, "Clinton and Allies Rediscover Their Voice in Writing Epitaph for Congress," *NYT*, October 9, 1994. The way that the Contract informed

relations between the Gingrich-led House and the Clinton White House is explored in Steven Gillon, *The Pact: Bill Clinton, Newt Gingrich, and the Rivalry That Defined a Generation* (New York: Oxford University Press, 2008), 123–134.

9. The poll sampled 1,147 adults on December 6–9, 1994, around a month after the midterms. Maureen Dowd, "Americans Like G.O.P. Agenda but Split on How to Reach Goals," *NYT*, December 15, 1994.

10. In 2012, Obama became the first Democratic president to win two terms with more than 50 percent of the vote since Franklin Roosevelt.

11. John B. Judis, "America the Liberal," *NR*, November 19, 2008, accessed January 25, 2018, https://newrepublic.com/article/60995/america-the-liberal.

12. Mark Gongloff, "The Reagan Era Is Over, the Obama Era Has Begun," *Huffington Post*, January 22, 2013, accessed March 25, 2016, http://www.huffingtonpost.com/2013/01/21/seven-and-a-half-things-you-need-to-know_n_2523273.html.

13. Julian E. Zelizer, "Rethinking the History of American Conservatism," *Reviews in American History* 38 (2010): 380, 387–389.

14. US Office of the Federal Register, *Public Papers of the Presidents of the United States: William J. Clinton, 1996, Book I—January 1 to June 30* (Washington, DC: National Archives and Record Service, 1997), 79.

15. Robert J. Samuelson, "Big Government Is Here to Stay," *WP*, June 21, 1995.

16. John E. Yang, "In Wake of Watergate, Reformers Charged Hill," *WP*, June 15, 1992.

17. Yang, "In Wake of Watergate, Reformers Charged Hill."

18. John Fogarty, "Burton: No Relaxing, No Regrets," *WP*, January 3, 1977.

19. Henry Waxman, "Rep. Henry Waxman: The Reason I'm Leaving Congress," *Washington Post*, January 31, 2014; Ron Elving, "Congressman's Exit Closes Book on 'Watergate Babies,'" *It's All Politics: Political News from NPR*, January 31, 2014, accessed September 15, 2014, http://www.npr.org/blogs/itsallpolitics/2014/01/30/269003155/congressmans-exit-closes-book-on-watergate-babies.

20. Richard Simon, "Rep. Henry Waxman to Retire from Congress," *LAT*, January 30, 2014; David Rogers, "Henry Waxman Hands Off the Torch," *Politico*, February 10, 2014; David A. Graham, "Henry Waxman's Retirement: A Bad Sign for House Democrats in 2014," *Atlantic*, January 30, 2014, http://www.theatlantic.com/politics/archive/2014/01/henry-waxmans-retirement-a-bad-sign-for-house-democrats-in-2014/283476/; Jonathan Cohn, "Farewell to Henry Waxman, a Liberal Hero," *NR*, January 31, 2014, accessed September 15, 2014, http://www.newrepublic.com/article/116418/henry-waxman-retiring-heres-why-well-miss-him.

21. In Martha Derthick's account of federal tobacco policy since the 1960s, the "liberal, tough, and resourceful" Waxman emerges as the "leader of the opposition" within Congress to Big Tobacco. Though critical of the pro-regulation forces, Derthick shows how Waxman was able to use his chairmanship of the House Commerce Committee's Subcommittee on Health and the Environment to press the issue relentlessly. Martha A. Derthick, *Up in Smoke: From Legislation to Litigation in Tobacco Politics* (3rd ed., Washington, DC, 2012), 19–21, 57–58, 114–115, 209.

22. Harold Myerson, "Henry Waxman, Liberalism's Legislative Genius," *WP*, February 6, 2014.

23. David Corn, "Waxman: Democrats' Eliot Ness," *Nation*, February 14, 2005; Ben McGrath, "The Scariest Guy in Washington," *The New Yorker*, August 31, 2009.

BIBLIOGRAPHY

MANUSCRIPT AND ARCHIVAL SOURCES
Atlanta, Georgia
    Jimmy Carter Presidential Library
        Office of Anne Wexler, special assistant to the president
        Office of the Assistant to the President for Communications
        Office of the Chief of Staff
        Office of the Congressional Liaison
        Office of Domestic Policy
        White House Central File
Berkeley, California
    University of California, Berkeley, Bancroft Library
        Papers of David Ross Brower
        Papers of Phillip Burton
        Papers of Alan Cranston
Boston, Massachusetts
    Boston College, John J. Burns Library
        Papers of Robert F. Drinan
        Papers of Thomas P. (Tip) O'Neill Jr.
    John F. Kennedy Presidential Library
        Papers of Adam Clymer
        Papers of Nancy F. Korman
        Papers of Frank Mankiewicz
        Papers of Theodore C. Sorensen
Boulder, Colorado
    University of Colorado, Boulder
        Papers of Gary W. Hart
        Papers of Timothy E. Wirth
Los Angeles, California
    University of California, Los Angeles, Department of Special Collections
        Papers of Augustus F. Hawkins
    University of Southern California, Los Angeles, Special Collections
        Papers of Edmund G. (Jerry) Brown Jr.
Lowell, Massachusetts
    University of Massachusetts, Lowell, Center for Lowell History
        Paul E. Tsongas Congressional Collection
Nashville, Tennessee
    Vanderbilt University
        Vanderbilt Television News Archive

St. Paul, Minnesota
  Minnesota Historical Society
      Papers of Hubert H. Humphrey
      Papers of Walter F. Mondale
Tucson, Arizona
  University of Arizona, Special Collections
      Papers of Morris K. Udall
Washington, DC
  Library of Congress, Manuscript Reading Room
      Papers of the Democratic Study Group
      Papers of Stuart Eizenstat
      Papers of the House Democratic Caucus
      Papers of Mary McGrory
      Papers of Patsy T. Mink
      Papers of Daniel Patrick Moynihan
      Papers of John F. Osborne
      Papers of Michael Pertschuk
      Papers of Norman Podhoretz
      Papers of Joseph L. Rauh
      Papers of Abraham Ribicoff
      Papers of Alice M. Rivlin

INTERVIEWS
All interviews were conducted in person unless otherwise stated.
Peter Bourne, Oxford, November 19, 2013
Joseph A. Califano, via telephone, April 10, 2012
M. Robert Carr, via Skype, March 14, 2013
Vernon Jordan, Washington, DC, March 29, 2012
Ann Lewis, Silver Spring, MD, February 12, 2012
Walter F. Mondale, Minneapolis, MN, April 21, 2010
Alice Rivlin, Washington, DC, January 9, 2012
Mark Siegel, Washington, DC, February 16, 2012
Henry A. Waxman, Washington, DC, January 13, 2012
Bruce Wolpe, Washington, DC, January 20, 2012

PRINTED PRIMARY SOURCES
Atlantic Monthly
Boston Globe
Carter, Jimmy, *White House Diary.* New York: Farrar, Straus and Giroux, 2010
Chicago Defender
Chicago Tribune
Christian Science Monitor
Commentary

Congressional Quarterly Almanac

Congressional Quarterly Weekly Report

Congressional Record

Congressional Serial Set

CQ Press, *Guide to U.S. Elections, Volume I.* 6th ed. Washington, DC: CQ Press, 2010

CQ Press, *Guide to U.S. Elections, Volume II.* 6th ed. Washington, DC: CQ Press, 2010

Dissent

Gallup, G. H. *The Gallup Poll: Public Opinion 1972–1977: Volume Two, 1976–1977.* Wilmington, DE: Scholarly Resources, 1978

Gallup, G. H. *The Gallup Poll: Public Opinion 1980.* Wilmington, DE: Scholarly Resources, 1981

Gallup, G., Jr. *The Gallup Poll: Public Opinion 1985.* Wilmington, DE: Scholarly Resources, 1986

Gallup.com, http://www.gallup.com/

Harper's Monthly

iPoll Databank, Roper Center for Public Opinion Research, University of Connecticut, http://www.ropercenter.ucon.edu/ipoll.html

The Living Room Candidate: Presidential Campaign Commericals, 1952–2012, Museum of the Moving Image, http://www.livingroomcandidate.org/

Los Angeles Times

Moynihan, Daniel Patrick, and Steven R. Weisman, eds., *Daniel Patrick Moynihan: A Portrait in Letters of an American Visionary.* New York: PublicAffairs, 2010

The Nation

National Journal

National Review

The New Republic

New York Amsterdam News

The New Yorker

New York Magazine

New York Times

Public Interest

Reagan, Ronald. *Speaking My Mind: Selected Speeches.* London: Hutchinson, 1990.

Reagan, Ronald., and Douglas Brinkley, ed. *The Reagan Diaries.* New York: HarperCollins, 2007

The Reporter

Rosenman, Samuel I. *The Public Papers and Addresses of Franklin D. Roosevelt: 1944–45, Victory and the Threshold of Peace.* New York: Russell & Russell, 1950

Time

US Department of Labor, *The Negro Family: The Case for National Action.* Washington, DC: US Government Printing Office, 1965

U.S. News & World Report

US Office of the Federal Register, *Public Papers of the Presidents of the United States.* Washington, DC: National Archives and Record Service

Wall Street Journal
Washington Post
Washington Post-Times Herald

PRINTED SECONDARY SOURCES

Abbott, Carl. *The New Urban America: Growth and Politics in Sunbelt Cities.* Chapel Hill: University of North Carolina Press, 1981.

Agnew, Jean-Christophe, and Roy Rosenzweig. eds. *A Companion to Post-1945 America.* Malden, MA: Blackwell, 2006.

Alterman, Eric. *Why We're Liberals: A Political Handbook for Post-Bush America.* New York: Viking, 2008.

Alterman, Eric, and Kevin Mattson. *The Cause: The Fight for American Liberalism from Franklin Roosevelt to Barack Obama.* New York: Viking, 2012.

Andelic, Patrick. "Daniel Patrick Moynihan, the 1976 New York Senate Race, and the Struggle to Define American Liberalism." *Historical Journal* 57, no. 4 (December 2014): 1,111–1,133.

Andrew, John A., III. *The Other Side of the Sixties: Young Americans for Freedom and the Rise of Conservative Politics.* New Brunswick, NJ: Rutgers University Press, 1997.

Asbell, Bernard. *The Senate Nobody Knows.* New York: Doubleday, 1978.

Ashby, LeRoy, and Rod Gramer. *Fighting the Odds: The Life of Senator Frank Church.* Pullman: Washington State University Press, 1994.

Baer, Kenneth S. *Reinventing Democrats: The Politics of Liberalism from Reagan to Clinton.* Lawrence: University Press of Kansas, 2000.

Bailey, Stephen K. *Congress in the Seventies.* 2nd ed. New York: St. Martin's Press, 1970.

Barker, Lucius J., and Ronald W. Waters, eds. *Jesse Jackson's 1984 Presidential Campaign: Challenge and Change in American Politics.* Urbana: University of Illinois Press, 1989.

Barnard, John, *American Vanguard: The United Auto Workers during the Reuther Years, 1935–1980.* Detroit: Wayne State University Press, 2004.

Barone, Michael, and Grant Ujifusa. *The Almanac of American Politics, 1982.* Washington, DC: Barone, 1981.

———. *The Almanac of American Politics, 2000.* Washington, DC: National Journal, 1999.

Barone, Michael, Grant Ujifusa, and D. Matthews. *The Almanac of American Politics, 1974.* London: Macmillan, 1974.

Barry, John M. *The Ambition and the Power.* New York: Viking, 1989.

Bell, Daniel. *The Coming of Post-Industrial Society: A Venture in Social Forecasting.* Special anniversary ed. New York: Basic, 1999 (orig. 1973).

Bell, Jonathan. *California Crucible: The Forging of Modern American Liberalism.* Philadelphia: University of Pennsylvania Press, 2012.

———. *The Liberal State on Trial: The Cold War and American Politics in the Truman Years.* New York: Columbia University Press, 2004.

Bell, Jonathan, and Timothy Stanley, eds., *Making Sense of American Liberalism*. Urbana: University of Illinois Press, 2012.

Bendavid, Naftali. *The Thumpin': How Rahm Emanuel and the Democrats Learned to Be Ruthless and Ended the Republican Revolution*. New York: Doubleday, 2007.

Berkowitz, Edward D. *Mr. Social Security: The Life of Wilbur J. Cohen*. Lawrence: University Press of Kansas, 1995.

———. *America's Welfare State: From Roosevelt to Reagan*. Baltimore: Johns Hopkins University Press, 1996.

———. *Robert Ball and the Politics of Social Security*. Madison: University of Wisconsin Press, 2003.

———. *Something Happened: A Political and Cultural Overview of the Seventies*. New York: Columbia University Press, 2006.

Berman, Ari. *Herding Donkeys: The Fight to Rebuild the Democratic Party and Reshape American Politics*. New York: Farrar, Straus and Giroux, 2010.

Berry, Jeffrey M. *The Interest Group Society*. Boston: Little, Brown, 1984.

Biles, Roger. *The Fate of Cities: Urban America and the Federal Government, 1945–2000*. Lawrence: University Press of Kansas, 2011.

Biven, W. Carl. *Jimmy Carter's Economy: Policy in an Age of Limits*. Chapel Hill: University of North Carolina Press, 2002.

Bloodworth, Jeffrey. "Senator Henry Jackson, the Solzhenitsyn Affair, and American Liberalism," *Pacific Northwest Quarterly* 97, no. 2 (Spring 2006): 67–77.

———. "Fred Harris's Neo-Populism and the Demise of Heartland Liberalism." *The Chronicles of Oklahoma* 88, no. 2 (Summer 2010): 196–221.

———. *Losing the Center: The Decline of American Liberalism, 1968–1992*. Lexington: University Press of Kentucky, 2013.

Blumenthal, David, and James A. Morone. *The Heart of Power: Health and Politics on the Oval Office*. Berkeley: University of California Press, 2009.

Bollens, John C., and G. Robert Williams. *Jerry Brown: In a Plain Brown Wrapper*. Pacific Palisades, CA: Palisades Publishers, 1978.

Bolling, Richard. *House Out of Order*. New York: Dutton, 1965.

Borstelmann, Thomas. *The 1970s: A New Global History from Civil Rights to Economic Inequality*. Princeton, NJ: Princeton University Press, 2012.

Bourne, Peter G. *Jimmy Carter: A Comprehensive Biography from Plains to Post-Presidency*. New York: Scribner, 1997.

Bowles, Nigel. *The White House and Capitol Hill: The Politics of Presidential Persuasion*. Oxford: Clarendon, 1987.

———. *Nixon's Business: Authority and Power in Presidential Politics*. College Station, TX: Texas A&M University, 2005.

Boyarsky, Bill. *Big Daddy: Jesse Unruh and the Art of Power Politics*. Berkeley: University of California Press, 2008.

Boyd, Tim S. R. *Georgia Democrats, the Civil Rights Movement, and the Shaping of the New South*. Gainesville: University Press of Florida, 2012.

Brandt, Karl Gerard. "The Ideological Origins of the New Democrat Movement." *Louisiana History: The Journal of the Louisiana Historical Association* 48, no. 3 (Summer 2007): 273–294.

———. *Ronald Reagan and the House Democrats: Gridlock, Partisanship, and the Fiscal Crisis.* Columbia: University of Missouri Press, 2009.

Brennan, Mary C. *Turning Right in the Sixties: The Conservative Capture of the GOP.* Chapel Hill: University of North Carolina Press, 1995.

Brinkley, Alan. "The Problem of American Conservatism," *American Historical Review* 99, no. 2 (April 1994): 409–429.

———. *The End of Reform: New Deal Liberalism in Recession and War.* New York: Alfred A. Knopf, 1995.

———. *Liberalism and Its Discontents.* Cambridge, MA: Harvard University Press, 1998.

Broder, David S. *Changing of the Guard: Power and Leadership in America.* New York: Simon & Schuster, 1980.

Brownlee, W. Elliot, and Hugh Davis Graham. *The Reagan Presidency: Pragmatic Conservatism and Its Legacies.* Lawrence: University Press of Kansas, 2003.

Bumpers, Dale. *The Best Lawyer in a One-Lawyer Town: A Memoir.* New York: Random House, 2003.

Burnham, Walter Dean. *Critical Elections and the Mainsprings of American Politics.* New York: Norton, 1970.

Califano, Joseph A., Jr. *Inside: A Public and Private Life.* New York: PublicAffairs, 2004.

Cannato, Vincent J. *The Ungovernable City: John Lindsay and His Struggle to Save New York.* New York: Basic, 2002.

Cannon, Lou. *Ronnie and Jesse: A Political Odyssey.* Garden City, NY: Doubleday, 1969.

———. *President Reagan: The Role of a Lifetime.* New York: Simon & Schuster, 1991.

Canon, David T. *Actors, Athletes, and Astronauts: Political Amateurs in the United States Congress.* Chicago: University of Chicago Press, 1990.

Caro, Robert A. *The Years of Lyndon Johnson: Master of the Senate.* New York: Vintage, 2002.

Carroll, Peter N. *It Seemed Like Nothing Happened: America in the 1970s.* New Brunswick, NJ: Rutgers University Press, 1990.

Carson, Donald W., and James W. Johnson. *Mo: The Life & Times of Morris K. Udall.* Tucson: University of Arizona Press, 2001.

Carter, Dan T. *The Politics of Rage: George Wallace, the Origins of the New Conservatism, and the Transformation of American Politics.* New York: Simon & Schuster, 1995.

———. *From George Wallace to Newt Gingrich: Race in the Conservative Counterrevolution, 1963–1994.* Baton Rouge: Louisiana State University Press, 1996.

Carter, Jimmy. *Keeping Faith: Memoirs of a President.* Fayetteville: University of Arkansas Press, 1995.

Chafe, William H. *Never Stop Running: Allard Lowenstein and the Struggle to Save American Liberalism.* Princeton, NJ: Princeton University Press, 1998.

————, ed. *The Achievement of American Liberalism: The New Deal and Its Legacies.* New York: Columbia University Press, 2003.

Champagne, Anthony, Douglas B. Harris, James W. Riddlesperger Jr., and Garrison Nelson. *The Austin/Boston Connection: Five Decades of House Democratic Leadership, 1937–1989.* College Station: Texas A&M University Press, 2009.

Chester, Lewis, Godfrey Hodgson, and Bruce Page. *An American Melodrama: The Presidential Campaign of 1968.* New York: Viking, 1969.

Chisholm, Shirley. *The Good Fight.* New York: Bantam, 1973.

Clymer, Adam. *Edward M. Kennedy: A Biography.* New York: Harper Perennial, 2009.

Cochran, Thomas C. "The 'Presidential Synthesis' in American History." *American Historical Review* 53, no. 4 (July 1948): 748–759.

Cohen, Adam, and Elizabeth Taylor. *American Pharaoh: Mayor Richard J. Daley; His Battle for Chicago and the Nation.* Boston: Little, Brown, 2000.

Cohen, Lizabeth. *A Consumers' Republic: The Politics of Mass Consumption in Postwar America.* New York: Knopf, 2003.

Cohen, Michael A. *American Maelstrom: The 1968 Election and the Politics of Division.* New York: Oxford University Press, 2016.

Collins, Robert M. *More: The Politics of Economic Growth in Postwar America.* Oxford: Oxford University Press, 2000.

Conkin, Paul. *The New Deal.* New York: Thomas Y. Crowell, 1967.

Conn, Steven, ed. *To Promote the General Welfare: The Case for Big Government.* New York: Oxford University Press, 2012.

Corbin, David A. *The Last Great Senator: Robert C. Byrd's Encounters with Eleven U.S. Presidents.* Washington, DC: Potomac, 2012.

Courtwright, David T. *No Right Turn: Conservative Politics in a Liberal America.* Cambridge, MA: Harvard University Press, 2010.

Cowie, Jefferson. *Stayin' Alive: The 1970s and the Last Days of the Working Class.* New York: New Press, 2010.

Cowie, Jefferson, and Nick Salvatore. "The Long Exception: Rethinking the Place of the New Deal in American History." *International Labor and Working-Class History* 74 (Fall 2008): 1–32.

Cox Han, Lori, and Diane J. Heith. *Presidents and the American Presidency.* New York: Oxford University Press, 2012.

Cramer, Richard Ben. *What It Takes: The Way to the White House.* New York: Vintage, 1993.

Crespino, Joseph. *In Search of Another Country: Mississippi and the Conservative Counterrevolution.* Princeton, NJ: Princeton University Press, 2007.

Dallek, Matthew. *The Right Moment: Ronald Reagan's First Victory and the Decisive Turning Point in American Politics.* New York: Oxford University Press, 2000.

Dalton, Russell J. *The Apartisan American: Dealignment and Changing Electoral Politics.* Thousand Oaks, CA: CQ Press, 2013.

Dark, Taylor E. *The Unions and the Democrats: An Enduring Alliance.* Ithaca, NY: ILR, 1999.

Davidson, Roger H., ed. *The Postreform Congress*. New York: St. Martin's Press, 1992.

Davies, Gareth. *From Opportunity to Entitlement: The Transformation and Decline of Great Society Liberalism*. Lawrence: University Press of Kansas, 1996.

———. *See Government Grow: Education Politics from Johnson to Reagan*. Lawrence: University Press of Kansas, 2007.

———. "Towards Big-Government Conservatism: Conservatives and Federal Aid to Education in the 1970s." *Journal of Contemporary History* 43, no. 4 (2008): 621–635.

Davis, Charles E. *Western Public Lands and Environmental Politics*. Boulder, CO: Westview, 1997.

Davis, Lanny J. *The Emerging Democratic Majority: Lessons and Legacies from the New Politics*. New York: Stein and Day, 1974.

Delton, Jennifer A. *Making Minnesota Liberal: Civil Rights and the Transformation of the Democratic Party*. Minneapolis: University of Minnesota Press, 2002.

Derthick, Martha. *Policymaking for Social Security*. Washington, DC: Brookings Institution, 1979.

———. *Up in Smoke: From Legislation to Litigation in Tobacco Politics*, 3rd ed. Washington, DC: CQ, 2012.

Deverell, William. *A Companion to the American West*. Malden, MA: Blackwell, 2004.

Diemer, Tom. *Fighting the Unbeatable Foe: Howard Metzenbaum of Ohio; The Washington Years*. Kent, OH: Kent State University Press, 2008.

Diggins, John Patrick, ed. *The Liberal Persuasion: Arthur Schlesinger, Jr. and the Challenge of the American Past*. Princeton, NJ: Princeton University Press, 1997.

DiSalvo, Daniel. "The Politics of a Party Faction: The Liberal-Labor Alliance in the Democratic Party, 1948–1972." *Journal of Policy History* 22, no. 3 (2010): 269–299.

Dionne, E. J. *They Only Look Dead: Why Progressives Will Dominate the Next Political Era*. New York: Simon & Schuster, 1996.

Dodd, Lawrence C., and Bruce I. Oppenheimer, eds. *Congress Reconsidered*. New York: Praeger, 1977.

Doherty, Brendan J. *The Rise of the President's Permanent Campaign*. Lawrence, KS: University Press of Kansas, 2012.

Domitrovic, Brian. "Gross as a Mountain." *Journal of Policy History* 23, no. 3 (2011): 438–443.

Dorrien, Gary J. *The Neoconservative Mind: Politics, Culture, and the War of Ideology*. Philadelphia: Temple University Press, 1993.

Drew, Elizabeth. *Senator*. New York: Simon & Schuster, 1979.

Dumbrell, John. *The Carter Presidency: A Re-evaluation*. 2nd ed. Manchester: Manchester University Press, 1995.

Edsall, Thomas B., and Mary D. Edsall. *Chain Reaction: The Impact of Race, Rights, and Taxes on American Politics*. New York and London: Norton, 1992.

Ehrenhalt, Alan, ed. *Politics in America: Members of Congress in Washington and at Home 1984*. Washington, DC: CQ Press, 1983.

Ehrman, John. *The Rise of Neoconservatism: Intellectuals and Foreign Affairs, 1945–1994.* New Haven, CT: Yale University Press, 1995.

———. *The Eighties: America in the Age of Reagan.* New Haven, CT: Yale University Press, 2005.

———. "The Age of Reagan? Three Questions for Future Research." *Journal of Historical Society* 11, no. 1 (March 2011): 111–131.

Ehrman, John, and Michael Flamm. *Debating the Reagan Presidency.* Lanham, MD: Rowman & Littlefield, 2009.

Erenberg, Lewis A., and Susan E. Hirsch, eds. *The War in American Culture: Society and Consciousness During World War II.* Chicago: University of Chicago Press, 1996.

Farber, David R. *The Rise and Fall of Modern American Conservatism: A Short History.* Princeton, NJ: Princeton University Press, 2010.

Farrell, John A. *Tip O'Neill and the Democratic Century.* Boston: Little, Brown, 2001.

Fenno, Richard F., Jr. *Senators on the Campaign Trail: The Politics of Representation.* Norman: University of Oklahoma Press, 1996.

Ferguson, Thomas, and Joel Rogers. *Right Turn: The Decline of the Democrats and the Future of American Politics.* New York: Hill and Wang, 1986.

Fink, Gary M., and Hugh Davis Graham, eds. *The Carter Presidency: Policy Choices in the Post-New Deal Era.* Lawrence: University Press of Kansas, 1998.

Finn, Chester E., Jr. *Troublemaker: A Personal History of School Reform Since Sputnik.* Princeton, NJ: Princeton University Press, 2008.

Flamm, Michael W. *Law and Order: Street Crime, Civil Unrest and the Crisis of Liberalism in the 1960s.* New York: Columbia University Press, 2005.

Flamming, Douglas. *Bound for Freedom: Black Los Angeles in Jim Crow America.* Oakland: University of California Press, 2004.

Flippen, J. Brooks. *Jimmy Carter, the Politics of Family, and the Rise of the Religious Right.* Athens: University of Georgia Press, 2011.

Foster, Carroll B. "The 'Sagebrush Rebellion' and the Alaska Lands Bill in the U.S. Congress." *Legislative Studies Quarterly* 8, no. 4 (November 1983): 655–672.

Frank, Thomas. *What's the Matter with Kansas?: How Conservatives Won the Heart of America.* New York: Metropolitan, 2004.

———. *The Wrecking Crew: The American Right and the Lust for Power.* London: Harvill Secker, 2008.

Fraser, Steve. *The Limousine Liberal: How an Incendiary Image United the Right and Fractured America.* New York: Basic, 2016.

Fraser, Steve, and Gary Gerstle, eds. *The Rise and Fall of the New Deal Order, 1930–1980.* Princeton, NJ: Princeton University Press, 1989.

From, Al. *The New Democrats and the Return to Power.* New York: Palgrave Macmillan, 2013.

Frum, David. *How We Got Here: The 70's; The Decade That Brought You Modern Life (For Better or Worse).* New York: Basic, 2000.

Frymer, Paul. *Black and Blue: African Americans, the Labor Movement, and the Decline of the Democratic Party*. Princeton, NJ: Princeton University Press, 2008.

Fuller, Adam L. *Taking the Fight to the Enemy: Neoconservatism and the Age of Ideology*. Lanham, MD: Lexington, 2012.

Funigiello, Philip J. *Chronic Politics: Health Care Security from FDR to George W. Bush*. Lawrence: University Press of Kansas, 2005.

Geary, Daniel. *Beyond Civil Rights: The Moynihan Report and Its Legacy*. Philadelphia: University of Pennsylvania Press, 2015.

Geismer, Lily. *Don't Blame Us: Suburban Liberals and the Transformation of the Democratic Party*. Princeton, NJ: Princeton University Press, 2014.

Germond, J. W., and J. Witcover. *Wake Us When It's Over: Presidential Politics of 1984*. New York: Macmillan, 1985.

Gillon, Steven M. *Politics and Vision: The ADA and American Liberalism, 1947–1985*. New York: Oxford University Press, 1987.

———. *The Democrats' Dilemma: Walter F. Mondale and the Liberal Legacy*. New York: Columbia University Press, 1992.

———. *Boomer Nation: The Largest and Richest Generation Ever and How It Changed America*. New York: Free Press, 2004.

———. *The Pact: Bill Clinton, Newt Gingrich, and the Rivalry That Defined a Generation*. New York: Oxford University Press, 2008.

Ginsburg, Helen Lachs. "Historical Amnesia: The Humphrey-Hawkins Act, Full Employment and Employment as a Right." *Revolutionary Black Political Economy* 39 (2012): 121–136.

Glazer, Nathan, and Daniel P. Moynihan. *Beyond the Melting Pot: The Negroes, Puerto Ricans, Jews, Italians, and Irish of New York City*. Cambridge, MA: MIT Press, 1963.

Gordon, Linda. *Pitied But Not Entitled: Single Mothers and the History of Welfare, 1890–1935*. New York: Free Press, 1994.

Gottlieb, Sanford F. *Red to Blue: Congressman Chris Van Hollen and Grassroots Politics*. Boulder, CO: Paradigm, 2009.

Gould, Lewis L. *The Most Exclusive Club: A History of the Modern United States Senate*. New York: Basic Books, 2005.

Graham, Otis L., Jr. *Toward a Planned Society: From Roosevelt to Nixon*. New York: Oxford University Press, 1976.

Green, Matthew N. *The Speaker of the House: A Study of Leadership*. New Haven, CT: Yale University Press, 2010.

Greenberg, Stanley B., and Theda Skocpol, eds. *The New Majority: Toward a Popular Progressive Politics*. New Haven, CT: Yale University Press, 1997.

Greenstein, Fred I. *The Hidden-Hand Presidency: Eisenhower as Leader*. New York: Basic Books, 1982.

———. *The Presidential Difference: Leadership Style from FDR to George W. Bush*. 2nd ed. Princeton, NJ: Princeton University Press, 2000.

Gurock, Jeffrey. S. *Jews in Gotham: New York Jews in a Changing City, 1920–2010*. New York: New York University Press, 2012.

Hale, Jon F. "The Making of the New Democrats," *Political Science Quarterly* 110, no. 2 (Summer 1995): 207–232.

Hamby, Alonzo L. *Beyond the New Deal: Harry S. Truman and American Liberalism.* New York: Columbia University Press, 1973.

———. *Liberalism and Its Challengers: F.D.R. to Reagan.* New York: Oxford University Press, 1985.

Hart, Gary. *The Thunder and the Sunshine: Four Seasons in a Burnished Life.* Golden, CO: Fulcrum, 2010.

Hays, Samuel. P. *A History of Environmental Politics Since 1945.* Pittsburgh: University of Pittsburgh Press, 2000.

Hayward, Steven F. *The Age of Reagan: The Fall of the Old Liberal Order, 1964–1980.* Roseville, CA: Forum, 2001.

———. *The Age of Reagan: The Conservative Counterrevolution, 1980–1989.* New York: Crown Forum, 2009.

Heale, M. J. "The Sixties as History: A Review of the Political Historiography." *Reviews in American History* 33 (2005): 133–152.

Heclo, Hugh. "The Mixed Legacies of Ronald Reagan." *Presidential Studies Quarterly* 38, no. 4 (December 2008): 555-574.

Heilbrunn, Jacob. *They Knew They Were Right: The Rise of the Neocons.* New York: Doubleday, 2008.

Hemmer, Nicole. *Messengers of the Right: Conservative Media and the Transformation of American Politics.* Philadelphia: University of Pennsylvania Press, 2016.

Hersh, Burton. *The Shadow President: Ted Kennedy in Opposition.* South Royalton, VT: Steerforth, 1997.

Hess, Stephen. *The Professor and the President: Daniel Patrick Moynihan in the Nixon White House.* Washington, DC: Brookings Institution, 2015.

Hill, Dilys M., Raymond A. Moore, and Phil Williams, eds. *The Reagan Presidency: An Incomplete Revolution?* Basingstoke: Macmillan in association with the Centre for International Policy Studies, University of Southampton, 1990.

Hodgson, Godfrey. *All Things to All Men: The False Promise of the Modern American Presidency.* London: Weidenfeld and Nicolson, 1980.

———. *The World Turned Right Side Up: A History of the Conservative Ascendancy in America.* Boston: Houghton Mifflin, 1996.

———. *The Gentleman from New York: Daniel Patrick Moynihan, A Biography.* Boston: Houghton Mifflin, 2000.

———. *America in Our Time: America from World War II to Nixon.* Princeton, NJ: Princeton University Press, 2005.

Hofstadter, Richard. *The Paranoid Style in American Politics, and Other Essays.* New York: Knopf, 1965.

Hudson, Cheryl, and Gareth Davies, eds. *Ronald Reagan and the 1980s: Perceptions, Policies, Legacies.* New York: Palgrave Macmillan, 2008.

Humphrey, Hubert H. "Notes and Memoranda: The Senate on Trial." *American Political Science Review* 44, no. 3 (September 1950): 650–660.

————. *The Political Philosophy of the New Deal*. Baton Rouge: Louisiana State University Press, 1970.

————. *The Education of a Public Man: My Life and Politics*. New York: Garden City, 1976.

Huntington, Samuel P. *American Politics: The Promise of Disharmony*. Cambridge, MA: Belknap, 1981.

Isserman, Maurice. *The Other American: The Life of Michael Harrington*. New York: PublicAffairs, 2000.

Isserman, Maurice, and Michael Kazin. *America Divided: The Civil War of the 1960s*. 3rd ed. New York: Oxford University Press, 2008.

Jacobs, John. *A Rage for Justice: The Passion and Politics of Phillip Burton*. Berkeley: University of California Press, 1995.

Jacobs, Meg. *Panic at the Pump: The Energy Crisis and the Transformation of American Politics in the 1970s*. New York: Hill and Wang, 2017.

Jacobs, Meg, William J. Novak, and Julian E. Zelizer, eds. *The Democratic Experiment: New Directions in American Political History*. Princeton, NJ: Princeton University Press, 2003.

Jacobs, Meg, and Julian E. Zelizer. *Conservatives in Power: The Reagan Years, 1981–1989; A Brief History with Documents*. Boston: Bedford/St. Martin's, 2011.

Jencks, Christopher, and Paul E. Petersen. *The Urban Underclass*. Washington, DC: Brookings Institution, 1991.

Jenkins, Philip. *Decade of Nightmares: The End of the Sixties and the Making of Eighties America*. Oxford: Oxford University Press, 2006.

Johnson, Haynes. *In the Absence of Power: Governing America*. New York: Viking, 1980.

Jones, Charles O. *The Trusteeship Presidency: Jimmy Carter and the United States Congress*. Baton Rouge: Louisiana State University Press, 1988.

Jordan, Hamilton. *Crisis: The Last Year of the Carter Presidency*. New York: Putnam, 1982.

Kabaservice, Geoffrey. *Rule and Ruin: The Downfall of Moderation and the Destruction of the Republican Party, from Eisenhower to the Tea Party*. New York: Oxford University Press, 2012.

Kahlenberg, Richard D. *Tough Liberal: Albert Shanker and the Battles over Schools, Unions, Race, and Democracy*. New York: Columbia University Press, 2007.

Kalman, Laura. *Right Star Rising: A New Politics, 1974–1980*. New York: W. W. Norton, 2010.

Kamarck, Elaine C. *Primary Politics: How Presidential Candidates Have Shaped the Modern Nominating System*. Washington, DC: Brookings Institution, 2009.

Kamen, Scott, "Rethinking Postwar Liberalism: The Americans for Democratic Action, Social Democracy, and the Struggle for Racial Equality," *The Sixties: A Journal of History, Politics, and Culture*, 11, no. 1 (2018): 69–92.

Kato, Kenneth, and Elizabeth Rybicki. "Congressional History: A Literature Review," *OAH Magazine of History* 12, no. 4 (Summer 1998): 5–12.

Katzmann, Robert A., ed. *Daniel Patrick Moynihan: The Intellectual in Public Life*. Washington, DC: Woodrow Wilson International Center, 1998.

Katznelson, Ira. *When Affirmative Action Was White: An Untold History of Racial In-equality in Twentieth-Century America*. New York: W. W. Norton, 2005.

Kaufman, Burton I., and Scott Kaufman. *The Presidency of James Earl Carter, Jr..* 2nd ed., rev. ed. Lawrence: University Press of Kansas, 2006.

Kaufman, Robert G. *Henry M. Jackson: A Life in Politics*. Seattle: University of Washington Press, 2000.

Keller, Morton, and R. Shep Melnick, eds. *Taking Stock: American Government in the Twentieth Century*. Cambridge: Cambridge University Press, 1999.

Kennedy, Edward M. *True Compass: A Memoir*. New York: Twelve, 2009.

Kessler-Harris, Alice. *In Pursuit of Equity: Women, Men, and the Quest for Economic Citizenship in 20th-Century America*. New York: Oxford University Press, 2001.

Key, V. O. "A Theory of Critical Elections." *Journal of Politics* 17, no. 1 (February 1955): 3–18.

Killen, Andreas. *1973 Nervous Breakdown: Watergate, Warhol, and the Birth of Post-Sixties America*. New York: Bloomsbury, 2006.

Kraft, Michael E. *Environmental Policy and Politics*. 2nd ed. New York: Longman, 2001.

Kristol, Irving. *Neoconservatism: The Autobiography of an Idea*. Chicago: Elephant, 1999.

Krugman, Paul. *The Conscience of a Liberal*. New York: W. W. Norton, 2007.

Kruse, Kevin M. *White Flight: Atlanta and the Making of Modern Conservatism*. Princeton, NJ: Princeton University Press, 2005.

———. *In God We Trust: How Corporate America Invented Christian America*. New York: Basic, 2015.

Kuttner, Robert. *The Life of the Party: Democratic Prospects in 1988 and Beyond*. New York: Viking, 1987.

Lachman, Seymour P., and Robert Polner. *The Man Who Saved New York: Hugh Carey and the Great Fiscal Crisis of 1975*. Albany: State University of New York Press, 2010.

Lasch, Christopher. *The Culture of Narcissism: American Life in an Age of Diminishing Expectations*. London: Abacus, 1980.

Lassiter, Matthew D. *The Silent Majority: Suburban Politics in the Sunbelt South*. Princeton, NJ: Princeton University Press, 2006.

Lassiter, Matthew D., and Joseph Crespino, eds. *The Myths of Southern Exceptionalism*. New York: Oxford University Press, 2010.

Lasswell, Harold D. *Politics: Who Gets What, When, How*. New York: Peter Smith, 1950.

Laursen, Eric. *The People's Pension: The Struggle to Defend Social Security Since Reagan*. Oakland, CA: AK, 2012.

Lechner, Zachary J. "'Fuzzy as a Georgia Peach': The Ford Campaign and the Challenge of Jimmy Carter's Southernness" *Southern Cultures* 23, no. 4 (Winter 2017): 62–81.

Lerner, Mitchell B., ed. *A Companion to Lyndon B. Johnson*. Malden, MA: Wiley-Blackwell, 2012.

Lesher, Stephen. *George Wallace: American Populist.* Cambridge, MA: Perseus, 1994.

Leuchtenburg, William E. *In the Shadow of FDR: From Harry Truman to Barack Obama.* 4th ed., rev. and updated, Ithaca, NY: Cornell University Press, 2009.

Levine, Suzanne Braun, and Mary Thom. *Bella Abzug: How One Tough Broad from the Bronx Fought Jim Crow and Joe McCarthy, Pissed Off Jimmy Carter, Battled for the Rights of Women and Workers, Rallied Against War and for the Planet, and Shook Up Politics along the Way.* New York: Farrar, Straus and Giroux, 2007.

Lichtenstein, Nelson. *The Most Dangerous Man in Detroit: Walter Reuther and the Fate of American Labor.* New York: Basic, 1995.

———. *State of the Union: A Century of American Labor.* Princeton, NJ: Princeton University Press, 2002.

Lipset, Seymour Martin, and William Schneider. *The Confidence Gap: Business, Labor, and Government in the Public Mind.* New York: Free Press, 1983.

Loomis, Burdett. *The New American Politician: Ambition, Entrepreneurship, and the Changing Face of Political Life.* New York: Basic, 1988.

Lowi, Theodore J. *The Personal President: Power Invested, Promise Unfulfilled.* Ithaca, NY: Cornell University Press, 1985.

Lowitt, Richard. *Fred Harris: His Journey from Liberalism to Populism.* Lanham, MD: Rowman & Littlefield, 2002.

Lowndes, Joseph E. *From the New Deal to the New Right: Race and the Southern Origins of Modern Conservatism.* New Haven, CT: Yale University Press, 2008.

Lytle, Mark H. *America's Uncivil Wars: The Sixties Era from Elvis to the Fall of Richard Nixon.* New York: Oxford University Press, 2006.

Mackenzie, G. Calvin, and Robert Weisbrot. *The Liberal Hour: Washington and the Politics of Change in the 1960s.* New York: Penguin, 2008.

MacNeil, Neil, and Richard A. Baker. *The American Senate: An Insider's History.* New York: Oxford University Press, 2013.

Mann, Robert. *The Walls of Jericho: Lyndon Johnson, Hubert Humphrey, Richard Russell and the Struggle for Civil Rights.* San Diego: Harcourt Brace, 1996.

Mann, Thomas E., and Norman J. Ornstein, eds. *The New Congress.* Washington, DC: American Enterprise Institute for Public Policy Research, 1981.

Marlin, George J. *Fighting the Good Fight: A History of the New York Conservative Party.* South Bend, IN: St. Augustine's, 2002.

Martin, Bradford D. *The Other Eighties: A Secret History of America in the Age of Reagan.* New York: Hill and Wang, 2011.

Mason, Jim. *No Holding Back: The 1980 John B. Anderson Presidential Campaign.* Lanham, MD: University Press of America, 2011.

Mason, Robert. *Richard Nixon and the Quest for a New Majority.* Chapel Hill: University of North Carolina Press, 2004.

———. *The Republican Party and American Politics from Hoover to Reagan.* Cambridge: Cambridge University Press, 2012.

Massey, Douglas S. *Return of the "L" Word: A Liberal Vision for the New Century*. Princeton, NJ: Princeton University Press, 2005.

Mattson, Kevin. *When America Was Great: This Fighting Faith of Postwar Liberalism*. New York: Routledge, 2004.

————. *Rebels All!: A Short History of the Conservative Mind in Postwar America*. New Brunswick, NJ: Rutgers University Press, 2008.

————. *"What the Heck Are You Up To Mr. President?": Jimmy Carter, America's "Malaise," and the Speech That Should Have Changed the Country*. New York: Bloomsbury, 2009.

Matusow, Allen J. *The Unraveling of America: A History of Liberalism in the 1960s*. New York: Harper & Row, 1984.

Mayhew, David R. *Congress: The Electoral Connection*. New Haven, CT: Yale University Press, 1974.

McGarr, Kathryn J. *The Whole Damn Deal: Robert Strauss and the Art of Politics*. New York: PublicAffairs, 2011.

McGirr, Lisa. *Suburban Warriors: The Origins of the New American Right*. Princeton, NJ: Princeton University Press, 2001.

McGovern, George. *Grassroots: The Autobiography of George McGovern*. New York: Random House, 1977.

McPherson, Harry. *A Political Education*. Boston: Little, Brown, 1972.

Michelmore, Molly C. *Tax and Spend: The Welfare State, Tax Politics, and the Limits of American Liberalism*. Philadelphia: University of Pennsylvania Press, 2012.

Micklethwait, John, and Adrian Wooldridge. *The Right Nation: Why America Is Different*. London: Penguin, 2004.

Mieczkowski, Yanek. *Gerald Ford and the Challenges of the 1970s*. Lexington: University Press of Kentucky, 2005.

Milkis, Sidney M., and Jerome M. Mileur, eds. *The New Deal and the Triumph of Liberalism*. Amherst: University of Massachusetts Press, 2002.

————. *The Great Society and the High Tide of American Liberalism*. Amherst: University of Massachusetts Press, 2005.

Milner, Clyde A., II, Carol A. O'Connor, and Martha A. Sandweiss, eds. *The Oxford History of the American West*. New York: Oxford University Press, 1994.

Miroff, Bruce. *The Liberals' Moment: The McGovern Insurgency and the Identity Crisis of the Democratic Party*. Lawrence: University Press of Kansas, 2009.

Moffitt, Kimberly R., and Duncan Andrew Campbell, eds. *The 1980s: A Critical and Transitional Decade*. Lanham, MD: Lexington, 2011.

Mondale, Walter F., and Dave Hage. *The Good Fight: A Life in Liberal Politics*. New York: Scribner, 2010.

Moore, Jonathan, ed. *Campaign for President: The Managers Look at '84*. Dover, MA: Auburn House, 1986.

Morgan, Iwan W. "Hubert Humphrey's Last Hurrah: The 1977 Senate Leadership Election and the Decline of the New Deal Tradition." *Mid-America: An Historical Review* 79, no. 3 (Fall 1997): 287–317.

————. "Unconventional Politics: The Campaign for a Balanced-Budget Amendment Constitutional Convention in the 1970s." *Journal of American Studies* 32, no. 3.1 (December 1998): 421–445.

————. *The Age of Deficits: Presidents and Unbalanced Budgets from Jimmy Carter to George W. Bush.* Lawrence: University Press of Kansas, 2009.

————. "Monetary Metamorphosis: The Volcker Fed and Inflation." *Journal of Policy History* 24, no. 4 (2012): 545–571.

Moynihan, Daniel P. *Coping: Essays on the Practice of Government.* New York: Random House, 1973.

————. *The Politics of a Guaranteed Income: The Nixon Administration and the Family Assistance Plan.* New York: Vintage, 1973.

————. *Came the Revolution: Argument in the Reagan* Era. San Diego: Harcourt Brace Jovanovich, 1988.

Moynihan, Daniel P., and S. Weaver. *A Dangerous Place.* Boston: Little, Brown, 1978.

Neustadt, R. E. *Presidential Power: The Politics of Leadership.* New York: Wiley, 1960.

Nutter, Kathleen Banks. "'Militant Mothers': Boston, Busing, and the Bicentennial of 1976." *Historical Journal of Massachusetts* 38, no. 2 (Fall 2010): 52–75.

Nye, J. S., P. D. Zelikow, and D. C. Kin, eds. *Why People Don't Trust Government.* Cambridge, MA: Harvard University Press, 1997.

O'Neill, Thomas P., Jr., and W. Novak. *Man of the House: The Life and Political Memoirs of Speaker Tip O'Neill.* New York: Random House, 1987.

O'Neill, William L. *Coming Apart: An Informal History of America in the 1960s.* Chicago: Ivan R. Dee, 2005.

Ornstein, Norman, "The Permanent Democratic Congress," *Public Interest* (Summer 1990): 4–44.

Packer, George. *The Unwinding: Thirty Years of American Decline.* London: Faber & Faber, 2013.

Patterson, James T. "The New Deal in the West." *Pacific Historical Review* 38, no. 3 (August 1969): 317–327.

————. *Grand Expectations: The United States, 1945–1974.* New York: Oxford University Press, 1996.

————. *Restless Giant: The United States from Watergate to Bush v. Gore.* New York: Oxford University Press, 2005.

————. *Freedom Is Not Enough: The Moynihan Report and America's Struggle over Black Family Life from LBJ to Obama.* New York: Basic, 2010.

Perlstein, Rick. *Before the Storm: Barry Goldwater and the Unmaking of the American Consensus.* New York: Nation, 2001.

————. *Nixonland: The Rise of a President and the Fracturing of America.* New York: Scribner, 2008.

————. *The Invisible Bridge: The Fall of Nixon and the Rise of Reagan.* New York: Simon & Schuster, 2014.

Phillips, Kevin. *The Emerging Republican Majority.* New Rochelle, NY: Arlington House, 1969.

Phillips-Fein, Kim. "'If Business and the Country Will Be Run Right': The Business Challenge to the Liberal Consensus, 1945–1964." *International Labor and Working-Class History* 72 (Fall 2007): 192–215.

————. *Invisible Hands: The Making of the Conservative Movement from the New Deal to Reagan.* New York: W. W. Norton, 2009.

Phillips-Fein, Kim, and Julian E. Zelizer, eds. *What's Good for Business: Business and American Politics Since World War II.* New York: Oxford University Press, 2012.

Pickens, Donald K. *Leon H. Keyserling: A Progressive Economist.* Lanham, MD: Lexington, 2009.

Podhoretz, Norman. *Ex-Friends: Falling Out with Allen Ginsberg, Lionel & Diana Trilling, Lillian Hellman, Hannah Arendt, and Norman Mailer.* New York: Free Press, 1999.

Radosh, Ronald. *Divided They Fell: The Demise of the Democratic Party, 1964–1996.* New York: Free Press, 1996.

Rae, Nicol C. *The Decline and Fall of the Liberal Republicans: From 1952 to the Present.* New York: Oxford University Press, 1989.

Ranney, Austin, ed. *The American Elections of 1984.* Durham, NC: Duke University Press, 1985.

Rarick, Ethan. *California Rising: The Life and Times of Pat Brown.* Berkeley: University of California Press, 2005.

Rauch, Jonathan. *Government's End: Why Washington Stopped Working.* New York: PublicAffairs, 1999.

Reagan, Patrick. *Designing a New America: The Origins of New Deal Planning, 1890–1943.* Amherst: University of Massachusetts Press, 1999.

Reichard, Gary W. "Mayor Hubert H. Humphrey." *Minnesota History: The Quarterly of the Minnesota Historical Society* 56, no. 2 (Summer 1998): 50–67.

Reichley, A. James. *Conservatives in an Age of Change: The Nixon and Ford Administrations.* Washington, DC: Brookings Institution, 1981.

Remini, Robert V. *The House: The History of the House of Representatives.* New York: Smithsonian, 2006.

Ritchie, Donald A. *Reporting from Washington: The History of the Washington Press Corps.* New York: Oxford University Press, 2005.

Rivlin, Alice M., ed. *Economic Choices 1984.* Washington, DC: Brookings Institution, 1984.

Rodgers, David T. *Age of Fracture.* Cambridge, MA: Belknap, 2011.

Roof, Tracy. *American Labor, Congress, and the Welfare State, 1935–2010.* Baltimore, MD: Johns Hopkins University Press, 2011.

Rosenbaum, Herbert D., and Alexej Ugrinsky, eds. *The Presidency and Domestic Policies of Jimmy Carter.* Westport, CT: Greenwood, 1994.

Ross, Steven J. *Hollywood Left and Right: How Movie Stars Shaped American Politics.* New York: Oxford University Press, 2011.

Rothenberg, Randall. *The Neoliberals: Creating the New American Politics.* New York: Simon & Schuster, 1984.

Rutland, Robert A. *The Democrats: From Jefferson to Carter*. Baton Rouge: Louisiana State University Press, 1979.

Sabato, Larry. *Feeding Frenzy: How Attack Journalism Has Transformed American Politics*. New York: Free Press, 1991.

Sale, Kirkpatrick. *Power Shift: The Rise of the Southern Rim and Its Challenge to the Eastern Establishment*. New York: Random House, 1975.

Sandbrook, Dominic. *Eugene McCarthy: The Rise and Fall of Postwar American Liberalism*. New York: Alfred A. Knopf, 2004.

———. *Mad as Hell: The Crisis of the 1970s and the Rise of the Populist Right*. New York: Alfred A. Knopf, 2011.

Sandel, Michael J. *Democracy's Discontent: America in Search of a Public Philosophy*. Cambridge, MA: Belknap, 1996.

Sanders, Randy. *Mighty Peculiar Elections: The New South Gubernatorial Campaigns of 1970 and the Changing Politics of Race*. Baton Rouge: Louisiana State University Press, 2007.

Savage, James D. *Balanced Budgets & American Politics*. Ithaca, NY: Cornell University Press, 1988.

Scammon, Richard M., and Ben J. Wattenberg. *The Real Majority*. New York: Coward-McCann, 1970.

Schlesinger, Arthur M., Jr. *The Cycles of American History*. London: Deutsch, 1987.

———. *The Imperial Presidency*. Boston: Houghton Mifflin, 1989.

———. *Journals, 1952–2000*. Edited by A. Schlesinger and S. Schlesinger. London: Atlantic, 2007.

Schlesinger, Arthur M., Sr. *Paths to the Present*. New York: Macmillan, 1949.

Schoen, Douglas. *Pat: A Biography of Daniel Patrick Moynihan*. New York: Harper & Row, 1979.

Schoenwald, Jonathan M. *A Time for Choosing: The Rise of Modern American Conservatism*. New York: Oxford University Press, 2001.

Schulman, Bruce J. *From Cotton Belt to Sunbelt: Federal Policy, Economic Development, and the Transformation of the South, 1938–1980*. New York: Oxford University Press, 1991.

———. *The Seventies: The Great Shift in American Culture, Society, and Politics*. New York: Free Press, 2001.

Schulman, Bruce J., and Julian E. Zelizer, eds. *Rightward Bound: Making America Conservative in the 1970s*. Cambridge, MA: Harvard University Press, 2008.

Self, Robert O. *All in the Family: The Realignment of American Democracy Since the 1960s*. New York: Hill and Wang, 2012.

Sellers, Christopher C. *Crabgrass Crucible: Suburban Nature and the Rise of Environmentalism in Twentieth-Century America*. Chapel Hill: University of North Carolina Press, 2012.

Shafer, Byron E. *Quiet Revolution: The Struggle for the Democratic Party and the Shaping of Post-Reform Politics*. New York: Russell Sage Foundation, 1983.

———, ed. *The End of Realignment? Interpreting American Electoral Eras*. Madison: University of Wisconsin Press, 1991.

———. *The Two Majorities: The Issue Context of Modern American Politics*. Baltimore, MD: Johns Hopkins University Press, 1995.

———. *The Two Majorities and the Puzzle of Modern American Politics*. Lawrence: University Press of Kansas, 2003.

Shafer, Byron E., and Richard Johnston. *The End of Southern Exceptionalism: Class, Race, and Partisan Change in the Postwar South*. Cambridge, MA: Harvard University Press, 2006.

Shapiro, Ira. *The Last Great Senate: Courage and Statesmanship in Times of Crisis*. New York: PublicAffairs, 2012.

Shermer, Elizabeth Tandy. *Sunbelt Capitalism: Phoenix and the Transformation of American Politics*. Philadelphia: University of Pennsylvania Press, 2013.

Shrum, Robert. *No Excuses: Concessions of a Serial Campaigner*. New York: Simon & Schuster, 2007.

Sides, Josh. *L.A. City Limits: African American Los Angeles from the Great Depression to the Present*. Berkeley: University of California Press, 2003.

Sinclair, Barbara. *Party Wars: Polarization and the Politics of National Policy Making*. Norman: University of Oklahoma Press, 2006.

Smith, Hedrick. *The Power Game: How Washington Works*. New York: Random House, 1988.

Soffer, Jonathan. *Ed Koch and the Rebuilding of New York City*. New York: Columbia University Press, 2010.

Solberg, Carl. *Hubert Humphrey: A Biography*. New York: Norton, 1984.

Stanley, Timothy. *Kennedy vs. Carter: The 1980 Battle for the Democratic Party's Soul*. Lawrence: University Press of Kansas, 2010.

Stein, Judith. *Pivotal Decade: How the United States Traded Factories for Finance in the Seventies*. New Haven, CT: Yale University Press, 2010.

Steinfels, Peter. *The Neoconservatives: The Origins of a Movement*. Rev. ed. New York: Simon & Schuster, 2013 [orig. 1979].

Stockman, David A. *The Triumph of Politics: How the Reagan Revolution Failed*. New York: Harper & Row, 1986.

Sugrue, Thomas. *The Origins of the Urban Crisis: Race and Inequality in Postwar Detroit*. Princeton, NJ: Princeton University Press, 1996)

Sundquist, James L. *The Decline and Resurgence of Congress*. Washington, DC: Brookings Institution, 1981.

Taylor, Jeff. *Where Did the Party Go?: William Jennings Bryan, Hubert Humphrey, and the Jeffersonian Legacy*. Columbia: University of Missouri Press, 2006.

Teles, Steven M. *The Rise of the Conservative Legal Movement: The Battle for Control of the Law*. Princeton, NJ: Princeton University Press, 2008.

Thomas, Clive S., ed. *Politics and Public Policy in the Contemporary American West*. Albuquerque: University of New Mexico Press, 1991.

Thompson, Hunter S. *Fear and Loathing on the Campaign Trail '72*. London: Harper Perennial, 2005.

Thurber, Timothy N. *The Politics of Equality: Hubert H. Humphrey and the African-American Freedom Struggle*. New York: Columbia University Press, 1999.

Tomasky, Michael. *Left for Dead: The Life, Death, and Possible Resurrection of Progressive Politics in America*. New York: Free Press, 1996.

Troy, Gil. *See How They Ran: The Changing Role of the Presidential Candidate*. Rev. and expanded ed. Cambridge, MA: Harvard University Press, 1996.

———. *Morning in America: How Ronald Reagan Invented the 1980s*. Princeton, NJ: Princeton University Press, 2005)

———. *Moynihan's Moment: America's Fight against Zionism as Racism*. New York: Oxford University Press, 2013.

Tsongas, Paul E. *Journey of Purpose: Reflections on the Presidency, Multiculturalism, and Third Parties*. New Haven, CT: Yale University Press, 1995.

Turner, James Morton. "'The Specter of Environmentalism': Wilderness, Environmental Politics, and the Evolution of the New Right." *Journal of American History* 96, no. 1 (June 2009): 123–148.

———. *The Promise of Wilderness: American Environmental Politics Since 1964*. Seattle: University of Washington Press, 2012.

Turque, B. *Inventing Al Gore: A Biography*. Boston: Houghton Mifflin, 2000.

Udall, Morris K., B. Neuman, and R. Udall. *Too Funny to Be President*. New York: H. Holt, 1988.

Vaïsse, Justin. *Neoconservatism: The Biography of a Movement*. Trans. Arthur Goldhammer. Cambridge, MA: Belknap, 2010.

Van den Berg, E. "Supersalesman for the Great Society: Vice President Hubert H. Humphrey." *American Studies International* 36, no. 3 .(October 1998): 59–72.

Warnke, Paul C. "Apes on a Treadmill." *Foreign Policy* 18 (Spring 1975): 12–29.

Waterhouse, Benjamin C. *Lobbying America: The Politics of Business from Nixon to NAFTA*. Princeton: Princeton University Press, 2014.

Wattenberg, B. *Fighting Words: A Tale of How Liberals Created Neoconservatism*. New York: Thomas Dunne, 2008.

Wattenberg, M. P. *The Decline of American Political Parties, 1952–1980*. Cambridge, MA: Harvard University Press, 1984.

Waxman, Henry, and Joshua Green. *The Waxman Report: How Congress Really Works*. New York: Twelve, 2009.

Wehrle, Edmund F. "Guns, Butter, Leon Keyserling, the AFL-CIO, and the Fate of Full Employment Economics." *Historian* 66, no. 4 (2004): 730–748.

Weidenbaum, Murray L. "The Case Against the Humphrey-Hawkins Bill," *Challenge* 19, no. 4 (September/October 1976): 21–23.

White, Richard. "*It's Your Misfortune and None of My Own*": A History of the American West. Norman: University of Oklahoma, 1991.

White, William S. *Citadel: The Story of the U.S. Senate*. New York: Harper & Brothers, 1956.

Wilentz, Sean. *The Age of Reagan: A History, 1974–2008*. New York: Harper, 2008.

Wills, Garry. *Reagan's America: Innocents at Home*. Garden City, NY: Doubleday, 1987.

———. *Under God: Religion and American Politics*. New York: Simon & Schuster, 1990.

———. *Lead Time: A Journalist's Education.* Boston: Mariner, 2004.

Wilson, James Q. *The Amateur Democrat: Club Politics in Three Cities.* Chicago: Chicago University Press, 1966.

Witcover, Jules. *Marathon: The Pursuit of the Presidency, 1972–1976.* New York: Viking, 1977.

———. *The Making of an Ink-Stained Wretch: Half a Century Pounding the Political Beat.* Baltimore, MD: Johns Hopkins University Press, 2005.

———. *Joe Biden: A Life of Trial and Redemption.* New York: William Morrow, 2010.

Wolfe, Alan. *One Nation, After All: How Middle-Class Americans Really Think About God, Country, Family, Racism, Welfare, Immigration, Homosexuality, Work, the Right, the Left, and Each Other.* New York: Viking, 1998.

Wolfe, Tom. *Mauve Gloves & Madmen, Clutter & Vine.* Toronto: Bantam, 1977.

Wolpe, Bruce C., and Bertram J. Levine. *Lobbying Congress: How the System Works.* 2nd ed. Washington, DC: Congressional Quarterly, 1990.

Woods, Randall Bennett. *Fulbright: A Biography.* Cambridge: Cambridge University Press, 1995.

Worster, Donald. *Rivers of Empire: Water, Aridity, and the Growth of the American West.* New York: Oxford University Press, 1985.

Zelizer, Julian E. *Taxing America: Wilbur D. Mills, Congress, and the State, 1945–1975.* Cambridge: Cambridge University Press, 1998.

———. *On Capitol Hill: The Struggle to Reform and Its Consequences, 1948–2000.* Cambridge: Cambridge University Press, 2004.

———, ed. *The American Congress: The Building of Democracy.* Boston: Houghton Mifflin, 2004.

———. *Jimmy Carter.* New York: Times, 2010.

———. "Rethinking the History of American Conservatism." *Reviews in American History* 38 (2010): 380, 387–389.

———, ed. *The Presidency of George W. Bush: A First Historical Assessment.* Princeton, NJ: Princeton University Press, 2010.

———. *Governing America: The Revival of Political History.* Princeton, NJ: Princeton University Press, 2012.

UNPUBLISHED THESES

Merton, J. D. *"Ethnic Power!": The Rise and Fall of the Politics of White Ethnicity, 1964–1984.* DPhil thesis, University of Oxford, 2009.

www.ingramcontent.com/pod-product-compliance
Lightning Source LLC
Chambersburg PA
CBHW050336270326
41926CB00016B/3479